ADDRESSING LEVINAS

Northwestern University

Studies in Phenomenology

and

Existential Philosophy

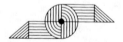

ADDRESSING LEVINAS

Edited by Eric Sean Nelson, Antje Kapust, and Kent Still

Northwestern University Press
Evanston, Illinois

Northwestern University Press
Evanston, Illinois 60208-4170

Printed in the United States of America

10   9   8   7   6   5   4   3   2   1

ISBN 0-8101-2046-1 (cloth)
ISBN 0-8101-2048-8 (paper)

Library of Congress Cataloging-in-Publication data are available from the
Library of Congress.

∞ The paper used in this publication meets the minimum requirements of the
American National Standard for Information Sciences—Permanence of Paper
for Printed Library Materials, ANSI Z39.48-1992.

Contents

Preface

Eric Sean Nelson and Antje Kapust

The title of this anthology presents us with a seemingly simple question: How should his readers address Emmanuel Levinas and the collection of books, articles, and interviews that bear his name? Given the rapidly growing interest in Levinas, one might also ask: What is Levinas's significance for us such that "we" need to address and be addressed by him? This question is not only an issue of addressing and being addressed but also one of responsiveness. It is a question of whether and how "I" or "we" can respond to our "other." The question of the other is especially acute when it is not just any other, or pious and sentimental talk about the general other, but the concrete other who is encountered as radically different than myself. This is the other who *I* ignore, push aside, marginalize, exclude, fear, or despise—and it is this other for whom *I* am in some sense responsible.

What is the import of this word "address"? This question can be approached through Levinas's early reception and later critique of Husserl's phenomenology of intentionality (as discussed in more detail in the introduction to this volume) and Heidegger's hermeneutical phenomenology of care. The early work of Martin Heidegger already linked address (*ansprechen* as distinguished from *besprechen,* which is discussion "about" something) with the question "who?" Who is the being-there (*Dasein*) who is addressed? Heidegger replied that only that being that is a question for itself, that can address and be addressed, is a who—i.e., that being whose very existence is a response to the question "who?" Levinas famously throws Heidegger's discourse into question for its violence and ethical poverty. This is not the place to examine the justice or injustice of his critique of Heidegger, particularly as a number of contributions to this volume investigate this question more fully. But it should be asked whether the responsiveness to things suggested by Heidegger fails to articulate the ethical core of the question "who?" We can still ask *with* Levinas whether the "who" and, as such, the address is primarily ethical rather than ontological. Heidegger's failure to articulate the ethical character of address and responsiveness is perhaps itself closely connected with a deeper failure in ethical thought and conduct. This responsibility for the self, which is "each time my own" in Heidegger's words, is questioned through a responsibility that grips me and refers me to the other such that responsibility is "each time my other."

Traditionally, in the history of Western philosophy, responsibility has been identified with autonomy or rational freedom. Levinas powerfully criticizes the failure of autonomy and spontaneity in Western ontology from the Greeks through Heidegger. These concepts are ethically inadequate insofar as they are intrinsically self-centered, given the self's ethical dependence on the other. Levinas speaks of passivity beyond passivity, beyond even the most passive intentionality or synthesis, and dependence prior to all independence. But is such an ethical responsiveness totally incompatible with spontaneity? Is there anything immanent in the world or in the human being that allows it to be interrupted by and morally respond to alterity? Why should otherness ever appear *as* other? For Heidegger, the interruption of alterity—from the broken hammer to the uncanniness of my own death—always addresses some aspect of my being such that I can potentially recognize and respond to it. Appropriation is always tied to that which cannot be appropriated.

In the preface to *Totality and Infinity*, Levinas describes being and ontology as a condition of violence and war. One's own being is tied to self-interest to the exclusion of concern for the other. The question of being is not the question of the other. Yet is there anything in being and in one's own being that allows one to be addressed by the other and that allows the ethical to interrupt and challenge self-interest? What is it about the face that singles me out and motivates me to act for the sake of that other? The ancient Chinese philosopher Mengzi (Mencius), reformulating the *ru* tradition that we call Confucianism, argued for the possibility of a spontaneity which is intrinsically moral and inherently responsive to the concrete suffering and need of the other, no matter who they are. Prior to all reflection and calculation, one is compelled to answer to the other in acting for her, as when one leaps without thinking to save a child who falls into a well or river without considering the risks or rewards of such an action. Could such an ethical spontaneity reflect the human side of the interruption of violence and war, of the "thou shall not kill" of the face?

Levinas's criticisms of autonomy and his inclusion of heteronomy should not be understood as an abandonment of freedom. Levinas was one of the first authors to develop a philosophical critique of National Socialism and totalitarianism, and this critique is informed by the notion of the freedom and spontaneity of the individual endangered by fascism. Levinas was not only influenced by the phenomenological and the Judaic, but by the French liberal philosophical heritage of the early twentieth century and the French republican tradition with its vision of liberty, equality, and fraternity for all. Levinas's ethics can even be understood as a radical rethinking and deepening of the ideas of 1789.[1] Instead of grounding liberty, equality, and fraternity in individual autonomy or rational self-interest, Levinas reorients this revolutionary trinity through the encounter of self and other in order to expose how these ideas have been devalued and deformed in twentieth-century political discourses and practices. Levinas is not only a thinker who applies ethics to politics, but also one who shows an acute awareness of political realities from the rise of fascism to the Holocaust and from the Cold War to the Israeli-Palestinian conflict. The question of responsibility is tied to the question of *how* to respond and, as such, the ethical is a *way* of responding to the reality and even cruelty of the political.

This brief reflection on the question of responsiveness already begins to indicate both the complexity of his philosophy as well as more subtle ways of reading Levinas. In the latest stage of the reception of Levinas, as found in the contributions to this volume, we can discover deepening articulations, criticisms, and extensions of his thought. We can read and address Levinas as a philosopher not simply engaged in easy or naive moral criticisms of political realities or mere reversals of traditional concepts. We can find a thinker who is not engaged in constructing static oppositions between autonomy and heteronomy, spontaneity and passiveness, totality and infinity, or ethics and violence. It is precisely the nuanced character of Levinas's philosophy, as well as his ethical directness and immediacy, that should address us. These call us to read him more critically and more thoroughly.

Addressing Levinas accordingly indicates an ongoing task that is not without its risks. This responsibility requires a critical encounter with his thought, as well as unfolding possible responses to his critics. This is particularly necessary given how radically different his ethics appear to be in contrast to the ethical discourses dominant in contemporary philosophy. Both in Europe and in North America, the field of ethics is focused on questions of normativity and justification: What is the "ought" and how can it be legitimated? Levinas, however, does not seem to speak of generally binding norms and ethical foundations. Even worse, secular intellectuals fear the possible "divinization" of ethics, or re-smuggling of religion into ethics, when they see Levinas mention and discuss God, the Torah, and its rabbinical commentaries.

Yet it should be argued that the different focus of Levinas's ethics is salutary in the face of the emptiness of current ethical discourses that seem irrelevant to anyone's actual ethical concerns. Levinas's ethics has its own strengths, and its difference in tone and substance is one of them. This also helps account for the increasing interest in his works. Levinas articulates the "ought" not at the general formal level so typical of contemporary ethics, but in the relationality and asymmetry of self and other. Rather than challenging egoism with arguments about self-interest and consensus, which ultimately only reaffirms identity rather than opening up its questionability, Levinas traces how the ethical and the "ought" already occur in the encounter between self and other. Levinas advocates different ways of thinking about ethics when he shows that normativity and justification cannot be adequately articulated through notions of autonomy and self-interest, social contracts and consensus. The ethical event occurs prior to how we construct it. A number of the contributions to this volume pursue these questions further by developing Levinas's relevance to moral and political theory, as well as issues in applied ethics such as the environment and war.

For Levinas, *I* am responsible. Responsibility is tied to responsiveness, or how *I* respond to the infinity and alterity intimated in the face of the other. Yet can an ethics oriented towards the face of the other hinder the bullet, the suicide vest, or the bulldozer? Of course, in one sense this question misses the point, since the face is not a phenomenal appearance or an empirical fact. The face, in its irreducible infinity and facticity, presents an ethical obligation according to Levinas. Nonetheless, some readers might want to pursue this question in another sense by asking whether Levinas, with his reliance on the language of Judaism and monotheism, is part of the current problem rather than offering resources to respond to it. How can an ethics so closely aligned with the language of monotheism—as is the case with Levinas even in the most secular of readings—be of benefit to us when we see and experience so much of the apparent intolerance and perilous consequences of monotheistic religions in terrorism and war, violence and social-political injustice? How can speaking of *God* be helpful if it is discourses about *God* that are the problem?

Levinas showed the ethical character of Judaism and of monotheistic language in general—of God as beyond, as excess, and as other—in the face of the destructive and totalitarian paganism of the twentieth century. He analyzed this paganism in the destruction and horrors of Stalinism and especially of National Socialism. The Holocaust was not just an accident of human history but is part and parcel of the West, of its ontology, its anti-Semitism, and in particular its revival of pagan rootedness in blood and soil.

Yet if National Socialism and the Holocaust are *his* questions, is not the question for us the violence and intolerance seen in the monotheism of the peoples of the Book and the Word? What of the physical and moral violence perpetrated by those claiming to represent the heritage of Christianity, Islam, and Judaism? In other words: How can the face halt religious justifications of intolerance against homosexuals and militant excuses for war? How can the face halt someone using himself as a bomb or shooting children? How can the face halt a bulldozer destroying homes or rolling over a person? Given the dominant tone of contemporary discourses, where there is a God *and* everything seems to be permitted, it might be appropriate to ask what ethics is there in speaking of God, monotheism, and religion? Don't we need to keep these out of ethics precisely for the sake of the ethical?

Despite the failure of Levinas to confront injustices such as colonialism and neocolonialism, as Robert Bernasconi examines in this volume, it can be argued that Levinas's approach is not in fact inappropriate given recent events, but is all the more trenchant. For it is Levinas who demonstrated the ethical character of monotheism that seems to be in such danger of being forgotten. It is Levinas who articulated how the prophetic voice does not speak against the downtrodden and marginalized, as it might seem from the daily news, but exists precisely to witness and give testimony to these persons in *their* pain and *their* trauma without excuses. The prophetic voice speaks out of my responsibility for the other that calls me to respond. Levinas's prophecy speaks specifically of those who have been ravaged and traumatized by war, terrorism, occupation, prejudice, and injustice. Levinas at his most orthodox still articulates a moral challenge to the narcissism inherent in religious fundamentalism, since it fails to address and respond to the other. The radically ethical character of "religion" in Levinas forcefully calls religious enthusiasm and unethical religious beliefs and practices into question. Levinas's ethics calls us to a greater responsibility for the other, the concrete other no matter how foreign to us or vilified by us as the "enemy." Although the political application of religion may appear to owe more to Carl Schmitt than Levinas, it is Levinas who contests the idolatry of a religion without the ethical and the construction of the other as an internal or external enemy.

This ethical challenge to our personal and national egoism and self-interest, including those of religiosity and faith, is for Levinas inherent in the language and practices of monotheism itself, which are oriented towards the other and to difference rather than the self and the same. If monotheism is the problem, Levinas suggests how it can also be a needed response. For Levinas, it is the alterity of God in and through the encounter with the human face who interrupts and calls into question the belief in our own ethical superiority and our dehumanization of others. If the ethical is the religious and the religious the ethical, then his philosophical and religious writings—as well as the corresponding secular and religiously oriented readings of Levinas's works—might have more in common with each other than is often thought. Levinas does not offer a religiously grounded ethics. He does not ask us to believe in God for the sake of the ethical, nor does he preach being religious or ethical. He does, however, ask us to look at ourselves in how we relate to others, to look at the other in examining oneself. This other is not lesser than me; the other is not an indifferent equal. It is this concrete other who addresses me and calls me to respond and be responsible.

The essays in this volume undertake in their own unique ways such an address and response. They wager a response by questioning and articulating the various dimensions of Levinas's thought—the Judaic, the phenomenological, the ethical and political. The authors explore the philosopher's relationship to a wide range of traditions and issues, including the philosophy of culture and religion, Jewish thought from the Torah to his own contemporaries, psychoanalysis, the history of philosophy, phenomenology, deconstruction, and contemporary feminism. Although they enact a critical encounter with Levinas, they also call us to think more carefully about what Levinas is saying beyond the reification and caricature of the said and stated. They show further possibilities for both thinking with Levinas and beyond him, of addressing Levinas as well as the excess and other of Levinas.[2]

Notes

1. Howard Caygill develops the political context of Levinas's thought in his *Levinas and the political.* (London: Routledge, 2002).

2. We wish to thank Alice A. Frye and François Raffoul for their comments on a draft of this preface.

Acknowledgments

The essays gathered in this anthology were originally presented at the "Addressing Levinas: Ethics, Phenomenology, and the Judaic Tradition" conference, held on the campus of Emory University in Atlanta, Georgia, October 15–17, 1999. It is a testimony to the interdisciplinary and international relevance of Levinas's thought that this conference, inspired by discussions with Antje Kapust and originally conceived as a small panel discussion featuring a few Levinas scholars, went on to feature speakers from no less than ten different disciplines and five different countries. We deeply regret that only a small number of the many excellent and important papers presented at the conference could be included in this volume.

The assistance received from Robert Bernasconi and David Michael Kleinberg-Levin has been beyond measure. We are especially appreciative of their early commitment to participate in the conference, their recommendations of young scholars doing significant work on Levinas's thought, and their continued support and encouragement with the volume.

Special mention must be made of Cynthia Willett of the Department of Philosophy at Emory University. Her generous sponsorship of the "Addressing Levinas" conference made that conference and this anthology possible.

We are very grateful for the assistance provided by the faculty and staff of Emory University. Rudolf A. Makkreel, chair of the Department of Philosophy, was especially helpful, not only with regard to the conference, but also throughout the publication process. We are especially grateful for all of his efforts. In addition, we would like to thank Dalia Judovitz, chair of the Department of French and Italian at the time of the conference. The Graduate School of Arts and Sciences, the programs in Comparative Literature and Jewish Studies, and the Graduate Department of Religion also provided generous support. And the staff of the Department of Philosophy—namely, Pat Redford, Brenda Costner, and Minal Singh—provided much-needed assistance.

It should be noted that the "Addressing Levinas" conference was organized and run by a group of immensely gifted young scholars who were graduate students in various departments and programs at that time—including Chris Anadale, Michael Buckley, Elizabeth Butterfield, Amy Coplan, Firmin Debrabander, Aaron Fichtelberg, Mark Fischer, Alex Hall, Courtney Hammond, Angela Hunter, Richard Oxenberg, Petra Schweitzer, Saul Tobias, Jennifer Vanderpool, Chad Wilson, Eric Wilson, and Coleen Zoller, among many others. Matt Dance and Henry Dyson graciously took on several especially heavy burdens. Karreem Khalifa was immensely helpful and deserves special recognition, as does Ian Oakes. In addition, the conference would not have been possible were it not for William Edelglass and Tam Parker, whose support, especially in the early stages, was crucial and cannot be emphasized enough. In a testament to their generosity and friendship, Kaiya Ansorge and Eric Jepsen provided assistance time and again, before any request was made. And it will come as no surprise to anyone who knows her that, throughout the organization of the conference and the preparation of this anthology, Alice A. Frye has always been, and remains, a pillar of support to one and all. Special acknowledgments are also owed to Julie Piering and Apostolos Vasilakis, both of whom took on task after task with such grace that they made their supererogatory efforts seem utterly effortless.

We are also grateful to Jeanne Marie Kusina, a graduate student at the University of Toledo, for proofreading the manuscript. Finally, we wish to express our gratitude to Anthony Steinbock for his steady guidance and the editors and staff at Northwestern University Press for their hard work and constant support in publishing this volume.

Abbreviations of Works by Emmanuel Levinas

AE   *Autrement qu'être, ou au-delà de l'essence* (The Hague: Martinus Nijhoff, 1974).

BPW   *Emmanuel Levinas: Basic Philosophical Writings,* ed. Adriaan Peperzak, Simon Critchley, and Robert Bernasconi (Bloomington: Indiana University Press, 1996).

BV   *Beyond the Verse: Talmudic Readings and Lectures,* trans. Gary D. Mole (Bloomington: Indiana University Press, 1994).

CPP   *Collected Philosophical Papers,* trans. Alphonso Lingis (Pittsburgh: Duquesne University Press, 1998).

DE   *De l'existence à l'existant* (Paris: Vrin, 1947).

DF   *Difficult Freedom: Essays on Judaism,* trans. Seán Hand (Baltimore: Johns Hopkins University Press, 1990).

DL   *Difficile liberté: Essais sur le judaïsme,* 2nd ed. (Paris: Albin Michel, 1976).

DMT   *Dieu, la mort et le temps,* ed. Jacques Rolland (Paris: Grasset, 1993).

ED   *En découvrant l'existence avec Husserl et Heidegger* (Paris: Vrin, 1967).

EE   *Existence and Existents,* trans. Alphonso Lingis (The Hague: Martinus Nijhoff, 1978).

EN   *Entre nous: Essais sur le penser-à-l'autre* (Paris: Éditions Grasset et Fasquelle, 1991).

ENT   *Entre Nous: Thinking of the Other,* trans. Michael B. Smith and Barbara Harshav (New York: Columbia University Press, 1999).

HH   *Humanisme de l'autre homme* (Montpellier: Fata Morgana, 1972).

N   *Nouvelles lectures talmudiques* (Paris: Éditions de Minuit, 1996).

OB   *Otherwise Than Being, or Beyond Essence,* trans. Alphonso Lingis (The Hague: Martinus Nijhoff, 1981).

S   *Du sacré au saint: Cinq nouvelles lectures talmudiques* (Paris: Éditions de Minuit, 1977).

TA   *Le temps et l'autre* (Paris: Presses Universitaires de France, 1983).

TI   *Totality and Infinity: An Essay on Exteriority,* trans. Alphonso Lingis (Pittsburgh: Duquesne University Press, 1969).

TeI   *Totalité et infini: Essai sur l'extériorité* (The Hague: Martinus Nijhoff, 1961).

TO   *Time and the Other,* trans. Richard Cohen (Pittsburgh: Duquesne University Press, 1987).

Introduction: Addressing Levinas

Kent Still

"Philosophy itself," Emmanuel Levinas writes in *Totality and Infinity*, is "a discourse always addressed to another" (*TI* 269). "What we are now exposing," he adds, "is addressed to those who shall wish to read it." If, as Levinas contends, philosophers have previously attempted to give a systematic, complete and self-enclosed discourse, those tightly woven tapestries of propositions are always breached by the fact that such discourse is addressed to another—to the reader.[1]

This *address* provides the guiding thread that runs through the following essays on the writings of Emmanuel Levinas. Indeed, it is a thread that already runs throughout his works, as perhaps most succinctly formulated in the following passage,[2] given in an interview: "*Language is above all the fact of being addressed . . . which means the Saying much more than the Said*" (*PL* 170). For Levinas, what is most important about language is not its designative function, nor even its communicative function, but rather that it is through language, through discourse, that the other (*Autrui*) addresses me (*moi*). Or, to formulate it in the terms of his distinction between the Saying and the Said, Levinas emphasizes the fact of being addressed (the Saying) "much more" than the propositions stated in discourse (the Said). This is not to say that the Said is not important; indeed, he insists on the necessity of paying attention to the Said. What matters, however, is that there is an excess, a "much more," that is here attributed to the Saying: the fact of being addressed exceeds, or overflows, the stated propositions.

The claim that the address is always in excess of the stated proposition requires, then, a reconsideration of our guiding thread. Although an emphasis on the fact of being addressed is not external to Levinas's writings, neither is it simply internal to them. Instead it might be understood as a loose thread, a thread that runs throughout his writings, but which also leads outside them. Indeed, Levinas suggests that such a loose thread runs in and out of every philosophical discourse. To the extent that it is addressed to another, every philosophical discourse, no matter how tightly wound, leads beyond its stated propositions.

This volume attempts to draw out that thread. In doing so, the contributors not only open up Levinas's admittedly difficult works, giving a glimpse into how his arguments are stitched together, but also take up those arguments, extending them in new directions. This approach goes hand in hand, however, with critical assessments of his texts, which consider whether his arguments fall short at times and which propose ways of redressing those shortcomings. In both of these gestures, Levinas's writings are extended beyond themselves.

Indeed, for Levinas, the address involves precisely such an approach. In the terms of *Totality and Infinity*, it is as if the Same could not simply reside in itself, could not simply avoid the Other, and could not remain in an allergic avoidance of the Other. Or, in the terms of *Otherwise than Being*, the address involves substitution: one for the other. Such descriptions might sound too metaphysical, or, conversely, too literary. They are, however, elaborated in terms of rigorous phenomenological descriptions of how the address exceeds the thematizing intentionality of consciousness, overflowing every theme.

This overflowing of every theme accounts for the difficulties posed by Levinas's works: if his writings are resistant to categorization, it is because, in every stated determination of a theme, the address is in excess of those propositions, extending beyond their theme. For that reason, although Levinas emphasizes the differences between the two issues, his discussion of *ethics*, often taken to be the theme of his writings, overflows into a discussion of *justice*.

Consider, for instance, his discussion of *ethics*. Although Levinas is most often categorized as a "philosopher of ethics," such a categorization threatens to be misleading, reductive. After all, in contrast to much of what is commonly considered to constitute "ethical philosophy," Levinas's discussions of ethics do not emphasize propositions that may serve as directives. Instead, he emphasizes the fact of being addressed. Language— that is to say, the fact of being addressed—is the occurrence of ethics, the occurrence of the ethical. Or to put it otherwise, the encounter with the Other (*l'Autre*) is the ethical. But even this formulation can be misleading, insofar as the Other remains perhaps too much of a metaphysical category. The claim that the encounter with the Other is the ethical, then, calls for a further formulation: the encounter with the Other (*Autre*) is always an encounter with the other (*Autrui*), with the other human, who addresses me.

Such a description of ethics will surely sound puzzling, if not outright mistaken, to those who understand the task of ethical philosophy to be the articulation of criteria for deciding whether a particular action can be said to be "ethical" or not. Indeed, Levinas does not, for the most part, issue directives or criteria for deciding between competing directives. And on the occasions when he does turn his discussion to particular prescriptions, such as "thou shalt not kill," he claims that such propositions are already announced before any word is said: those prescriptions are "revealed" already in the very saying of the address.

Thus, even the categorization of Levinas's philosophy in terms of "ethics" is not entirely unproblematic. Since his writings neither issue nor attempt to legitimize particular ethical directives, they hardly belong to that philosophical genre whose stake is to articulate such rules and to argue for their acceptance. Moreover, the difference between such a project and Levinas's approach is exacerbated by the increasing emphasis that Levinas places on what he calls "bad conscience."

If the task of ethical philosophy were merely to articulate rules for behavior, one need only follow those rules to evade pangs of conscience. Of course, there are many competing criteria of ethical behavior, from which one must choose. But, if one's motivation is to evade pangs of conscience, one's path of evasion is clear: simply pick a criterion that legitimates the way in which one already behaves. For this reason, Robert Bernasconi, in a recent article,[3] has gone so far as to claim: "Much of what passes for ethics are simply different ways of evading the truth that accuses" (*EP* 34). In other words, the formulation of such rules (and the casuistry often involved in such formulations) is an attempt to evade what Levinas calls "bad conscience." And, if such a project is described under the name of "ethics," Bernasconi rightly suggests that Levinas's thought would instead have to be understood as "an 'ethics of suspicion' or even 'an ethics against ethics'" (*EP* 34).

Such a thesis, however, leads to further questions. For instance, if Levinas's ethical philosophy emphasizes the fact of being addressed, the Saying and not the Said, one might wonder how an "ethical philosophy" would even be possible. Philosophy, after all, is a discourse that is obliged to give reasons. Thus, while it is always addressed to another, and hence involves the Saying, philosophy is also firmly entrenched in the Said. In other words, even a philosophy that emphasizes the Saying is obliged to formulate itself in the Said. And, for his part, Levinas himself acknowledges that the Saying can be thematized, showing itself as a Said, that even in his own discourse the Saying is betrayed, insofar as the fact of being addressed becomes the theme of stated propositions. Indeed, Levinas not only acknowledges this betrayal of the Saying in the Said, but goes so far as to claim that it is necessary: because the giving of reasons and judgments is necessary for *justice*.

The claim that an excess overflows every philosophical determination of a theme, then, also holds for Levinas's own work, as evidenced by the way in which his discussion of ethics leads to discussions of justice, despite the fact that, at times, Levinas, especially in *Otherwise than Being, or Beyond Essence,* describes ethics and justice in seemingly contradictory terms. Ethics, according to Levinas, involves responsibility to the singular other, whereas justice concerns the other of the other, all the other others. Justice also involves the use of reason and judgment in an attempt to arrive at rules that govern just and equitable action. Obviously, the Said is of great importance here; the propositions advanced as Law must be judged, as to their justness. Such an account of justice, of course, sounds quite similar to the type of argumentation about rules for conduct, of which Levinas is suspicious. How, then, should one understand the way in which Levinas's discussion of ethics overflows into a discussion of the theme of justice? And what sense can be made of his insistence upon both ethics and justice?

Here Levinas's emphasis on bad conscience is instructive, especially when contrasted with the traditional philosophical dictum: know thyself! Some maintain that respect for "the other" must be founded upon respect for the self (indeed, some go so far as to claim that the self, what philosophers call "the subject," is also an "other" or, in a more metaphysical formulation, "Other"). Levinas, of course, is suspicious of such an emphasis upon the self, or "the subject," opposing those claims, which he views as an evasion of the responsibility for the other. But, trained in a phenomenological method that he himself extends, Levinas does not reject every notion of "subjectivity," as his emphasis on "bad conscience" attests. It is as if bad conscience were a feeling that threw "the subject" into question, threw "me" into question. And the question is: Have I lived up to my responsibility for the other? The answer, it seems, is always "no," insofar as Levinas insists that the responsibility to the other is infinite; more is always required, which may help explain why he describes ethical responsibility to the other as an "accusation," and even a "persecution." Such claims, obviously, are quite controversial. And they are, in fact, subjected to critical appraisals in several of the essays that follow. But to momentarily grant Levinas this claim, one might construct the following argument. If ethical responsibility to the other is infinite, then an ethical response would not result in good conscience, allowing me to content myself with the reassurance that I have been ethical; to the contrary, a more intense feeling of bad conscience would manifest itself, revealing that more is required. In other words, in order to be ethical, I must be attentive to the extent to which I have not yet been ethical. This line of argumentation could then be extended to the question of the place of ethics in the field of philosophy, which is, after all, the field of argumentation and of judgment, and which, as such, always has—and must—concern itself with the Said, insofar as such judgments are necessary for justice. One could conclude, analogously, that in order to be just, one must be attentive to the extent to which justice has not yet been achieved, to the work that remains to be done. Indeed, at times, Levinas suggests such an account of the relation of ethics to justice: "It is ethics which is the foundation of justice. Because justice is not the last word; within justice, we seek a better justice" (*PL* 175).

This understanding of the relation of ethics to justice, in turn, illustrates what "addressing Levinas" might mean, what a serious philosophical engagement with Levinas, whether pro or con, would look like: the giving of reasons in a philosophical discourse would be motivated not by the attempt to legitimate and justify that discourse, but out of an obligation to further accomplish the work that remains to be done. The work of extending Levinas's philosophy to new topics would involve an acknowledgment of the work to be done as well as a call for others to extend this work even further. "Addressing Levinas," moreover, would not rule out a critical appraisal of his work; it would demand it.

This is even suggested by the ambiguity of the English "to address." In this introduction, it has been used in a sense that more or less overlaps with what Levinas calls the Saying. Such delimitation of the term "address" is in keeping with Levinas's own use of the French *addresser*. In this sense, the title of this volume might be understood as responses to Levinas. The English term "to address," however, has taken on another meaning: to deal with or treat a problem, to redress it. In this sense, the title of this volume would imply identifying and correcting what may be problematic in Levinas's thought. The title of this volume invokes both of these senses. "Addressing Levinas," then, involves responding to Levinas in a manner that is responsible, by giving as generous a reading as possible, while also critically appraising where his thought falls short and attempting to redress those shortcomings.

For instance, do Levinas's descriptions of "the feminine" simply perpetuate traditional, hierarchical stereotypes of gender? Does his emphasis on language preclude responsibility to animals and the environment? Do his descriptions of ethical responsibility in terms of "persecution" and being taken "hostage" serve, instead, to perpetuate oppression? And, more generally, how is the relation between ethics and justice to be negotiated, especially when his description of the ethical relation seems to run counter to egalitarian and universalistic presuppositions of justice? Do his descriptions of the address as an "interruption" of philosophical discourse, of ethical responsibility as a "doing before understanding," and other such claims lead to irrationalism? The essays collected here respond to these questions, both attesting to the resources in Levinas's writings and redressing what may be problematic in his work.

The editors have refrained from dividing the following essays into discrete sections, from placing them under different headings. Such headings would have occluded what we wished to highlight in the arrangement of these essays: that the overflowing of every theme holds not only for Levinas's works but also for the essays collected in this anthology. Throughout the following essays, the discussion of one theme keeps overflowing into another. For instance, the volume begins with a number of essays that consider the distinction that Levinas himself makes between his phenomenological writings and what he calls his "confessional" texts. That discussion extends into a series of appraisals of the more general question of the relation of Levinas's thought to other genres of discourse, considering, for example, how the ethical imperative revealed in the address relates to the disciplinary imperatives that structure academic writing and, more broadly, the various cultural and economic imperatives that structure society. These questions stretch to assessments of the place of Levinas's philosophy in relation to a specific discipline: that of phenomenology, especially as practiced by Husserl and Heidegger. The discussion of Levinas's relation to Heidegger leads to some of the more overtly political discussions. And this is continued in a number of essays that consider Levinas's account of ethical responsibility as involving "persecution" and "trauma." In turn, the discussions of trauma lead to assessments of the relation of Levinas to psychology and psychoanalysis. Levinas's account of embodiment and temporality, which is so crucial to an understanding of the psychological import of his thought and his relation to psychoanalysis, is then extended in the last two essays, both of which critically assess his work with regard to the question of sexual difference. The summary that follows illustrates how the contributed essays both fit into these topics and—perhaps more important—extend beyond them.

Jill Robbins opens the volume with a discussion of the relation of Levinas's "confessional" or religious texts to his more overtly philosophical works. Robbins begins by noting Levinas's contention that, although he forbids himself from giving a Talmudic or biblical verse as a reason for a philosophical claim, the verse may nevertheless motivate the search for a reason. Indeed, Robbins suggests that Levinas's commitment to discourse and the giving of reasons may be read in the epigraph to *Difficult Freedom,* a line which, insofar as it is inscribed at the beginning of that collection of his earliest confessional texts, may even be said to point in the direction taken by his subsequent Talmudic readings and occasional essays. This epigraph, however, might seem to threaten the very relevance of religion for an ethical philosophy, insofar as Levinas takes this epigraph from a Talmudic commentary on the verses in Leviticus that narrate the violent death of two of Aaron's sons. Indeed, they are said to have died in a fire that came forth from the Lord, as punishment for crimes that are— to say the least—difficult to specify. It is, in other words, precisely the type of verse that raises the suspicions that some philosophers may have about any use of religious texts in a discourse about ethics, suspicions concerning the legitimization of violence in the name of religion. Having dramatically presented the dangers that some find lurking in the use of religious texts in the course of an elaboration of ethical responsibility, Robbins proceeds to offer a careful and critical exegesis that responds to those concerns and, in doing so, exemplifies the dual senses of "addressing Levinas." On the one hand, she explicates how Levinas's confessional texts are precisely an effort to critique the type of religious pathos that would occlude responsibility to the other and even lend itself to such legitimizations. Indeed, she demonstrates that, on the reading that Levinas seems to endorse, Nadab and Abihu were themselves guilty of the type of enthusiasm that gives rise to violence in the name of religion, the verses narrating their deaths serving as a lesson about the ethical dangers of religious pathos. On the other hand, in a subtle and understated gesture, Robbins suggests another possible response to those deaths, a response that might be a more Levinasian response than the one Levinas himself endorses.

Continuing the discussion opened by Robbins, the essays by Claire Katz, James Hatley, Wayne Froman, and Michael B. Smith call attention to Levinas's philosophical works, considering them in relation to biblical and Talmudic verses. This is not to say, however, that the grave stakes raised by Robbins are diminished, as dramatically demonstrated by Claire Katz's discussion of the story of Abraham and Isaac. Katz compares Kierkegaard's interpretation (which emphasizes Abraham's responsibility to God) with Levinas's critique of Kierkegaard (which emphasizes, instead, the ethical responsibility to the other, in this case to Isaac). Although such a comparison seems to suggest a dilemma between religion and the ethical responsibility to the other, Katz arrives at a synthesis of the interpretations offered by both Levinas and Kierkegaard, arguing that religious responsibility requires ethical responsibility.

Otherwise than Being, the most sustained presentation of Levinas's later philosophy, is explicated through readings of biblical and Talmudic verses in the essays by James Hatley, Wayne Froman, and Michael B. Smith. And, as in the contributions by Robbins and Katz, their readings of these verses attest to the severity of the stakes raised by Levinas. This is well demonstrated by James Hatley's essay, one of several essays in this volume that critically assess Levinas's controversial description of ethics as involving "persecution." Hatley does not try to minimize the problem; to the contrary, he begins by demonstrating that Levinas's insistence upon my

responsibility even to the one who persecutes me is a radical intensification of the already severe depiction of responsibility offered earlier in *Totality and Infinity*. Yet, although such a notion of responsibility may sound
extreme, Hatley presents a moving defense of Levinas's claims through
his consideration of the opposite case, namely, the case of the persecutor,
who evades responsibility for the persecuted one, an argument that he illustrates through a reading of the story of Cain.

The discussion of *Otherwise than Being* is continued by Wayne Froman, who shows how Franz Rosenzweig's reading of the biblical story of
creation is helpful for understanding Levinas's discussion of the Saying,
the self, and freedom. In addition to offering a rewarding explication of
some of the more difficult passages of Levinas's writing, including passages that even Levinas himself characterizes as "strange," Froman contributes an important defense of the import of biblical and Talmudic texts
for practical philosophy. More specifically, in contrast to some of the abstract, invariant, and idealistic presuppositions of ancient Greek philosophy, Froman emphasizes the importance of understanding "creation" as
a work that must be renewed each day.

Michael B. Smith, for his part, suggests that at least some of the difficulties of *Otherwise than Being* are due to the disciplinary concerns that
lead philosophers to neglect Levinas's attention to religious writings.
Smith offers an instructive explication of *Otherwise than Being* through a
reading of the story of Job. And his careful attention to the importance of
religious texts for understanding Levinas's philosophy is, in turn, illustrative of what he calls the "transdisciplinarity" of Levinas's thought. Indeed,
Smith's essay is one of the most explicit assessments of the import of Levinas's thought for disciplines other than philosophy.

Margret Grebowicz, Bernhard Waldenfels, and Alphonso Lingis
raise a related question: if the address may seem to be clothed with all
sorts of other types of directives (disciplinary imperatives, social norms,
etc.), what import does this have for Levinas's insistence that the address
reveals a specifically ethical imperative? For instance, using Jean-François
Lyotard's analyses of different discourses in terms of their stakes (i.e. cog-
nitive, ethical, aesthetic, etc.), Margret Grebowicz considers the differences between Levinas's philosophy and deconstruction. Focusing on
Jacques Derrida's recent text, *Adieu to Emmanuel Levinas,* in which Derrida
writes of the "debt" that is owed to Levinas, Grebowicz explicates this debt
in a manner that neither reduces the ethical import of Levinas's distinction between the Saying and the Said to the mediation that deconstruction finds at work in all signification, nor denies the ethical stake of Derrida's writings.

Bernhard Waldenfels reconsiders the distinction between the Saying and the Said in terms of linguistic pragmatics. More specifically, Waldenfels demonstrates the ways in which the Saying may be haunted by the sedimentation of cultural traditions and idioms within language, making it difficult to determine who speaks, and resulting in an anonymous speaking in which the distinction between myself and the other who addresses me is blurred. This does not mean, however, that the responsibility for the other disappears into a faceless anonymity; instead, Waldenfels elaborates a notion of "creative responsivity," which involves "a Saying which interrupts itself, leaving room for another Saying and for the Saying of others." And, in a gesture that might be seen as performing the type of "creative responsivity" that he elaborates in his essay, Waldenfels neither rejects everything Levinas says nor acts as if Levinas said it all; rather, he suggests a creative intertwining of Levinas's account of ethical responsibility as "one-for-the-other" with what Husserl calls "one-within-the-other" (*Ineinander*).

Alphonso Lingis mounts a resourceful defense of Levinas's description of the face of the other who addresses me as a "signification without a context," a claim that critics take as implying an abstract notion of the other and a lack of attention to the various cultural, social, and even economic directives within the contexts of various projects. Written in that singular Lingis style, his essay counters this charge in its very mode of writing, which conjures up a series of singular faces—the face of a destitute woman in São Paulo clutching a doll, the face of an injured neighbor knocking at my door asking to be taken to the hospital, the face of an old woman caught in the latest war as she stares at me on the news. All these faces appear indeed within specific cultural, ethnic, and social contexts that his writing underlines strikingly. But they also break through and strip away the contexts within which they appear, a stripping away that is not a reification but a concretion of each singular face. Through these individual faces, a "bare humanity" (as the title of his essay suggests) appeals to me—"bare" in the sense of stripped of contexts, facing me as a succession of singular faces outside the practical field of the collective work defined by our interchangeability and difference from one another, apart from any pragmatic or cultural context, radically extracted from the communities those contexts establish. As he accounts for the imperative force that comes from the naked face, Lingis is attentive to the need and suffering revealed by the face; indeed, in moving descriptions and narratives, Lingis puts a face—indeed, a plurality of singular faces—on poverty, disease, war, and abuse. There is, however, also an emphasis on how my response to that poverty may allow me to discover a wealth of previously unknown resources with which to respond. Lingis describes this as a certain type of "birth," that is, a capacity for interruption, for disconnection from my past projects, and hence for commencement. In other words, the suffering other does not only interrupt my project but also opens me to new possibilities, new ways of responding. Thus, if Lingis goes on to criticize other aspects of Levinas's thought, perhaps even interrupting Levinas's project by attesting to a responsibility for animals and the environment, his essay should also be read as revealing new possibilities within Levinas's philosophy, including previously unknown resources in Levinas's thought for bearing witness to the ethical obligations due to animals and the environment.

How, then, should one understand Levinas's philosophy with regard to the specific disciplinary imperatives of phenomenology? Does his ethical philosophy constitute an interruption of phenomenology? And if so, might this interruption still reveal new possibilities and previously unknown resources within phenomenology? Leslie MacAvoy shows that if Levinas's phenomenology is itself a description of the "reversal of intentionality" involved in the address, then Levinas's descriptions of this reversal, and the critique of the thematizing nature of intentionality that accompanies it, can be viewed as a radicalization—and not a rejection—of Husserl's phenomenological method. Indeed, MacAvoy goes on to demonstrate the ways in which Levinas extends strategies developed within Husserlian phenomenology.

Anthony Steinbock continues the discussion of the innovations that Levinas introduces into the method of phenomenological description. In contrast to interpretations that find the Other to be primarily a disruptive force, one that exceeds phenomenological disclosure, Steinbock contends that such accounts must be reconsidered in terms of Levinas's distinction between "disclosure" and "revelation." Steinbock demonstrates that what Levinas calls "revelation" should be understood as a distinctive mode of phenomenological givenness, one which cannot be reduced to disclosure.[4] Indeed, Steinbock argues that revelation is a mode of phenomenological givenness upon which disclosure itself is founded, and one within which the address of the Other is not, in fact, interruptive but is, instead, instructive. And, as Steinbock himself instructively points out, teaching is an address, one recognized as such in *Totality and Infinity*, in which it is phenomenologically described in terms of revelation.

The next several essays concern the relation of Levinas to Heidegger's phenomenology. Here is Levinas's most widely known account:

> If at the beginning our reflections are in large measure inspired by the philosophy of Martin Heidegger, where we find the concept of ontology and of the relationship which man sustains with Being, they are also governed by a profound need to leave the climate of that philosophy, and by

the conviction that we cannot leave it for a philosophy that would be pre-Heideggerian.[5]

The essays by François Raffoul, David Wood, and Robert Bernasconi, however, complicate this account. For instance, François Raffoul contests a certain way of categorizing Heidegger and Levinas (one suggested by Levinas himself) that treats Heidegger's thought as a thinking of the Same (or ontology) and Levinas's thought as a thinking in response to the Other (or ethics). Raffoul complicates such a categorization through a provocative rereading of both thinkers. On the one hand, Raffoul argues that Levinas leaves certain ontological presuppositions unquestioned, presuppositions that are "Cartesian" and "egoistic." On the other hand, in his reading of Heidegger's descriptions of *Mitsein* and the finitude of *Dasein*, Raffoul is attentive to a concern for the dying of the other that makes itself heard in Heidegger's works. Raffoul's essay, then, might be described as tracing Heidegger's path out of the ontological assumptions of Levinas's philosophy, albeit not for one that is pre-Levinasian—at least, provided that a Levinasian philosophy is characterized by such a responsibility for the other.

David Wood, for his part, traces a different trajectory. Like Raffoul, Wood argues that Levinas leaves certain ontological presuppositions unquestioned, thereby suggesting that Levinas moves back to a pre-Heideggerian philosophy, one that is Cartesian. These covert presuppositions, Wood argues, foreclose any sort of obligation to beings otherwise than human, such as animals and the environment. Wood wants to undo these presuppositions and argues that a different ontology—and a different understanding of the relation of ontology to ethics—is required. Accordingly, and as his title suggests, Wood asks his "Levinasian friends" to leave the climate of Levinas's philosophy, albeit not for a philosophy that would be pre-Heideggerian.

Robert Bernasconi's essay begins with a consideration of Levinas's remarks about Heidegger's politics. More specifically, Bernasconi argues that Levinas's insistence upon leaving the climate of Heidegger's thought must be understood in terms of Levinas's suggestion that Heidegger's thought, National Socialism, and social Darwinism are symptoms of "the struggle for existence" that prevails throughout Western thought and that gives rise to racism. Yet, as Bernasconi explains Levinas's need to leave the climate of Heidegger's philosophy, he does not fail to question the climate of Levinas's own philosophy, bringing attention to Levinas's discussion of struggle and war at the end of *Otherwise Than Being*, a discussion that is explicitly addressed to "us Westerners."[6] The Eurocentrism of this particular address (and other similar passages in Levinas's writings), itself an exclusionary gesture, prompts Bernasconi to argue that it is necessary to leave the climate of Levinas's philosophy, albeit not for a philosophy that would be pre-Levinasian.

The topic of politics is also explicitly discussed in the next essay, in which John Drabinski explicates the technical meaning of Levinas's term "utopia" and, more specifically, its place, as it were, in his philosophy. Drabinski is critical of the way in which Levinas's conception of justice unfolds in terms of an account of a messianic temporality; nevertheless, he argues that there are resources in Levinas's thought for a concrete ethical politics: a justice of redistribution and reparation. For Drabinski, this involves undoing Levinas's distinction between the ethical responsibility to the other person (as exemplified by charity) and the universality of justice for all (as exemplified by law). In order to be just, Drabinski argues, the law must become charitable, redressing the injustices produced by economic disparity.

Together, Bernasconi and Drabinski present two of the more overtly political essays; the discussion of political topics is not, however, limited to only their texts. Indeed, it is precisely for this reason that this anthology is not divided into discrete sections that would separate, for instance, the essays that discuss Levinas's accounts of ethical responsibility from those that discuss the political implications of his thought. As I have emphasized throughout this introduction, Levinas's discussion of ethics overflows into a discussion of justice or, in other words, politics. And, much as Levinas's discussion of ethics leads beyond ethics and specifically to questions of justice, the essays in this volume, even when they seem to focus on Levinas's accounts of ethical responsibility, also extend to political questions, thereby overflowing any discrete and separate topical organization. For instance, in a text that appears early in the volume (amongst the essays that most explicitly concern the tensions between the phenomenological and religious aspects of Levinas's thought), James Hatley explicates Levinas's description of ethical responsibility as a "persecution" in a way that brings Levinas's account to bear on instances of political persecution. And, in this way, Hatley's reading of the story of Cain is a dramatic example of the ways in which the essays that appear earlier in this volume also extend to political topics.

So too with the essays following the contributions by Bernasconi and Drabinski. For instance, like Hatley, David Michael Kleinberg-Levin extends Levinas's description of ethical responsibility as involving "persecution" to a discussion of persecution on the basis of racial, ethnic, and religious differences, thereby illustrating the contention, advanced throughout this introduction, that Levinas's account of ethics does lead to the discussion of urgent political questions. Kleinberg-Levin's account of

Levinas's ethics may even be read as a response to some of the political worries that Drabinski raises about what Levinas calls "messianic temporality," insofar as Kleinberg-Levin's essay is a powerful testimony to the promise that remains in Levinas's account of "messianic temporality." Yet, like Drabinski, Kleinberg-Levin's essay is attentive to the various ways in which Levinas's concerns may be occluded within the polis. And, like Kleinberg-Levin, Antje Kapust emphasizes the recurrent violence that may result from such an occlusion. Indeed, Kapust considers a wide range of discussions of war and peace and calls attention to the various ways in which those accounts—including those that are advanced as calls for peace—may involve exclusionary gestures that serve to perpetuate the recurrence of violence.

Kleinberg-Levin and Kapust, however, also open another topic: the import of Levinas for psychology and psychoanalysis. For instance, Kleinberg-Levin demonstrates how the distinction that Levinas makes between ego (*moi*) and self (*soi*) complicates Levinas's notion of persecution; indeed, he carefully untangles no less than four different senses of persecution in Levinas's thought, which then allows him to explicate the precise sense in which ethical responsibility can be described as a "persecution" and a "trauma." Kleinberg-Levin goes on to argue that Levinas's account implies a similarly complex narrative of moral development, one in which embodiment is shown to play a major role, and which Kleinberg-Levin carries forward in his elaboration of that account in terms of a moral psychology. Kapust, for her part, emphasizes the difficulties posed by the effects of trauma. Although her attention to cases such as the one discussed in Merleau-Ponty's *Phenomenology of Perception* (that of Schneider, who suffered brain damage from a shell fragment in World War I) is certainly in keeping with Levinas's insistence upon an attention to the other's vulnerability, Kapust might also be read as asking whether Levinas pays enough attention to the other's vulnerability. Akin to Wood's concern for animals, who are incapable of articulated discourse, Kapust suggests that any account of ethical responsibility as revealed in discourse must also consider the extent to which the effects of persecution and trauma make it difficult for the survivors to speak.

Given the differences between, on the one hand, Kleinberg-Levin's elaboration of Levinas's discussion of "trauma" in terms of moral psychology and, on the other hand, Kapust's emphasis upon a "traumatology" that would be attentive to the damage done by exposure to trauma, Bettina Bergo's contribution, in which she considers the differences between Levinas's description of ethics as involving a "traumatism" and Freud's psychoanalytical case studies of trauma victims, could not be more timely. Acknowledging the complications posed to such a study by both

Levinas's repeated repudiations of psychoanalysis and Freud's equally insistent suspicions regarding philosophy, Bergo presents a careful consideration of the confluences between Levinas's ethical philosophy and psychoanalytical discourses, the interpenetration of their concepts, and the
validity of their critiques of one another, in an essay that is important for
understanding their different senses of "trauma."

Diane Perpich devotes further discussion to issues concerning embodiment, a topic that Kleinberg-Levin, Kapust, and Bergo also touch
on in their essays. Perpich, however, goes on to ask whether Levinas acknowledges not only that the ethical relation must be embodied but also
that it necessarily involves sexual difference. While recognizing that Luce
Irigaray has been widely read as criticizing Levinas for lacking an ethics of
sexual difference, Perpich suggests that Irigaray's text, "The Fecundity of
the Caress," may also be read as enacting the very notion of "fecundity"
that Irigaray develops in that text. More specifically, Perpich demonstrates
how Irigaray may be said to make Levinas's ethics "fecund" in Irigaray's
own sense of that term; that is to say, she regenerates Levinas's philosophy,
showing it to be already shaped by and within a matrix of sexual difference.

Tina Chanter concludes the volume with an essay that draws out
many of the themes raised throughout this anthology: from questions
about the relation of Levinas's thought to that of Heidegger and Derrida,
to questions about how social structures may condition the relation to the
other. For the purposes of this introduction, however, I will limit myself to
a few remarks regarding the way in which Chanter's response to the question of sexual difference by way of her consideration of Levinas's discussion of "the feminine" involves a gesture that, while unique to her own
philosophical approach to such questions, might also be regarded as emblematic of the dual senses of "addressing Levinas." On the one hand,
Chanter advances what she calls a "charitable" reading, according to
which "the feminine" is demonstrated to function as a structural principle
that interrupts traditional philosophical categories, such as totality and
identity, and which, as such, is an ethical response that extends to the political. On this interpretation, which emphasizes the contribution that
Levinas's thought can make to feminist philosophy, Chanter demonstrates how Levinas's philosophy may be extended beyond those topics
with which he has largely been associated. But, on the other hand,
Chanter also advances what she calls a "less than generous" reading, according to which the feminine, while interrupting totality, is confined to
a merely preparatory role in service to the higher purpose of the transcendent masculine relationship established in both ethics and politics.
In other words, Chanter's "less than generous" reading is an important re-

minder that "addressing Levinas" must mean more than merely responding to Levinas; indeed, "addressing Levinas" must also mean redressing
what remains problematical in his thought.

These introductory remarks have attempted to bring out the ways in
which a plurality of themes are woven throughout the following essays.
This thematic description is bound, however, to be exceeded not only by
the many other themes that the essays address but also by the very fact of
their being addressed. Indeed, each of the following essays is an address,
a discourse addressed to another. As such, they exceed the attempt to cir-
cumscribe them to a set of propositions, and overflow even the minimal
theme under which they have been collected, the theme provided by the
title of this anthology: namely, that of *addressing Levinas*. Yes, in their essays, the contributors respond, each in his or her own singular voice, to
Levinas. These essays, however, are also addressed to all the other others.[7]

Notes

I wish to thank Eric Nelson for his helpful comments and suggestions on an early
version of this introduction.

1. Such a claim might appear to subsume "the other" under the figure of "the
reader." For Levinas, "the other" is precisely *other*, that is, other than me, and apart
from any context that I might share with the other. In contrast, "the reader" might
be seen to be implicated within a hermeneutical context, one involving a shared
language, etc.; moreover, due to the reiterability of language, one may even be
said to be one's own reader. Within the limits of these introductory remarks, I will
be unable to discuss this tension at length; I would argue, however, that, if my gesture seems to assimilate "the other" to "the reader," this tension is itself subsum-
able under the larger question of the problematic relation of "ethics" (which, for
Levinas, is the relation to the singular other) and "justice" (which, for Levinas,
does involve contexts, and concerns not only the other but all the others, including oneself). On the more specific question of address within writing, see note 4
to this introduction, which suggests one route such a discussion could take; see
also the works cited in note 7 to this introduction.

2. T. Wright, P. Hughes, and A. Ainley, "The Paradox of Morality: An Interview
with Emmanuel Levinas," in *The Provocation of Levinas*, ed. R. Bernasconi and
D. Wood (London: Routledge, 1988), 168–80. Hereafter cited in the text as *PL*.

3. R. Bernasconi, "The Truth that Accuses: Conscience, Shame and Guilt in
Levinas and Augustine," in *The Ethics of Postmodernity*, ed. G. Madison and M. Fair-
bain (Evanston: Northwestern University Press, 1999), 24–34. Hereafter cited in
the text as *EP*.

4. It should also be noted that Steinbock goes on to distinguish a third mode
of phenomenological givenness, namely, "manifestation," which is neither merely

"disclosive," nor quite the same as "revelation." Written works, to the extent that they involve an address (the Saying) and hence cannot be reduced to mere propositions (the Said), would be instances of what Steinbock calls "manifestation."

5. Emmanuel Levinas, *Existence and Existents,* trans. Alphonso Lingis (The Hague: Martinus Nijhoff, 1978), 19.

6. Emmanuel Levinas, *Otherwise Than Being, or Beyond Essence,* trans. Alphonso Lingis (The Hague: Martinus Nijhoff, 1981), 177.

7. See also Simon Critchley, "'*Bois*'—Derrida's Final Word on Levinas," in *Re-Reading Levinas,* ed. R. Bernasconi and S. Critchley (Bloomington: Indiana University Press, 1991), 162–89; and Jill Robbins, *Altered Reading: Levinas and Literature* (Chicago: University of Chicago Press, 1999), esp. 10–19.

ADDRESSING LEVINAS

Strange Fire

Jill Robbins

Difficult Freedom, a collection of essays on Jewish topics that Emmanuel Levinas published in 1963 and in a second, expanded edition in 1976, is the first of Levinas's "nonphilosophical" or "confessional" works. He keeps these works separate from his philosophical works, as the difference between an exegetical adherence to a tradition on the one hand, and a phenomenological inquiry aware of its own presuppositions on the other. While arguably this distinction between the two kinds of writing is not absolute (it breaks down, in any case, after 1975 with the publication of essays eventually collected in *Of God Who Comes to Mind*), it is important to understand why Levinas takes the distinction seriously. As he would later formulate it in a 1986 interview with François Poirié:

> A philosophical truth cannot be based on the authority of a verse. The verse must be phenomenologically justified. But the verse can allow for the search for a reason.[1]

This assertion of the distinction between the philosophical and the nonphilosophical does not go without acknowledging the possibility of a certain interplay between them. The search or "midrash" (a term which the French biblical scholar Renée Bloch translates as *recherche*), the starting point of which is the scriptural verse, may—indirectly, of course—"motivate" the ethical thought which, in turn, "must" receive phenomenological description. More generally, this might be a way in which Levinas's philosophical works can be said to be inflected by Judaism. The forty-seven essays collected in *Difficult Freedom*—which date from the late 1940's through the early 1960's, namely, from a time when Levinas was developing his mature ethical philosophy, represented by the 1961 *Totality and Infinity*—were originally published in French Jewish periodicals such as

Evidences, Arche, Les nouveaux cahiers, and *Information juive.* In these post-war essays, which register the impact of the Nazi genocide of the Jews, Levinas addresses questions of Jewish education, assimilation, and identity. Suffice it to say that in this context, Levinas feels free to let the Jewish exegetical tradition engage him.

The epigraph to part 1 of *Difficult Freedom* is from the medieval French Jewish commentator Rashi. The opening moment of a book cannot be inconsequential. At the opening of his book, at the very opening of the opening, Levinas offers his reader an inscription, Rashi's comment on Leviticus 10:2: "Let them not enter the sanctuary drunk." This is a telling motto for an ethical philosopher who always tries to keep intoxication and the ludic at arm's length. I have evaluated the consequences of this for Levinas's philosophical work, especially as it concerns the relation between ethics and aesthetics, elsewhere.[2] In this essay, I am concerned with the meaning of the epigraph for *Difficult Freedom.* There are no further direct references in that work to Rashi's comment, and although it would appear that Levinas endorses the interpretation of the scriptural text that it implicitly advances, he never does come right out and say so.[3] What is irrefutable is this: the inscription with which Levinas opens his work calls upon us to ask, and gives us to think, what it means to read and interpret. To read the inscription is necessarily to read Levinas reading Rashi reading previous rabbinic commentators reading scripture, i.e., to read reading. This inscription also suggests something about the modality of interpretation, as a relation to a "word always already past," as Levinas put it in an interview, "in which transmission and renewal go hand in hand" (*IR* 275).

The Leviticus passage which provoked the interpretive comment belongs to one of the few extended narrative portions in the book of Leviticus, which is primarily comprised of legal material. According to Jacob Milgrom, while Exodus presents us with a static picture of the people receiving instructions for the building of the tabernacle, Leviticus gives us its living context.[4] The focus of Leviticus is on the priests. Chapters 1–7 contain the laws about sacrifice and the distinctions between different kinds of offerings. The narrative portions, chapters 8–10, recount how Moses's brother Aaron, along with four of Aaron's sons, undergo consecration as priests, the inaugural service of the tabernacle, and what Milgrom calls "the tragic aftermath of the Inaugural Service," in which two of the sons, Nadab and Abihu, are killed. Chapters 11–16 detail the impurity system. The authorship of Leviticus is generally attributed to the P (Priestly) writer, who, in Genesis, favors genealogies and has a statistical bent. The author of the first, rather than the second, creation account in Genesis, P has a heaven-centered view.[5] Within a hierarchy of biblical authors and styles, P is something of a bookkeeper.

The major theological effort of Leviticus, according to Milgrom, is a negation of paganism. "Impurity is eviscerated of its magic power" and "devitalized" (*ABL* 261). It is still dynamic—as in regard to sancta encroachment—but no longer demonic. Leviticus "severs impurity from the demonic and reinterprets it as a symbolic system" (*ABL* 47). The world of demons is abolished, leaving only one being with demonic powers, the human being. This demonization of man is a central contribution of the Priestly theology (*ABL* 43).

The context of the verse commented upon is especially important because of the ironic juxtapositions it contains. The last few verses of chapter 9, verses 22–24, recount a blessing and theophany—appearance of God—at the conclusion of the inaugural service of the tabernacle:

> Then Aaron lifted his hands toward the people and blessed them; and he came down after sacrificing the purification offering, the burnt offering and the well-being offering. Moses and Aaron then entered the Tent of Meeting. When they came out, they blessed the people; and the Glory of the Lord appeared to all of the people. Fire came forth from before the Lord and consumed the burnt offering and the suet pieces on the altar. And the people saw, and shouted for joy, and fell on their faces.
> (Milgrom translation)

The appearance here of the divine glory (*kabod*) necessarily recalls the cloud-encased fire (by day only the cloud is visible; at night the fire can be seen) which guided the Israelites in the wilderness (*ABL* 588–89). It recalls a similar theophany on Mount Sinai: "Now Mount Sinai was completely enveloped in smoke, for the Lord had come down upon it in fire. Its smoke rose like the smoke from a kiln, and the whole mountain trembled violently" (Ex. 19:18). God is not a fire but *like* a fire (Num. 9:15; Ex. 24:17), and it is precisely not God who is visible but his fire (*ABL* 574–75). In Exodus 24:15–18, we read:

> Then Moses went up the mountain and the cloud covered the mountain. The glory (*kabod*) of the Lord settled on Mount Sinai and the cloud covered it six days. On the seventh day he called to Moses from the midst of the cloud. Now the appearance of the glory (*kabod*) of the Lord was like a devouring fire on the top of the mountain in the sight of the people of Israel.[6]

Here the *kabod* is expressly identified with the fire, and its destructive power is emphasized. A few verses earlier, Exodus 24:9–11, an even more direct theophany is described:

> Then Moses and Aaron, Nadab and Abihu, and seventy of the elders of
> Israel went up and they saw the God of Israel, and under his feet as it
> were a pavement of sapphire stone, like the very heaven in purity. Yet he
> did not lay a hand on the leaders of the Israelites, but they beheld God,
> and they ate and drank.[7]

This passage is not without its difficulties. Astonishing for its anthropo-
morphism and for what Brevard Childs calls "its bluntness"[8] (e.g., "And
they saw the God of Israel"), the text seems to acknowledge the unique
and extraordinary nature of this meeting by observing that God "did not
lay a hand on the leaders of the Israelites," "as might have been expected."[9] In Exodus 24:11, Moses, Aaron, Nadab and Abihu, and the elders even share a covenant meal, "a communion which," for Childs, "is in
stark contrast to the burning terror of the theophany in Ch. 19."[10] According to Milgrom, Exodus 24:9–11e comes from a tradition which suggests that Moses penetrated into the divine cloud to receive the Deca-
logue, which encounter made Moses's face radiant (*ABL* 136). It must be
harmonized with the other places in scripture (even later in the same passage, Ex. 24:17) that assert that Moses saw only the *kabod* (fire-cloud) that
envelops God (Num. 9:15) or that Moses hid in the cleft of the rock while
the presence of the Lord passed him by (Ex. 33:22–23).

The analogy between the theophany at Sinai and that in the tabernacle is significant for several reasons. First, it establishes a certain equivalence: the tabernacle, suggests Milgrom, may be understood as a por-
table Sinai. As at Sinai, at the tabernacle theophany, the *kabod* and the fire
are associated ("And the Glory of the Lord appeared to all the people.
Fire came forth from before the Lord and consumed the burnt offering
and the suet pieces on the altar," Lev. 9:23–24). As at Sinai, where God
speaks to Moses who speaks to Aaron who, in turn, speaks to the people,
revelation proceeds by way of a chain of communicators, sometimes with
unpredictable results. In Leviticus 6:1, the typical structure is in place:
"The Lord spoke to Moses, saying, 'Command Aaron and his sons thus.'"
When the *kabod*, as Milgrom details, separates itself from its nebulous en-
casement and consumes the sacrifices in the sight of all the people (*ABL*
575), this is a sign—depicted in drastic and miraculous terms—of divine
approbation.[11] No wonder the people "saw, shouted for joy, and fell on
their faces," in the words of verse 24. Hence the *kabod* theophany in Leviticus 9:24 signifies a legitimation of Aaronic priesthood.

At this point we are ready to appreciate the ironic juxtaposition of
9:22–24 (blessing and theophany) and 10:1ff. (the tragic aftermath of the
inaugural service). No sooner has the ritual order been inaugurated, than
"systems failure"—as Everett Fox puts it—occurs.[12] Divine approbation

becomes wrath, joy becomes grief. Chapter 10 (verses 1–3) of Leviticus begins:

> Now Aaron's sons, Nadab and Abihu, each took his pan, put coals in it, and laid incense on it; and they offered before the Lord unauthorized coals (*eš zerah*), which he had not commanded them. And fire came forth from the Lord and consumed them; thus they died before the Lord. Then Moses said to Aaron, "This is what the Lord meant when he said: 'Through those near to me I shall sanctify myself and before all of the people I shall glorify myself.'" And Aaron was silent. (Milgrom translation)

The sin or error committed by Aaron's sons is unspecified, but its consequences are violent and irreversible. The question—what did Nadab and Abihu do?—has received a range of exegetical answers, to which I will return. However, one should note that the very fact that the biblical account does *not* specify the priestly error serves to direct attention to the inherent asymmetry in divine/human relations, what Kierkegaard called "the edification implied in the fact that man is always in the wrong before God."[13] (Indeed, the ironic juxtaposition of Leviticus 9:22–24 and 10:1ff. recalls a previous ironic juxtaposition back at the Sinaitic theophany. While Exodus 31:18 recounts the giving of the tablets, the subsequent verse, Exodus 32:1ff. recounts the fashioning of the golden calf. One midrashic commentator finds that the two events were simultaneous: "While Israel were standing below engraving idols to provoke their Creator . . . God sat on High engraving for them tablets which would give them life."[14] Suffice it to say that perhaps this simultaneity of donation and betrayal is constitutive.) Milgrom argues that "against the backdrop of the wilderness narratives, the story of Nadab and Abihu is the Priestly counterpart to the episode of the golden calf" (*ABL* 632); that is, this story, too, points to man's inherent inability to be righteous.

But let not these edifying reflections distract us from what is disturbing and recalcitrant in the episode. David Damrosch notes that it is shocking not only in its timing but in the stature of the victims.[15] God's sudden wrath, the violence of the episode, the family tragedy unfolding—these are the elements that make a reading encounter with the Hebrew Bible deeply strange and unfamiliar, rendering it less of a complacent and customary possession, as Franz Rosenzweig noted in a letter written to Gertrud Oppenheim in June 1922:

> The people who wrote the Bible apparently thought about God in a similar manner as did Kafka. I have never read a book that so much

reminded me of the Bible as his novel *The Castle*. Reading it also can certainly not be called a pleasure.[16]

Is it Kafka who reminds us of the Bible or the Bible which reminds us of Kafka? The irreducible similarity between the Bible and Kafka imposes itself upon Rosenzweig when he is confronted with the biblical authors' style in the full radicality of the original Hebrew—with its distinctive syntax and sound-patterning. Arguably, this similarity between the Bible and Kafka imposes itself on all modern readers. Harold Bloom refers to J, the uncanny Yahwistic writer (in distinction from P, the Priestly author), as the legitimate ancestor of Kafka's K., and argues that a Kafkan facticity governs our awareness of the biblical tradition.[17] In the case of the Nadab and Abihu episode, what seems Kafkan is not simply the fact that we begin with a punishment in search of a crime, which may lead, as will be seen, to an infinite proliferation of deadlocked interpretations. It is the uneasy sense that, as in Kafka, guilt is never to be doubted; "guilt," as Henry Sussman puts it, "is an ineluctable family legacy."[18]

The matter-of-fact way in which commentators countenance the interpretive possibility (attributed to Rashbam and Hazzequni [quoted in *ABL* 599]) "that the same divine fire that consumed the sacrifices also struck down Nadab and Abihu in its path" may be disconcerting. Everett Fox calls the fire that destroys Nadab and Abihu "an ironic echo of the positive divine fire that came down and completed the sanctifying of the priesthood."[19] Searching out the scriptural cross-references for divine fire does little to allay this essential ambiguity. In *The Legends of the Jews*, Louis Ginzberg reports:

> Upon twelve occasions did God send a Divine fire upon earth, six times as a token of honor and distinction, but as many times as a punishment. To the first class belong the fire at the consecration of the tabernacle, at the offering of Gideon as at that of Manoah and of David; at the dedication of Solomon's Temple, and at the offering of Elijah upon Mount Carmel. The six fatal fires are the following: the fire that consumed Nadab and Abihu; that which wrought havoc among the murmuring and complaining multitude; the fire that consumed the company of Korah; the fire that destroyed Job's sheep, and the two fires that burned the first and the second troops which Ahaziah sent against Elijah.[20]

Following out any of these local references in which, comparably, God's fire is a token of honor or punishment, may well be of interest. Yet there is something folkloristic about the "six and six" patterning, as if the actual number is less important than the fact that they cancel each other out. This "six of one, half a dozen of the other" quality discourages interpretive assurance. Another rabbinic discussion, from *Leviticus Rabbah* 11.7, no doubt has the impending tragedy in mind when it comments on scripture's account of the beginning of the day of the inaugural service, Leviticus 9:1, "And it came to pass on the eighth day that Moses called Aaron and his sons and the elders of Israel and he said unto Aaron, etc.":

> R. Tanhuma in the name of R. Hiyya said, as also R. Berekiah in the name of R. Eleazar of Modin: The following homiletical interpretation was brought back with us from the Exile. Wherever the words *wayyehi* ["and it came to pass"] are used [in scripture], there is misfortune [related].

There is something deliberately irrelevant about researching this phrase, one of the commonest in the entire Bible and the very basis, if you will, for the famous biblical parataxis, coordinate rather than subordinate construction. Nor does this hermeneutic operation eventuate in a resolution when, later in the same discussion, "Simeon b. R. Abba says in the name of R. Johanan: Wherever [in scripture] it is said, *wayyehi* ['and it came to pass'] it serves to indicate either a misfortune *or* an occasion of rejoicing." Such evenhandedness is a bit vertiginous. The midrashic argument concludes, in short: even the positive instances of *wayyehi* (such as "And it came to pass on the eighth day") are not occasions of unalloyed rejoicing, "for on that day Nadab and Abihu died."

What, then, was the guilt of Nadab and Abihu? The wording of the first half of verse 1, Leviticus 10, suggests that it lies in their bringing forth *eš zerah* what Milgrom renders as "unauthorized coals," often translated as "strange fire,"[21] "alien fire,"[22] or "outside fire."[23] Incense offering was part of the normal course of worship and one of the normal cultic functions of the priests. But this instance was an illicit incense offering, or so they "discovered." It seems that "instead of deriving from the sacrificial altar, the coals came from a source that was 'profane' or 'outside'" (*ABL* 598). "They took the fire for their censers 'from somewhere,' but not from the altar fire, which alone was legitimate."[24] Since the incense altar was "standard equipment for Canaanite temples" (*ABL* 236), and since in Assyrian astral worship "it was customary to offer incense on the rooftops of private homes" (*ABL* 628), the Nadab and Abihu episode may represent a polemic against paganism, a warning about "the susceptibility of incense offerings to 'foreign' influences."[25] The second half of verse 1 has as important an explanatory function as the first: "They offered before the

Lord strange fire, which He had not commanded them." That is, it was not a matter of their being commanded not to do a particular thing, they were commanded not to do what they were not commanded.

The penalty for their infraction was the same as that for sancta encroachment: death. This is the perspective of the resumptive retelling of Leviticus 16:1: "The Lord spoke to Moses after the death of the sons of Aaron who died when they drew *too close* to the presence of the Lord." But Moses's explanation to Aaron immediately following his sons' death (Lev. 10:3)—"This is what the Lord meant when he said: 'Through those near to me I shall sanctify myself'"—is terribly enigmatic. Rashi asks "But where did he say it?" for indeed there is no such biblical passage. However, Moses's statement becomes, in the commentary, one of several bases for the interpretation that they died a sanctifying death ("From the Holy of Holies issued two flames of fire, as thin as threads, then parted into four, and two each pierced the nostrils of Nadab and Abihu").[26]

The interpretation that Levinas cites for the unspecified crime of Nadab and Abihu in Leviticus 10:2 is based on a contiguous passage, Leviticus 10:8–9: "And the Lord said to Aaron: 'Drink no wine or ale, you or your sons after you, when you enter the Tent of Meeting, lest you die.'" This is how the interpretation appears in Rashi:

> 10.2 "And fire came forth . . ." Rabbi Eliezer said: the sons of Aaron died only because they gave decisions on religious matters in the presence of their teacher, Moses. Rabbi Ishmael said: They died because they entered the Sanctuary intoxicated by wine. You know that this is so, because after their death he admonished those who survived that they should not enter when intoxicated by wine (vv 8–9). A parable! It may be compared to a king who had a bosom friend, etc., as is to be found in Leviticus Rabbah (ch. 12).[27]

One may hold, as does Edward Greenstein, that "the fact that the biblical text presents this law after the death of Nadab and Abihu has no chronological bearing."[28] Or one may understand the reversal of the chronological order as precisely the point which the parable of the king elaborates:

> R. Simeon taught: The sons of Aaron died only because they entered the Tent of Meeting drunk with wine. R. Phinehas said in the name of R. Levi: This may be compared to the case of a king who had a faithful attendant. When he found him standing at tavern entrances, he severed his head in silence, and appointed another attendant in his place. We would not know why he put the first to death, but for his enjoining the second thus: "You must not enter the doorway of taverns"; whence we

> know that for such a reason he had put the first to death. Thus [it is said], "And there came forth fire from before the Lord, and devoured them, and they died before the Lord" (Lev. 10:2), but we would not know why they [i.e., Nadab and Abihu] died, but for His commanding Aaron: "Drink no wine nor strong drink . . ." We know from this that they died precisely on account of the wine. (*Leviticus Rabbah* 12.1)

Even so, would not this law, "grasped" only in death or by the survivors, be indistinguishable from cruelty? It does not ethically awaken; it annihilates.

"And the Lord said to Aaron: 'Drink no wine or ale when you enter the tent of meeting.'" This is the sole time in the entire Bible where God speaks to Aaron solely. Usually his younger brother Moses serves as an intermediary. Damrosch shows how the "family politics of the patriarchal period" are being played out in the Nadab and Abihu episode.[29] The reversal of primogeniture—the passing over the right of the firstborn son (to whom special privileges accrue) in favor of the younger one—is still operative. In Exodus 4 when God commissions the reluctant Moses and designates Aaron as Moses's spokesman unto the people, he adds: "behold, he [Aaron] is coming out to meet you and when he sees you he will be glad in his heart" (v. 14), as if to draw attention to the possibility that, as the passed-over elder brother, he need not have been glad at all! Hence, with regard to Leviticus, Rashi reads the fact that "the divine address was made to him alone and not to Moses also" as "a reward" he received for his silence following the terrible event (*Rashi* 38).

Subsequently Moses forbids Aaron and his remaining sons to mourn, because their priestly duties take precedence. In what Milgrom terms "the squabble over the purification offering" (*ABL* 635), Moses becomes angry upon discovering that Aaron's surviving sons have failed to eat the goat of the sin offering, as they were supposed to do. The timing of Moses's anger—which is, of course, legendary—is as perplexing as God's in initiating a conversation with the grief-stricken father:

> And Aaron spoke to Moses, "See, this day they brought their purification offering and burnt offering before the Lord, and *such things have befallen me!* Had I eaten the purification offering today, would the Lord have approved?" And when Moses heard this, he approved. (Milgrom translation)

In Damrosch's reading, here the focus shifts "from Aaron's sons to Aaron himself, and specifically in Aaron's sense that the death of his sons is something that has befallen *him*."[30] For Damrosch, this episode is all about

Aaron, and can be referred back to his role in the golden calf episode. Since Aaron was responsible for the making of the golden calf, his sons are punished for their father's crime in "a classic case of the biblical confrontation of the present in the form of the past."[31] After all, "Nadab and Abihu have no existence apart from Aaron; this is their one action in the Pentateuch, apart from accompanying Moses and Aaron on Sinai."[32]

Indeed, according to some rabbinic commentators, the crime for which Nadab and Abihu are punished can be traced back to their activities at Sinai:

> Even at Sinai they had not conducted themselves properly, for instead of following the example of Moses, who had turned his face away from the Divine vision in the burning bush, they basked in the Divine vision on Mount Sinai.[33]

Their crime is, they basked, that is, they did not acknowledge their proper limits in relation to God. Similarly, on the day of the inaugural service, they were "carried away by the universal rejoicing at the heavenly fire, approached the sanctuary with the censers in their hands."[34] Moreover, in the words of Leviticus 10:1, "they each took his fire pan and put fire in it and laid incense on it. They offered before the Lord strange fire, which he had not commanded them." That is, they did not consult with each other; each one acted on his own—individually. Moreover, God had not commanded it; that is, they improvised. They did this not out of malicious intent to transgress the word of the Lord, "but out of a superabundance of joy" or religious ecstasy.[35] Hence, they were drunk after all; they were drunk on God.

The tendency among rabbinic commentators is to magnify and amplify the crimes of Nadab and Abihu: man always in the wrong before God. But despite the edification implied in this thought, are not these readings too apologetic with regard to a God who is arbitrary, wrathful, and violent? To say that Nadab and Abihu died because they entered the sanctuary intoxicated—literally or metaphorically—is not this reading authoritarian, legalistic, pharisaical? Does not the reading seek to rule out all spontaneity and affect in relation to the divine? Does not the reading draw attention to everything within Judaism, especially around what we call the law, that seems negative and lacking?

Here Levinas's overall project in *Difficult Freedom* becomes pertinent: to render explicit the "hidden resources" of the Judaic tradition, resources that have been "hidden" to the extent that they have been covered up by the dominant Greco-Christian tradition. Within a hermeneutic of Judaism that I have elsewhere termed "reinscription,"[36] Levinas argues that perhaps what seems a deficiency is in fact an alternative intelligibility. Perhaps Judaism can be understood, according to the formulation Levinas offers in *Difficult Freedom*, as "a passion distrusting its pathos" (*une passion se méfiant de son pathos; DL* 18–19). Perhaps the function of Jewish ritual life is to break up spontaneity, and therein lies its dimension that can be termed "ethical" in the sense that Levinas gives it in *Totality and Infinity*, "the putting into question of my spontaneity, of my joyous possession of the world by the presence of the other" (*TI* 43). A passion distrusting—or interrupting—its pathos would be precisely the ethical contribution of a reinscribed Judaism. It is no accident that the entire part 1 of *Difficult Freedom* (where the epigraph from Rashi is found) is entitled "Beyond Pathos" ("Au-dela du pathétique"). Levinas's hermeneutic of Judaism explicitly announces itself as a going beyond pathos.

In the essay "A Religion for Adults," he states that the entire effort of Judaism

> consists in understanding the holiness [*sainteté*] of God in a sense that stands in sharp contrast to the numinous meaning of the term. . . . The numinous annuls the links between persons by making them participate, albeit ecstatically, in a drama not brought about willingly by them. . . . The sacred [*le sacré*] that envelops and transports me is a form of violence. (*DL* 29)

The distinction asserted here in 1952 between the sacred and the holy indeed runs through all of Levinas's subsequent discussions of religion. The title of the second collection of talmudic writings, *Du sacré au saint* (1977), not only makes the passage from the one to the other explicit (*from* the sacred *to* the holy), it identifies this passage with extracting the ethical meaning from the Bible over and against any numinous sense. Similarly, in the 1975 essay "God and Philosophy," "fear and trembling" is opposed to the "dis-interestedness of holiness." In short, if to study the Torah in ceaseless dialogue with previous commentators means to be a Pharisee, so be it. He writes, in an essay called "The Pharisee Is Absent":

> The Pharisee draws from the source but does not confuse himself with it. He is not possessed by the forces which tear apart, alter, and dissolve [*Il n'est pas possédé par les forces qui déchirent, altèrent, et dissolvent*]. . . . The liquor that he drinks quenches his thirst without drunkenness [*La liqueur qu'il boit désaltère sans ivresse*]. (*DL* 49)

The verb *alterer* means both "to alter" and also "to make thirsty." The liquor which Levinas's Pharisee drinks is said to *désaltère*, it unmakes thirst, it quenches, without producing drunkenness. One should not miss this important emphasis. Here, as in his implicit interpretation of the Nadab and Abihu episode, Levinas situates himself among the *mitnagdim,* the traditional opponents of Hasidic mysticism and forms of spirituality. (And this polemic against Hasidism, which runs through his work, shows that the difference between the pathetic and the nonpathetic is not reducible to the difference between Christianity and Judaism; rather it is internal to Judaism.) Levinas's Judaism is intellectualist, not emotional. For the *mitnagdim* it was forbidden to contemplate God's essence. It was enough to study the Torah and obey its commandments. For Levinas, ethics is sobriety itself; his Judaism, as he states in *Difficult Freedom,* is not lyrical, but "prose": "To lyrical Judaism . . . , let us oppose a few words in prose" (*DL* 78).

Rashi's reading of Leviticus 10:2 gives the "plain sense" of the scriptural verse, but not to the exclusion of all others. On the contrary, the "plain sense" makes possible all other senses and is traced by them. When Levinas cites Rashi, he necessarily invokes all the rejected opinions about the death of Nadab and Abihu, of which he is certainly aware.[37] With regard to Leviticus 10:2, he appears to be delighting in the search, or midrash.

In my view, the place where the Nadab and Abihu story reverberates most in a Levinasian way is not verse 2: "And fire came forth from the Lord and consumed them; thus they died before the Lord," but the second half of verse 3: "And Aaron was silent." "Stupefied," glosses Milgrom (*ABL* 604). In a book on biblical silence, André Neher describes this as the most eloquent silence in all of biblical literature. He writes:

> One can detect in his [Aaron's] silence, no doubt, a religious touch of submission to the divine will, but it is far more probable that by this brief phrase the Bible wished to portray the physiological moment of petrification. As with the Patriarch Jacob there was with Aaron a momentary stopping of the heart, a suspension of intellectual and moral reaction. . . . Aaron was nothing more at that moment than a statue of stone. If we accept this interpretation however, then it might be reasonable to assume that the "petrification" of Aaron followed not the fatal accident but the theological explanation which Moses had attempted to give to it: "Through those near to me I shall be sanctified. . . ." Here we put our finger on a biblical attitude which the example of Job precisely illustrates in a remarkable manner, namely, that the silence of God in the event is less painful than His silence in the interpretation, and that men can accept that God keeps silent but not that other men should speak in His place.[38]

In short, Moses's *theological* explanation of Aaron's sons' death is too pat, too totalizing. But in Aaron's silence, might not one read the beginning of a response, or responsibility, to the disaster?

Notes

1. Jill Robbins, ed., *Is It Righteous to Be? Interviews with Emmanuel Levinas* (Stanford: Stanford University Press, 2001), 62. Hereafter cited in the text as *IR*.

2. Jill Robbins, *Altered Reading: Levinas and Literature* (Chicago: University of Chicago Press, 1999).

3. Levinas's attribution of this interpretation to Rashi is itself problematic. First of all, Rashi (after having cited Rabbi Eliezer) is quoting the view of R. Ishmael. This particular interpretation, which refers us to the parable of the king in Leviticus, is followed by an "etcetera." In other words, Rashi mentions at least two rabbinic interpretations of the Nadab and Abihu episode without necessarily singling out this one. Moreover, the interpretive passage that Levinas cites is not in all printed editions of Rashi. In the critical edition by Berliner and Chavel, the passage is in brackets. Thanks to Michael Berger for drawing my attention to these issues.

4. Jacob Milgrom, *The Anchor Bible: Leviticus 1–16* (New York: Doubleday, 1991). Hereafter cited in the text as *ABL*.

5. E. A. Speiser, *The Anchor Bible: Genesis* (New York: Doubleday, 1964), xxiv–xxv.

6. Translation by Martin Noth in *Exodus: A Commentary,* trans. J. S. Bowden (Philadelphia: Westminster, 1962).

7. Translation by Brevard Childs in *The Book of Exodus* (Philadelphia: Westminster, 1974).

8. Childs, *Exodus,* 506.

9. Noth, *Exodus,* 196.

10. Childs, *Exodus,* 507.

11. See Martin Noth, *Leviticus: A Commentary,* trans. J. E. Anderson (Philadelphia: Westminster, 1965), 82.

12. Everett Fox, ed. and trans., *The Five Books of Moses* (New York: Schocken, 1995), 546.

13. Søren Kierkegaard, "Ultimatum," in *Either/Or Part II,* trans. Howard V. Hong and Edna H. Hong (Princeton: Princeton University Press, 1987).

14. *The Midrash Rabbah,* trans. and ed. H. Freedman and Maurice Simon (London: Soncino, 1977), 41.1.

15. David Damrosch, "Leviticus," in *The Literary Guide to the Bible,* ed. Robert Alter and Frank Kermode (Cambridge: Harvard University Press, 1987), 70.

16. *"Die Leute, die die Bibel geschrieben haben, haben ja anscheinend von Gott ähnlich gedacht wie Kafka. Ich habe noch nie ein Buch gelesen, das mich so stark an die Bibel erinnert hat wie sein Roman "Das Schloß." Den zu lesen is deshalb auch kein Vergnügen."* Franz Rosenzweig, *Briefe,* ed. Edith Rosenzweig (Berlin: Schocken, 1935), 596.

17. Harold Bloom and David Rosenberg, *The Book of J* (New York: Grove Weidenfeld, 1990).

18. Henry Sussman, *The Trial: Kafka's Unholy Trinity* (New York: Twayne, 1993), 37.

19. Fox, *Five Books of Moses,* 548.

20. Louis Ginzberg, *The Legends of the Jews* (Philadelphia: Jewish Publication Society, 1928), 3:243–44.

21. Noth, *Leviticus,* 82.

22. Baruch A. Levine, *The JPS Torah Commentary: Leviticus* (Philadelphia: Jewish Publication Society, 1989), 58.

23. Fox, *Five Books of Moses,* 548.

24. Noth, *Leviticus,* 85.

25. Ibid.

26. Ginzberg, *Legends,* 3:187.

27. *Pentateuch with Rashi's Commentary,* trans. M. Rosenbaum and A. M. Silbermann (Jerusalem, 1932), 38. Hereafter cited in the text as *Rashi.*

28. Edward Greenstein, "Deconstruction and Biblical Narrative," *Prooftexts* 9 (1989): 70.

29. Damrosch, *Leviticus,* 72.

30. Ibid., 70.

31. Ibid., 71.

32. Ibid.

33. Ginzberg, *Legends,* 3:187–88.

34. Ibid., 3:187.

35. Nehama Leibowitz, *Studies in Vayikra* (Jerusalem: World Zionist Organization, 1980), 67.

36. Jill Robbins, *Prodigal Son/Elder Brother: Interpretation and Alterity in Augustine, Petrarch, Kafka, Levinas* (Chicago: University of Chicago Press, 1991); and Jill Robbins, "An Inscribed Responsibility," in *MLN,* "Comparative Literature Issue," vol. 106, no. 5 (1991).

37. See Daniel Boyarin, *Carnal Israel: Reading Sex in Talmudic Culture* (Berkeley: University of California Press, 1993), 26–30. This is another reason why it would be problematic to let a single proper name or signature ("Rashi") stand in for an irreducible rabbinic polyphony.

38. André Neher, *The Exile of the Word: From the Silence of the Bible to the Silence of Auschwitz,* trans. David Maisel (Philadelphia: Jewish Publication Society, 1981), 35.

The Responsibility of Irresponsibility: Taking (Yet) Another Look at the Akedah

Claire Elise Katz

> No man is an island, entire of itself; every man is a piece of the continent, a part of the main . . . any man's death diminishes me, because I am involved in mankind.
> —John Donne

> I love him [God], but I love even more his Torah.
> —Yossel ben Yossel, cited by Levinas in *Difficult Freedom*

> Can we still be Jewish without Kierkegaard?
> —Emmanuel Levinas

> Abraham both awes and repulses me.
> —Kierkegaard/de Silentio

The Torah, or Hebrew Bible, is usually read as a story about the creation of the world as such, about cosmogony. But there are passages in the Midrash, the rabbinic commentary on the Bible, that allow for the possibility of another interpretation. Rashi, for example, explains the creation of the world in terms of the giving of the Torah itself—what we know as the Hebrew Bible.[1] Rashi's worry is that the mention of water at the start of the book of Genesis comes with no explanation of its creation. Thus, the creation of the world must be about something other than a chronological retelling of the story. The term "Torah" is often translated, or mistranslated, as "Law." A better translation is one offered by Hermann Cohen: instruction, path, or ethics, but specifically the instruction and knowledge of morality.[2] My point here is that if we alter the reading of Genesis from cosmogony to "ethogony," that is, from an emphasis on the world created as such to an emphasis on the creation of a moral universe, then we can also ask about the ways in which the stories that follow the first chapter of Genesis are altered.[3]

For example, let us take the story of Cain and Abel. What do we say about Cain's responsibility? That he is responsible might not change, though many of us might need to examine the anachronistic methods we use to hold Cain responsible. The codified rules of the Ten Commandments were not yet available, in fact they do not arrive until Exodus, and there is nothing written in the text which indicates Adam and Eve either knew about moral codes or were teaching them to their children. But if we understand the Creation story as the creation of an ethical world, we might conceive of ethics differently than we have traditionally. If we understand the Ten Commandments to be a codified set of rules for practices that were already taking place and for behavior that could be expected of people without having moral training, we can then interpret the story a bit differently than we have. By altering the way we understand the ethical, we might also see the gravity of murder in a different light. We could say that the punishment of Cain indicates that the commandment "thou shalt not kill" was something Cain should have known, but to which he failed to respond. The face of Abel spoke to Cain, but Cain did not hear it. We could say that the "thou shalt not kill" expressed in the face of the other is so profound that the prohibition against murder is not something that needed to be taught. It is precognitive.

And if we understand murder in this regard, we can understand the Judaic view that murder is *the* unforgivable act. Mishna Sanhedrin 4:5 give us an indication of the profound nature of murder: "To save a life is as if to save the world," accompanies the expression, "Whoever takes a single life destroys thereby an entire world."[4] This passage responds to the use of the word "bloods," written in Hebrew in the plural, when God says to Cain, "your brother's bloods cry out to me from the ground." The rabbis tell us that the Hebrew word for "blood," written here in the plural, indicates that it is not just Abel who is lost, but all of his future generations.[5] According to one Judaic view, acts that are committed by a person against another person cannot be forgiven by God; they can only be forgiven by the one against whom the act was perpetrated. Murder makes this forgiveness impossible, since no one can stand in as proxy for another. If murder is so grave, so profound, then how are we to understand the Akedah, the biblical story of the binding of Isaac in which the killing/murder is commanded by God?

What does Judaism do with this story, which is not only part of its holy text, but also has as its main character Abraham, the man with whom Judaism begins? How does Judaism come to terms with a God who asks for a child to be sacrificed to it as part of a test? How does Judaism respond when the sacrifice is to indicate one's love for God? This essay will revisit the Akedah by viewing it first through Kierkegaard's reading of it and then through Levinas's response to Kierkegaard, a response informed by his own Jewish background. Thus, I also invoke and integrate Jewish sources into my discussion. In particular, I wish to engage themes from Emmanuel Levinas's philosophical and confessional writings so that we may glimpse an unorthodox, if you will, reading of the binding of Isaac. I argue that this task can be better accomplished by taking seriously Søren Kierkegaard's reading of Abraham found in *Fear and Trembling*.[6] Though I sympathize with Levinas's concerns with Kierkegaard's reading, it is Kierkegaard who gives us the strong reading of Abraham, a man before whom we fear and tremble. I claim that it is precisely Kiekegaard's reading which ultimately serves to give force to Levinas's concern. My task, then, is to examine the possibility of locating a "genesis" of the ethical and to explore Levinas's conception of responsibility by using the images we find in the Akedah, but to do so by synthesizing Kierkegaard, Levinas, and Judaism.[7] I embark on this task with the strong disclaimer that this is a Jewish approach and not *the* Jewish approach, since Judaism comprises a plurality of views.

The Akedah is one of the more troubling stories that we find in the Torah, for it tells the story of God's demand that Abraham willingly sacrifice his (Abraham's) child to God in order to prove his faith.[8] The test, as Abraham understands it, is to take Isaac, his beloved son, the son through which God has promised the fulfillment of the covenant, up to Mount Moriah where he is to be offered as a sacrifice. It is in the absurdity of the situation that Abraham's faith is tested, for God has promised that Canaan will be delivered through Isaac, but now God is asking that Isaac be sacrificed. Because of God's initial promise, Abraham must believe Isaac will be returned to him, though this seems impossible. It is in light of this absurdity that Abraham starts with Isaac up the mountain.

The story took on new force with Kierkegaard's attention to it in *Fear and Trembling*. Writing under the pen name Johannes de Silentio, Kierkegaard calls into question whether we can truly understand the anguish Abraham must have felt at having to comprehend and pass such a test. For Silentio, the kind of faith Abraham exhibits is not the faith talked about in modern days, where faith is too easy. Thus, for Silentio/Kierkegaard, the heart of the story is revealed in Abraham's faith in the absurdity of the situation: that God will take Isaac and that Isaac will be returned to him. Silentio sees the absurdity in the story as a paradox that consists of the sacrifice and the necessary return of Isaac. By focusing on this element of the story, Kierkegaard sees in the narrative a story about Abraham's faith that he will lose Isaac and somehow get him back—but the return of Isaac, as Silentio expresses it, is necessary only for the fulfillment of the covenant. That is what makes the asking for the sacrifice an absurdity. Even in the section of *Fear and Trembling* called "The Attunement," when Silentio is trying to help us to see what Abraham must be struggling with, the focus is on the fear that it will be Isaac who will lose faith in God. Silentio's concern is with the logical possibility, or impossibility, of the situation. But we might ask if he has glossed over the real concern: the father of Judaism has just been asked by God to kill his own son, for no reason other than for a test. And for the moment, I wish to leave open what this test is.[9]

Let us refocus our attention back to Kierkegaard's reading of Abraham, for it is in Kierkegaard's insight that we should take Abraham seriously that we will find our answers. If we follow Kierkegaard in this reading, we can ask after Kierkegaard's own question: Why do we tremble before Abraham? One attempt at an answer is to say that we fear and tremble before Abraham because we fear and tremble before God. This is where I part company with Silentio. Silentio cannot move forward because his focus remains on Abraham and of what Abraham is capable. This focus distracts him (and us) from a larger question, namely, of what is God capable? For whatever reason, and we can speculate about numerous reasons, Silentio does not entertain the possibility that God is variable. He focuses on Abraham so that neither he, nor his reader, looks behind Abraham at God. But it is by looking at God that we come to the possibility of admiring Abraham, while also giving up what Kierkegaard terms the "teleological suspension of the ethical." It is the suspension of the ethical understood as a universal, and this suspension is in the name of something higher, namely, the experience of the religious. Though Silentio wants to mock Christianity, he does so by keeping the ethical structure as he understands it in place; thus his challenge falls flat.

From Silentio's perspective, if we are to admire Abraham as a man, we must allow for the possibility of what he calls the "teleological suspension of the ethical," a suspension that Abraham enacted when he raised the knife to Isaac. Silentio wants to take seriously Abraham's struggle, which Christianity wants to ignore by reconceiving faith. According to Kierkegaard's reading of Christianity, faith, or rather God, and by implication, faith, cannot ask us to do what it asked Abraham to do; it cannot ask us to be unethical. I suggest that it is by reading Kierkegaard seriously that we actually find a way out of the conclusion at which he arrives: that we fear and tremble before Abraham because there can be a teleological suspension of the ethical. I suggest that there is another possibility, one which disallows the teleological suspension of the ethical.

The teleological suspension of the ethical is precisely the feature that makes Levinas uncomfortable; and he is in good company, for most of the rabbis are also uncomfortable.[10] One rabbi's discomfort can be seen in the following midrash, where Rabbi Aha questions Abraham's interpretation of God's command. Abraham has problems fitting together three things: (1) God's promise to fulfill the covenant through Isaac; (2) God's command to offer Isaac as a sacrifice; and (3) God telling Abraham not to continue with the sacrifice. God responds by saying that he will not change any part of what he has commanded. Rabbi Aha provides the following speculative dialogue between Abraham and God in which Abraham wonders about God's indulgence in prevarications. God, according to the rabbi, says, "O Abraham, my covenant will I not profane, And I will establish My covenant with Isaac. When I bade thee, 'Take now thy son,' etc. Did I tell thee, Slaughter him? No! But, 'take him up.'[11] Thou hast taken him up. Now take him down." In other words, the rabbi speculates that, for whatever reason, God merely asked Abraham "to take Isaac up," not to offer him up as a sacrifice. The root from which this word is rendered consists of the Hebrew letters *ayin, lamed, heh*. The root could be rendered as *aliyah*, which translates literally as "to take up," a word used to describe the action when a Jew goes up to the *bimah* to read from the Torah, or when someone makes a religious trip to Israel. But its root can also be rendered as *la'ola*, "to offer up," as in a sacrifice. So the rabbi here speculates that Abraham misunderstood God's command, and the command to sacrifice Isaac was fabricated by Abraham, not commanded by God. The rabbi's attempt to "save" God, and Judaism, from the violence that would accompany a request for such a sacrifice reveals just how troubling this story is to Judaism. But this midrash, as humorous and sincere as it is, does not do justice to the story; nor does it do justice to Abraham, who is presented here as a buffoon. In the effort to "save" God by making God less frightening, the rabbi here does not take Abraham seriously, and therefore, does not take God seriously. Moreover, what could we make of a religion in which the message of God was to be followed literally, but the chosen of the chosen to carry out God's will misunderstood that message? If Abraham does not get it, where does that leave the rest of us?!

For Levinas, among others, a suspension of the ethical which allows for the sacrifice/murder of another cannot be tolerated. However, rather than say that God would not ask this kind of action of us, though Levinas assumes that God must be compassionate, Levinas focuses on *our* actions, on what we are supposed to do. Franz Rosenzweig makes a similar point when he claims that if humanity is to be truly free, God must also be truly free, and part of that freedom is the freedom to deceive us.[12] In addition, God must make God's own actions difficult, if not impossible, to understand, lest we be too willing to follow along God's will blindly. If this course of action were possible, then the fearful and the timid, those most likely to follow God's will out of fear of the repercussions, would be the most pious. In order to be free, we must be free to defy God's will.[13] We fear and tremble before a God who can ask us to commit a murder precisely because we are to choose not to do so. We fear and tremble before a God who is also free and who will not do our ethical work for us. As Levinas would say, it is a "difficult freedom."[14]

Levinas's criticism of Kierkegaard focuses on Kierkegaard's conception of the ethical. For Kierkegaard the ethical is defined as the universal, and the religious is the way one reclaims the particular. At the level of the religious, the particular is reclaimed, but in a higher form than the particular at the level of the aesthetic. In Kierkegaard's understanding of the ethical, the singularity of the self, and the other, is lost in a rule that is valid for everyone. Levinas's criticism rests on his claim that "the ethical is not where [Kierkegaard] sees it."[15] Similar to the rest of the history of philosophy, the ethical is characterized in terms of the universal, as that which applies to everyone. For Levinas, Kierkegaard's violence emerges precisely when he "transcends ethics," and ascends to the religious.[16] Although in Kierkegaard's account the religious reclaims the particular, this view of the religious cannot be seen as Levinas's account of the ethical. Although the religious reclaims the particular, and although the ethical that is suspended for Kierkegaard is the ethical understood as the universal, in Levinas's view, the religious still appears to suspend the ethical even as Levinas understands it. A conception of the ethical that accounts for the singularity of the *I,* and that poses the *I* as a unique individual, that implies an infinite requirement of a responsibility toward others, is still missing from Kierkegaard's religious stage. So one must ask, if the religious entails a suspension of the ethical, that is, the universal, but also allows for a renaming of murder so that a sacrifice can be made for the love (or is it fear?) of God, is there an account present of an ethics such as the one that Levinas puts forth? The answer would have to be no.[17]

Consequently, in Levinas's view, the dramatic moment of the story emerges when Abraham listens to the angel of the Lord who tells him, "Do not lay a hand on the lad." This moment in the story illustrates the turning point from the focus on Abraham to the focus on Isaac. The story is no longer about Abraham as a man of faith, about Abraham's perceived duty to God; rather, this moment in the story could be read as the need for our attention to be focused on the victims, on those who suffer the violence, not the administrators of that violence, even if, or maybe especially if, that violence is administered in the name of God. We can draw on Levinas's imagery of the Shoah—the too-tight skin, references to persecution, to being a hostage, to feeding the hungry—that appear in *Otherwise Than Being*, a text which explores in detail the tension between the ethical and the political, to support the claim that Kierkegaard's reading of this story is precisely the problem Levinas has with the history of philosophy and the moral theory that springs from it.[18] Levinas's worry about the history of philosophy fuels his belief that the focus of Western philosophy, its emphasis on rationality and the need to universalize, led to the sacrifice of the individual in the name of a greater good. We can see this enacted most clearly in the way national policy often sustains its own form of theodicy: the suffering of individuals is justified in the name of a greater good for everyone else concerned. From the events of Nazi Germany we have countless examples, including Eichmann at his trial in Jerusalem, of those who claimed "just to be doing their duty."[19]

The conflict between duty and responsibility appears in Kierkegaard's reading of the Akedah just as it appears in Nazi Germany. Levinas's concern issues precisely from this commitment to duty, even if, and maybe especially when, that commitment to duty is directed toward God. In *Fear and Trembling* this conflict is demonstrated in Silentio/Kierkegaard's characterization of the tragic hero, an individual contrasted with the knight of faith. But regardless of this distinction, the loss of the ethical in the name of duty is precisely what Levinas fears, and the Shoah, though certainly an extreme limit of this loss, nonetheless has its roots in a view that condones the subordination of the ethical to duty.

I do not mean to imply that the Nazis' obedience to their leader and to their cause resembles Kierkegaard's knight of faith, and I realize that Kierkegaard conceives a level higher than the ethical. Rather, I want to underscore Levinas's concern with regard to an ethical defined as such; I also want to underscore the danger in Kierkegaard's interpretation which tells us that, in spite of the anguish Abraham must have felt, he still felt compelled to obey God, and this obedience led to the potential sacrifice of his son. As Sartre also notes, Abraham certainly may have struggled with questions about the identity of who was asking him to commit this act.[20] Additionally, Abraham's action could be seen not only as selfless, but actually self-defeating, since all he had was invested in Isaac and Isaac's future. But Abraham nonetheless made the choice to take that leap of faith and obey God. This choice, this obedience to duty that we find in Kant and then reformulated but essentially taken up again in Kierkegaard, is

Levinas's worry. For both Levinas and Kierkegaard there is the concern that the ethical will be disrupted by such a suspension. But for Kierkegaard, this possibility must remain open. It is here that Levinas and Kierkegaard part company.

For Levinas there cannot be a teleological suspension of the ethical, since this suspension of the ethical may very well mean not simply the disruption, but also the annihilation of the ethical. Thus, we might ask if there is another way to engage this fear and trembling. Must this fear and trembling be brought on only because of the suspension of the ethical? It is here that we should not leave Kierkegaard behind, but precisely engage him. It is here that we should help Silentio further his inquiry. Silentio does not want to give up on Abraham. He sees him as an admirable figure, though whether Abraham is to be admired for his participation in this action is a curiosity, at best. For the Jews, he is an admirable figure, but for different reasons. In fact, Levinas comments that Kierkegaard never speaks of the Abraham who welcomes the stranger into his tent and who argues with God to save the possible pious who are in Sodom. Thus, although Silentio wants to proceed, he does not know how to proceed. Abraham is admired for his faith, but his faith is examined in light of his willingness to sacrifice Isaac. And yet, Silentio has his own well-motivated anxieties about Abraham, revealed in Silentio's comment that Abraham both awes and repulses him. If we take Kierkegaard's reading of the story seriously, we must imagine that it took all of Abraham's strength, emotional and otherwise, to get him to the point of raising that knife. Kierkegaard gives us an excellent psychological portrayal of Abraham. Kierkegaard reminds us of the time it took for Abraham to make the decision: that he had to lie to Sarah, travel up the mountain, cut the wood, and then bind Isaac. To read *Fear and Trembling* is, to be sure, not to take lightly what Abraham believes he is asked and commits himself to do. In light of this psychological profile and our understanding of what it must have taken to get Abraham to the point of accepting this demand such that he raises the knife to his own son, what must have happened that Abraham so easily puts the knife down, without so much as a question to the angel such as "How do I know *this* is what God wants?" If nothing else, inertia alone should have prompted him to go through with God's command.[21] Something crucial is missing from this story, but it can only be noticed if we complete a reading of this story which Kierkegaard began but did not finish.

So in spite of Kierkegaard's brilliant reading of this story, in spite of the effective way he teaches us to reread it, and maybe even teaches us to read it for the first time, to read it slowly, to fill in the gaps, or at least wonder about them, ponder them, and be troubled by what might be inserted, in spite of all these things, Silentio misses something.[22] It is this lack which

Levinas notices, and to which I turn. How can we retain an admiration for Abraham, but have a different motivation for doing so? It is here that I insert my own answer into the question. Let us look at the story again. Not the whole story, but just the part where the angel of the Lord tells Abraham to put the knife down and he does. What is going on here?

In order to address this question, we need to apply Kierkegaard's teaching in *Fear and Trembling*, which implores us not to read the Akedah too quickly, to his own reading of the story. We should take Kierkegaard at his word. We should read the story slowly and carefully, but we should also read it to the end! What dangers might await us if, by stopping halfway through the text, all we take away from Kierkegaard's insightful reading is the profundity of faith that we cannot understand without questioning the very command to kill Isaac that led to that faith, or without wondering why Abraham did not go through with the task set before him? We can read Kierkegaard back upon himself and discover another message in the text.

In "A Propos of 'Kierkegaard Vivant,'" a short essay by Levinas on Kierkegaard, Levinas writes, "that Abraham obeyed the first voice is astonishing: that he had sufficient distance with respect to that obedience to hear the second voice—that is essential."[23] Levinas's focus on Abraham's sensitivity to hear the second voice signals the difference in his reading from Kierkegaard's, and his insight mimics Kierkegaard/Silentio's lesson. Levinas does not want us to gloss over the fact that the sacrifice did not happen, that Abraham stopped when the angel of the Lord spoke to him. This distance from obedience, this receptivity to the other that Abraham displayed, is as extraordinary as his initial faith.[24] But Levinas's interest gains new strength if read against the backdrop of Kierkegaard's portrayal of Abraham. In light of this portrayal, I want to examine what it means that Abraham heard the second voice and that he put down the knife.

Levinas insists that responsibility presupposes response. Responsibility, indeed, a conception of ethics, cannot lose sight of "response," and it is precisely this conception of response that we see in Abraham at the point when Abraham aborts the intended sacrifice. An angel of the Lord says, "Abraham, Abraham."[25] Abraham replies to the angel, "here I am [*hineni*]." The angel then says, "Do not lay a hand on the lad." It is significant that while it was God who initiates this sequence of events, it is an angel who brings them to an end. Just as Sartre indicated that Abraham might have wondered if it really was God who issued the initial command, should not Abraham have wondered if this presence really was an angel of the Lord, an agent of the Lord, if you will; should Abraham not have wondered if stopping the sacrifice really was what God intended? The "here I am [*me voici*]," *hineni,* in Hebrew, implies a sensitivity, a total awareness, or an openness to respond, and in a sense, implies that the response actually precedes the utterance of the phrase.[26] To utter "here I am" is to be already ready to respond. This view is borne out by Levinas himself when he cites Isaiah's claim that "before they call, I will answer."[27] If we think through, again, what Abraham had endured in order to get to the point of actually raising the knife to his son in order to respond to a command given to him by God, then it is extraordinary that Abraham is ready to hear the second command, the command not to continue. This command given to him, not directly by God, but by a messenger of God, is significant for Silentio, since this means that Abraham is no longer in a relation of Absolute to Absolute; the relationship between Abraham and God is now mediated, and the immediate relationship has shifted to Abraham and Isaac, a relationship Levinas terms the "face to face." We might be able to interpret this story as Abraham having already turned back to the ethical, or maybe having turned toward it for the first time, if the ethical is to mean something different from what it means for Kierkegaard. In any case, it would not mean, for Levinas, a turning back to the universal. In other words, the Levinasian conception of the ethical would mean a fourth category for Kierkegaard. But might we not say that at the moment he raised the knife Abraham saw the face of Isaac in a way that demanded response, that commanded him in a way greater than God's command to respond to a face that signified the particularity of the Other, rather than the universal of a nation? Could we not say that Abraham's receptiveness to the second voice implies that Abraham had already turned toward the ethical, and could we not read this moment, as Levinas also suggests, as the essential moment in the story? Let us look again at the midrash which asks after the phrase, "Do not lay a hand on the lad." I suggest that this moment in the text indicates that Abraham had already put down the knife. The angel's voice, then, is less a command from above than it is a response to a response that is already in motion.[28]

We have two Abrahams, then: the Abraham who went up the mountain prepared to sacrifice his son, and the Abraham who countermands the command of God and who listens to an angel say "do not do this action." Why did Abraham not go through with the sacrifice? How did he know to listen to the angel? Something happened on Mount Moriah, and it is something not mentioned in the written text of the Torah, and it cannot be written into the text of the Torah. It is only through Abraham's bodily actions, through his preparations to sacrifice Isaac, that he has the epiphany of the ethical. And just as Abraham comes to understand *through* his actions, so too must we come to understand *through* the act of reading and reflecting.

If we read this part of the story, and Abraham's "here I am," as a sign of Abraham's turn toward the ethical, then the story could move in a variety of different directions. We could say that God saw the need to stop the action about to take place. But we could also say that Abraham might have defied God, even if the angel had not come to stop him.[29] In fact, we might say that Abraham did defy God. If we followed this latter alternative, we might approach Levinas's understanding of what it means to love the Torah more than God, to love the ethical more than God. Levinas illustrates what he means by this relationship when he affirms Yossel ben Yossel's remark that "even if I [Yossel ben Yossel] were deceived by him and became disillusioned, I should nevertheless observe the precepts of the Torah."[30] Levinas asks, "Is this blasphemy?" And he replies to his own question, "At the very least, it is a protection against the madness of a direct contact with the Sacred that is unmediated by reason. But, above all, it is a confidence that does not rely on the triumph of any institution, it is the internal evidence of morality supplied by the Torah. Loving the Torah even more than God means precisely having access to a personal God against Whom one may rebel—that is to say, for Whom one may die."[31]

If we reread Levinas's work *Totality and Infinity* into this story, we could say that the father-son relationship Levinas describes is playing itself in the Akedah, as it does nowhere else.[32] Nowhere in Judaism does fecundity mean more than it does in Abraham's relationship to Isaac, a relationship in which the son's life and the future of Israel are, literally, suspended in his father's hands. Thus, we might say that contrary to Kierkegaard's view, it is not faith that is the highest moment, but the turn toward the ethical; and it is not an ethical defined in terms of the universal as Kierkegaard describes it. Rather, it is a response to the other, an ethical that emphasizes responsibility to the other where the uniqueness of the "I" is such that one's responsibility is infinite and irreplaceable. In the "Preamble from the Heart," another section of *Fear and Trembling*, Kierkegaard/Silentio implies that Abraham must give Isaac up so that he can get Isaac back and receive him in a proper way. Could this story be telling us that, contrary to Kierkegaard's claim that Abraham suspended the ethical, in fact, Abraham did not understand, did not yet see the ethical at all?

I claim that it is in Abraham's actions that we have the genesis of the ethical. And contrary to the story of Cain and Abel in which the murder of Abel is necessary in order for the profundity of "thou shalt not kill" to be revealed to us, I claim that not only is it unnecessary that Isaac be sacrificed, but it is essential that Abraham abort the sacrifice. The ethical was present for Cain and Abel, but Cain was unable to hear its call and respond to the face of Abel. If Judaism is to begin with Abraham, then it is precisely at this moment that Abraham must love the Torah more than

God. Hermann Cohen offers a similar view when he says that to love God is to love the Torah. Love of God means knowledge of God, of God's attributes. To love God is to comprehend morality.[33] Rosenzweig follows Cohen so elegantly when he describes the movement of humanity from Adam, who did not hear God, to Abraham, who did. Rosenzweig describes this movement in terms of the recognition of responsibility. Adam, upon being asked what he had done, does not reply with an "I." He does not say, "I did it." Rather, he says, "she did it." But, according to Rosenzweig, "man . . . now called by his name, twice[34] in a supreme definiteness that could not but be heard, now he answers, all unlocked, all spread out, all ready, all-soul: 'here I am.'"[35] The "here I am" marks the moment of subjectivity.

We might say, then, that Abraham's actions, Abraham's willingness to sacrifice his child, *and* his receptiveness not to continue with the action, depict a necessary moment in the genesis of the ethical itself. Even if Levinas does not want to locate the ethical in an *arché*, even if responsibility is to be an-archical, there is nonetheless a sense in which the ethical calls for its own explanation. We can explain the ethical in developmental, or generative, terms. Such a view can synthesize the readings given by both Kierkegaard/Silentio and Levinas. We can concede that Abraham is the knight of faith; but we can also agree with Levinas that the essential moment of the story is that Abraham does not sacrifice Isaac. Thus, one possible way to look at this story is in terms of Abraham's movement from faith to ethics. We can say that Abraham needed to have faith in a compassionate God in order to offer Isaac up, only to see the face of the other in Isaac. That is, Abraham needed to have this extraordinary faith in order to come to the limit of committing a horrific act so that he could see, profoundly, what it is that God really wants, or rather, what it means to love God: that regardless of what it appears God tells us to do, we must first and foremost respond to the other. And we must keep in mind that this movement travels in one direction; this kind of faith is not preserved. If Abraham were asked to do this act again, he would not. The lesson he needed to learn was learned.[36] The religious is not merely suspended for something higher, namely, a reconceived ethical. Rather, this kind of religiosity is exchanged for the ethical, a new conception of religion, if you will.[37] For Levinas, the point at which Abraham hears that second voice is the moment that indicates Abraham has heard the voice that has led him to the ethical; it is this moment that is not only the essential moment, but "the highest moment in the drama."[38] Thus, is it not the case, as Levinas says, that we rise to the level of the religious precisely when we are ethical?[39]

In *The Gift of Death,* Derrida illuminates the aporia of responsibility: all responsibility entails irresponsibility. Thus, to be responsible to another is to be irresponsible to other others. Levinas recognizes this problem; however, for Levinas the movement between my responsibility to the other and to the other others is the movement between ethics and politics. In Levinas's view, this movement must, but typically does not, privilege the ethical. The ethical for Levinas takes precedence, even over God. This claim raises other questions insofar as God represents the ethical. But if, as Rosenzweig claimed, a religion is to be founded on those who are strong rather than on those who are weak and timid, God must be free and able to deceive; God must be free to command a murder so that we are free to choose not to commit that murder. We must be free to show that we are strong by being able to disobey God's unethical command. This, I claim, was the test Abraham had to pass.[40]

Kierkegaard's reading, although brilliant in its own right, also leaves us wanting. His exploration in *Fear and Trembling* is similar to what the rabbis did centuries before him. There is no doubt that he gives us a different reading than the collection of midrashim we have in the Judaic tradition; we might even say that he offers his own version of a midrash on Abraham's struggle. But I say Kierkegaard's reading leaves us wanting, for he does not abide by even his own rule to read the story slowly and to read it carefully, since he does not read it to the end. He stops precisely where the drama begins, namely, when Abraham hears the angel, when Abraham puts down the knife, when Abraham sees in the face of his son the true meaning of the religious, and when he sees that to love the Torah more than God, to love the ethical more than God, is actually to see the trace of God in the Other.[41] Kierkegaard's drama ends where for Levinas, and for me, the climax begins: when Abraham realizes that to be irresponsible to God and responsible to Isaac, is precisely to be responsible to God.

Notes

I would like to thank Antje Kapust, Eric Nelson, and Kent Still for providing me with the opportunity to work on the ideas in this paper and present them to a lively audience. I would also like to thank my colleagues in the Department of Philosophy and the Jewish Studies Program at Penn State for their feedback on this paper. Finally, I would like to thank Daniel Conway for pushing me on my interpretation of Kierkegaard.

1. "Rashi" stands for the initials of Rabbi Shelomo Yitzhaki, the foremost commentator on the Torah (AD 1040–1105).

2. See, for example, a collection of Hermann Cohen's writings, translated and

gathered by Eva Jospe, in *Reason and Hope* (Cincinnati: Hebrew Union College Press, 1993).

3. The word "ethogony" is my own neologism, and I am using it to refer to the "creation" or inauguration of morality.

4. This line is also used to indicate the significance of being created from one human species. There is no hierarchy, since no one can claim a different ancestry, but also, to kill one human is as if one killed the entire world. It also refers to the time when Adam was created and was alone. Had he been destroyed, all of humanity would have been destroyed. Thus, to kill one individual is as if to kill an entire world. See the *JPS Torah Commentary,* commentary by Nahum M. Sarna (Philadelphia: Jewish Publication Society, 1989), 13.

5. It should be noted that there is controversy among the rabbis as to whether Cain is in fact a murderer. Rashi claims Cain is, and that he is eventually punished as a murderer would be punished. Other rabbis claim that Cain is not only not a murderer, but should not be held accountable as a murderer. See the *Midrash Rabbah* on this theme.

6. Søren Kierkegaard, *Fear and Trembling,* trans. Alistair Hannay (London: Penguin, 1985).

7. I realize that Kierkegaard uses a pen name to write *Fear and Trembling,* and I am aware of the significance of taking seriously that he does use a pen name. However, I use Kierkegaard interchangeably with Johannes de Silentio throughout the paper, primarily for convenience, but also because Levinas does not draw this distinction.

8. To say that this text is troubling is an understatement. Judah Goldin, translator of Shalom Spielgel's *The Last Trial,* Spiegel's elegant commentary on both the Akedah and the poetry arising from the story of the Akedah, refers to the Akedah as the most terrifying narrative in all of scripture.

9. In other words, the story takes place as such, with the circumstances as such. But what if the absurdity were not present? What if there was nothing in God's relationship to Abraham that made it absurd that he would ask for Isaac's life, but only horrifying? One cannot help but wonder what Kierkegaard's reading of the story would be if the covenant had not been promised through Isaac. Is the teleological suspension of the ethical only an issue because of the promise of Canaan? What would we think of a God who had no reason to return the son to the father? What would we think of the father who was willing to sacrifice his son under that circumstance? Would faith still be a possibility? If so, what would it be like?

10. *The Midrash Rabbah,* trans. and ed. H. Freedman and Maurice Simon (New York: Soncino, 1977), 498.

11. The Hebrew reads "*V'ha-a-lay-hu* [and offer him up], *sham* [there] *l'olah* [as an offering]." The phrasing involves a word play, of sorts, on the Hebrew *aliyah,* which can be rendered in a variety of ways. One of these meanings would simply be "to go up" or "to take up."

12. See Franz Rosenzweig, *The Star of Redemption,* trans. William W. Hallo (Notre Dame: University of Notre Dame, 1970), 266.

13. We could contrast this view against the one Descartes give us in his *Medi-*

tations. For Descartes, God must be a being that does not deceive, and the avoidance of error comes precisely when he follows God's will.

14. I am making reference here to Levinas's work *Difficult Freedom*, trans. Seán Hand (Baltimore: Johns Hopkins University Press, 1990), 24–26; *Difficile liberté*, 2nd ed. (Paris: Albin Michel, 1976).

15. Emmanuel Levinas, "A Propos of 'Kierkegaard Vivant,'" in *Proper Names*, trans. Michael B. Smith (London: Athlone, 1996), 76.

16. Levinas, "A Propos," 76.

17. See Merold Westphal's article, "Levinas's Teleological Suspension of the Religious," in *Ethics as First Philosophy*, ed. Adriaan T. Peperzak (London and New York: Routledge, 1995), 151–60, for another perspective on the relationship between Levinas and Kierkegaard. In Westphal's view, Levinas makes a parallel move to the one made by Kierkegaard. Where Kierkegaard suspends the ethical, Levinas suspends the religious, if we think of what is suspended as that which is derivative of something higher than it. But the problem with Westphal's view is that he fails to take into account the places where Levinas tells us that religion is equated with ethics. See, for example, Westphal's "On Jewish Philosophy" in *In the Time of the Nations*. In failing to take this point into account, Westphal then makes the mistake of assuming that we would need to put Levinas and Kierkegaard together in order to have a more complete picture of the ethical, that is, in order to have both the ethical and the religious combined. But it seems that Levinas already assumes this point. To hear the call of the other is to respond to the trace of God, the infinite, in the other. These things, the ethical and the religious, are not mutually exclusive, and though Levinas is greatly indebted to Kierkegaard, he does not need Kierkegaard to save the religious from its suspension by the ethical. However, we might say, as I am arguing in the text of this essay, that Levinas's view comes from assuming implicitly what Kierkegaard is spelling out for us—that Abraham did raise his knife, and in light of how horrifying that is, that he put it down needs to be explained. For a similar reading of this view, see Jill Robbins's essay, "Tracing Responsibility in Levinas's Ethical Thought," in *Ethics as First Philosophy*, 173–83. Robbins suggests that

> if God can be understood as "not contaminated by being," as
> Levinas puts it, that is, in accordance with what can be called a
> "Judaic" non-ontotheological theology, then perhaps the non-
> manifestation of the revelation of God can be understood other-
> wise, as a differential constitution of (textual) traces, as the other-
> trace. Then perhaps we can begin to think God, in Levinas's
> work, as the *name*—unpronounceable if you like—for the diffi-
> cult way in which we are responsible *to* traces. (182)

18. Emmanuel Levinas, *Otherwise Than Being, or Beyond Essence*, trans. Alphonso Lingis (The Hague: Martinus Nijhoff, 1981); *Autrement qu'être, ou au-delà de l'essence* (The Hague: Martinus Nijhoff, 1974).

19. Levinas has a similar concern about the relationship between National Socialism and the kind of reading Kierkegaard gives us of Abraham. See Levinas, "A Propos," 76.

20. Jean-Paul Sartre, *Existentialism,* trans. Bernard Frechtman (New York: Philosophical Library, 1947), 23–24.

21. In fact, the Midrash has a similar concern, but for a different reason. The rabbis, in their meticulous attention to detail, wonder why the angel tells Abraham "not to lay a *hand* on the lad" (emphasis mine). Their response is that when Abraham raised the knife, the angels wept and their tears melted the knife. So Abraham responds to this by saying, "okay, I will strangle him then." Although the rabbis are trying to explain the change in "weapon," they also underscore Abraham's determination, which must have been present.

22. See Jill Robbins, *Prodigal Son/Elder Brother,* for another claim to the importance of Kierkegaard's reading of the Akedah. In fact, Robbins relates the question that Levinas asks, "Can one still be Jewish without Kierkegaard?" as if to imply that it is Kierkegaard who has taught us how to read the text in the first place.

23. Levinas, "A Propos," 77.

24. And could we not say that this distance from obedience, this sensitivity to hear a second voice—if there was one, is precisely what the Nazis lacked? Such a view can be seen in some of the speeches Himmler gave to the SS, speeches of encouragement so that they would continue with their duty in spite of their own horror at the Nazi activities. That the Nazis were able to squelch whatever response to the other they had in order to carry out Hitler's plan is the cause for Himmler's praise. Himmler himself saw his actions as a conflict between will and obligation (see William Shirer, *The Rise and Fall of the Third Reich* [New York, 1960], 937–38).

25. The repetition indicates that first the Lord speaks to Abraham, and second he speaks to all future generations. All generations to come will have men like Abraham and men like Jacob, Moses, and Samuel. Each represents philanthropy, service of God, study of Torah, and civil justice, respectively.

26. See Rashi: "It is the response of the pious. I am ready, an expression of humility and readiness" (*Ariel Chumash* [Jerusalem: United Israel Institutes, 1997], 138).

27. Isaiah 65:24, as cited in Levinas, *Otherwise Than Being,* 150; *Autrement qu'être,* 235.

28. We might even be able to use the term *teshuva,* a "turning back toward," to describe Abraham's actions.

29. A supreme case of civil disobedience? I would like to thank Doug Anderson for calling my attention to this conception of Abraham's action.

30. Levinas, *Difficult Freedom,* 144; *Difficile liberté,* 204.

31. Levinas, *Difficult Freedom,* 144–45; *Difficile liberté,* 204.

32. Emmanuel Levinas, *Totality and Infinity,* trans. Alphonso Lingis (Pittsburgh: Duquesne University Press, 1969); *Totalité et infini* (The Hague: Martinus Nijhoff, 1971; 1st ed., 1961).

33. See Cohen, *Reason and Hope,* 52.

34. A reference to God calling to Abraham.

35. Rosenzweig, *Star of Redemption,* 175–76.

36. My interpretation of this story follows Rosenzweig and the Jewish view in

general—women are exempt, though not forbidden from, reading the Torah, because they are closer to the ethical. Thus, it is men who have the lesson of morality to learn. I would suggest that Abraham was asked *because* he had this lesson to learn. That is, he had to learn the significance of Isaac's life, not because of the covenant, but because of the significance of an individual life. I want to thank Emily Grosholz for calling my attention to the poem "Sarah's Choice," by Eleanor Wilner. In the poem, it is Sarah who is asked to slay her son. Upon being asked she not only refuses, but also decides to pack up Isaac, Hagar, and Ishmael, and leaves the area. In the course of the poem, Sarah tells Isaac about the command. She offers the choice to Isaac, but makes it clear what will happen if he follows through on the command.

37. See Cohen, *Reason and Hope*. Here Cohen writes, "A religion's right to exist is derived from its concept of God. And this concept must be constantly reaffirmed and perfected. This is particularly true of Judaism which, as a matter of principle, makes no distinction between religion and ethics. For the God of Judaism is the God of morality" (45). Thus, we can have a sense of the Torah as the story which tells the story of the development of morality. Abraham moves from faith to ethics, from sacrifice of the other to response to the other.

38. Levinas, *Proper Names*, 77.

39. Ibid.

40. I would like to thank Doug Anderson for his wonderful characterization of Abraham as a "civil disobedient." A bit anachronistic in the terminology, but if my characterization of Abraham is correct, the term fits. See note 29 above.

41. I would like to thank Evelyn Barker for calling to my attention the possibility that I also end the interpretation of this story too soon. Barker reminded me that God does indeed provide the ram, a symbol, if you will, for an alternative to human sacrifice, in the broadest sense of the term. Thus, the symbolism could be that we can and must find other ways to "praise" God, ways other than sacrificing our fellow human beings and, in particular, our loved ones.

Beyond Outrage: The Delirium of Responsibility in Levinas's Scene of Persecution

James Hatley

> Obsession is a persecution where the persecution does not make up the content of a consciousness gone mad [*une conscience folle*]; it designates the form in which the ego is affected, a form which is a defecting from consciousness.
> —Levinas, *Otherwise Than Being*, 101

> Obsession traverses consciousness countercurrentwise, is inscribed in consciousness as something foreign, a disequilibrium, a delirium [*un delire*].
> —Levinas, *Otherwise Than Being*, 101

> Abel remains in the field. Cain remains Cain. And since it was decreed that he is to be a wanderer, he wanders diligently. Each morning he changes horizons. One day he discovers: the earth tricked him all those years. *It* had moved, while he, Cain, had walked on one spot. Had walked, jogged, run, on a single piece of ground exactly as big as his sandals.
> —Dan Pagis, "Brothers"

A Delirium That Is Not Madness

Could forgiveness put us in danger of madness, of delirium? Or put even more provocatively, is forgiveness itself the opening of a delirium that puts madness itself to shame? In *Otherwise Than Being*, Levinas's analysis of subjectivity centers on, becomes obsessed with, the scene of a persecution in which the persecuted, by the very undergoing of the persecutor's blow, offers expiation for he or she who persecutes.[1] In this scene, which is itself a reworking of the face-to-face scene of *Totality and Infinity,* the accused ego, the "I," who performs, or perhaps better put, is submitted to, Levinas's autobiographical text, no longer is placed in the role of the one who would murder but of the one to be murdered, and so, of the victim obsessed by the blow of the murderer. Going beyond his own temptation to murder, Levinas now turns to face the other who is succumbing to this very same temptation. In this shift of attention, the fear that Levinas had earlier identified with a consciousness and conscience no longer ecstatically taken up with its own state of being, a conscience that fears it may have already harmed the other, that is an assignation for-the-other, now finds the articulation of this assignation even more radical, more denucleated, more impoverished, more exposed, than that earlier analysis had explicitly made clear.[2] For now Levinas must fear not only for the possibility of his murdering the other, *but also for the other's plot to murder Levinas!* As in his earlier analysis of conscience and its affectivity, this newly articulated fear does not devolve to a fear *for* oneself, *as if* all that one owed to the other who would murder one is to save oneself from being murdered.[3] Rather, this fear is *for* the other, but now *for* the other's attempted dereliction of responsibility in the face of my own facing of him or her. My very persecution by the other is revealed to be my call to responsibility for the other. The mere fact of my innocence, that I have become a victim, does not save me from responsibility. In fact, persecution only intensifies my responsibility. Any thought of my own innocence does not remove me from the malice eating away at the human heart; in fact, it implicates me in it even more deeply!

This alteration of his earlier texts on the issue of responsibility and its affect, on the articulation of conscience as a preoccupation of and by the other, is itself a blow, a stunning displacement, a delirious turning of the original terms of Levinas's analysis.[4] It leads to the claim that the very articulation of my subjectivity lies beyond merely a concern for what I might do to the other, for how the other's vulnerability to my violence claims me, makes me restless for the other. Now I am also called to an attentiveness for what the other might do to me, for how my vulnerability tempts him or her. And in being called to this attentiveness, I am being called to that which is unique and irreplaceable about me. In Levinas's words: "The uniqueness of the self is the very fact of bearing the fault of another" (*OB* 112). And even more strongly put: "In its being carried toward the other, the subject is expiation and that which one would be tempted to take as my being is expiation" (*DMT* 218). If I am anything at all, I am responsibility for the other, an expiation.

In this intensification of the notion of his responsibility for the other, Levinas turns ambivalently, ambiguously, to the notion of obsession itself. Levinas's obsession for the other, as the two citations above make clear, borders on the edge of madness (*folie*), is itself a sort of madness (*delire*) and yet is to be distinguished decisively from madness. The delirium of persecution is a restlessness, etymologically, a "deviation from the furrow," from the straight and narrow preoccupations of rational consciousness, an affect driven astray. And yet this peculiar mode of restlessness does not lead one to mad folly, to a condition of the mind in which its very motion away from itself, its incapability of staying with itself, its *restlessness*, its "cellular irritability," becomes the articulation of mindlessness or oblivion, *as if* one could finally evade the disequilibrium by which one is burdened in one's subjectivity. In ethical delirium, in this obsession for the one who persecutes me, the movement of one's attention toward the other is itself prior to any threat against me that the other might unwittingly or even knowingly mount. No matter how great the other's assault against me might be, no matter how deeply wounded it might leave me, no excuse is given for that dereliction of attentiveness in regard to the other that madness in its usual sense implies.[5] Not the other's assault upon me but my vulnerability to him or her is the issue. My ethical delirium for the other does not cancel out my attentiveness to him or her or divert it away but intensifies it beyond any possible recall. Rather than leaving me shorn from the other or myself, this mode of delirium leaves me incapable of forgetting the other altogether and so of forgetting my unique responsibility to him or her. Even the other's delirium, the other's mode of attentiveness to my own vulnerability, is at issue now.

Two questions rise to the fore in the discussion that follows. First, why delirium at all? Why does Levinas insist on the use of this particular term, coupled with that of obsession, terms that in their normal usage imply crippled and disaffected forms of consciousness? In turning to this question, one must consider how "ordinary" or clinical madness and its delirium are themselves symptomatic of a more radical significance at work in consciousness than consciousness could itself account for. Madness is not simply a defect, a failure of consciousness to be adequately conscious of itself, but also the symptom of a radical movement, a counter-currentwise traversing of consciousness that always already has been disturbing consciousness's confident and intentional grasp upon the world. This counter-currentwise movement, which is not simply a defect of consciousness but an infinite exceeding of it, finds one of its expressions within Jewish discourse in midrashic discussions of exile and the search for a transcendent G-d, as well as in moments of wrongdoing and repentance. The disarray of such moments of submission to the infinite are moments of delirium so dangerous, so haunting, so overwhelming that they are in danger of destroying one's mind altogether, of undoing the soul of the one who becomes open to them. In the very idea of the infinite is an excession of reason that puts reason permanently in crisis.

But a second question also must be considered in regard to the scene of obsession advanced by Levinas: what of the persecutor's delirium? Or put otherwise, what of the other's rage? In the scene of persecution, the whole issue of delirium and its articulation may be doubled in a manner that Levinas hints at but does not, at least in this particular text, do much to unfold. For my delirium in the face of the other who persecutes me finds in that other's face another sort of delirium—in which the other attacks me *as if* he or she were not responsible. In the scene of persecution, my delirium is an obsession with my persecutor's delirium, particularly in his or her deluded fleeing of that delirium. Levinas implicitly raises this point in his analysis of the affect that is revealed in the persecutor's face and how the significance of that affect is transcended and transformed by my obsession with it. The "malice" in the other's face, Levinas claims, obsesses me "as something pitiful" (*OB* 111); my gaze into the hateful grimace of the other reveals its essential impotence, its overwhelming shamefulness, its unendurable self-consumption. In this manner, Levinas claims, persecution is rendered otherwise than as a provocation to war. Moving beyond outrage at the other's rage, one's very suffering of the other's blow offers the opening for expiation and beyond that, perhaps, for forgiveness. In order to understand how suffering serves the other who is filled with hate, which is to say, is insistent on denying any semblance of responsibility before the other's face, the situation of the persecutor in regard to his or her irresponsibility needs careful analysis.

An Oblivion That Cannot Forget Itself

In regard to the genesis of the persecutor's irresponsibility, Levinas at least once refers to how "the initial limitless responsibility" of one's subjectivity "can forget itself." Levinas goes on to argue:

> In this oblivion is born a consciousness as a pure possession of the self by the self—but this egoism or egotism is neither first nor ultimate . . . A memory lies in the depth of this oblivion. A passivity that is . . . the impossibility to escape, an absolute susceptibility, a gravity sans frivolity that is in reality the sense in the obtuseness of the being that constitutes itself in this oblivion. (*DMT* 214)

Notice the odd twist that an oblivion intent on its irresponsibility takes—even as it would forget itself, it would continually be reminded that it cannot forget itself. A "memory" lies in its depth. Thus, oblivion's very insistence on forgetting is precisely to forget that it cannot forget itself. The impossibility of this task in turn leads to its intensification as it is repeatedly frustrated in its attempt to be carried through. This is the "obtuseness" referred to above. The affect or distortion of affect that names this frustration in its irresponsibility is wrath. In this affect is given the very malignity of the persecutor's approach of the persecuted. For the persecutor acts *as if* only the persecuted could ever have been to blame, and that he or she, the persecutor, is actually without responsibility in the matter of the persecuted's betrayal. Ultimately, the denial of the other held in wrath goes so far as to pretend that there is no other, that no one has spoken or listened but the persecutor him or herself. The form of this denial is delusional; one attacks the other as if one were not responsible for the other even as that very responsibility is always already at the core of why one is attacking the other.

An example of this oblivion, as well as how its obtuseness makes its sense felt regardless of the intentions of the one engaged in the oblivion, can be found in Levinas's essay "Toward the Other."[6] There he reflects upon a midrashic account within the Talmud of a certain butcher who, infuriated, closes off the conciliatory approach of a concerned rabbi, Rab Zera, whom the butcher had previously insulted:

> He [Rab Zera] went there and remained standing before him [the butcher], who was sitting and chopping an [animal's] head. He [the butcher] raised his eyes and saw him [Rab Zera], then said: You are Abba; go away, I will have nothing to do with you. Whilst he was chopping the head, a bone flew off, struck his throat and killed him.
> (Yoma, 87a)

Levinas comments that "the game of offense and forgiveness is a dangerous one" ("TTO" 23). Levinas adds that the death of the butcher should not be interpreted as miraculous retribution, thunder and lightning rolling down upon a man who has not sufficiently respected G-d's power or commands, but as the failure of a concerned and humble man, namely Rab Zera, to respond carefully enough to the immensity of the malice he had encountered: "It [the story] . . . wants to speak to us of the purity which can kill, in a mankind as yet unequally evolved, and of the enormity of the responsibility which Rab took upon himself in his premature confidence in the humanity of the Other" ("TTO" 23).

The butcher's response is maddened to the point of delirium, as the outcome of an anger so beyond itself that it strikes against its own intentions willy-nilly. In lieu of carefully carving up the animal's flesh, the butcher in his rage at seeing Rab Zera repeatedly batters the animal carcass before him. The animal's head becomes a fetish. One imagines that the butcher imagines that if this crushing of an animal's skull could become so intensely a content of his consciousness and conscience that nothing else existed for him, then perhaps finally he could forget the plea for repentance and forgiveness in the Rab's mere approach to him. He would look up and no face would be before him, no words would have been addressed to him. And yet his every blow against the animal's head and, by proxy, the face of the Rab, necessarily reminds the butcher that what he is trying to forget is utterly incapable of being forgotten. The very blows against the animal indicate that the insistence of the other's voice, the inevitability of the other's face, have already made their impact, no matter how thoroughly the butcher dismisses Rab Zera, the address of Rab Zera remains. This in turn provokes yet even more violent blows against the animal's head. Thus each blow simply exacerbates the need to strike its blow yet again and brings the very giving of the blow to a repetition that intensifies itself in its very repetition. The very delirium of this action, its frenzied repetition, signifies the butcher would rather murder and die than admit he is needful of forgiveness, indeed, that an act demanding forgiveness has even occurred. His obsession with violence is preferable to becoming vulnerable to the Rab's gesture of reconciliation.

Given the extent of its chaos, its lack of control, that this frenzy ultimately turns against the butcher and murders him is not surprising. But ironically the butcher's delirium, even as it is unmeasured and chaotic, cannot outstrip the delirium instigated by the Rab's approach. No matter how frenetic and intense the butcher's delirium becomes, it fails to quell that erring without bounds, that restlessness that cannot be fixed that has always already turned the butcher away from his own intentions, his own safe place in the sun. In his willful delirium against the delirium of the other's approach, the butcher focuses upon the pig's head so repeatedly that in at least one dimension of his consciousness he does not diverge at all from his intention. His attentiveness becomes the inversion of a delirium that does not escape its furrow but instead fixes upon it. The butcher's delirium, insofar as it expresses a divergence from a reasonable approach to his perceived enemy, involves an intensification of fixation— he will not let go of his insistence upon his non-acknowledgment of, his indifference to the other, even as that insistence continually is frustrated by the very approach of the other. In this manner the butcher's gesture is both too delirious and not delirious enough and so becomes folly. In the end his affect is burnt away by his own wrath.

Cain's Wrath

In the book of Genesis, this struggle between an address that would provide reconciliation and a rage that will not relent in its single-minded insistence upon itself continually resurfaces in each new generation to question yet again the very meaning of what is begun in Genesis, the very beginning of beginning, Creation itself. In the prophetic tradition, the condition of a chaotic and yet increasingly repetitive affect in the aftermath of one's violation of the other would be termed hard-heartedness. In this condition the very animation of the soul is threatened.

Perhaps the most telling moment of hard-heartedness in Genesis is found in the story of Cain, where G-d, like Rab Zera, comes to a persecutor, the murderer of his own brother, in the aftermath of his offense and questions the offender concerning his state of mind *not* in regard to the Most High *but* in regard to the brother. Instead of speaking for the Almighty, the Almighty speaks in the place of Abel. In doing so, G-d also speaks for all other humans who exist or will exist and even those who will not have existed.[7] Among the many stunning aspects of the narrative that ensues is the tone of address G-d takes up in seeking out Cain in regard to his murder. Rather than being caught up in a rage over Cain's wrongdoing, G-d probes him with the most impossible and difficult and yet careful of questions: "Where is Abel thy brother?" (Gen. 4:9). Mirroring G-d's earlier question to Adam in the wake of his wrongdoing—"Where art thou?"—G-d's approach to Cain provides an ethical model of how the persecuted would seek out the persecutor: one takes responsibility so that the other might assume responsibility. In Rashi's words, G-d enters "into a friendly conversation with him: perhaps he might repent and say, 'I have killed him, and sinned against You.'"[8]

In doing so, G-d insists that Cain consider "where" he stands in relation to the one he has violated: "Where is Abel thy brother?" (Gen. 4:9). In this question, the "where" involved does not hint at a ground upon which one is firmly rooted but at a wherefore or whereto, a *whither* first oriented toward the other, a *whither* that takes one away from one's own place, or better, that addresses one into one's place only by having submitted one to the other. For the perpetrator, in his insistence of having avoided responsibility for the other, has convinced himself that he believes this question of his place in regard to the other can be and has been utterly forgotten. For the perpetrator, it would be *as if* one finds one's place in the sun only by obscuring the view of all the others who might covet my place in place of me. In G-d's tone of address to Cain, the assignation of his place, no longer and, in actuality, never having been his own in the sun, but always already *"for-the-other,"* is brought into issue. But Cain immediately dismisses the radicalness of this suggestion by clinging to the delusion that he has never even been submitted to it. The other, whether in the address of Cain or of G-d, had never been there at all. "I know not: am I my brother's keeper?" (Gen. 4:9).

In the first place, this sentence constructs an attempt to dismiss the relevance of Abel at a point before even the fact of his existence could ever have been at issue. For not only is Abel's existence irrelevant in Cain's state of mind, but the very possibility that it could be relevant, *should he have existed,* is also irrelevant. It is *as if* Cain's only place is in regard to where he himself stands, *as if* the place where the other stands has been absorbed by a soul who has burnt away all routes for being called elsewhere.

In the second place, this sentence is part of a strategy that would dismiss the relevance of G-d and of the whole of G-d's creation as well. Cain's response, infected with his wrath, is no more than the pretense of a response—ultimately, Cain responds utterly in order to avoid responding. Still speaking from out of his wrath, his words are filled with cunning and sober calculation.[9] He splits hairs rather than facing up to what is asked of him. And underlying this rationality, this careful phrasing of his case, is an ongoing plot to undo the effect of G-d's address by pretending to go along with it even as his every gesture dismisses it, as if it could be dismissed before its impact has been registered upon him.

According to the *Midrash Rabbah,* Cain's wrath is literally burning him up—the Hebrew word for his "wrath," *wayyichar,* being derived from the verb "to burn," *charah.* (*MR* 1:184).[10] This suggestion is then amplified in a reading of the falling of Cain's countenance that accompanies his wrath as literally referring to a firebrand blackened with its own fire, of a rage consumed within its own rage. By implication, Cain's inflammatory wrath is in danger of burning out his human countenance, of blackening over the animation of his face's expression. It is as if the face of the wrathful, of the man being consumed by his own malice, has become hollowed of expression, as if no expression remains at all but flesh burnt to a crisp, flesh crumbling into ash! This is, I would argue, the face that appears in Levinas's account of persecution when he speaks of "the face of the neighbor in its persecuting hatred" (*OB* 111). This face is one that is caught up in its own delusion of pretended invulnerability, of its maniacal insistence that no one faces it. Here we find a face insistent that there is no face. And the more it insists this, the more it must pretend that it has never insisted at all. And the more it finds its so-called place, the more it must pretend that there is no other place, no place away from here in which the other might stand before him.

In working out the extent and significance of this faceless rage, of its repetitive insistence in not being attentive to what utterly calls for attentiveness, the discussion of the *Midrash Rabbah* goes so far as to find Cain's wrath at issue in the first moment of creation. In explicating the meaning of the crucial words *tohu* and *bohu* from the line "Now the earth was unformed and void"—*tohu v'bohu*—Rab Judah ben Rab Simon interprets "void," *bohu*, as referring to and anticipating none other than Cain, who, it is claimed, "desired to turn the world back into formlessness and emptiness" (*MR* 1:16). In the first moment of creation, G-d hovers over the wrath of Cain. In his voiding of creation, Cain exceeds even the rebellion of his father Adam, who is as nothing (*tohu*) because of his sin but does not desire a return to formlessness. Adam's sin only involves *tohu*, but Cain's encompasses the full measure of rebellion—the formless and the void are articulated in his rage. Why is this so? Could it not be because Cain, unlike Adam, introduces wrath into the face-to-face relationship? Adam's pretense stems from envy of G-d and the shame that comes from the realization of his own powerlessness, his nothingness. Abel at least knows that he must hide himself from G-d for the *shame* of what he has done. But Cain does not admit to shame, even as he slyly clings to his wrath. He does not hide from G-d but acts, when G-d approaches, *as if* nothing at all has occurred, and *as if* no one has addressed him. Here, the void of *bohu* is best thought not as Heideggerian nothingness but as Levinasian facelessness. *Bohu* is without a face.

Cain's wrath would burn away the face of all created entities and then would forget he had done so. It would be *as if* G-d had hovered over the earth, commanding the light to be, and instead of the earth responding with light, G-d's words would have rung hollow into a void of wrathful self-consumption. And in the wake of this ringing hollow, it would be *as if* G-d would have never spoken at all! The very saying of one's words, their very wherefore and whereto or whither, their orientation as toward-the-other, would have never been articulated. Cain's wrath and his nonchalant tone toward G-d's question puts the very gesture of creation into question. Even more radical than Adam's sin against the Almighty is Cain's against his fellow man.

If we take this reading to heart, Rashi's claim that Cain never truly embraces repentance logically follows. When Cain finally responds to G-d and claims his punishment is too much to bear, Rashi hears in Cain's words a question loaded with arrogance: "You bear the worlds above and below, and is it impossible for You to bear my sin?" (*CRC* 18).[11] In bearing these worlds, G-d gives them their place. Why can he not then take Cain's place and relieve Cain from the weight of his murderous guilt? After G-d seemingly relents and makes a sign upon Cain in order to give him leave to wander the earth, Rashi goes on to interpret the passage "And Cain went away" as a departure made "in *pretended* humility, as though he would deceive the most high" (*CRC* 19). Rab Aibu, in this same vein, comments that the very notion of Cain going out, *as if there were someplace away from the Most High to which Cain could travel,* only shows "he [Cain] threw the words behind him and went out, like one who would deceive the Almighty." The editor comments: "He rejected G-d's reproof, as though murder was a light matter" (*MR* 1:191–92). Cain never repents, never even is moved to recognize the need for his repentance, even as he plays the game of repentance. He pretends and then pretends to forget he has pretended. He puts on the mantle of sincerity in order to hide away his outrageous insincerity.

Cain's wrath is the first gesture of a willful and calculated pretense in regard to all that faces it, even the Creator. Consumed by his lie, given to it with an intensity beyond what is a merely rational ploy, Cain pretends and then pretends that he does not pretend. This pretense doubles his negation of the other's address—for he not only ignores the other but then acts *as if* the other were not even involved in the logos of his speech. In this doubled pretense, Cain's wrathful expression would command the voiding of the very gesture of creation that addresses creatures into being by the simple command that they respond. Cain perverts speech, perverts the face-to-face address in a manner not unlike that described by Primo Levi in regard to the cold and calculated indifference with which the inmates of Monowitz were treated by their persecutors. When Levi recounts his having been shoved away for simply asking why something had occurred, it can be argued that the guard physically dismisses him not simply because Levi has spoken out of turn but because he has spoken at all. The guard desires, in his rage against Levi, to intimidate Levi to the point that he would not even dare to speak. The guard does not simply wish that Levi would obey him, he would have Levi behave *as if* he were faceless.[12]

But what becomes most disturbing in this interpretation of Cain's story is G-d's patience with Cain. G-d relents to Cain's complaint—in spite of Cain's ill will and continuing self-deception. For what reason is Cain given protection to wander about the face of the earth free from the threat of murder, when his own brother Abel did not receive this mark of sanctuary from G-d in the first place? It is as if the Most High has not registered the depth of Cain's deception, or the extremity of Cain's violence against Abel, a man who was, in the story's own words, pleasing to the Most High. The story of Cain, or at least this interpretation of it, threatens to become nonsensical in this glaring, scandalous inconsistency. How can G-d allow Abel to suffer the violence of murder and then protect Cain even as he deceives G-d with seeming impunity? How is it that G-d moves beyond outrage over the murder Cain has perpetrated without at the same moment forgetting the very scandal of a creation in which injustice becomes the order of the day, in which the innocent can be murdered and forgotten? Was it not G-d who stated in the first place that the very earth cried out with Abel's blood? In the echo of that exclamation of outrage, how could Cain be given leave to wander the earth? Why does G-d take Cain's protest seriously even as it is uttered in the tones of insincerity?

Responsibility That Cannot Be Fixed

Perhaps the answer to these questions lies in understanding how G-d's response suggests that outrage, even as it is inevitable and morally significant in the aftermath of violence, is not sufficient to address the folly, the fixed delirium, of the evildoer's malice. Hearing the outrage of the earth, its cry against Cain, G-d curses Cain, but the curse is itself lost upon Cain. Buried in Cain's response is this objection: "How can I stand up to a call that leaves me without a place? Being without a place leaves me open to being murdered." Again Cain's narcissism is at work. Still preoccupied with the power of murder to silence the other's voice and to subsume the other's place, Cain can only imagine an ordering of the world in which the strong seek out the weak to prey on them. Rather than turning to face his betrayal of his brother, Cain worries about how others might seek revenge or betray Cain himself. Cain still lives in a world where power struggles with power, where one is only capable of living with the other if the other can be made known in my own terms. The other must become a mode of my keeping my own place. What Cain refuses to grasp, even after he has been confronted with the fact of his having murdered, is how his very repentance for that murder would bring him to the point where his own place in the sun, his own preoccupation with the preservation of his ego *at any cost,* is itself without any justification. Creation is not about the maintenance of my place, my identity, my security.[13]

Creation, as both Levinas and the rabbis insist, is about response and responsibility,[14] about *teshuva,* a turning toward the other so caught up in its turning that it decenters, or as Levinas would put it, denucleates, one's self. In the logos of creation, one's self is not archaic, finding itself in the rational consideration of itself as its own measure, its own autonomy; it is obsessive, a response to the other that is without any possibility of anticipation or measure. Zornberg points out that *shogeh,* the Hebrew word for "obsession," is directly related to *shoga,* the word for "madness."[15] And yet she also points out that for Ramban love of G-d is *shogeh,* an obsession that borders on madness. This obsession that borders on madness in turn is given a powerful exemplar for Zornberg in Abraham's being called out into an indeterminate place by G-d, a call that both recalls and utterly reconfigures the curse of Cain. Like Cain, Abraham is seemingly bereft of place, but unlike Cain, Abraham takes on this lack of a place, this invitation into indeterminacy and alienation, this delirium that moves one out of the furrow, as a movement toward G-d. But this very movement puts into question every resolution of that movement in any single possible terminus. In response to the call of the Infinite, one is left groundless; for the very mode of what showing might turn out to be, of what really indicates G-d's intention as to one's place beyond what one thought had been one's place, is so transcendent as to elude all possible destinations. Revelation "reinforces the enigma" rather than resolving it. And this reinforcement or magnification of the enigma in turn reveals a world torn asunder. Would not Cain, in his state of mind, see the very call to which Abraham submits as a curse? It is *as if* Cain's ears are so attuned to his own place that the very issue of obsession, of a *shogeh* that calls one utterly beyond oneself to the other, is without any place whatsoever. Cain acts *as if* there is no voice but the voice that he can hear *in his own terms.* Any other voice drives him to wrath, to madness, and ultimately to murder.

Put in other terms, Abraham rather than Cain is the one who really suffers to suffer! Cain suffers but does not suffer this suffering. Cain's curse is to have turned away from his curse. Heard otherwise, Cain's curse is a call to repentance. Cain won't let the tone of G-d's saying register. If he were to do so, he would be caught up in a listening so unsettling, so restless, so indeterminate, that Cain would be utterly beyond himself, torn open, *shoga* and *shogeh.* G-d's tone, spoken in utter sincerity, calls for the sincerity of a listening that not only exposes itself to the address of the other but also exposes that exposure. Rashi speaks of G-d's address as *teruf,* as a rending of the human soul that is only granted to the righteous precisely because only the righteous are willing to suffer it unconditionally.[16] In Levinas's notion of *teruf,* of a rending obsession, of an exposing of exposure, one would find oneself always already restless for the plight of the other and the part one has played in the other's suffering. In this restlessness is given a philosophic translation of the Hebrew term *yirah,* the fear of the Lord.

This call to sincerity before the other, in the case in which that other is Cain as persecutor, would involve the revelation of Cain's face as pitiful. In being revealed as pitiful, Cain would not become an object of condescension, although he himself might be quick to jump to that very conclusion in his own mind. Being pitiful and the pity it inspires should not be confused with the modern tone of these words in which the hard- or narrow-heartedness of another's actions becomes an excuse for demeaning him or her. That mode of pity would merely be another form of rage, another manner of surreptitiously striking the other *as if* one had struck no one at all. But "pitifulness" and "pity," as Levinas understands them, hearken back to their usage in Shakespeare, where the lack of pity in the world of *King Lear* leads to the most excruciating forms of cruelty and ingratitude. To be rendered pitiful is to find oneself impotent at the very moment of one's greatest powers, to find the very issue of one's singularity, of one's significance, to have been utterly taken out of one's own hands. To be pitiful in turn commands pity, which is to say, commands a compassionate response of solidarity that is without bounds, that exposes its exposure to the other *no matter what conditions are involved*.[17] That there is no limit to the pity the other inspires, even the other who would murder oneself, leads Levinas to speak of the relationship articulated in pity as one of being hostage to the other. As in King Lear's declaration: "I should e'en die with pity / To see another thus" (*King Lear,* act 4, scene 7, line 52).

While Cain, in his discourse with G-d, makes use of pity as a ploy—You (G-d) are the one who orders the heavens and the earth; take care of me—that very ploy puts off the acknowledgment by Cain of his pitifulness. Cain willfully reinterprets his pitifulness as merely a possibility of being murdered, *as if* the worst that can occur to him is to suffer outrage at the hands of another. What Cain's response fully refuses to consider is the pitifulness of his own plight, the outrageousness of his doing outrage. As Cain, the one who has already murdered, considers the possibility of his own murder, he rejects the delirium of responsibility as it is played out in the persecuted soul who is called to steadfastly look into the face of his or her persecutor, the soul whose gaze, in Levinas's scene, renders the hateful grimace of the persecutor as pitiful. Cain, in moving from persecutor to persecuted, still remains unwilling to accept the danger and the adventure of his position, the utter gratuity of the sacrifice that is demanded of him in the order of creation. Because he is unwilling, he remains unable to imagine that transformation of the murderer's face, now his possible murderer, in which he, Cain, the persecuted, might move from "outrage" to "expiation." Levinas's scene of persecution demands that one suffer *to the quick* the very blow of the other against one's life, one's own survival and interests. One feels the full force of the other's betrayal and does not turn away but "endures" it (*OB* 111). But the enduring of this blow, instead of compelling recrimination and counterblow, instead of instigating an angry justice that would be maddened with its own sense of the other's injustice, inspires a response of pity in the one who suffers the blow, a pity stemming from beyond outrage. Only in this manner could the face that is obsessed by the willfulness of its own unfettered attack upon all that exists be revealed as something other than a pure threat to my own existence. One's very suffering of the other's blow shames the other's glee in his or her malice in a manner that any active resistance on one's part is incapable of doing.

Cain is not yet willing to turn toward the radical demands of a delirium that is truly responsible, to submit to that disorientation in the face of the other calling him beyond himself to the point that he is revealed to be the epiphenomenon of that call. And in the wake of this unwillingness Cain is also unwilling to listen radically to what G-d invokes. G-d's invocation of Cain in Genesis is not one stemming from an easy mercy that can do nothing more than relent to Cain's intransigency, but from an insistent and inspiring mercy that intensifies Cain's fault infinitely. If Cain were to truly listen to the Almighty's command, that casting out into the wastes that Cain hears as a curse, if he were not so quick to toss away G-d's words on behalf of Abel with a condescending and hypocritical affirmation, Cain would find his very capacity to remain within his own words and in his own place to be rent beyond repairing. For discourse is at its heart about being infinitely given over to the tones of the other's address, which is to say to the saying of the other as it makes its impact beyond one's own ken within one's own speaking. The words I say already carry a tone, which is to say, a mode of acknowledging how the other's address of me has already encumbered me and how I now sustain that encumbrance. My speaking is always already a tone of speaking, since it speaks toward another. Sincerity is given as that tone of speaking, in which the very saying of one's response to the other is always restless for how it might have failed to respond to the other. The saying fears for its own inattentiveness to its saying. The argument one makes, in the tones of sincerity, always already finds oneself in accusation and fearful of the other's betrayal.

To speak with the other, Levinas claims, is to engage in a "dangerous life" whose urgency is not the concern for one's own security but "the gratuity of sacrifice" (*OB* 120). Caught up in the tones of the other's discourse, one's own language is continually interrupted by that "sign of the giving of sign" (*OB* 119), that is, the *hineni,* the "here I am," in which the recognition that one's ear has already been given to the tones of the other's discourse is offered to the other. In the aftermath of one's *hineni,* one's "apology," one's self-justification as to why one has acted in a certain manner, is always already under "disqualification" (*OB* 121). In creation, the point of one's discourse with the other is not the justification of one's own place under the sun but the registering of the other's tone of address in one's own saying. One's saying is a whither, a being given over to the other that has no resolution, no final summation in one's own terms. In being "restless for the other" (*OB* 143) one finds oneself in "the extreme tension of a language" (ibid.) that lies beyond any self-indulgent babbling merely obsessed with its own tone, its own frustrations and needs. My proximity to the other, which is language itself, "closes in on me from all sides and concerns me even in my identity" (ibid.).

And beyond the singular confrontation with the singular other lies the multiplicity of all the other others. Ultimately, one's language, the very means by which one articulates one's presence to oneself and to the others one addresses, already speaks in all these other tongues as well. Because one's language is always already redolent with all the other others' tones of address, responsibility calls one to a hermeneutical instability in one's speaking and language of the most disruptive sort. One's speaking is never simply an exposition but is always already a witness, in which one's very tone of speaking is always already under accusation. Ultimately, in speaking of the other to all the other others, one is called to a speech of "incessant correction" (*OB* 158), in which philosophy, among other modes of discourse, is asked to "conceive ambivalence, to conceive it in several times" (*OB* 162). This is the "fine danger" Levinas would have us run.

Dan Pagis writes that no matter where Cain went, he stepped in the same place. And in the tone of that claim, could one not add that no matter what G-d said, Cain heard the same thing again and again? In dismissing G-d's address, Cain leaves himself under a curse that threatens at every moment to extinguish his existence. But if he were to listen in another tone to that curse, if he were finally to be rent by G-d's words spoken on behalf of the other, if Cain were to finally consent to that indeterminacy of responsibility to which he has been submitted no matter how willfully he denies his consent, then the very curse that G-d has left him under would also be heard as a call to repentance. As Dan Pagis's poem points out: "Abel remains in the field."[18] In being directed to wander about the face of the earth, Cain is being commanded to place his feet again and again upon Abel's grave, and upon the earth's very crying out in response to his murder. In a provocative reversal of the scene of creation, Cain is called to hover over the depths, but this time instead of over *tohu v'bohu,* formlessness and void, Cain would hover over the place of the other whom he has murdered but has still nevertheless failed to render silent in his heart of hearts.

Creation is not faceless after all. To turn toward this voice that still cries, if one is willing to hear it, is to move as Abraham would into the tearing and teeming indeterminacy of a responsibility that could never be stilled, that will require saying upon saying in a struggle for sincerity. If Cain were to listen to this voice, he would finally suffer willingly and without reserve what he is already suffering anyway. The problem with the murderer is that he or she is not willing to suffer the delirium of responsibility but consumes suffering in an insistence that will not let go of its own gesture of self-insistence. In calling Cain to a delirium of suffering, G-d's response moves far beyond outrage, which would only condemn the wrongdoer, *as if he too were faceless,* and offers expiation and mercy as well. If Cain were to submit to this address, he would come to understand that the earth had never been his own to have but was always already the other's earth, imbued with the other's voice. And perhaps that mark left so mysteriously on Cain's face could finally be seen by Cain himself as nothing other than his having been rendered pitiful, as the revelation of a call to responsibility, so weighted with suffering, so delirious in its movement toward the other, that only those who will be righteous can endure it.

Notes

The third epigraph for this chapter is from Dan Pagis, "Brothers," in *Points of Departure,* trans. Stephen Mitchell (Philadelphia: Jewish Publication Society, 1981), 5.

    1. Among the works by Emmanuel Levinas cited in this paper are *Otherwise Than Being, or Beyond Essence,* trans. Alphonso Lingis (The Hague: Martinus Nijhoff, 1981); and *Dieu, la mort et le temps,* ed. Jacques Rolland (Paris: Grasset, 1993). Hereafter cited in the text as *OB* and *DMT,* respectively.

    2. "Assignation" in this context refers to its meaning as "a summons to appear in court" (*The Compact Edition of the Oxford English Dictionary,* 1979). In this sense it reflects its French cognate, which is used by Levinas as a technical term for defining the subjectivity of the one who is responsible: one is an assignation, a for-the-other. The term is defined in French as "an order to present oneself for the purpose of being arraigned or giving testimony before a judge" (*Le petit larousse,* 1979; translation mine). While this meaning is related in its concept to the more common notion of "assignation" in English as a lovers' tryst (in that both senses of the word involve being summoned to a particular time and place), the term does not carry the latter connotation in its use by Levinas.

    3. See Emmanuel Levinas, "Bad Conscience and the Inexorable," in *Face to Face with Levinas,* ed. Richard Cohen (Albany: State University of New York Press, 1986).

    4. This alteration does not imply, to my mind, a replacement of one by the other, *as if* Levinas suddenly decided to deny his earlier analysis of the face-to-face relationship by means of the later. Rather, the later analysis offers a rereading of an earlier saying that, already devolved into a said, calls again for Levinas's own saying. The earlier saying concerning the face-to-face encounter takes place in relationship to one dimension of my own approach toward the other—that I might indeed become a murderer of the other. This possibility does not cease with the realization that the other might become my murderer as well. The two different

JAMES HATLEY

roles—murderer and murdered—do not cancel each other out but chiasmatically intertwine with and exceed one another. Even in being the persecuted, one must also worry about being the murderer. The two thoughts do not sit easily with one another and demand attentiveness to their diverging implications that keep both aspects of the other's face in mind.

5. These comments leave unaddressed the exact relationship in Levinas's thought between clinical madness and ethical delirium, a relationship that is referred to occasionally by Levinas but not developed in much detail. Generally Levinas is reluctant to give the psychological language of pathology much weight in his discourse about malignity and responsibility. In the preceding citations he brings up the issue of madness, but only to serve as a counter to what he actually discusses, which is the delirium of responsibility. Elizabeth Weber, in her account of the psychotherapeutic treatment of survivors of the Holocaust ("Persecution in Levinas's *Otherwise Than Being*," in *Ethics as First Philosophy*, ed. Adriaan Peperzak (New York: Routledge, 1995), treats the connection between pathology and ethical involvement, which is also discussed briefly in my book *Suffering Witness: The Quandry of Responsibility After the Irreparable* (Albany: State University of New York Press, 2000), chap. 6, ft. 2. See also Emmanuel Levinas, "And God Created Woman," in *Nine Talmudic Readings*, where Levinas claims: "Evil as psychoanalysis discovers it in sickness, would already be predetermined by a betrayed responsibility" (170). Whatever pathological madness might be, it does not explain the disturbance of that madness that comes in one's dereliction of responsibility, an event in the throes of which clinical madness can and does ensue.

6. Emmanuel Levinas, "Toward the Other," in *Nine Talmudic Readings*, trans. Annette Aronowicz (Bloomington: Indiana University Press, 1990). Hereafter cited in the text as "TTO."

7. The children who would have been born had Abel not been murdered are just as much at issue in G-d's confrontation of Cain as the children Cain will father!

8. *Chumash with Rashi's Commentary*, trans. A. M. Silberman and M. Rosebaum (Jerusalem: Silberman Family, 1984), 18. Hereafter cited in the text as *CRC*.

9. See Levinas, *Otherwise Than Being*, 10, where he explicitly links what he terms "Cain's sober coldness" with the rejection of a responsibility for the other that transcends one's own interest. And consider Rashi's argument that Cain "persuades himself he could deceive the Most High" who is implicitly beyond deception. It is *as if* Cain is talking to no one but himself. (*Chumash*, 18).

10. *The Midrash Rabbah*, vol. 1, ed. H. Freedman (London: Soncino, 1983). Hereafter cited in the text as *MR*.

11. This line of reasoning here differs from one advanced by Levinas in regard to Cain. See his "A Religion for Adults," in *Difficult Freedom* (Baltimore: Johns Hopkins University Press, 1990), 20. There the insolence of Cain's response to G-d is downplayed and Cain's need to be instructed in the significance of murder, since no human had heretofore confronted its possibility, is emphasized. The divergence between the two readings in turn reflects midrashic disagreement over whether Cain truly repents or not. But in spite of this divergence, both readings underscore how murder is an attempt to escape the address of the other, to ren-

der the world as faceless. And in both readings, G-d cannot take Cain's place, but Cain must be submitted to atonement, to suffering, to expiation meant for him uniquely.

12. See the discussion of this point in my book *Suffering Witness,* especially chap. 3. The story from Primo Levi is found in his *Survival in Auschwitz,* trans. Stuart Woolf (New York: Collier Books, 1961), 25.

13. See Levinas's own words on this matter: "The responsibility for the other is the locus in which is situated the null-site of subjectivity, where the privilege of the question 'Where?' no longer holds" (*Otherwise Than Being,* 10). It has been suggested above that although the question of "Where?" no longer holds preeminence, that of "Whither?" or "Whence?" of a where already caught up in an orientation toward the other, does: "Where is thy brother?"

14. The German term, *Verantwortung,* seems preferable here to the English word "responsibility." The German word hints at an intensification of response to the point of being utterly taken up in answering what calls one, whereas the English term's etymology suggests that the ability to respond limits the call to respond. As a logos, the creation is not tuned to being-able but to being-called. If the Creator had waited until creatures were able to respond, the creation would have been a failure, would have reverted immediately to *tohu v'bohu.*

15. See Zornberg's discussion of this term in Avivah Zornberg, *The Beginnings of Desire: Reflections on Genesis* (New York: Doubleday, 1995), 91.

16. As is argued at the paper's end, responsibility calls one to radical indeterminacy in one's very language and so to hermeneutical instability of the most disruptive sort. If one turns to von Westernhagen's account of Nazi perpetrators, one finds how those who are unrepentant, who simply act *as if* nothing has occurred after World War II ends, often lapse into psychosis and other highly dysfunctional states when confronted with their evildoing. Could it be argued these persons cultivate psychosis precisely because the reality of the call to the other and the instability it works in one's own identity seem even more extreme to them? Psychosis is far more comfortable than responsibility! And far less delirious! (Dörte von Westernhagen, *Die Kinder der Täter: Das Dritte Reich und die Generation danach* [Munich: Kösel, 1987]). See also my "Impossible Mourning," *Centennial Review* 35, no. 3 (Fall 1991): 445–59.

17. "It is through the condition of being hostage that there can be in the world pity, compassion, pardon and proximity—even the little there is, even the simple 'After you sir'" (Levinas, *Otherwise Than Being,* 117).

18. Pagis, "Brothers," 5.

The Strangeness in the Ethical Discourse of Emmanuel Levinas

Wayne Froman

Toward the very end of *Otherwise Than Being, or Beyond Essence,* Emmanuel Levinas characterizes the discussion that he has conducted in that text as "strange." He writes:

> The emphasis of exteriority is excellency. Height is heaven. The kingdom of heaven is ethical. This hyperbole, this excellence, is but the for-the-other in its interestedness. This is what the strange discussion conducted here about the signification in the one-for-the-other of the subject sought to say.[1]

What I want to do in this paper is to elicit just what it is that is strange about this discussion. I will do so in terms of what I take to be three focal points of that strangeness: the first is the status of "self," the second is the status of "saying," and the third is the status of freedom. Having done so, I will try to specify the sense of strangeness found in each of these.

The strangeness of the discourse is intimately related, I think, to the role played in *Otherwise Than Being* by the sense of creation. Creation has long been a particularly significant issue in addressing the question of the compatibility or incompatibility of the Judaic tradition and the philosophical tradition stemming from Greece. In that regard, in the medieval period, it was necessary for Maimonides to qualify the Aristotelian teaching concerning the eternality of the world. In the twentieth century, Franz Rosenzweig, in *The Star of Redemption,* addresses the issue in a very suggestive way. Rosenzweig finds that philosophy, from the beginning, has not had the wherewithal to decide whether divinity, or the soul, or the world lies deepest.[2] Following Schelling in his adaptation of the Kantian transcendental identification of those three elements as ideas of pure reason, Rosenzweig turns to the biblical themes of creation, revelation, and redemption as narrative means of addressing the interactions among God, humanity, and world, given that the three do not form a system that is amenable to the type of analysis that works for physical systems. In regard to creation, taking it as given that the world has always been, Rosenzweig finds that creation can be understood as an addition to the world, namely, the addition of existence (*SR* 118–22). His reading of the biblical Hebrew regarding creation is that creation is performed "on the world." Rosenzweig distinguishes the addition of existence in creation from the dynamic of "grounding" in Being that he associates with redemption, while he associates revelation with the disclosure of the means for that "grounding" (*SR* 218–19, 169–71). All three are understood in terms of a narrative approach to the interactions among the three primordial elements of God, humanity, and world, of which philosophy cannot specify the one that lies deepest. When creation, revelation, and redemption, which are traditionally addressed by theology, get drawn into the philosophical field in the manner indicated here, the result is what Rosenzweig calls *das neue Denken,* "the new thinking," which he specifies is neither theology, nor philosophy, in any traditional sense.[3]

On the first page of *Totality and Infinity,* Levinas makes it known that the book is indebted to Rosenzweig on every page, so much so that to provide the references was a practical impossibility.[4] In *Totality and Infinity,* creation is specified as creation ex nihilo, the idea that sets the biblical tradition and the philosophical tradition apart. It is precisely because creation is creation "out of nothing" that it accounts, according to *Totality and Infinity,* for the possibility of atheistic thinking.

In the context of "the new thinking" as understood by Rosenzweig, it will only be possible to characterize creation as creation ex nihilo when creation will no longer take place. In *Otherwise Than Being,* I find, creation plays an expanded role, one that makes it more consistent with what Rosenzweig says in regard to an addition of existence to a world that has always been, and that this expanded role of creation is intimately related to the strangeness of Levinas's ethical discourse in that later work. In return, Levinas provides, I find, elements for a reading of the sense of creation that comes from phenomenology, a philosophical mode of thought that Rosenzweig did not adopt.

In order to identify, first, what is strange in regard to the status of "self," as understood in *Otherwise Than Being,* it is necessary to understand how the self is related to the central dynamic in that text, namely, the dynamic of substitution. Beginning with the approach of the other, Levinas describes my sensibility to the other who approaches in terms of passivity, a passivity that is even more passive that any capacity of receptivity by me. This sensibility makes for a disturbance; indeed, it becomes a persecution, one that expels me from any sense of being at home to myself, and strips me of any of my resources for responding. I am accused, in effect, without having any basis for appeal, either in a set of conditions that would allow me to thematize the sensibility and thereby gain, in effect, a perspective on it, or in establishing that I am, in fact, innocent. The extreme passivity found here, the thoroughgoing incapacity to escape this accusation, makes it seem to me that the accusation itself is coming from me, that I am accusing myself in this way.

In this way, I take upon myself the responsibility for the other, even to the point of being responsible for the other's accusation of me. Levinas describes how the effect is a gnawing away at myself. This is an undoing, an eating away at the Ego, the "I" of control, which takes me to the point where I am substituted for the other, insofar as this is my expiation for the extreme expulsion, the persecution by an inescapable accusation by the other, which by virtue of the unlimited passivity involved here, is as though it were coming from me. At this point, the proximity of the other turns out to be a substitution of the one-for-the-other.

That there is no one other than I myself who can be substituted indicates how the undoing of the Ego has brought me to my Self. In effect, this is the other side of the asymmetry of the approach of the other, as understood by Levinas, in keeping with what he had said in *Totality and Infinity* concerning "the face," in particular with regard to how I always encounter the other at a height relative to me. In the chapter on "Substitution" in *Otherwise Than Being*, Levinas writes in regard to the liberation of my Self:

> Through substitution for others, the oneself escapes relations. At the limit of passivity, the oneself escapes passivity or the inevitable limitation that the terms within relation undergo. In the incomparable relationship of responsibility, the other no longer limits the same, it is supported by what it limits. Here the over-determination of the ontological categories is visible, which transforms them into ethical terms. In this most passive passivity, the self liberates itself ethically from every other and from itself. Its responsibility for the other, the proximity of the neighbor, does not signify a submission to the non-ego; it means an openness in which being's essence is surpassed in inspiration. It is an openness of which respiration is a modality or a foretaste, or, more exactly, of which it retains the aftertaste. Outside of any mysticism, in this respiration, the possibility of every sacrifice for the other, activity and passivity coincide. (*OB* 115)

It should not be overlooked, I think, that the finding of that responsibility, to the point of substitution, is an available way toward liberation of the

Self, and is consistent with the Judaic precept that the crucial content of revelation—namely, that one should love the neighbor, i.e., anyone who is nearest, as one's Self—does not mean that one should lose one's Self in this love. Rather, that crucial content of revelation tells us that the other is, no more and no less than am I, a Self. The other's freedom is not any more self-originating than is my freedom, and that is to say that the other is a creature just as I am a creature. It is not by accident that the sense of creatureliness gets drawn into the discussion by Levinas of the sense of uniqueness, of the strong sense of individuality, of Selfhood, as tied up with the ethical dynamic of substitution.

It is the liberation of the Self that I want to emphasize in eliciting what is strange in this ethical discourse. This Self is not a resting within itself, a being at home in itself. Rather, it is the very restlessness associated with the fission of the Ego, the "I" of control, which comprises the Self. At the same time, however, Self must involve a sense of sameness. The fission or the restlessness is what amounts to an other within the Self. But to say this is to say that the other is in fact, in this sense, within the Self. It is precisely this sameness of Self that is, after all, strange. It is strange because the very disturbance brought on by the approach of the other, the persecution that precludes recourse to any resources, is what brings on the liberation of my Self and a sense of sameness that would appear not to amount to a sameness with anything that has preceded it. This is where to find the meaning of a past that never has been present. In the course of the discussion of witnessing, Levinas addresses this sameness that would appear not to amount to a sameness with anything that has preceded it, as the very subjectivity of a subject. He writes:

> The subjectivity of the subject . . . is a recurrence which is not self-consciousness, in which the subject would still be maintained distant from itself in non-indifference, would still remain somehow in itself and be able to veil its face. This recurrence is not self-coinciding, rest, sleep or materiality. It is a recurrence on the side of oneself; prior to indifference to itself. It is substitution for another. In the interval, it is *one* without attributes, and not even the unity of the one doubles it up as an essential attribute. It is one absolved from every relationship, every game, literally without a situation, without a dwelling place, expelled from everywhere and from itself, one saying to the other "I" or "here I am." (*OB* 146)

Consequently, the Self that is liberated in the dynamics of substitution exists in a sense without its being in Being, without its being tied to an essence that would be ultimately what makes it what it is. And this is precisely what is strange. The point that makes this strange is not so much that the liberation of a Self is associated with the inescapable persecution to the point of full responsibility, but rather that the Self that is a sameness in its restlessness exists at all without being in Being, without somehow realizing its essence. One would ordinarily expect that only that which is in Being could exist in any sense at all.

What Levinas says about Saying in contrast to the Said basically reflects the same sense of strangeness as that found in the dynamics of the liberation of the Self. Saying itself, or in other words, Saying divested of any Said, is, itself, signifying. This means that it is not by virtue of any "already Said" that Saying signifies initially. In this way, Saying does not follow upon any prior articulation, does not draw out or draw up any such prior articulation into a Said. The Saying must also be distinguished from any Said that results from it. Levinas understands this divesting of the Said from Saying, or this recursion to Saying from the Said, as the basic trajectory of phenomenological reduction.

Saying, understood in this way, is what follows from the persecution or the intrusion of the other who approaches, leaving me without any resources to which I can appeal. Here there is no "already Said" that would constitute resources of that nature. Because of this, the Saying is paradoxically the extreme passivity that is even more passive than the passivity distinguished from activity. Levinas writes: "To maintain . . . that saying is to respond to another . . . is to catch sight of an extreme passivity, a passivity that is not assumed, in the relationship with the other, and, paradoxically, in saying itself" (*OB* 47). The substitution associated with the unlimited responsibility of the for-the-other takes place with the signifying of Saying understood in this way. Pain always comes with Saying understood in this way. Saying is an exposure to the other without limit that marks my irremediable vulnerability.

It is Saying that expiates for the persecution by the other. Saying understood in this way as expiation will not be absorbed or assimilated totally by a Said, and it is precisely in this way that it is the mark of the Self that we found to exist prior somehow to its being in Being.

Insofar as Saying, by itself, is signifying, there should be some sense in which there is a constancy, understood primarily as a constancy of place, that would characterize the Saying. That is, it should have a place in a context of signification. In fact, given the way that Levinas identifies Saying with substitution, there would appear to be provision for that context in what he says in regard to Saying divested of the Said. In other words, substitution does imply context. But at the same time, the absence of resources for this Saying means that there is no constancy of place involved here. Once again, as was the case in considering the liberation of a Self by virtue of the unlimited responsibility for the other, what we catch a glimpse of here is a mode of constancy that would appear not to be dependent on anything that has preceded it. In other words, what we catch a glimpse of here is what is meant by "a past that has never been present," and in the same sense, an "always already."

Levinas understands prophecy as illustrative of this sense of Saying. He writes: "We call prophecy this reverting in which the perception of an order coincides with the signification of the order given to him that obeys it" (*OB* 149). And then:

> An obedience preceding the hearing of the order, the anachronism of inspiration or of prophecy is, for the recuperable time of reminiscence, more paradoxical than the prediction of the future by an oracle. "Before they call, I will answer," the formula is to be understood literally. In approaching the other I am always late for the meeting. But this singular obedience to the order to go, without understanding the order, this obedience prior to all representation, is precisely the other in the same, inspiration and prophecy, the *passing itself* of the Infinite. (*OB* 150)

For Levinas, the question concerning language, the question of its origin, ultimately comes down to the "anachronism" illustrated in prophecy.

Saying as Levinas understands it does not continue an articulation that precedes it, does not involve a "that which is to be said," and consequently, even as it signifies and so displays a certain constancy, it occupies no place in an order of signification. That is its strangeness. This strangeness persists despite how, in effect, the Saying gets absorbed by a Said. That absorption occurs via "thematization," as understood by Levinas, and is illustrated by the way in which that which is first and foremost not thematic turns out to be themes in Levinas's text. The strangeness persists nonetheless.

What Levinas says about freedom is the third focus of the strangeness in his discourse. Levinas proposes that his understanding of the dynamics of substitution provides a more adequate means of understanding "finite freedom" than those analyses that concentrate on the limitation of the will. In those other analyses, although the will is found limited, the freedom, Levinas points out, is still, in effect, a pure freedom. Levinas proposes that his analysis understands freedom as finite in a way that qualifies the freedom itself while still understanding it as genuine freedom. What qualifies the freedom is that it is not freedom understood in terms of self-possession or in terms of recovery of a point of origin. In fact, Levinas understands freedom in terms of the approach of the other that becomes a persecution that divests me of any and all of the resources of an Ego to the point at which a "gnawing away at myself" occurs, amounting to my own responsibility for the other, a responsibility that is unlimited by virtue of the fact that I am without resources to contest it. These are the dynamics of substitution. They entail a point that is outside of essence. Levinas writes:

> Essence, in its seriousness as *persistence in essence,* fills every interval of nothingness that would interrupt it. It is a strict book-keeping where nothing is lost nor created. Freedom is compromised in this balance of accounts in an order where responsibilities correspond exactly to liberties taken, where they compensate for them, where time relaxes and then is tightened again after having allowed a decision in the interval opened up. Freedom in the genuine sense can be only a contestation of this book-keeping by a gratuity. This gratuity could be the absolute *distraction* of a play without consequences, without traces or memories, of a pure pardon. Or, it could be responsibility for another and expiation. (*OB* 125)

Expiation takes place "on a point of the essence [where] there weighs the rest of the essence, to the point of expelling it" (*OB* 125).

Freedom does not involve the recovery of a point of equilibrium that is prior to the intrusion and the persecution by the other. Any such recovery, if in fact there were such a prior point of equilibrium, is ruled out by the nature of the intrusion and persecution. But at the same time, freedom must be equal to the task of expelling "the rest of the essence," it must, so to speak, be up to the gratuity of freedom. The point from which the expulsion that marks the gratuity of freedom occurs must be a point of balance because it must, as Levinas says, *support* the intrusion by the other that crushes the Ego. It must sustain this. But the question is just how that can take place when previously no equilibrium was even possible. The answer, once again, lies in a past that was never present. It is by virtue of this past, where, "since an 'immemorial time,' anarchically, in subjectivity, the by-the-other is also the for-the-other" (*OB* 125), that there is a point at which the intrusion and persecution of the other get supported despite the fact that no recovery occurs.

The effect of freedom as understood by Levinas is the expulsion of all that lies within essence and along with it the suffering and cruelty that come from the violence of non-freedom, of not being capable of taking possession of essence, that is, of concentrating it in such a way as to be invulnerable to that suffering and cruelty. This is freedom's dignity, as Levinas puts it. What is strange in this freedom is that it is effective in this way even while it is altogether gratuitous. This is basically what Levinas means when he identifies this freedom as "ontologically impossible." There is freedom, which is ontologically an impossibility.

In each instance—that of the Self, that of Saying, and that of freedom—the strangeness of this discourse derives from the quality of a "past that was never present," an "always already," a "time immemorial." Each of these is an indication of the "anachronism" associated with the sense of "creation." To note that each of these involves an "anachronism" is to make the point that what is at issue is not first and foremost a point, so to speak, before all others that cannot be recaptured. Rather, "a past that was never present" refers to a past that comes with the dynamics of substitution even though it had not been present. This is its "anachronistic" sense, and this is how proximity, substitution, and expiation make us aware of what we may call the "creation dynamic." Proximity, substitution, and expiation proceed in the first place because like myself, the other does not reach to his or to her origin, i.e., the other is, like myself, a "creature." The reason why the "creation dynamic" is Good is that it is the very lack of self-origination that entails the existence of Self outside Being, the Saying, and the genuine freedom that comes with substitution.

The sense of the "always already" gives us an indication of what, in effect, is most strange about Levinas's description, in *Otherwise Than Being*, of the dynamics of proximity, substitution, and expiation. If the "always" does not refer first and foremost to a point, so to speak, before all others, which is beyond recapturing, but rather to how the "already" always will come with the dynamics of proximity, substitution, and expiation, we catch a glimpse of how the dynamics of essence is always going to exert a reappropriating tendency upon the existence of the Self outside Being, the Saying divested of the Said, and the gratuity of freedom. Levinas refers to the particularly enigmatic way in which prophecy, the illustration of Saying, will circulate eventually as "information." The awareness of the reappropriating tendency involved in the sense in which an "already" will always come about puts us in touch with a traditional Judaic reading of the creation narrative in the Bible, where the fact that it is said only in regard to the creation of human beings that creation is *very* good, in contrast to simply good, is understood as a reference to the way that death crowns creation and is the last word of creation. That awareness puts us in touch with an irreducible strangeness in the relation of the world to ourselves. Ultimately, I think, this opens the question of whence comes the voice of Emmanuel Levinas in this strange discourse concerning proximity, substitution, and expiation, a voice that says "here I am."

Finally, insofar as Levinas's ethical discourse does remain descriptive, and thus remains phenomenological, the strangeness of that discourse, understood in terms of a past that has never been present but is, all the same, indissociable from proximity, substitution, and expiation, which is to say, in terms of the "always" character of this "already," or in terms of the "since" of the "since time immemorial" by virtue of which the "by-the-other" is also the "for-the-other," amounts to a clue for a phenomenological understanding of a primary feature in the idea of creation, one that Franz Rosenzweig emphasizes strongly, namely, the daily character of creation, that is, how the work of creation is renewed each and every day.

Notes

1. Emmanuel Levinas, *Otherwise Than Being, or Beyond Essence,* trans. Alphonso Lingis (The Hague: Martinus Nijhoff, 1981), 183. Hereafter cited in the text as *OB.*

2. Franz Rosenzweig, *The Star of Redemption,* trans. William W. Hallo (Boston: Beacon, 1971), 83–93. Hereafter cited in the text as *SR.*

3. See *Franz Rosenzweig: His Life and Thought,* presented by Nahum N. Glatzer (New York: Schocken Books, 1953), 196–208, for a discussion of the "new thinking" and its relation to philosophy and to theology. (This is a translation of excerpts from Rosenzweig's essay "Das neue Denken: Einige nachträgliche Bemerkungen zum Stern der Erlösung," in *Kleinere Schriften* [Berlin: Schocken, 1937]).

4. Emmanuel Levinas, *Totality and Infinity,* trans. Alphonso Lingis (Pittsburgh: Duquesne University Press, 1969).

Levinas: A Transdisciplinary Thinker

Michael B. Smith

Levinas's oeuvre cannot be properly understood, much less appreciated, without consideration of both the philosophical (Greek) and the spiritual (Judaic) sides of his work. This may not seem like a particularly earth-shaking observation, but I believe that the interdependence of these two aspects is often overlooked.

There are several reasons for this. First, Levinas himself has said, during interviews, that he never uses religious texts to substantiate any-thing of a philosophical nature, and that he even uses different publishers for those two types of reflection. Second, and more important, the struc-ture of the academic establishment often discourages a form of discourse that, seen from the precincts of a form of clarity purchased at the price of innovation, must appear muddled. Spirituality is (rightly or wrongly) con-sidered a suspect element in philosophical circles, and theology, an area which is generally conceded as participating in both styles of research, is sometimes viewed as a kind of intellectual miscegenation. Furthermore, Judaism, in America in particular, seems to show little interest in Levinas's philosophical speculation, or even in his Talmudic contributions—in spite of that author's lifelong attempt to awaken present-day Judaism to its distinguished intellectual *mitnagim* tradition, which has by and large lacked the picturesque attraction of the countervailing Hasidic one that Martin Buber, Marc-André Schwartzbart, and more recently Elie Wiesel have brought to the attention of the larger Jewish and non-Jewish public.

A point of terminology: If I have avoided the term "interdiscipli-nary" in favor of "transdisciplinary," it is because I do not believe there is much authentic intrinsic distinctness in the academic disciplines in the first place—none at least that goes beyond the contingencies of the his-tory of the European university and the peculiarities of a local tradition of thought—so that a mixture of disciplines would be doubly fictitious. By

MICHAEL B. SMITH

the term "transdisciplinary" I wish to point beyond that historical specificity to an *apeiron* (which Merleau-Ponty called "wild being") that is prior
to any specific cultural organization into disciplines. Hence, rather than
to think of a return to such an originary domain by means of "mixing" disciplines, I have preferred the idea of transcending them.

In order to give a brief account of this transdisciplinary field, which
is truly central to Levinas's thought, I draw from two texts, one by Levinas
and one (see "A Critique of Ontology" below) by Catherine Chalier. The
first is Levinas's "Transcendence and Intelligibility," a lecture given in
Switzerland in 1983.[1] The fact of its frank suspension of the usual depart-
mentalization of disciplines is due in part perhaps to the setting. It is one
of a number of talks that were given on that occasion under the general
theme "Truth and Illusion of Metaphysics." Metaphysics—a term exiled
from current philosophical research, only to be seen occasionally as a
bookstore rubric between Horoscope and New Age. The lecture in question was given at the University of Geneva, and was followed by amiable
discussion between Jews, Christians, and atheists. Its orientation is philo-
sophico-theologico-religious.[2]

Transcendence and Intelligibility

In "Transcendence and Intelligibility," Levinas sets out from the premise
that philosophy is based on an understanding of the human psychism as
"knowledge" (*savoir*). This will be perceived as a limitation, of course,
later on in Levinas's exposition. This is not particularly surprising, for in
a general sense we are aware, whether from the recognition of the finitude
of human understanding in mystic thought (e.g., Pseudo-Dionysius's
Cloud of Unknowing) or from negative theology, that there is a point of view
from which knowledge can be seen as a limitation, despite the prima facie paradox this seems to raise, namely: Is not the recognition of the limitations of knowledge immediately incorporated into the corpus so characterized? This "tar baby" syndrome of knowledge, which is paralleled by
that of immanence, is one of Levinas's major themes. Another term that
will be presented in a way that is more limiting than is the norm is "experience"—following the usage of Martin Buber in *I and Thou*. It may be
noted in passing that Levinas does not follow Merleau-Ponty by formulating his project as one of extending the meaning of knowledge, nor of
pushing on to a level of hyper-reflection that would include the subjectivity of the knower. What Levinas claims is that knowledge does not cover

the range of the meaningful, the *sensé*, as he calls it. As Levinas himself points out, what he means by "knowledge" is more or less what Descartes meant to be covered under the cogito: thinking, doubting, conceiving, affirming, denying, wanting, not wanting, imagining, and feeling. Although "remembering" is not in Descartes' enumeration, I think it safe to presume that Levinas would include it as well, since he often speaks of an "immemorial past," which would be out of the reach of knowledge. This leads us to the next element of Levinas's critique: the present.

On the question of presence, Levinas's critique takes on the commonsense notion of temporal and spatial immediacy, but it is clear that the role of presence as *Dasein* is also meant, or co-meant. Theories of representation, based on the idea of knowledge as adequation, and the understanding of past and future as deficient—or at least attenuated—modes of the present (here Levinas is more Bergsonian than Husserlian) or as somehow simultaneous in transcendental understanding, are rejected. But that rejection takes on a more Levinasian terminology, which is at the same time a more classical one, with the introduction of the terms "Same" and "Other," capitalized. Levinas quotes the *Timaeus* as confirmation of an age-old prejudice: the "circle of the Same encloses that of the Other." Indeed, this succinct formula seems to reflect the basic thought behind the movement of knowledge, which assimilates the new, the other, the external, to the same. The etymological force of the *Begriff* (from *greif-fen,* "to grasp" or "to grip firmly") and of the concept (*cum-capio,* "like taking," or "taking together") affirm this traditional thought mode.

This movement of knowledge as a taking together moves in the direction of the world, or the totality, the unity of which is assured by that of its correlate, the ego.

That which is given is also taken, in perception: *per-cipio,* again a prefixed member of the *capio* family, the family of taking. What Levinas calls the *emphase,* the "emphasis," of this taking, a secured and thematized having, is satisfaction, the culminating point in this rapid phenomenology of immanence.

A Phenomenology of the Other

But here Levinas introduces his own view, characteristically in the form of a question, or in the proviso that Levinas readers have come to recognize as heralding the thesis to which Levinas will hold: "*à moins que . . .*" ("unless it is the case that . . ."). "Unless it is the case that the intelligibility of the alterity of the other, of transcendence, calls for a different phenomenology, and even if that other phenomenology, and that phenomenology of the other, should prove the destruction of the phenomenology of appearance and of knowledge."[3]

Hence we have in Levinas's own philosophy an essentially prior transcendence, accessible, if at all, through ethics, and in Levinas's version of "the received philosophy," an essentially present immanence, which always triumphs in its own realm.

This is not to say that Levinas believes himself to be the author of an entirely new direction of thought. His works are shot through with perhaps a half dozen references to passages by earlier philosophers who have transmitted a glimmer of the "otherwise than being" or the "beyond being" that becomes central to Levinasian thinking. These loci are Plato's reference to the Good that is "beyond being" in the *Republic*,[4] Descartes' reference to infinity as being contained in finite human thought,[5] and two passages from Pascal.[6] These latter references are not to matters concerning ontology, however. What they tend to show is that the ego's aggressiveness toward the other is close to being the principle of all evil. But it should be noted that even here there is an ontological implication: that it is the struggle to be and to possess that brings conflict; that being itself, in its "simultaneity," is struggle.

Two other prior philosophical elements that Levinas enlists in his direction of thought are Kant's "primacy of practical reason"[7] and Bergson's "duration" (*durée*).[8] It is because Kant, despite his declaration that metaphysics was over, pursued his ethical thought under the more immediate auspices of practical reason that Levinas finds a kinship with him, despite many other contrasts.[9] As for Bergson, Levinas grants him a valid intuition of the spontaneity of absolute newness in his notion of *durée* despite the former's failure to see this "spirituality of transcendence" as anything more than a subjective phenomenon.

Levinas takes his cue from religion, rightly understood, to give an account of the non-relation to the absolute. And it is on the basis of the notion of the infinite that Levinas attempts to evoke that non-relation. As opposed to normal forms of transcendence (those that fit the intentionality model), the thought of the infinite or the idea of God does not stop at an adequate noetic object. This "deportation" or transcendence has that in common with a simply failed transcendent act that misses its mark. Here consciousness, being always (in Husserl's words) consciousness "of" something, must be left behind. Further, the unconscious, which is the negation of consciousness, can be of little help, since negation still carries too much of the dust of positivity on its sandals. What is needed is a way of thinking that disengages itself from being more radically than does negation: dis-inter-estedness. Consciousness, knowledge, and perception are all left behind here. What remains is the optics of an ethical thought: a mode of thought that Levinas does not hesitate, at this late time in his career, to refer to as theological. A theological thought that Levinas prunes of anything resembling thought as adequation, or being as an expression of excellence, or the synthesis of transcendental apperception, however. Those forms of thought are deemed essentially atheistic, in that they tend fatally to draw the transcendent into immanence.

Instead of the passivity of experience being transformed by the activity of a knowing subject, it is the finite (man) that is affected by the Infinite (God). This being affected by the Infinite cannot be expressed in terms of an apparition, nor as a participation in a content, a comprehension of any kind. In the final analysis, the comparison of this affection with a transcendent act that misses its object must be abandoned. This is a thought thinking more than it thinks, or doing better than thinking. A going to the Good. The plurality of sociality is better than any oneness, and proximity is better than merger or adequation.

Here Levinas's descriptions seem to have for their aim to cut off the movement from the subject to the object, and to describe an inverse and irreversible movement from other to same, in which the Same is awakened by, or troubled by, the Other. It is the Other at the heart of the Same.

One obvious result of this for ethical thought is that ethical action is a response, the act of assuming responsibility, or the hearing of a call. "Here I am" (*Hineni,* in Hebrew).

A Critique of Ontology

Catherine Chalier's slender volume, *Levinas: The Utopia of the Human (Lévinas: L'utopie de l'humain)*, highlights the tension referred to earlier.[10] It takes up the question of whether there can be any philosophically legitimate meaning to "inspiration," or whether reason, the logos, contains all there is of intelligibility or meaningfulness. The second chapter of this sympathetic but incisive presentation of Levinas, entitled "A Stranger to Being," brings out the rather complex relationship between Levinas and Heidegger in the ontological realm.

The main elements to be considered in specifying Levinas's relation to ontology are the following. (My comments draw on, but do not summarize, Chalier's treatment of these themes.)

MICHAEL B. SMITH

A Critique of Being

Evil is not construed by Levinas as a lack (of being) as it has been in the philosophical tradition of the West since Aristotle. On the contrary, being is alien to man, and the emphasis on being is evil. Examples would be war, which shows the terrible "simultaneity" of being, and to a lesser degree commerce, since it too displays the competitive and aggressive nature of being. An interesting late summary of this metaphysical view of being as *conatus essendi* is the following text from Levinas's introduction to *Entre Nous*.

> Origin of all violence, varying with the various modes of being: the life of the living, the existence of human beings, the reality of things. The life of the living in the struggle for life; the natural history of human beings in the blood and tears of wars and between individuals, nations, and classes; the matter of things, hard matter; solidity; the closed-in-upon-itself, all the way down to the level of the subatomic particles of which physicists speak.[11]

It is clear that Levinas is thinking in the metaphysical mode. Being is given a characteristic, that of a certain impermeability, a self-centeredness, a hardness. But this way of characterizing being is indicative of a move beyond being, which can no longer be taken as an "all-in-all." In fact, Levinas will move from a revision of being to an abandonment of ontology.

The Abandonment of Ontology

In commenting on the ontological language he adopted in *Totality and Infinity*, Levinas said that he had adopted that language in order to avoid psychological language. In other words, the assumed philosophical commitments of psychology could only be transcended by moving to ontology; but once being is characterized as an active force, with a will, an aggressiveness, and certain other traits—at that point it becomes both possible and necessary to find a way of exiting being. Already in his very early work *On Evasion* (1935), Levinas evokes the necessity of "exiting being by a new path" (*sortir de l'être par une nouvelle voie*).[12]

A Critique of Heidegger

Levinas credits Heidegger with giving us an "ear" for being. This being is not the abstraction of what all beings have in common, but is describable.

The *il y a,* or "there is," is an anonymous sort of being that we are caught up in and cannot escape. This notion of the *il y a,* which Levinas shares with his friend Maurice Blanchot, sets the negative setting for being as enrootedness and fixation on self that Levinas criticizes in a work he nonetheless deeply admires: Heidegger's *Being and Time.*[13] But it should be noted that Levinas's critique of ontology is a critique of a critique—i.e., it is post-Heideggerian. The ontology Levinas is critiquing is not that of classical philosophy (Plato, Aristotle), which was the ontology of a reason "liberated from temporal contingencies," and therefore a naive reason. The ontology he critiques is that of existential phenomenology: the ontology of existence and of facticity, of man who is the being for whom being is a concern.

A Critique of Freedom

Levinas's critique of being is accompanied by a critique of freedom. The sort of freedom found wanting is the one that proceeds from a sense in the individual of his or her autonomy and self-assertive right to be. "My place in the sun," as Levinas never tires of pointing out after Pascal, is the beginning of the usurpation of the entire earth.

But can there be such a thing as freedom that is not based on the notion of autonomy? The title of Levinas's collection of studies on Judaism, *Difficult Freedom,* indicates the direction of his thought.[14] This sense of freedom is really a liberation from the tyranny of the self, riveted to its self-interest and its struggle to be, but called to a higher vocation by listening to the command of the other. The responsibility for the other is what makes us most distinctively ourselves. This freedom is at antipodes from the freedom of the wild, unspoiled domain of nature, which is dependent on a disregard of the other, and an unreflective assertion of that concentrated sense of being that makes up the ego of each being. It is also distinct from the freedom felt by the resolute *Dasein* that faces its own death authentically. My death is no longer the issue. I do not know the freedom from all cares of those for whom death has no meaning, however. Rather, I enter into a different sort of disquietude, a solicitude for the other. It is a "difficult" freedom, because it binds me to obligations I never entered into voluntarily.

Thus the view that there can be no morality without freedom (in the sense of choice) is not refuted, but superseded by a morality that precedes any sort of decision on my part. This movement from the bond of self-interest to that of non-indifference toward the other is designated by

Levinas as the "marvel of the ego rid of itself and fearing God,"[15] the conversion of the ego (*moi*) to the self (*soi*), transfigured by the invasion, the accusation, the persecution of the same by the other. The result is described as the situation of the hostage. We are hostage to the other human being.

Another aspect of the critique of freedom is that of the sort of autonomy reflected in the ideal of Stoic philosophy—even-mindedness or even *ataraxia,* "indifference." A more general ideal of philosophy has been the attainment of serenity, tranquility of soul—an inner sanctum, secret and beyond the reach of the outside world.[16] It is the situation of Gyges in Plato's *Republic,* the man with the ring that he could put on and see without being seen; the question there was whether or not such a person would be moral.[17] But in a deeper sense we are all in the position of Gyges, since we can conceal our thoughts.

The Who and the What

Looking at existentialism after Levinas, is it possible to understand that movement's refinement of the concept of being—its development of a specifically human mode of being called *Existenz*—as symptomatic of an *Aufhebung* in which the notion of being is conserved/destroyed in some higher idea? This interpretation would, however, remain too much within the realm of ontology for Levinas, because the "work" of the negative can never leave its positive starting point entirely behind. It is not "wholly otherwise." Still, it may be legitimate to see in this development the symptom of an inadequacy leading to a new level, similar to the way in which the paradoxical expression "virtue is its own reward" leads naturally to the suspicion that such a notion of virtue critiques and eventually surpasses the concept of reward altogether.

A more adequate view, in my opinion, is to consider Heideggerian ontology as translating in its own terms a phenomenon essentially foreign to it: a "science of the who" into the "science of the what." This division, rigorously abstracted from Talmudic thought by Georges Hansel, suggests that the development of dialogical philosophy in the twentieth century need not be annexed to ontology to be given philosophical "weight," although a question does arise about the relationship between ontology and whatever parallel term may be appropriate to the human.[18] But the network of internal relations that makes up our philosophical tradition, and perhaps language itself, seems to require that everything be expressible in terms of everything else. Hence the inevitability, but inevitably problematic nature, of the question posed by Frederick Olafson's recent Heideggerian work, *What Is a Human Being?*[19]

Levinas raises the question of thing/person in *Otherwise Than Being*. There the situation of questioning, a who interrogating a what, is posited, but it is not the most fundamental level.

The other to whom the petition of the question is addressed does not belong to the intelligible sphere to be explored. He stands in proximity. Here is where the *quis*-nity of the "what" excepts itself from the ontological quiddity of the "what" sought which orients the research. The same has to do with the other before the other appears in any way to a consciousness (*OB* 25).

This "having to do with" the other refers to something prior to and other than consciousness.

Thus Levinas takes the meaning of "who" a step farther. He hesitates within the dilemma of whether the "who" should or should not be included in being (*OB* 28). He will in the final analysis exclude the "who" from being; thus his research in this field cannot be called ontological. It is this work, *Otherwise Than Being, or Beyond Essence* (1974), that presents Levinas's most organized effort to trace a path to the edge of philosophy as the exploration of being, and to move beyond being.

One of the perplexing questions that arises in connection with my relation to my neighbor, the fellow man—that *autrui* of whom Levinas has so much to say—is whether it is a "personal" relation. Or is the "neighbor" another word for the "stranger"? Levinas answers this question in *Otherwise Than Being:*

> Absolving himself from all essence, all genus, all resemblance, the neighbor, *the first one on the scene,* concerns me for the first time (even if he is an old acquaintance, an old friend, an old lover, long caught up in the fabric of my social relations) in a contingency that excludes the a priori. Not coming to confirm any signaling made in advance [I would prefer "description" to "signaling" as a translation of the French *signalement*], outside of everything, a priori, the neighbor concerns me with his exclusive singularity without appearing, not even as a *tode ti*. (*OB* 86)

Levinas has inserted a footnote after the term "a priori" to explain the apparent contradiction in my concern for the other. The other concerns me outside all a priori—but perhaps *before all a priori,* prior to all a priori. This would be in an absolute passivity.

Hence we come back to the question of passivity. In the more traditional view, morality applies to acts, and acts are not passive. If my relation to the other is more passive than any passivity, how can it be moral at all?

What terms could possibly be available to designate those psychic (non-)entities that have hitherto been falsely ascribed to being? Obsession, for example: "Obsession is not consciousness, or a species or a modality of consciousness, even though it overwhelms the consciousness that tends to assume it" (*OB* 87). One of the striking elements of this relation to the other is the intrinsic lack of preparation. We are taken by surprise. "Extreme urgency is the modality of obsession—which is known but is not a knowing" (*OB* 88). It is difficult not to think in terms of the general scientific evolutionary worldview, according to which matter is primary and man a latecomer. That is the usual way in which the primary situation has been conceived in philosophy. The philosopher is confronted with the world. He must end up thinking he is part of the world, or the world a part of him; or a kind of mutual inclusion—transcendence in immanence.

One of the most basic concepts in moral behavior would seem to be reciprocity and equality. I have neither more nor less rights than any other human being (ideally, that is). How is it, then, that Levinas insists upon an inequality of status between myself and the other? The other is always greater than myself. From an objective or third-person point of view this would seem to be nonsensical, since we would, from each other's point of view, have to be greater than each other, which is logically untenable. Is Levinas's thought such that it is impossible to put oneself in another's place, thereby attaining a less personal perspective? Surely not, since he stresses the notion of substitution, the one-for-the-other, which would be impossible if we were irremediably stuck in our own individual perspectives.

According to Levinas, "the word *I* means *here I am,* answering for everything and for everyone" (*OB* 114). But it is important to remember that

> these are not events that happen to an empirical ego, that is, to an ego already posited and fully identified, as a trial that would lead it to being more conscious of itself, and make it more apt to put itself in the place of others. (*OB* 116)

It is being turned inside out.[20] The Self (*Soi*), an original passivity, older than the ego (*Moi*), is a religiosity "beyond egoism and altruism." Therefore we must regard these descriptions not as psychological, but as metaphysical.

The "after you, sir."[21]

It is being based on sense, rather than the opposite.

An open-eyed ignorance.[22]

Job, or Responsibility without Freedom

The book of Job has been at once a stumbling block and a provocative source of new interpretations. It is the story of a pious man upon whom endless suffering is heaped, despite the fact that he cannot think of anything he has done wrong. His friends, traditionally referred to as the "false comforters," tell him that he has probably forgotten his misdeeds.

What is disturbing about the story is that it seems to constitute a roadblock to all theodicy. How can this treatment of Job be justified, if not as his "just reward" for some evil act on his part?

Both the Jewish Bible and the Jewish tradition uphold the notion of justice such that good and pleasant things happen to those who do good. The second scriptural passage contained in every mezuza, affixed to the doorpost of traditional Jewish homes, and that is frequently a part of Jewish liturgy (Deut. 11:13–21) specifies that obedience to the law, the Torah, will be rewarded by rain in its proper seasons, "that thou mayest gather in thy corn, and thy wine, and thine oil. And I will give grass in thy fields for thy cattle, and thou shalt eat and be satisfied." Conversely, rain will be withheld if other gods are served. The principle of just recompense seems so basic to our sense of morality that we may well feel quite disoriented by any suggestion that it be put in question. It is this conviction that makes Job's friends (and Job himself) think that the calamities befalling him are the consequence of evil deeds. (When I say "consequence" I do not mean to imply anything on the order of a "natural" consequence: I am not addressing the question of some sort of immanent justice here.)

The context in which Levinas introduces the question of Job is that of freedom. There seems to be general agreement among philosophers that the concept of responsibility has no meaning without freedom. If I make a promise freely, I am obliged to keep it. Coercive conditions, on the other hand, such as those in which a prisoner is forced to make promises, do not carry the weight of moral obligation. The idea of human freedom and the possibility of choosing evil have always been central to Judeo-Christian theological and ethical thought.

But as we shall see in the following passage, Levinas interprets the book of Job as accusing Job precisely of this sort of thinking—that limits responsibility to obligations freely entered into.

I quote from *Otherwise Than Being*, the translation being slightly modified:

> We have been accustomed to reason in the name of freedom of the
> ego—as though I had witnessed the creation of the world, and as though
> I could only be in charge of a world that has issued out of my free will.

These are presumptions of philosophers, presumptions of idealists! Or evasions of the irresponsible. That is what the Scripture reproaches Job with. He would have been able to explain his calamities if they could have come from his misdeeds. But he never wished evil! His false friends think as he does: In a meaningful world one cannot be held answerable when one has done nothing. So Job must have forgotten his misdeeds. But the subjectivity of a subject come late into a world not issued from his projects does not consist in projecting, or in treating this world as one's project. The "lateness" is not insignificant. To support the universe is a crushing charge, a divine discomfort. (*OB* 122)

Could it be that the problem of a self-imposed limit to freedom is rooted in this philosophical preference for autonomy? If I decide to limit my freedom by a commitment, have I thereby limited my freedom? If I have not, why should you trust me? If I have, is not the ethical value of my actions in fulfillment of my promise diminished or annulled, by virtue of the principle that all ethical acts must be chosen by a free agent? But perhaps we can conceptualize this dilemma of the promise as an incorporation of heteronomy within autonomy, or, in Levinas's words, the Other in the Same.

Except for a small number of readers, Levinas is generally rejected as being too metaphysical to be of serious philosophical interest. Those who are courageous enough to seek an alternative to the naturalistic-scientific philosophy of physicalism that is so dominant in this country attempt rather to enlarge or enrich the notions of the physical (the lived body) or of presence (Heidegger's *Dasein*) in a way that gives some foothold to an account of human being. This is not to say that there are not other readings of Levinas in this country that are more sympathetic than the strictly philosophical one. He has an appeal to those interested in hermeneutics, theology, and Judaism, and even, despite some of his positions that make such a reading problematic, to feminists, political scientists, and literary or artistic theorists.

Notes

1. Emmanuel Levinas, *Transcendance et intelligibilité* (Geneva: Labor et Fides, 1984); "Transcendence and Intelligibility," in *Emmanuel Levinas: Basic Philosophical Writings*, ed. Adriaan Peperzak, Simon Critchley, and Robert Bernasconi (Bloomington: Indiana University Press, 1996).

2. See Catherine Chalier's *L'inspiration du philosophe: "L'amour de la sagesse" et*

sa source prophétique (Paris: Albin Michel, 1996) for an excellent treatment of the relationship between philosophy and spirituality in Levinas, and *simpliciter.*

3. My translation of Levinas's *Transcendance et intelligibilité* (Geneva: Labor et fides, 1964), 18. Cf. S. Critchley's translation, in *Emmanuel Levinas: Basic Philosophical Writings,* ed. Adriaan Peperzak, Simon Critchley, and Robert Bernasconi (Bloomington: Indiana University Press, 1996), op.cit., 153. In the course of a discussion following another lecture, "God and Philosophy," published in 1975, Levinas responds to some very probing questions by the Dutch phenomenologist Th. de Boer on the precise nature of the differences between his phenomenology and the Husserlian variety. It remains a phenomenology however, Levinas claims, because it is still essentially the exploration of the horizon of meaning out of which phenomena emerge. But Levinas's area of investigation goes back to before ontology as it is normally understood, to a domain he qualifies as ethical, and as rooted in a "spiritual intrigue." Compare his *De Dieu qui vient à l'idée* (Paris: J. Vrin, 1986), 138–43. Although the lecture itself has been translated as chapter 10 of the *Collected Philosophical Papers,* trans. Alphonso Lingis et al. (Dordrecht: Martinus Nijhoff, 1987), the ensuing discussion is not included.

4. Compare Plato, *The Republic,* esp. 509b, but also 517b, 518d.

5. René Descartes, *Discourse on Method and the Meditations,* trans. F. E. Sutcliffe (London: Penguin, 1968), 130–31.

6. These two passages appear in Emmanuel Levinas, *Otherwise Than Being, or Beyond Essence,* trans. Alphonso Lingis (The Hague: Martinus Nijhoff, 1981), vii. Hereafter cited in the text as *OB.*

7. Levinas, *Basic Philosophical Writings,* 154.

8. Levinas, *Basic Philosophical Writings,* 154.

9. See Catherine Chalier's detailed study of the relationship between Levinas's and Kant's ethical thought in *Pour une morale au-delà du savoir: Kant et Levinas* (Paris: Albin Michel, 1998).

10. Catherine Chalier, *Levinas: L'utopie de l'humain,* published by Albin Michel (Paris, 1993) in the series "Présences du Judaïsme."

11. Emmanuel Levinas, *Entre Nous: Thinking of the Other,* trans. Michael Smith and Barbara Harshav (New York: Columbia University Press, 1998), xii.

12. Emmanuel Levinas, *De l'évasion* (Montpellier: Fata Morgana, 1982), 99.

13. I have not been able to determine at this writing whether this use of the term *il y a* appears first in Blanchot or in Levinas. Levinas's use dates back at least to 1946, since it is the title of an article in *Deucalion* 1:141–54. This material was incorporated into his *De l'existence à l'existant* the following year. Robert Bernasconi seems to share my uncertainty on this point. In commenting on Merleau-Ponty's use of *il y a* in the early pages of his essay "Eye and Mind," he surmises that the term is quite probably borrowed "from Levinas (or Blanchot)." See Bernasconi's *Ontology and Alterity in Merleau-Ponty* (Evanston: Northwestern University Press, 1990), 73.

14. Emmanuel Levinas, *Difficult Freedom: Essays on Judaism,* trans. Seán Hand (London: Athlone, 1990).

15. E. Lévinas, *De Dieu qui vient à l'idée* (Paris: J. Vrin, 1986), 265. Quoted by

C. Chalier, *L'utopie de l'humain* (Paris: Albin Michel, 1993), p 103. For a slightly different translation of this passage, cf. *Of God Who Comes to Mind,* trans. B. Bergo (Stanford: Stanford University Press, 1998), 177.

16. Chalier treats this Levinasian theme in her *De l'intranquilité de l'âme* (Paris: Payot et Rivages, 1999).

17. Plato, *Republic,* 359d–360d.

18. Georges Hansel, "Sciences du quoi et science du qui," in *Explorations talmudiques* (Paris: Editions Odile Jacob, 1998), 39–52, esp. 46–47.

19. Frederick Olafson, *What Is a Human Being?* (Cambridge, Eng., and New York: Cambridge University Press, 1995).

20. Levinas, *Otherwise Than Being,* 117.

21. Ibid.

22. Ibid.

"Between Betrayal and Betrayal": Epistemology and Ethics in Derrida's Debt to Levinas

Margret Grebowicz

Derrida's "Adieu," a text so remarkable for its brevity, intimacy, and feeling that I hesitate to invoke it, ends with the acknowledgment of a debt. Unlike the debt Levinas claims to regretfully owe Heidegger, Derrida tells us, "The good fortune of our debt to Levinas is that we can, thanks to him, assume it and affirm it without regret, in a joyous innocence of admiration."[1] Of course, the notion of debt is one of the things Derrida's work has caused us to reconsider over the years, even as recently as during his address here, two weeks ago, at the colloquium for Jean-François Lyotard. In spite of this, or perhaps because of it, the relationship between Levinas and Derrida is often, and appropriately, mapped according to the trajectory not of interlocution, but of debts and demands.

The question of the ethics of deconstruction has been a particularly popular occasion for this mapping, which typically leads to the conclusion that if Derrida's thought is intertwined with that of Levinas, this is the case insofar as deconstruction is an "ethical" discourse—or if we say that deconstruction is an ethical discourse, we mean it is ethical in the Levinasian sense. This is the shape which Derrida's debt to Levinas appears to have taken in the academic imagination: Levinas as the ethical motor of deconstruction. See, for example, the final pages of Christopher Norris's book *Derrida,* which turns to Levinas in order to "make good the claim" that "there is an ethical dimension to Derrida's writings."[2] See also the editors' introduction to *Re-Reading Levinas,* which presents Levinas's essay "Wholly Otherwise" as a possible response to the charge that deconstruction's commitment to problems of language results in its having no ethical force. The editors write: "It is hoped that 'Wholly Otherwise' will raise the vital issue of the ethics of deconstructive reading and prepare the way for the consideration of Derrida as an ethical thinker, understood in the particular sense Levinas gives to the word 'ethics.'"[3]

Their hope appears to have been more or less fulfilled—not only has this "vital" question been raised, but it has repeatedly been answered in the affirmative. Perhaps it is for this reason that the question concerning the debt Derrida owes to Levinas's thought—"is deconstruction an ethical discourse in the Levinasian sense?"—should keep us up at night: not because we are not convinced of the answer, but because we *are*—a certainty which has succeeded in extinguishing the question's very vitality. On the other hand, revisiting this question opens the possibility of at least two dangers. The negative answer—"no, deconstruction is not an ethical discourse in the Levinasian sense"—may eventually lead us back to the criticism that deconstruction does not have an ethical force. After all, if deconstruction is an ethical reading, but this is not an ethics in the Levinasian sense, then what kind of ethics is it? The positive answer—"yes, deconstruction is ethical in the Levinasian sense"—appears to be the more popular, and so the danger to which it potentially gives rise is more worrisome: the danger of failing to attend to the particularity of Levinas. In an effort to show the affinities between Derrida and Levinas, we may forget what makes Levinas's thought so radical that it suffers from an essential incommensurability with the theoretical idiom, any theoretical idiom, even deconstruction.

In "Violence and Metaphysics," Derrida himself initially appears to fall prey to precisely this danger, in a gesture he presents as the Levinasian gesture par excellence: "we must let the other speak."[4] We might wonder, in an aside, to what extent this is a Levinasian gesture. After all, Derrida uses this gesture to articulate the implications of Husserl's and Heidegger's discourses because Levinas rejects them on charges of violence. First of all, then, letting the other speak is and is not consistent with Levinas's critique in *Totality and Infinity*—the first of the paradoxes which make "Violence and Metaphysics" an impossible essay. This gesture consistently frustrates the possibility of attributing to Derrida any of the positions Derrida articulates—something to keep in mind when approaching this essay.

In the course of letting several others speak, Derrida famously gives voice to Husserl's phenomenology. The exchange which Derrida constructs between Husserl and Levinas begins with what Derrida presents as the "fundamental disagreement" between them: namely, the nature of the experience of the other. Husserl maintains the other as part of the ego's phenomenal sphere, as something whose alterity appears to me. In Derrida's words, "It is this appearance of the other as that which I can never be, this originary non-phenomenality, which is examined as the ego's intentional phenomenon." And while Levinas would object that the intentional schema of meaning neutralizes alterity, Derrida offers several readings of Husserl which save him from the charge of violence.

I will concern myself with the most provocative of these—Derrida's turn to a phenomenological notion of meaning as a way of easing into the problem of the intelligibility of Levinas's text: "One could neither speak, nor have any sense of the totally other, if there was not a phenomenon of the totally other" ("VM" 87). This is the position Derrida ascribes to Husserl, and to phenomenological discourse in general: in order for the other to be meaningful to me, as other, it must take place in the form of a phenomenon, as part of my intentional, meaning-bestowing sphere. Derrida makes this point in several ways. "By acknowledging the infinitely other as such (appearing as such) the status of an intentional modification of the ego in general, Husserl gives himself the right to speak of the infinitely other as such, accounting for the origin and legitimacy of his language." Derrida points out that Levinas speaks "*in fact,*" but without right: "by refusing to acknowledge an intentional modification of the ego (which would be a violent and totalitarian act for him) he deprives himself of the very foundation and possibility of his own language" ("VM" 125). If Levinas relies on the evidence of brute experience, he is forced to adhere to the notion that meaning takes place as a modification of the ego. If he renounces the notion of egoity, Levinas deprives himself of the foundation for meaning, and is unable to account for the legitimacy of his speech. Levinas may speak "in fact," but, Derrida writes, "No philosophy responsible for its own language can renounce ipseity in general" ("VM" 127, 131).

If we take Derrida to suggest that these are legitimate responses from the Husserlian position to the Levinasian, he appears to miss what I have been calling Levinas's particularity, or that aspect of his thought which renders each of these defenses essentially irrelevant. In an effort to determine the outlines of this particularity, we might provisionally describe the difference between Husserl and Levinas in terms of stakes. Husserl's stake, in the position which Derrida lays out for him, is epistemological. Levinas's stake, on the other hand, is, we might say, ethical—although I will temporarily suspend the question of what that means. I here obviously borrow the idiom of stakes from the work of Lyotard, but Derrida's own formulation demonstrates the difference in question: Levinas renounces egoity not because he takes issue with Husserl's epistemology, but because describing the other as a modification of my ego "*would be a violent and totalitarian act for him.*" In other words, according to Levinas's position, Husserl is "wrong," but not in the sense that he is mistaken.

Is the distinction on the level of stakes the same one which Paul Feyerabend wishes to illuminate in *Against Method,* when he tells us that his aim in writing the book is "to support people, not to 'advance knowledge'"?[5] This claim seems more curious to me each time I read it. We know from Lyotard that the stakes of a discourse matter, and, importantly, that they determine its relationship with other discourses. From Levinas we know that the distinction between the ethical stake and the epistemological stake is *imperative*—that it must be adhered to rigorously in order to allow for the possibility of ethics as first philosophy, uncontaminated by the violence of epistemology. Thus, it is not Feyerabend's distinction itself which strikes me as odd, but his suggestion that a book, a theoretical work, could have any stake other than to advance knowledge. Even a philosophy which "supports people" would do it by first of all "advancing knowledge"—is that not simply what philosophy does? In the case that this question, my question, sounds unsophisticated and certainly un-postmodern, recall Lyotard's criticism of Thomas Kuhn's notion of the incommensurability of scientific theories. *Pace* Kuhn, Lyotard claims that scientific theories are not truly incommensurable because incommensurability takes place between genres of discourse, which have different stakes. Lyotard claims that scientific paradigms invariably have a common stake: to know.[6] Say, for the moment, that Lyotard is correct—something of which I am not convinced, if only because "knowing" could be a profoundly different kind of stake for Ptolemy than it is for contemporary astronomers and theoretical physicists. If he is correct, however, would this not mean that the stake of philosophy is also, in the end, to know? And if not, what might it be? Could the stake of a philosophy ever legitimately be "to support people?"

Of course, Levinas's work, perhaps better than anyone's, indicates the possibilities for a philosophy whose stake would not be "to know." Even he, however, has trouble maintaining the distinction between ethics and epistemology—particularly, I suggest, in the essay intended to underline the affinity between his thought and deconstruction. In "Wholly Otherwise," as Robert Bernasconi notes, Levinas appears to offer a response to the challenge posed by the position Derrida presents as the Husserlian, phenomenological criticism of Levinas. The position that Levinas cannot speak meaningfully of the other unless he accepts the other's phenomenality is strikingly similar to the reductio ad absurdum argument used to refute skepticism throughout the history of philosophy. The argument, which silences the skeptic by showing that the statement, "I know that nothing can be known," is a contradiction, fails to account for what Levinas describes as "the incompressible nonsimultaneity of the Said and the Saying." This nonsimultaneity is what saves skepticism from the fate of "the contradiction between what is signified by its Said and what is signified by the very fact of articulating a Said."[7] Levinas's response to the argument takes two different forms. First, he shows that, as it insists on the simultaneity of the Said and the Saying, the position Derrida outlines for

Husserl suffers from the logic of logocentrism. Since Levinas, at least provisionally, reads the Husserlian position as Derrida's own, this reversion to the logocentric logic which deconstruction seeks to frustrate would commit Derrida's critique to a contradiction. Second, and more interesting, Levinas indicates the ultimate impotence of this kind of refutation of skepticism by calling on the fact that skepticism consistently "returns" as a philosophical position throughout the history of philosophy—returns as "the legitimate child of philosophy."[8] As Bernasconi points out, this is not a historical claim, but a structural one—Levinas insists that skepticism is a kind of not-so-dark underbelly of philosophical thought, that the non-simultaneity of the Saying and the Said is as essential to theory as theory's relentless repression of their nonsimultaneity. In this respect, Bernasconi shows, skepticism functions as a "metaphor or 'model'" for how to respond to "what [Levinas] understands to be the 'polemic' of 'Violence and Metaphysics.'"[9] Ultimately, "Wholly Otherwise" leaves us with the impression that both deconstruction and Levinas's work are moments in the return of skepticism in the face of refutation.

It is here, I suggest, in the course of tracing the affinities between ethics as first philosophy, deconstruction, and skepticism—the "legitimate children" of philosophy, which have in common an attention to the nonsimultaneity of the Saying and the Said—that Levinas fails to attend to the stakes of his own discourse. Skepticism is an epistemological position. Its negative claim, that nothing can be known, is not an ethical one—it is not asserted on the grounds that "knowing" is a violent relation with the other. And it is precisely due to skepticism's epistemological stake that the refutation which Levinas is quick to dismiss has been relatively successful. The forms of skepticism which resurface in spite of the refutation ultimately shut down philosophical thought and shift their emphasis to praxis, as in Hume's work on the "common life." Precisely because of its philosophical legitimacy, skepticism is impotent as an epistemological position.

In an effort to maintain the parallel between the skeptic and Levinas, Bernasconi calls our attention to skepticism's interest in praxis. Like skepticism, which, he reminds us, "was as much a way of life as a philosophical position," the ethical relation with the other is "an ethical behavior and not a theology, not a thematization" ("SPF" 150). Bernasconi's emphasis on the importance of praxis, however, fails to address the difference between discourses on the level of stakes because it leaves behind the order of discourses. Levinas's engagement with skepticism is not on the level of behavior, but on the level of philosophical discourses. By his own account, skepticism ends up legitimized as a philosophy, not as a way of life. In other words, the emphasis on praxis fails to address the possibility of a philosophy whose stake is ethical in the Levinasian sense. In question here is the possibility of a theory, not of a practice, whose stake is ethical. Skepticism's stake, even the one of interest to Levinas—namely, skepticism's insistence on the difference between the Saying and the Said—may, at most, be ethical in, if you will, the vulgar sense, the sense of how to live the "good" life. Presumably, if Levinas's thought were reduced to a series of prescriptions for how to live one's life, this would hardly signal the "survival" of his thought in the face of logocentrism.

Derrida's reading, on the other hand, does a better job of attending to the particularity of Levinas's stake. "Violence and Metaphysics" invokes a less legitimate child: mysticism. He addresses the traditional ineffability claim as something which distinguishes Levinas's predicament from that of the mystic. Unlike the tradition of mysticism, Derrida points out, Levinas cannot speak "in a language resigned to its own failure." The mystic's "autodestruction of language which [advocates] silent metaphysical intuition" allows her to speak only "in fact," only contingently, illegitimately. Unlike the skeptic, who inhabits philosophy legitimately, the mystic gives herself the right to "travel through philosophical discourse as through a foreign medium." "But," Derrida asks, "what happens when that right is no longer given, when the possibility of metaphysics is the possibility of speech? When metaphysical responsibility is responsibility for language . . . ?" ("SPF" 116). Levinas's commitment to the notion that "justice is a right to speak," or, in Derrida's words, that "only discourse is righteous," leads Derrida to insist on the difference between Levinas's relationship with language and that of the mystic.[10] Ultimately, mysticism is too illegitimate—it fails to respect the signification of the Saying, and rejects not only the Said, but also the Saying.

It is the stake of the rejection, however, which makes mysticism relevant to Levinas's position. Levinas rejects the right, to borrow Derrida's paraphrase, to speak in the name of an advocation of the "autodestruction of language" for the reasons that discourse is "righteous" and that speech is the possibility of "justice." These are not epistemological claims concerning language—they are ethical. Although Derrida abandons the problem of mysticism here, I suggest that it is precisely the notion of stakes which illuminates the relevance of mysticism for the problematic with which Derrida, Levinas, and Bernasconi are concerned. Skepticism is focused on epistemology, and, of course, living. Mysticism's negative claim, that the experience of God is ineffable, also develops on the epistemological level, and on the practical—note the thousands of years of contemplatives' doctrine about how to live in the service of God's visitations. In addition, however, mysticism's negative claim develops on a level we might call ethical, at least in the sense that the rejection does not take place on epistemological grounds. The stake which separates the Said and the Saying for the contemplative is an ethical one: it is *wrong* to think that language can accommodate the truth of God. This may not be ethics in the Levinasian sense, but it is also not ethics in the vulgar sense—the sense of how to live the good life. From the perspective of the notion of stakes, skepticism may be less relevant to his project than Levinas thinks, and mysticism more relevant to his project than he would allow.

In "At This Very Moment in This Work Here I Am," Derrida continues to experiment with the possibility that Levinas's is a discourse with a nonphilosophical stake. Can there be a responsible speech which is not merely the violence of thematization? He formulates the problem as the question of the "responsibility" of Levinas's writing itself, of the "response in deed" that is his writing.[11] However, the motif which Derrida introduces in "Violence and Metaphysics" and revisits here is that of Levinas's work as precisely not a response, but a question. In both essays, Derrida turns the traditional interrogative format of a scholarly reading inside out. In "Violence and Metaphysics," Derrida describes what has traditionally been taken to be his critique of Levinas as "questions put to *us* by Levinas," and in "At This Very Moment," it is "[Levinas's] responsibility—and what he says of responsibility—that interrogates us."[12] This difference would be of little more than rhetorical interest were it not for Derrida's consistent return to the trope of the question throughout his engagements of Levinas, even in his recent "A Word of Welcome." Taking the difference seriously means considering the possibility that it is the responsibility of the *questions* posed by Levinas that Derrida's reading interrogates.

Indeed, the notion of the question in Levinas's thought occasions two simultaneous trajectories in Derrida's reading: it serves to address the issue of the responsibility of discourse, as well as to thematize the relationship between Levinas's work and his own. Already at the start of "Violence and Metaphysics," Derrida describes the philosophical community in which Levinas takes part as "a community of the questions about the possibility of the question." The community "consists," if we can say this, of those who face the death, past or future, of philosophy—assembled as a sort of jury that is indefinitely "out" on the question of the status, value, and limits of theoretical discourse. These questions concerning the very possibility of philosophy, Derrida writes, "should be the only questions today capable of founding the community within the world of those who are still called philosophers" ("VM" 79–80). According to his specification, skepticism and deconstruction would find themselves within the outlines, however provisional, of this community.

In "A Word of Welcome," Derrida revisits the notion of the question—this time, in the figure of the third in Levinas's thought. The third,

the question, or justice—in the relationship of non-synonymous substitution—are, Levinas writes, "necessary." This necessity, Derrida continues,
"reintroduces us, as if by force, into places ethics should exceed: the visibility of the face, thematization, comparison, synchrony, system, co-
presence before a 'court of justice.'"[13] The face to face may be without question, but it does not properly precede the question—"the question, but
also, as a result, justice, philosophical intelligibility, knowledge . . . [are]
there from the 'first' epiphany of the face in the face to face" ("WW" 31).

Thus, the question, which Derrida also describes as "the passage
from ethical responsibility to juridical, political—and philosophical—responsibility," is not derivative of the "purity of ethical desire" ("WW" 31–
32). Philosophical responsibility and mediation are not merely perver-
sions of ethical responsibility and immediacy. Derrida here employs the
same logic of the supplement at work in *Of Grammatology,* in which the apparently derivative, secondary, perverted element serves as the condition
for the possibility of the original, primary, pure element. More important,
his reading suggests that this logic is at work in Levinas's text. Finally, the
boundaries between Derrida and Levinas run together to such a degree
that Derrida infuses the notions of ethics and justice with the language of
early deconstruction, describing the face-to-face relationship as an "oath
before the letter," and justice as "perjury" ("WW" 33). To Derrida's knowledge, he tells us, "perjury is not a theme in Levinas, nor is oath." They are,
however, themes in *Of Grammatology*—perhaps not by name, but as moments in that work's general problematic of the presence and absence at
work in meaning. Derrida's reading of Levinas unfolds along the same
lines as his development of the supplement at the origin: the third, the
question, philosophical intelligibility are all moments in the "necessary,"
"pre-originary" perjury which makes possible the oath of the ethical relation ("WW" 33–34).

Does not Derrida's recourse to the logic of the supplement amount
to the most violent reading possible—one which does not respect the particularity of Levinas's thought, but instead takes the nonsimultaneity of
the Saying and the Said to be the same thing as the mediation at work in
all signification? If what Levinas's work teaches us about discourse is indistinguishable from what deconstruction teaches us about discourse,
that meaning is conditioned by mediation, then the claim that Levinas is
the ethical force of deconstruction amounts to nothing more than a neu-
tralization of the particular nature of the ethical relation, of its difference
from all other relations. Ethics becomes one of the formal, epistemological or metaphysical, problems of language with which deconstruction
deals.

Even in the case of "A Word of Welcome," reading Derrida's reading with the help of the notion of stakes offers an alternative. It offers the possibility that Derrida's recourse to the logic of the supplement is not the same in the case of Levinas as it is in *Of Grammatology*, where perjury would be structurally necessary, as the condition of the possibility of the oath. Here, instead, the pre-originary perjury of the third, of justice and philosophical intelligibility, is necessary—not structurally, but because "the absence of the third would threaten with violence the purity of ethics in the absolute immediacy of the face to face with the unique." "The third," Derrida writes, "would thus *protect* against the vertigo of ethical violence itself" ("WW" 32–33, emphasis mine). The necessity of the third thus has the force of an imperative, as opposed to the force of the description of a structural fact. This would not be the imperative of prescription, or of ethics in the vulgar sense—since we are not dealing with the practical, or even with the Good—but rather, an imperative constitutive of the discourse itself, of an ostensibly philosophical discourse. In this respect, Levinas's thought would be radically unlike, and perhaps incommensurable with, the discourses of skepticism and deconstructive reading.

I propose that this stake, the stake of this imperative, which is not the same as the stake of the third, the question, justice, and philosophical intelligibility, is a sort of "blind spot" which Derrida consistently, self-consciously revisits in his readings of Levinas. He is particularly attentive to it when indicating the respect in which Levinas's work is *unlike* that of any other thinker. When Derrida writes that "almost the entirety of Levinas's discourse, for example, *almost* the entire space of its intelligibility for us, appeals to this third," to what does this mysterious "almost" refer? I suggest that this stake, the illegitimate, unphilosophical stake of Levinas's discourse, is the unthinkable remainder, falling outside of the order of the third ("WW" 30, emphasis mine).

I will conclude by once again raising the question of Derrida's debt to Levinas. If we take seriously the idea that the stake of Levinas's discourse is not epistemological, we face the possibility that this discourse is incommensurable with deconstruction, and the breakdown of the idea of Levinas as the ethical motor of deconstruction. Working through these difficulties would require showing that deconstruction's stake is also ethical. In that case, it would not suffice to write *about* justice and responsibility. We would have to take seriously the possibility of writing in such a way that the intelligibility of discourse would not merely appeal to the third, but instead, would appeal to an order in which imperatives, protections, and violations are the critical terms. In the end, I think, Derrida struggles with precisely this challenge throughout the course of his engagement with Levinas. In "At This Very Moment" he writes, "I don't yet know how to qualify what is happening here between him, you, and me that doesn't belong to the order of questions and responses."[14] Bernasconi translates the "I don't yet know" as "I am still ignorant," and reads this ignorance as the sign of a contemporary skepticism ("SFP" 159). At the end of "Adieu," however, addressing the debt which we all owe Levinas, Derrida writes, "We often addressed to one another what I would call neither questions nor answers, but . . . a sort of 'question-prayer.'"[15] Does that which in deconstruction exceeds the order of questions and answers belong to the ignorance of skepticism, or to the unknowing prayer of a mysticism?

What I wish to insist on is neither one, nor the other, but on the difference between them as a difference in stakes, and on the value of reading Derrida's engagement of Levinas with this difference as a resource. What I will suggest, more tentatively, is that perhaps Derrida's debt to Levinas amounts to nothing more than the possibility of reading and writing with this difference in mind. Even more tentatively, I will conclude with an imperative: If Levinas's thought is to "survive" logocentric refutations, it is a debt we—the "we" to which Derrida appeals in the "Adieu"— should owe actively, in the course of our scholarly engagements with the problems of responsibility, justice, and the experience of the other.

Notes

1. Jacques Derrida, "Adieu," in *Adieu to Emmanuel Levinas,* trans. Pascale-Anne Brault and Michael Naas (Stanford: Stanford University Press, 1999), 13.

2. Christopher Norris, *Derrida* (Cambridge: Harvard University Press, 1987), 228.

3. See "Editors' Introduction" in *Re-Reading Levinas,* ed. Robert Bernasconi and Simon Critchley (Bloomington: Indiana University Press, 1991), xiv.

4. Jacques Derrida, "Violence and Metaphysics," in *Writing and Difference,* trans. A. Bass (Chicago: University of Chicago Press, 1978), 87. Hereafter cited in the text as "VM."

5. Paul Feyerabend, *Against Method* (Verso, 1993), 3.

6. Jean-François Lyotard, "A Bizarre Partner," in *Postmodern Fables,* trans. G. Van Den Abbeele (Minneapolis: University of Minnesota Press, 1997), 133.

7. Emmanuel Levinas, "Wholly Otherwise," in *Re-Reading Levinas,* 5.

8. Levinas, "Wholly Otherwise," 5.

9. Robert Bernasconi, "Skepticism in the Face of Philosophy," in *Re-Reading Levinas,* 157–58. Hereafter cited in the text as "SFP."

10. Bernasconi, "Skepticism," 116; and Levinas, *Totality and Infinity,* 298.

11. Jacques Derrida, "At This Very Moment in This Work Here I Am," in *Re-Reading Levinas,* 17.

12. Derrida, "Violence and Metaphysics," 84; and Derrida, "At This Very Moment," 17.

13. Jacques Derrida, "A Word of Welcome," in *Adieu to Emmanuel Levinas,* 30. Hereafter cited in the text as "WW."

14. Derrida, "At This Very Moment," 17.

15. Derrida, "Adieu," 13.

Levinas on the Saying and the Said

Bernhard Waldenfels

The distinction between *the Saying* and *the Said* seems to be one of the strongest motives in Levinas's later work. In contrast to earlier distinctions, like those between existence and the existent or between totality and infinity, this related distinction originates immediately *from speaking and language itself,* without being a mere linguistic distinction. In addition, we are confronted with a sort of *self-differentiation of speech.* Speech itself is split into the Saying and the Said, and this occurs as a result of a certain diachrony of speaking. There is a self-delay of discourse, a *diachrony* of the Saying that goes beyond the *synchrony* of things being said. To put it in Platonic terms: the *dihairesis* prevails over the *synopsis* or synthesis. The *syn-*, which stands for the composition of order, becomes dislocated.

Certainly these are ideas that open new and rich perspectives. Nevertheless, there are some ambiguities that have to be discussed. I shall do so, focusing on the alternative between a *Saying without the Said* and a *Saying with-out the Said* (i.e., within and without at once). The latter alternative, which I want to defend, runs against every purism of pure Saying. It must be mentioned that such a pure Saying runs the risk of a certain ethical foundationalism.

I shall proceed in the following way. After a linguistic prelude, I shall analyze three problematic aspects of speech: (1) the difference between the speech event and the speech content, (2) the distance between the speaker and the listener, and (3) the difference between *that to which* we respond and *that which* we answer when responding to the Other's demand. In other words, I deal with the difference between the Saying and the Said, with the plurality of the sayers, and with the difference of demand and response.

1

Beginning with Levinas's relation to linguistics, I will respond to just one passage in which Levinas explained his ideas in a highly concentrated way: the preface of *Otherwise Than Being, or Beyond Essence* (*Autrement qu'être, ou au-delà de l'essence*).[1] Rather vaguely, Levinas speaks here of "the correlation of the Saying and the Said, i.e., the subordination of the Saying to the Said within the linguistic system and within ontology." It is true that he does not strictly repudiate this sort of subordination, which he accepts as "the price which manifestation requires" (*AE* 7). However, in the same context we read that Saying "precedes the verbal signs which it connects," it precedes "the semantic tickling," coming forth as the "fore-word of languages" (*AE* 6). Before exploring this anteriority attributed to Saying, and the price the Saying has to pay, let us look into linguistics, even though Levinas pushes linguistics away in such a global way—as if linguistics were a reign of traitors who betray the Saying by translating it into the Said.

If we take into account the well-known *theory of speech acts,* we become aware that, even within the frame of this linguistic pragmatics, the process of saying takes place neither inside nor outside language. On the one hand, a speech act like "I promise you to be here tomorrow" certainly does not occur *outside language,* as if it consisted of something we were speaking about. The speech act as such is not included in the propositional content, it is not a part of what is said. On the other hand, it is just as little *inside language,* as if it were a linguistic element, bound to syntactical rules and endowed with semantic features. The promise I give is, rather, an *event of the language itself.* It coincides with speaking in *actu,* with the very *event* of speaking. As soon as something gets said something happens which belongs neither to the realm of words nor to the realm of things, but moves between words and things. But that is not all: the link between the Saying and the Said is co-indicated by linguistic tools such as demonstrative pronouns (here, now), by the tense of verbs (I promise), and by personal pronouns (I/to you). According to Karl Bühler's theory of language, the field of symbols is anchored in a field of pointing (*Zeigfeld*). In a similar way, Emile Benveniste admits "instances of discourse" which transform language into discourse. But while *indicated* in what is said, the Saying *surpasses* what is said. The Saying can neither be reduced to things, which are given, nor to acts fulfilled by myself or by the other. I thus distance my argument from the theory of speech *acts* by taking the Saying as an *event.* Acts are all too quickly appropriated when they are attributed to a certain person.

Finally, there is a last step to take. This is the most important one, and again we can take our cue from linguistic hints. In accordance with the linguistic distinction of *énonciation* and *énoncé,* the instances of discourse are *doubled.* In Oswald Ducrot's book *The Saying and the Said* (*Le Dire et le Dit*), published in 1984, this distinction is conveyed even by Levinas's own terms, although the name of Levinas is never explicitly mentioned. Let us illustrate this new aspect by again referring to the promise. Explicitly formulated, the promise is internally doubled under three aspects: (1) "*I* promise to you that I shall help you," (2) "I promise *to you* that I shall help *you*" and (3) "I *promise* to you that I *shall* help you." Not only is the addressee split into *I* and *Me,* into the *je de l'énonciation* and the *je de l'énoncé;* the addressed—and the time and place—of speech are split as well. They are split into the Here and Now of speaking functions, as zero-points, before being "betrayed" by local and temporal data. Here and Now are thus not simply given; rather, they mark the place-time of giving space and time.

These linguistic sketches demonstrate that the distinction between the Saying and the Said is an occurrence that does not simply lie outside the field of linguistics. The absorption of the Saying by what is said cannot be taken as a failure of linguistics, but it is due to certain practices and techniques of speaking and writing which take "as true being what is only a method." Certainly, linguistics plays its part in the process of self-forgetting that our speech undergoes. But verdicts like "science does not think" or "linguistics submits the Saying to the Said" are not more than half-truths.

2

After this linguistic prelude, I shall return to Levinas's texts in order to articulate some open questions. If we take as our starting point the event of speaking, then we should not simply presume that there is a sort of *Saying before and without that which is said*—unless we conceive the anteriority of saying as a *self-precedence* of speaking and interpret this "without" as an *outburst* of speaking itself. Otherwise the saying would degrade into *being* outside of what is said, i.e., being *said* in its own way, belonging to a sort of *Hinterwelt* or *Überwelt,* as Levinas himself remarked (*AE* 6).

Assuming the distinction between the Saying and the Said, we must assume as much—that there is no pure Saying and no pure Said at all. There are only certain *border-experiences* that come near to such extremes. Our speaking approximates what is merely said the more it turns into the pure reproduction of what has already been said, i.e., repeating given patterns and applying existing rules—ending with *stereotypes* or *automatisms.* However, speaking approximates the pure Saying the more it leaves space for the invention of what has never been said and for deviations from rules. This nearly pure speaking would end with *exclamations,* with *crying* or, less pathetic, with *salutations* (see *AE* 183). Levinas does not refrain from defending a sort of "speaking in order to say nothing" (*parler pour ne rien dire*), which evokes the "speaking in order to speak" repudiated by Plato. By the way, salutations like *adieu* follow certain rules as well; they can be interpreted as enclaves within the field of what is said or as kinds of overtures and finales, which open and close the ongoing intercourse. They can thus be characterized as "rituals of accessibility."[2] But let us consider the extreme case of crying: crying, when one is in pleasure or pain, in joy or sorrow, has no sense and does not follow any rule. In this and only in this sense does the crying of a tortured human being stand for the possibility of a Saying without anything said. In summary, the Saying may tend toward the limit of *saying* nothing by purely repeating what has been said, or it may tend toward the limit of saying *nothing* by refusing what has been said. More can hardly be said about that.

However, someone may make the following objection. When dealing with a Saying before and without something said, Levinas is not interested in speaking as signifying something, be it by repetition or innovation; instead, he focuses on the "significance of signification" directed toward the Other (*AE* 6).[3] To this objection, I would answer as follows: one cannot jump directly from speaking *about* the Other to speaking *to* the Other. The different dimensions of speech mentioned above are closely interconnected. We only have to recognize the fact that our speech may be alternatively *dominated* by one function or the other, as Bühler and Jakobson assume. So the speaker's utterance may be classified as primarily exhibitive, appellative, or self-expressive. In any case, the Other—*to whom* I address or *by whom* I am addressed myself—will never emerge from outside those orders which define what can and cannot be said, and the same holds true for myself as a speaker or a listener. We are unable to *skip* the order of things, which is spelled in the order of words; we can only *transgress* the limits of order, and even this only to some extent. Regarded from this perspective, the alienness or otherness of whomever and whatever appears, strictly speaking, as *extra-ordinary.* The extra-ordinary always presupposes the ordinary it exceeds. The excess takes place when normality yields to anomalies, when the extra-ordinary de-viates from the ordinary and de-ranges the existing orders. Levinas's *dire sans le dit* only makes sense when connected with the "order of things" and with the order of discourse analyzed by Michel Foucault. Because historical discourses and cultural life-worlds are impregnated by scientific methods, technical dispositives, and cultural patterns, we cannot reduce the Said to the Saying without passing again and again through the orders of what is said. "Passing through" means more than mentioning such orders. It means more than simply relying on certain traditions.

3

Other questions arise when we consider the fact that for Levinas, saying means *speaking to the Other* before and beyond saying something. This implies giving, proposing, responding, and this means not only to the Other but also *for the Other* (see *repondre d'autrui, AE* 60). Levinas does not tire of displaying a series of verbs that all vary, even celebrate, the *dative*—the case of giving.[4] The gesture of giving by far surpasses what is given. This is a fascinating issue, which I do not want to discuss in detail here.[5] I only want to ask *who speaks* when speaking is happening. Levinas asks this question too. He nearly uses Lacan's terms when he claims that what is at stake here is the "who of the saying" (*le qui du dire; AE* 60). It is the "sayer," so to speak, who does not coincide with the "speaker" or "emitter," who functions within a communication or information system. Hence, the event of saying gets split in a new way. It gets split into the *who* and the *to whom* or *for whom* of the saying. The classical subject, functioning as the source or bearer of speeches and actions, loses his or her central place while being involved in an "intrigue of responsibility." In this regard, the Saying—which precedes what is or can be said—means the "proximity of one to the other: involvement of approximation, one for the other" (*AE* 6).

One for the other—but how does somebody becomes some*one*? Being oneself should not be confused with the uniqueness (*Einmaligkeit*) of individual beings or events. It means a sort of singularity "for which the plural makes no sense,"[6] it means to be singled out by the appeal or the demand of the Other, by a sort of creative election. It seems to be difficult to miss the religious tone suggested by this vocabulary. What Levinas indicates is my own birth out of the Other's demand. To exist means to subsist for the Other; institutions turn into substitutions. So it becomes clear that Levinas tries to change the very status of the human being and not only his or her aspirations and duties.

However, just as we persist in the distinction between the Saying and the Said, we have to ask about the manner in which the event of saying splits into my own Saying and the Saying of the Other. Consequently, the difference turns into a process of differentiation, the remoteness into a process of distantiation, and such processes presuppose a certain graduation, including a certain *overlapping* of one's own and the alien. Once more, Levinas tends to skip the problem. While asking the question of who fulfills the pre-original saying, he mentions something like a pure "speaking language" (*langage qui parle*), a pure "it speaks" (*cela parle*) which would be "nobody's saying" (*AE* 60–61). But he only mentions it in order to reject it. Instead he looks for a "Sayer" within the Saying: "We have to show within the Saying . . . the de-position or de-situation of the subject which however remains an unsubstitutable uniqueness, and we have to show within the Saying the subjectivity of the Subject" (*AE* 61). Levinas does not take into consideration at all the *In-ein-ander* between me and the Other and that this "in-one-another" might presuppose a certain *anonymity*, i.e., a certain kind of non-difference. This anonymity—which constitutes the social background of the *Einander*, of the "one to the other"—cannot be disqualified as an unethical sort of indifference.[7]

I do not intend to discuss the problem of an "operative sociality" (*fungierende Sozialität*) in all its details. I shall only attend to the question of an *anonymous speaking*. Our speaking does not only depend on linguistic orders, which decide what can and cannot be said; it is also embedded in certain traditions, idioms, and institutional texts. And all of this is only more or less invidualized, taking the features of a *Man*. Being born means being born into a world—which means being already spoken, inasmuch as everybody is already spoken by others, before speaking with his or her own voice.

One could refer to the use of personal pronouns, which differ considerably from age to age, from social status to social status, from culture to culture. For example, the Japanese language offers many forms of "I" and "thou," the uses of which remain highly contextual. We cannot simply claim: "The pro-noun disguises already the unique which is unique while speaking, it subsumes him under a concept" (*AE* 72). Even if we accept that "there is *nothing* which is named I [*je*]; I is said by someone who speaks" (ibid.), there are still different ways of saying "I." In addition, while stressing the unicity of the speaker (i.e., *his* indeclinability), Levinas also effaces the gender difference, simply using the masculine.

We can take a further step, considering a phenomenon that Merleau-Ponty described as social *syncretism*. Learning the use of personal pronouns or other linguistic devices, we pass through introjections, projections, and transferences in such a way that the question "Who speaks?" remains open. What Merleau-Ponty calls "intercorporeity" includes multiple interferences between my own and the Other's behavior. Let us consider an example that reminds us of Levinas's own analysis of violations. When a little girl, after having slapped the face of her playmate, claims to have been beaten, she certainly does not draw as sharp a distinction between her own and the Other's action as the judge does when he pronounces a judgment. Were she to do so, she would deny what is too obvious to be denied in a normal way. What Merleau-Ponty tries to illustrate by this example is something else. He points to the fact that words and actions gear into each other, that they pass into each other by a sort of transitivism, which does not stop at the borderlines of our sphere of ownness. The attitude of jealousy, which persists beyond the threshold of childhood, looks similar. So Merleau-Ponty concludes: "Every human relation irradiates. There are no relations two by two."[8] When we read in Levinas that "The One exposes him/herself to the Other like a skin exposes itself to what it hurts, like a cheek to what it knocks" (*AE* 63), we should add that the hyperbolic descriptions of vulnerability cannot replace the descriptions of what is going on between different people, who are never completely individualized.

Finally, even on the level of responsible speech we meet with a plurivocity, a plurality of voices. Different voices interfere with each other, as in the case of quotation (which remains implicit to some extent), in the case of irony (where one takes distance from one's own words), or in the case of theater (which finds its echo in the scenarios of everyday life). With regard to this multiplication and proliferation of voices, Mikhail Bakhtin evokes an inner dialogicity of speech: each word we utter or write down is a "half-alien word," and our speech is crowded by "hybrids" that belong neither to this nor to the other side.[9] In his book *The Saying and the Said,* Ducrot elaborates these ideas with the help of contemporary linguistics. Accordingly, the empirical speaker is doubled by the *locuteur,* who takes responsibility for what is said. And in the background there is a third figure, the *énonciateur,* who incorporates certain points of views and attitudes, while widely exceeding the inventions and capacities of each individual speaker. Ervin Goffman arrives at similar results in his analyses of the social frames within which we speak and act.

In general, Levinas's *one-for-the-other* presupposes something like a *one-within-the-other* which Husserl calls *Ineinander.* So we reach an intercorporeity that includes the intertwining of speaking and listening. The borderlines between one's own and the Other's behavior are more or less blurred. This does not imply that all responsibility seeps away into a faceless anonymity. It only means that each responsibility is going to be measured out in correspondence to the specific organization of the given speech field or action field. Were we to overlook these inner limits of speaking and acting, we would fall into an overmoralization, as if every speech or action would simply return to a single speaker or actor. Nietzsche is right to warn us against any morality that forgets its origins, turning it into a moralistic compulsion. It seems to me that the separation between myself and the social world, presupposed in *Totality and Infinity*, has to be reinterpreted in terms of dis-entanglement (*Entflechtung*), which precisely implies some entanglement (*Verflechtung*), connecting what belongs to me and others. I do not find the Other only in myself, I also find myself in the Other. What I call response and responsivity arise from this chiasm between one's own and the alien, even in the case when victims are confronted with their persecutors.[10] The order in twilight I have analyzed elsewhere allows us to speak as well of morals in twilight. There is no clear-cut distinction between dog and wolf. On the contrary, we live *entre chien et loup*.[11]

4

There is a last question left, which aims at the heart of Levinas's ethics. Having discussed how speech splits into the Saying and the Said, and having shown how the process of Saying becomes socially differentiated, the "response of responsibility" (*AE* 180) remains to be considered. We have to ask how the *response* I give is related to the *demand* I am confronted with. To put it in my own terms, we have to find out how the *Antwort* and the *Anspruch* (taken in the double sense of appeal and claim) are interconnected.

The well-known dialogical scheme that confronts the speaker with the listener may be helpful here. According to this scheme, the partners of a dialogue are basically independent of each other. Everybody is invited to speak in his or her own name, in his or her own voice. Everybody is expected to give reasons for what has been said or done. And these reasons refer to the common reason we are all participating in.[12] To this extent, the one gives what the other literally has already in mind, except empirical information which does not reach the level of the veritable dialogue. Thus we understand Levinas's remark that the Platonic dialogue is "the reminiscence of a drama rather than the drama itself" (*AE* 25). Similar things could be said about the argumentative discourses on which the discourse-ethics of Habermas relies. It is thus to be suggested that we approximate the Other step-by-step: we hear what the Other says; we understand more or less what is going to be said; we respond with yes and no; we come to an agreement, and if not we continue. This step-by-step model allows for changing roles. The hearer becomes the speaker and vice versa. By means of the reversibility of standpoints (following Piaget) or by means of the reciprocity of perspectives (following Schutz), one's own speech gets coordinated with that of the Other, at least in the long run, notwithstanding a lot of accidents, which can be produced by ignorance, error, bad will, or violence. Obviously it is just this kind of dialogical homology (*homologia*) that Levinas attacks with so much vehemence. In his view, such a dialogical agreement makes everyone separate the Other from his or her own body.[13] Or conversely, referring to Levinas's image of the skin, the ego feels much too well at home within his or her own skin (*AE* 137). There is nothing which really goes under one's skin, and there is no place for something like a "skin trade."[14] Every sort of dialogical harmony or personal intangibility, however, is put into question by statements like this: "[The Other] gives orders to me before being recognized" (*Il m'ordonne avant d'être reconnu; AE* 109). The Other's order precedes our mutual understanding. The Other takes my words precisely out of my mouth—my speaking begins elsewhere, outside myself.

In my view, Levinas is again right in what he tries to show. Indeed, entering into a dialogue is not a part of the dialogue itself—just as in a similar way concluding and keeping a contract does not belong to what is contracted—as if the saying could be absorbed by what is said. As in the case of speaking, we have to distinguish between *hearing something* and *listening to*. Listening to the Other's words is more than a prestep which leads to responding; it is rather itself a sort of responding, relating to the Other's demand. Even Husserl speaks of a "responding looking at and listening to."[15] Listening is never completely up to me, it is provoked by what has already been said and done. Once confronted with the Other's demand, one cannot not respond, much as, according to Paul Watzlawick, one cannot not communicate. We are trapped by the Other's gaze or word. My exposition to the Other includes a certain inevitability, a practical sort of *ne-cessitudo* (*Un-ausweichlichkeit*). My own speaking and that of the Other will never be integrated into a unity without fissure, they will never be synthesized. Rather, the Other's demand and my own response form a double event—similar to a double word—marked by a hyphen (*Bindestrich*) that functions at once as a dash (*Trennungsstrich*). Hence Maurice Blanchot insists on the fact that interruptions, pauses, and intervals are constitutive features of every sort of "enter-tainment," of *entre-tien*. Our Saying is not only plurivocal, it crosses a threshold of silence—unless we are sticking with what has already been said—as if words could be frozen in time.

However, Levinas seems to go too far again, overemphasizing the part of the Other. I certainly do not think that Paul Ricoeur is right when he assumes that Levinas simply reverses one's own role and that of the Other, although Levinas sometimes comes rather close to that. What Levinas seems to intend is not a new bargain, an exchange between the egoism and the altruism, as if to revive the eighteenth century's debates.

Nevertheless, there are other aspects that remain doubtful, such as the distinction between *gravité* and *jeu*. Whereas gravity is reserved for the Saying, play turns to what is said and to Being (compare *AE* 6, 148, 154). This distinction itself goes back to Plato, who opposes the seriousness (*spoude*) of the vivid voice of the logos to the mere play (*paidia*) of writing. But Levinas does not merely repeat Plato's view, he goes his own way. First, he avoids the use of the common term for seriousness, *sériosité*—as in *Being and Nothingness*, when Sartre opposes the *esprit de sérieux* to the *esprit de jeu*. Simultaneously, Levinas keeps a distance from the normal seriousness of speech acts. The gravity he is looking for has more to do with the forces of experience than with the quality of existential projects and mental states. The term "gravity" connotates the forces and fields of gravitation. With regard to the face-to-face situation, Levinas already remarked in *Totality and Infinity:* "That is not a play of mirrors, but my responsibility, i.e., an existence already obliged. It locates the center of a being's gravity outside that being."[16] This reminds us of Nietzsche's eagerness to transform the "weight of things," or of Simone Weil's reflections that oscillate between weight and grace.[17] In any case, what Levinas has in mind is not a new gravity of Being (and even less Kundera's "unbearable lightness of Being"); what he has in mind is a *gravity beyond Being*.

This may be so, but what about the other side? First, we should ask whether to render *jeu* as "play" or as "game"? Levinas does not spend much time distinguishing different forms of *jeu*. What he tries to lower are all kinds of gratuity and frivolity, all "liberty without responsibility," including Eugen Fink's *Spiel der Welt* (compare *AE* 148). The real target of his attack seems to be the attitude of a player who only dis-plays the range of possibilities, devoting himself to an aesthetics of existence. Levinas thus puts aside rule-guided games, including all kinds of *Sprachspiele,* which could be taken as a sort of secondary gravity, typical of beings whose center of gravity is inside themselves.

But here we run into a peculiar kind of Rubicon. If we understand the ethical responsibility as an obligation—delivered from every play or game, freed as well from every *Spielraum* and every sort of free play—we really shall end up with a dubious form of ethical foundationalism. The movement of passing outside myself would be hypostasized into an outer world. We would fly into a moral *Hinterwelt.*

It is true that Levinas would be the last to accept this consequence, one that he explicitly and permanently repudiates. For him, ethics has nothing to do with any sort of escapism. But is the risk of escape really banished? I do not think this question can be answered by a clear yes or no. In any case, raising the question may make us read Levinas's texts more cautiously.

Levinas permanently confronts us with the question of arbitrariness. But we should look for a way to avoid the Scylla of bondage as well as the Charybdis of arbitrariness. I agree with Levinas when he persists in maintaining that all our speaking and acting starts elsewhere, that it starts where we have never been and where we will never be. It is just this speaking and acting from elsewhere that I call "response." The responsivity that is at work here has to be distinguished from any moral or legal responsibility, which relies on a given order. However, responding, which starts from elsewhere without being grounded there, culminates in the paradox of creative responsivity, which resembles Merleau-Ponty's paradox of creative expression.[18] This creative aspect, dependent on the contingency of orders that call for invention and creation, remains simply underdetermined in Levinas's thinking. Levinas seems to be right when he emphasizes that we do not create that to which we respond, but he neglected the fact that we do create to some extent that which we give as response. Consequently, there is no Saying without something said; at best there is a Saying with-out what is said. But even when this is accepted, it is not so easy to keep hold of the small edge that separates arbitrariness from bondage and bondage from arbitrariness. Our history demonstrates that one extreme reinforces the other. There is no conclusive solution, but what we need is what Levinas calls *redire*, i.e., a sort of Saying which interrupts itself, leaving room for another Saying and for the Saying of others.

Notes

1. Emmanuel Levinas, *Autrement qu'être, ou au-delà de l'essence* (The Hague: Martinus Nijhoff, 1978), 49. Hereafter cited in the text as *AE*.

2. E. Goffman, *Relations in Politics* (New York: Basic Books, 1971).

3. Concerning the unusual word *signifiance* and its linguistic context, compare Th. Wiemer, *Die Passion des Sagens: Zur Deutung der Spache bei Emmanuel Levinas und ihrer Realisierung im philosophischen Diskurs* (Freiburg and Munich: K. Alber, 1988), 196–202

4. The case of providing contrasts with the accusative, as the case of accusing, and this contrast is not easily explained.

5. More about this can be found in my book *Antwortregister* (Frankfurt am Main: Suhrkamp, 1994), chap. 3, p. 13; and in my comments about Derrida's *La fausse monnaie* in "Das Un-ding der Gabe," in *Einsätze des Denkens: Zur Philosophie von Jacques Derrida*, ed. H.-D. Gondek and B. Waldenfels (Frankfurt am Main: Suhrkamp, 1997).

6. Edmund Husserl, *Die Krisis der europäischen Wissenschaften und die transzendentale Phänomenologie* (Husserliana 6) (The Hague: Martinus Nijhoff, 1954), 146.

7. See my reflections on the relation between Merleau-Ponty and Levinas in "Verflechtung und Trennung," in *Deutsch-Französische Gedankengänge* (Frankfurt am Main: Suhrkamp, 1995), chap. 20. I refer further to an excellent book dealing with this topic: Antje Kapust, *Berührung ohne Berührung: Ethik und Ontologie bei Merleau-Ponty and Levinas* (Munich: W. Fink, 1999).

8. Maurice Merleau-Ponty, *Merleau-Ponty à la Sorbonne: Résumé de cours 1949–1952* (Grenoble: Cynara, 1988), 97.

9. See Mikhail Bakhtin, "Das Wort im Roman," in *Die Ästhetik des Wortes*, ed. R. Grübel (Frankfurt am Main: Suhrkamp, 1999). I make use of this essay in my analysis of the quotation in chapter 7, "Hybride Formen der Rede," of Bernhard Waldenfels, *Vielstimmigkeit der Rede: Studien zur Phänomenologie des Fremden*, vol. 4 (Frankfurt am Main: Suhrkamp, 1999).

10. See, for example, Jorge Semprun's novel on Buchenwald, *Quel beau dimanche* (Paris: Grasset et Fasquelle, 1980).

11. The French expression *entre chien et loup* means "in the twilight." See the preface to my book *Ordnung in Zwielicht* (Frankfurt am Main: Suhrkamp, 1987); *Order in Twilight*, trans. D. J. Parent (Athens: Ohio University Press, 1996).

12. Compare the Greek expressions *logon didonai* and *logon lambanein*, i.e., the giving and taking of the logos.

13. In German we say *Sich den Anderen vom Leibe halten*.

14. Compare the German expression *die eigene Haut zur Markte tragen*, and see J. O'Neill, *Sociology as a Skin Trade* (London: Heinemann, 1972).

15. See Edmund Husserl, *Zur Phänomenologie der Intersubjektivität. Dritter Teil: 1929-1935* (Husserliana 15) (The Hague: Martinus Nijhoff, 1973), 462. There is something like an *"antwortendes Hinsehen und Hinhören,"* responding to the call (*Anruf*) of the Other.

16. Emmanuel Levinas, *Totalité et infini* (The Hague: Martinus Nijhoff, 1971), 158.

17. Weil turns the Platonic schema of ascent and descent into a paradox when she writes: "S'abaisser, c'est monter à l'égard de la pesenteur morale. La pesenteur morale nous fait tomber vers le haut" (Simone Weil, *La pesanteur et la grâce* [Paris: Plon, 1948], 13).

18. Compare chap. 7, "Das Paradox des Ausdrucks," in *Deutsch-Französische Gedankengänge*.

Bare Humanity

Alphonso Lingis

We live in a world where there are six billion similar beings of our species. Our bodies have been conceived and grown in the bodies of others, and our children grow in our own bodies. We have learned to mobilize our limbs, to shape and release feelings, we have indeed caught on how to focus our eyes and see things from others. We have acquired thoughts and opinions by learning speech, vocabulary, grammar, and rhetoric from others. We pick up thoughts from others, pass them on to others. We recycle in our minds the thoughts and feelings of people dead for centuries. We stand and act in different places in the world, but we can exchange places and equipment with one another. Looking at one another, we put ourselves in another's place and envision things as others see them. We sign permissions for doctors to salvage, when we die, whatever organs they can to transplant into the bodies of strangers. We are equivalent and interchangeable.

There are always perceptible differences among us. Even our identical twin has a body marked by a sunburn, a scar of which ours is free; his body feels a wrinkle under his belt ours does not feel. Even working on an assembly line, we do not see quite the same perspective on the factory building our coworker sees. We occupy different positions in the spatial layout of the practicable world.

Each of us foresees that he and she will die, as others have died and die. We envision that death as an event in the common world, where our living body is immobilized into a corpse, which will lie there in the midst of perceptible things and be handled by others. But the anxiety that gives me a sense of my own vulnerability and mortality anticipates my being cast into the void, the whole supporting network of the world giving way and disappearing. The whole world will not be annihilated, only my perceptual and practical field.

In envisioning this event, the ending of my whole life in the world, I realize the limited circumference of my perceptual and practical field. By envisioning the blank abyss of death that lies somewhere ahead of me, at some point in the next ten or forty years, I envision the time open to me still offering possibilities for initiatives, before that brink of impossibility. In envisioning what may lie on this side of that brink, I disengage my future from the futures of others. The black shadow of death separates in the world that extends as so many possibilities a layout of possibilities that are yet possible for me, cut out in the outlying field of what is possible for others. My children will harvest the fruit from the orchard I am planting; others will verify the effectiveness of this vaccine against Ebola fever I am culturing. Addressing myself to the possibilities open to me, I find in what has come to pass in my life the resources and momentum to address that future. I acquire a sense of my own lifetime. Others—my parents, my children, my associates, strangers—have different futures ahead of them, each time delimited by their deaths. The fact that the death destined for others is deferred relative to my death, makes us, in our practical equivalence and interchangeability, different. We act in discontinuous fields, dealing with different possibilities.

When we interact, we recognize both our interchangeability and our difference from one another. Strangers at a stalled car in the road turn to us and say: "Hey give us a hand!" A colleague, working out an engineering problem, says: "I've made a wrong calculation somewhere, see if you can locate it." In the theater company, we are enthusiastic, sure that each of us has a role that he and she can play to perfection, but we absolutely have to get Beatrice to play Ophelia. We coordinate our different perceptions and skills in common projects and in institutions. We work together and build a community with what we are in common and what we have in common. We come to the assistance of our collaborators who are injured at their post.

As we work, we take our respective positions, our bodies coordinate the rhythms and force of their movements, signaling to one another. In a complex undertaking where people with different skills and tasks are enlisted, the coordination requires someone to oversee the work; she coordinates the work with verbal and kinesic signs. Her hands and manpower are not engaged with us in the work; she confronts us with her face. Her face, like a blank surface pulled over the pulsations and circulations of her head, over the hungers, thirsts, and pleasures of her body, expresses signs—linear sequences of words that are directives. Her eyes are not only organs to survey the collective work; they judge and sanction, we look to them to see approval or disapproval.

The work, in the course of its edification or operation, reveals material requirements. The one who oversees formulates those requirements into orders. The directive force of her indications, her authority, is that of the collective work in which we are engaged and to which we have committed ourselves.

A neighbor knocks on my door; he has suffered a fall and is bleeding. I see that I can drive him to the hospital. I also realize that I ought to. Facing me, he addresses an appeal to me; his wound, his mortality is a demand put on me. His question, his appeal, binds me, his presence, facing me, has imperative force.

Coming to knock on my door, facing me, he singles me out. In facing me, he intrudes in my fields of concerns, interrupts my activities. Turning to face me, he calls upon my attention. He contests me in the closed sphere of my own tasks and pleasures. Already when, while walking down the street, I look up to answer his greeting, I recognize his rights over me. To decline to answer his greeting requires a justification.

A moment ago, I was entangled in the task before me, or absorbed in the character of a television drama, or I was relaxed and dissolved in an anonymous revelry. Now I must arise, mobilize my resources. I find myself summoned forth, called upon to be *I,* a responsible and responsive agent, before an other. His act of facing me that singles me out singularizes me. In being faced, I discover resources with which to answer the appeal and demand put to me. I discover that I have resources, that I am a resource.

The act of facing is an event in the phenomenal field. It is in his facing me that I find myself confronted with an imperative. The imperative may be formulated in the grammatical and rhetorical forms of language, or in certain kinds of gestures. But the indicative and informative meaning and referents of all he says, in the measure that they are addressed to me, have vocative and imperative force. They call for my attention, and direct and order my understanding. They already direct and order my action. This vocative and imperative force is not an immaterial and ideal meaning connoted by the sensorial signs he makes, his utterances and gestures. It is the force of his approach and the movement with which he faces that give his utterances their vocative and imperative force. I see myself singled out and held in the focus of his eyes; I see the nakedness of those eyes that search and appeal. I see the empty-handedness of his gestures turned to me. I hear his voice addressed to me, the frailty and transitoriness of his voice without causal force that solicits.

This injured one is not a collaborator in a common project to which I am committed. I recognize that he is a neighbor. In moving into this neighborhood, I have committed myself to a social contract: committed myself to participate in the neighborhood utilities services, to conform to zone regulations. Have I not also committed myself to conform to neighborhood practices of civility and reciprocal respect, and reciprocal assistance when needs arise?

To get rid of my television set, I call up the garbage collection office of my neighborhood; I am not appealing to the woman who answers the phone, but to the town ordinances. She tells me to put it out for pickup on Thursday, in conformity with the regulations that schedule refuse pickup. But the one who knocked on my door was not simply showing me a copy of the rules.

The social contract is not a contract made with "the neighborhood." I find myself obligated to respond to this individual who knocked on my door and faces me. My social contract is nothing else than my foreseeing that he and others who live here may face me and put demands on me by facing me—demands that bind me.

If I shut the door on my neighbor who needs a ride to the hospital or even the airport, he may say to the others that I am not a real neighbor, that I am not civilized, that I do not recognize ordinary humanity. It is as a human being, an adult, someone who speaks the language, that I respond to his late-night knock on my door. Being adult, being rational, being a member of humanity, as facts, do not by themselves constitute obligations to every human being or every rational agent. But in recognizing myself to be, and in living, as an independent adult, a person with a mind of his own, a human being, have I not committed myself to a whole set of social contracts? I drive a reliable car others have agreed to manufacture and I to pay for; I make myself an evening meal with food and wine others have agreed to produce according to standards; in speaking I call upon a body of information supplied by schools and workplaces; in pursuing my solitary reveries I plan my pleasures with thoughts articulated in English. Is it then the commitment I made to the working economy, the community of those who treat one another as adults, the animal species that communicates with intelligible and informed language, the neighborhood, that binds me in the appeal the neighbor has made? Shall we say that it is the social order, order itself, rational order, that I committed myself to that I now recognize to bind me?

It is one thing to recognize the force of my own commitment. It is another to acknowledge the imperative force of that to which I am committed. To recognize myself bound only by laws that I myself legislate for myself is simply to commit myself to a program. This commitment involves an acknowledgment of the logical and physical laws that will have to be conformed to if I am to carry out my program. But my program itself binds me only in the sense that I have not revoked it.

One will object, with Immanuel Kant, that rationality, the imperative for the universal and the necessary, is not a simple project I set before myself. As soon as thought arises, it recognizes that it must conceive things consistently and relate them coherently. It finds it must commit itself to this program because it finds itself from the first subject to this imperative. This imperative is a fact, which thought recognizes in an intellectual sense of respect. But is not my decision to think, to act thoughtfully, a resolution that rests on my own freely revocable will?

The one who says that in turning him away I do not recognize ordinary humanity is saying that humanity is imperative, makes claims on me. But I do not make a social contract with *humanity*. Is my membership in humanity anything else than the succession of my responses to individuals who face me, putting demands on me? Is it not then that recognizing ordinary humanity is acknowledging that anyone who knocks on my door and faces me puts demands on me?

Being faced is encountering someone who is not simply similar to me but in another place—occupying a different point of view, acting in a different practical field, in which the time marked by his oncoming death encloses him. It is encountering someone who appeals to me and puts demands on me which bind me. In his appeal, his demand, he stands apart, other. He is other with the otherness of an imperative. An imperative is a force that binds me that does not have its source in my own initiative.

The experience of being faced loses nothing of its nature when it occurs out of context. It was not a neighbor who knocked, but an injured stranger who speaks no English. It was a lost child. It was someone mentally retarded, in whose bag we found the airplane ticket. In the ruins of the neighborhood, devastated by an earthquake, in the charred outskirts of Hiroshima fuming in radioactive cinders, it was a stranger whose face is charred and from whose throat no voice issues, who turns to me and reaches out to me across the years and the oceans.

On the face of the one who faces us in the midst of a collective work, whose part in the work is to oversee it and direct it, the whole context of the collective work is exhibited. All the lines of force of the work meet in his eyes. He turns to us a face invested with authority. But the one who turns to greet me outside the field of a common work turns to me the nudity of his face. For him to face me is to exhibit want and need that require me. His face is abstract and absolute, Emmanuel Levinas says, disconnected from the supporting relations with things. To turn to face me is to extract himself from the substance of the world, to denude himself. He faces me in poverty and destitution.

In facing me, he not only shows himself to be different from me—in the midst of a different situation, envisioning a different future from the momentum of a different past—but other than me and other than the substantial space and time of the phenomenal world. In his want and need he is other. I do not see his visible and tangible face as the side and contour of his physiological substance, nor do I see it as a sign designating something conceptually grasped: his functional identity. I see it as the visible and tangible mark of a lack, a need. For him to face me is to present me, in that phenomenal *trace* which is his visible and tangible face, with a lack, a need, an absence.

By identifying the otherness, and thus the force of contestation, in the poverty and destitution of the other, the nakedness of his face, Levinas disengages an ethical imperative from cultural and ethnic imperatives, from community imperatives. My judge is any stranger. Each one in the nakedness of his face contests me and puts demands on me. The more divested and destitute, the more the ethical imperative imposes imperiously with all its own force. But is this force the force of that poverty and destitution?

The recognition of needs and wants, of poverty and destitution, is not simply the recognition of negativities. The presentation of a void, a nothingness of itself can simply motivate our avoiding it, or retreating and recoiling from it. The observation of emptinesses and weaknesses is the recognition of possibilities for us to apply our substance and insert our force. The recognition of needs and wants is the perception of beings which are in the course of evolution or achievement.

It is not only their needs, but what has been achieved in them that appeal to us and put demands on us. When they greet us and call for our attention, our attention is turned to the force of life in them, which has grown and striven—the force of an individual life. This attention is acknowledgment and concern. We see a life that enjoys living, that finds goodness in living. We find ourselves called upon to let this life be, to respect its space, to let it flourish, to care about it and care for it. We see facing us someone in whom nature has achieved something: we see hale and hearty physical heath and vigor, vibrant sensibility, beauty. We also see someone who has done something with her life, protected and nourished, built, repaired, restored, rescued. We see someone who has cared for a sick relative, maintained a farm, been a devoted teacher, is a loyal friend. We see someone who has not achieved anything materially, but who knows that he or she is a good person, steadfast, open-minded, with a good head and a good heart, has dared to break the rules and make mistakes, has a sense of his or her worth. We see facing us someone who has suffered the worst oppressions of the social system and the worst destructions of disease or nature and who has been able to endure suffering and awaits death with lucidity and courage. We see someone who has the vitality to laugh over absurdities and his own failures, has the strength to weep over the loss of a lover and over the death of a child in another land. It is then not simply need and want that imperatively contest us when someone turns to us. Is it not the particular and intrinsic goodness of the life that approaches us that gives force to his contestation of our personal concerns?

For Levinas, someone who faces me shows me what I have to say and do, because to face me is to appeal to me, to expose wants and needs, to expose the spasms, wrinkles, scars, wounds, of his or her skin. When I turn to someone who faces me, I am immediately afflicted with these wounds, these wants, this suffering. For Levinas the fundamental imperative, the sole imperative, is to respond to the needs and wants and suffering of someone of my species with all the resources of the environment.

Yet the suffering I see may well be a suffering that does not seek to be consoled. Nietzsche warned against imagining that we should alleviate a suffering which another needs and clings to as his or her destiny—the inner torments of Beethoven, the hardships and heartaches of the youth who has gone to join the guerrillas in the mountains, the grief of someone who has to grieve the loss of her child. To be afflicted with his or her suffering requires that we care about the things he or she cares for.

Another's words of greeting open a silence for our words but also for our reticence and our tact before the importance, urgency, and immediacy of the demands of things. The suffering of the one who faces me, a suffering visible in the bloodless white of her anguished face, may well be not the suffering of her own hunger and thirst, but a suffering for the animals in her care dying of the drought or the peregrines in the poisoned skies, a distress over the crumbling temple and for the nests of seabirds broken by the tidal wave, a grieving for the glaciers melting under skies whose carbon dioxide layers are trapping the heat of the sun.

Do we not see, in the hand of another who reaches out to us for support, an appeal of a fellow earthling to answer the summons of the earth? When another greets us, with a voice that trembles with the dance of springtime or threnody of winter, his or her voice invites us to hear the murmur of nature that resounds in it. When someone turns his eyes to us, he does not only look in our eyes for the map of the environment; his eyes seek out first the vivacity and delight of the light in them that summons him forth. Does not the gaze of another, which touches us lightly and turns aside, and invokes not the glare of our gaze but the darkness our eyes harbor, refract to us the summons of the impersonal night?

Is it only his suffering that appeals urgently to us, has importance, and afflicts us immediately? Is there not always joy in the one who faces us, even joy in his suffering—the joy of finding us? Joy is an upsurge that affirms itself unrestrictedly, and affirms the importance and truth of the face of the landscape illuminated by joy. The one who faces us in joy does not only radiate his joy, which we find immediately on ourselves; it requires a response. The thumbs-up that the Brazilian street kid—his mouth too voraciously gobbling our leftover spaghetti to smile or say *obrigado*—gives is a gift given us that we must cherish in the return of our smile, a gift that we have no right to refuse. But the joy of the street kid is not only a contentment in the satisfaction of his hunger; it is a joy of being in the streets, in the sun, in the urban jungle so full of excitements, and it is in his laughter pealing over the excitements of the urban jungle and the glory of the sun reigning over the beaches of Rio that gives rise to his hunger and his relishing the goodness of restaurant spaghetti.

Yet does not the immediacy of a face that faces us in all its nakedness, divested of any pragmatic or cultural context, isolate the imperative experience in all its distinctive force? A lost child comes up to us. Someone mentally retarded faces us. A leper, outside the restaurant in a country where we came for a vacation, reaches out to us. In the nightly broadcasts from the refugee camps in Albania and Rwanda, images of people driven from their farms, their homes burnt, robbed of their jewelry and clothing, stripped of their identity papers, their birth certificates and marriage licenses, the force of the ethical imperative stood forth, a powerful and undeniable reality in the world. It was from the extremity of destitution and helplessness that the searing appeal and demand and accusation gripped us. Before their eyes facing us, our secured appropriation of the resources of the planet appears as a usurpation and expropriation.

In the ruins of senseless war, we see the most advanced scientific and technological reason turning into the destruction of the constructions of reason and of the validities established by reason. We see societies and industries integrated and mobilized for their mutual destruction. We see the dialectical advances of history feeding the incineration of history. In the extremities of poverty and destitution, we see the breakdown of social contracts, the disintegration of the economic and social edifice, the current of historical force spilling over and sinking into festering swamps.

In an infant we see need and dependency, but we also see birth. But birth shows us just as much the nondialectical, nonprogressive time of nature and of history. It is birth that requires death. Birth too is discontinuity, unreason, violence. Birth marks the interruption of the continuities of material and physiological causality. Every birth is a disconnection of the vectors of the past, a consignment of the momentum of the past to nothingness.

Birth is disconnection. This life to be sure did not arise by spontaneous generation; it is the life given to the child by the parents, it is the very life of the parents but disconnected, alienated from them. In the course of our life, what we have passed through remains with us, is our past; it clings to us. All our past states of consciousness are hooked to one another and cling to the present consciousness; to recall something is to reactivate one of those states of consciousness which never lets go of us. All our mistakes, failings, compromises, betrayals, mark us and remain on us like a habitus. Our initiatives have passed but remain inertly with us. We cannot shift about in the present, orient ourselves out of it toward new spaces, without carrying with us the weight and inertia of our past.

Our life can free itself from the weight and inertia of its own initiatives and achievements only by giving birth. Our child, Levinas says, lives with our life, but in our child our life is new and alienated from our life. His birth, the innocence and newness of existence in him, is of itself irresponsibility and revolt against the past. A child is, without being on his own. He leaves the burden of carrying on the projects initiated in the past and the task of securing resources for the future to his parents. He plays out his existence.

Birth is also commencement. There is a break, a cut, in the continuity of time; the past is disconnected, and in this hiatus a new life upsurges with a force that begins with it. Is it not this leap of force that commences in birth that appeals to us and commands us in the nakedness of the child that faces us? Is it not commencement itself, newness of birth without a context, that puts an imperative on us?

Walking in the roads of South Africa, how overwhelmed we are by all the crimes committed in this land, by these people, crimes that cling to the hearts of these people. How impossible it seems that a new, rainbow nation could be created out of such a history! Yet to see the children is to see that possibility. The children are born without these crimes, this past. Each child is a new beginning, a cut in the continuity of time, a presence without a past, a commencement.

Each time someone turns to face us, there is something of a birth he realizes. We had observed him, situated him in the social and practical field, watched how he oriented himself, toward what implements and what goals he moved; we had interpreted and synthesized. Now he turns to face us. His turning to face us interrupts the continuity of our interpretations, predictions, and judgments of him. His move tears through the picture we had composed of him. His turning to face us is not simply his entry into our world; it is his birth into our world. He speaks by banishing the picture we had composed of him. We may well see the person who has now a good character, a good head and a good heart, but because the whole past of that person is inaccessible to us, we see in that person someone who was born and is being born now in the theater of our life.

The camera shows us the landscape of burnt villages and barns reduced to ashes. Then it shows us a child. We see a vivacity of life in the eyes that look out to us, that is innocent, without a past, a new beginning. There is the same kind of childlikeness in the face of the old woman the camera shows us. Destitute now, her past is gone from her, as from us who have never had any access to it. We see her on TV, we feel the impulse to drop everything and rush over there and make her a hot meal. Not set out to recover her past; her life would be reborn. Her life is already being born in us. We would open our eyes in the morning on an Albanian or Eritrean landscape with her, like a newborn child.

Thus the exceptional force of someone who enters our life from nowhere. This backpacker met in the dust one afternoon in the Sahel; he is an adult, but he is newborn in our life. And something of him is born in us. Our own adulthood, with all its history, its experiences and skills, its initiatives and burdens, falls away; we feel a backpacker got born in us. We join him in the innocence of his birth.

But do not other animals, plants, landscapes, rivers, and clouds, in what is achieved in them, and in their birth (*nature* etymologically is what is born)—in their bare materiality—appeal to us and put demands on us, address their imperatives to us?

On a side street in downtown São Paulo, there is a woman of about thirty, not unattractive, seated on some flattened cardboard boxes against a doorway. She has a baby, a large doll. You see her when you go out of your hotel, she is there when you go out in the morning, in the evening, when you come back in the night. She never looks at you or holds open a hand to you. A few times you have seen her wash in the fountain in the adjacent square. You have noticed the waiter from a cafeteria at the corner bring her a plate of food after mealtimes. She does not cling to the doll, rock it and coo over it, like a little girl does; often it is left to her side as she contemplates the passing scene. Like a real baby, it often seems to tire her, or bore her. It is always warm in São Paulo; a fixed awning overhead shelters her from the rain. She has a pile of extra clothes. She sees you, occasionally your looks cross. She seems to have all she needs. She never begs. She is not a little girl. There is nothing she needs that she does not have. There is nothing she wants. Except someone, something to love. Haggard, unrelenting, aching, craving to love.

You eat, sometimes, in the adjacent cafeteria. The waiter is young, vigorous, his face has a certain charm. He is certainly ill paid. In another country he would be a student, or apprenticed to a trade. He certainly does not live around here; he must take a long bus ride here each morning from the far-flung favelas that extend the city. After the meal hour, he takes her a plate of food, handing it to her, not looking at her, not speaking to her. He understands it is not the craving to be loved that is in her.

She must have learned as an infant. She must have learned, playing with a stray puppy, that her frail body is full of pleasures to give. Holding that puppy but not too tight, her baby hand learned tenderness. She must have learned that her hands are organs to give pleasure. She must have learned, in contact with the puppy mouthing and licking her legs and fingers and face, that her lips are organs that give, give the pleasures of being kissed. Ordered to watch a baby sister while her mother went off to labor all day, she must have learned that her hands, her thighs, her belly are organs that give pleasure. In a slum childhood, abandoned to the streets, she learned how little she needed or wanted. Picked up, fucked, left by a fifteen-year-old, and by how many men since, she learned how little she needed or wanted. How much all that tenderness, all that pleasure she learned she has to give aches in her now!

One day she was gone. You blamed the police. This is the center of the city; was there some business conference for foreign investors in town, so that the police were ordered to clean up the streets, chase away the riffraff? Was there some national commemoration to be made—some historical event to be celebrated, some statue to be unveiled?

But a few days later, you saw her again. Seated at the same doorway. With the same doll.

One day you left São Paulo. You saw her as you left the hotel with your bags. She is still there. You still see her. She, who did not need you or want you, got born in you. You who had no need of or desire for her, found her to care about and care for. You who after all have so much tenderness and tact, kisses and caresses, to squander.

The Other Side of Intentionality

Leslie MacAvoy

In critiquing Western philosophy, Levinas engages himself largely with the phenomenological tradition which construes subjectivity in terms of intentionality. Against the background of this critique, Levinas offers an alternative account of subjectivity as sensibility, which receives its most explicit formulation in *Otherwise Than Being* but is thematic in a number of shorter pieces leading up to this work.[1] Although Levinas is critical of phenomenology, his work remains strikingly phenomenological, and his debt to Husserl is substantial. Indeed, I suspect that Levinas's work represents more of a radicalization of phenomenology than a destruction of it. Accordingly, I would expect the idea he puts forward of subjectivity as sensibility to be linked to the idea of subjectivity as intentionality. In this paper I will trace this linkage, first, by investigating the emergence of the notion of sensibility out of Husserl's notion of sensation; and, second, by exploring how Levinas attempts to effect a reversal of intentional subjectivity in the notion of proximity.

Levinas strives to differentiate intentionality from the relation with the other with which he is concerned. The discussions of proximity in *Otherwise Than Being* and of desire in *Totality and Infinity*[2] are motivated by the contrast with intentionality.[3] Moreover, Levinas distinguishes the intentional object, which signifies as a phenomenon, from the face, which signifies as a trace or enigma. A phenomenon acts as a sign which makes the essence of the object present to consciousness, thereby allowing the subject to glide over the object in its singularity toward its universal meaning. The Other as enigma signifies in a way which does not make present or does not make anything transparent. The Other presents itself as absent or withdrawn; it is beyond the grasp of consciousness.[4]

This "beyond" is something which Levinas maintains cannot be thought within the domain of intentionality. Intentionality entails a relation in which the subject is oriented toward the object or phenomenon, the essence or being of which is disclosed to varying degrees to the subject. Through the application of techniques of phenomenological reduction, the essence of the object can be more fully disclosed and grasped by the subject. This essence is the meaning of the object and is always graspable in principle, if not in fact. According to accounts of subjectivity based on intentionality, the meaning of the phenomenon is equated with its being or essence, and furthermore, the being of a phenomenon lies in its presentation to consciousness. This implies that there is effectively no meaning which *in principle* outstrips consciousness; nothing lies beyond consciousness. From Levinas's perspective this is problematic, for it indicates that there is no beyond, there is no infinite, there is no alterity.

But rather than abandoning the phenomenological perspective altogether, Levinas searches for evidence that this intentional subjectivity is actually founded on something else which itself cannot be comprehended by consciousness and incorporated into ontology. Levinas finds what he is looking for in Husserl's notion of sensation.[5] As Levinas reads Husserl, the sensible content which is given in an act of intuition is necessary for being to be present and for an intention to be fulfilled. This sensible content is founded on the stream of lived experience, *Erlebnisse,* which is not thought, but simply provides the background for what is thought.[6] The implication, then, is that the sensuality of lived experience lies behind intentional acts of consciousness and contributes necessarily to their meaning. This stream of lived experience is effectuated through a non-thematizing consciousness characterized by the intentionality of retention and protention. Through retention and protention, consciousness makes sensations, which are already past or which have not yet occurred, present to it such that experience is made coherent and continuous rather than fragmented into single moments of sensuous impression. Thus, temporal consciousness and consciousness of sensation are intimately linked.[7] The upshot is that there is always a temporal gap between a sensation and the consciousness of that sensation such that consciousness is always recalling what has already passed in the stream of lived experience. Husserl realizes that none of this would be possible were the subject not corporeally situated and participating in a world. As Levinas puts it: "the subject faces the object and is *in complicity with it;* the corporeity of consciousness is in exact proportion to this participation of consciousness in the world it constitutes, but this corporeity is *produced* in sensation" ("IS" 145). These sensations are kinesthetic and characterize the subject as incarnated in the world, and this incarnation is necessary for Husserl's account of intentionality.[8]

While the role that Husserl gives to sensation is promising, Levinas thinks that he has missed an opportunity to make a more definitive break from traditional accounts of subjectivity. Husserl continues to maintain that all sensuous impressions can be grasped in principle by consciousness and incorporated into conscious experience, and he insists upon this view despite the fact that on his own account sensibility would have to precede consciousness because of the incarnate nature of the lived subject.

Levinas pursues this line of argument against Husserl in his discussion of the *Urimpression* in *Otherwise Than Being*.[9] Since Husserl maintains that consciousness is always consciousness of something and that this something must always have its source in sensuous life, it follows that at some point content enters consciousness via the *Urimpression,* which is the originary moment of sensation—an overlapping of the sensing and the sensed. Consciousness depends, first, upon the differentiation or displacement of sensing and the sensed and, second, on the retention of the sensed and its re-presentation to consciousness. It follows, then, that at the moment of the *Urimpression,* there is no consciousness of the *Urimpression;* there is only sensation.[10] Consciousness of the sensation follows through the retention of the sensed. According to Husserl it is possible for consciousness to recuperate the *Urimpression* through the mechanisms of protention and retention. Levinas disagrees. To be able to retain the *Urimpression,* there would have to be consciousness of it, but there is no such consciousness. Husserl, he argues, is wrong here: not everything can be incorporated back into conscious experience.

This point is important for Levinas. It points to an aspect of corporeity—namely sensibility—which lies at the origin of consciousness and time, and which cannot be recollected through cognition. This sensibility lies at the foundation of intentional subjectivity, yet is itself not intentional and cannot be taken up and comprehended through intentionality. As he puts it, this origin belongs to a past which is "older" than consciousness itself and cannot be recovered because it effectively belongs to a different time.

Levinas reaches this notion of sensibility by traversing Husserl's thought. He does not abandon it, but sees in it glimmers of something suggested beyond it. In *Otherwise Than Being* Levinas writes that:

> The intentionality involved in disclosure, and the symbolization of a totality which the openness of being aimed at by intentionality involved, would not constitute the sole or even the dominant signification of the sensible. The dominant meaning of sensibility should indeed enable us to account for its secondary signification as a sensation, the element of a

cognition. We have already said that the fact that sensibility can become "sensible intuition" and enter the adventure of cognition is not a contingency. The dominant signification of sensibility is already caught sight of in vulnerability, and it will be shown in the responsibility characteristic of proximity. (*OB* 64–65)

Levinas claims here that the condition for the possibility of a phenomenon like sensible intuition is sensibility. This sensibility is intimated in sensible intuition even if that phenomenal manifestation is not the "dominant signification of sensibility." The strategy indicated in the passage is quite phenomenological; Levinas wants to say something about the conditions for the possibility of certain phenomena, and he suggests that these conditions are intimated in these phenomena, even if they cannot themselves be reduced to phenomena or do not signify as phenomena. He uses strategies developed within phenomenology to search for essences in order to gesture at something yet more originary than essence, namely sensibility, which lies just on the other side of intentionality.

Levinas maintains that the sense of sensibility is proximity (*OB* 19). The term "sense" is suggestive. It preserves an ambiguity between the *meaning* of sensibility, which suggests that proximity is an interpretation of sensibility, and the *direction* or *orientation* of sensibility, which suggests that sensibility orients one toward the other in the manner of approach.[11] These notions of meaning and direction or orientation are usually associated with intentionality in classical phenomenology. The reference to proximity as the sense of sensibility suggests that although proximity is nonintentional, it remains implicated in intentionality. This suspicion is further supported when Levinas claims that proximity is to be described as an *inversion* of intentionality, and that this will be due to a passivity associated with exposure to the Other and the responsibility which issues from it (*OB* 47).[12] Continuing in this vein, Levinas writes in "Language and Proximity"[13] that the ethical "indicates a reversal of the subjectivity which is *open upon* beings and always in some measure represents them to itself, . . . into a subjectivity that enters *into contact* with a singularity, excluding identification in the ideal, excluding thematization and representation" ("LP" 116). This passage suggests that the inversion of intentionality is effected through this reversal of intentional subjectivity and results in ethical subjectivity.[14] What particularly interests me is this reversal. What does it mean to reverse this subjectivity, and in what sense is the subjectivity of sensibility and proximity such a reversal?[15]

The word "reversal" in this passage has been used to translate *retournement,* which can mean an abrupt change in attitude or opinion, an about-face. It can also mean a complete or sudden transformation of a situation, in the sense of a situation's having been reversed or the tables having been turned. Both senses imply a turning around. One does not hear this sense of turning as much in another word for "reversal" which Levinas might have used, but did not: *renversement*. *Renversement* suggests a switch in order, a turning things backward or upside-down. If we thought of the reversal of intentional subjectivity as a switching of the poles of the intentional relation, this would, I think, capture the sense of *renversement*. Indeed, it is tempting to think of the reversal in these terms. In the intentional account of subjectivity, the subject is sovereign and wields power over the Other. Its responsibility is rooted in its freedom. In Levinas's account, the subject is subjected to the Other, who seems to wield power over it insofar as it can make ethical demands of the subject and hold it accountable. Based on this comparison, one might claim that in the second account the subject finds itself at the object pole of the relation, as the object of another's intention, and one might think that this is what it means to reverse intentionality. However, while the poles of the relation are switched, the relation itself does not appear to be altered, and Levinas's reversal implies such an alteration. The use of *retournement* instead of *renversement* is suggestive. Why is the sense of turning or turning back emphasized?

I suggest that this turning should be understood to mean that the intention itself is turned back from the object at which it aims. The intention does not reach its object because that object passively resists it; it resists comprehension by consciousness because it signifies in the manner of an enigma, not in the manner of a phenomenon. In discussing the encounter with the face in "Meaning and Sense,"[16] Levinas writes that "a face confounds the intentionality that aims at it" ("MS" 54) and that "the wonder of the infinite in the finite of thought is an overwhelming of intentionality" ("MS" 55). These passages refer to the fact that the face defies the universal form through which intentionality would comprehend it, but they point out that this defiance of the form occurs through the defiance of the intention. The intention is turned away, and in this confounding the face signifies as enigma. The implication is that the intentional movement is initiated and then thwarted or frustrated because it fails to find completion in its object.[17]

The impenetrability of the Other not only deflects the intention, but throws consciousness into question. In "Meaning and Sense," Levinas stresses that "being called into question is not the same as becoming aware of this being called into question" ("MS" 54). In other words, the self is not called into question by the Other in such a way that it is *conscious of* this calling into question. To be conscious of being called into question implies that consciousness is no longer called into question. The calling of consciousness into question is a radical challenge to the sovereignty of the subject whose very sovereignty is rooted in consciousness. The resistance of the intention by its would-be object challenges the sovereignty of the subject and thereby calls consciousness itself into question. In a sense, the resistance of the object implies that consciousness loses its object. If consciousness is consciousness of . . . , then it should be arrested and brought to a halt when it no longer has anything of which to be conscious. It should collapse on itself or be thrown back on itself, although we can use this term "itself" only provisionally here.

When consciousness is called into question, it is submitted to critique, and critique pertains to the ethical. Pursuant to this idea, Levinas writes in "Language and Proximity" that "the orientation of the subject upon the object has become a proximity, the intentional has become ethical" ("LP" 116). A few lines later he states that the intentional mutates into the ethical, and this occurs at the point "at which the approach breaks through consciousness" (ibid.).[18] It would seem, then, that the turning back of intentionality through which consciousness is called into question is the point at which intentionality is transformed into the ethical.[19] By "ethical" Levinas means "a relationship between terms such as are united neither by a synthesis of the understanding nor by a relationship between subject or object, and yet where the one weighs or concerns or is meaningful to the other, where they are bound by a plot which knowing can neither exhaust nor unravel" ("LP" 116n6). The way to the ethical is through intentionality; the ethical is not so much a surpassing or overcoming of intentionality as a mutation and alteration of it.

The subjectivity that enters into contact with a singularity is the subjectivity of sensibility and proximity—a nonintentional subjectivity. This subjectivity is reached through a reversal of the subjectivity which represents beings to itself. The intentional orientation on beings through which representation occurs prevents the immediacy that would be required for this contact, and this obstacle is overcome by the turning away or deflection of the subject's intention. This deflection ruptures consciousness and clears the space for the proximity, contact, and approach with which Levinas is concerned.

This rupture of consciousness effects a transformation in the subjectivity of the subject because of the way in which it throws it into question. While intentional subjectivity produces the self as ego, which expresses itself in the nominative as "I," the self effected in proximity originates in a "me"—the self in the accusative case ("LP" 123). This is usually taken to mean that the self is formed through its responsibility to the Other, which precedes any action on its part. This responsibility is said to be anterior even to the very possibility of an act of will, which is why the subject is born only subsequent to the existence of this responsibility, and why it must exist in the accusative before it exists in the nominative. We should also consider, however, that this movement from the Other toward the self in which the self is accused is also partly the recoil of the thwarted intention, which has been turned away from the Other and is returning. But this return will never actually be fulfilled, because a return requires the possibility of going back to the point of departure which has, in the meantime, remained the same. This possibility is precluded by the interruption of consciousness through the turning away of the intention. In this boomerang movement, the self on the receiving end is not the same as the self at the beginning. This is why the turning which we hear in *re-tournement* cannot be heard as a *retour,* or return in the straightforward sense. The origin of the intentional movement is the intentional subject, but this subject is altered in the mutation of the intention into proximity.[20]

In some respects, it seems appropriate to speak of the overcoming of intentionality in the ethical as a destruction of intentionality. After all, the intentional object or phenomenon has been replaced with the enigma, the intention has been diverted, and consciousness has collapsed on itself. But I do not think that the destruction of intentionality is Levinas's goal. Levinas devotes considerable time to explaining the development of the interiority of the conscious subject who is concerned with its being. We cannot dispense with this subject, nor is it Levinas's intention to suggest this. Ethical responsibility as Levinas construes it must involve sacrifice if it is to have any significance. Sacrifice means taking from oneself and giving to another, and this kind of action will only be a sacrifice if the self in question cares for its being and goes without in order to care for the being of another. The significance of exteriority and its ethical hold on us would be completely effaced if interiority were eliminated. Levinas's point is simply that interiority cannot be the whole story about subjectivity; if it were, ethics would never really be ethical because it would always be rooted ultimately in self-interest.

In conclusion, I suggest that Levinas's work attempts to intimate what lies just on the other side of phenomenology and the subjectivity of intentionality. But according to Levinas we must traverse these domains, exploring their furthest limits in order to approach, though not comprehend, what lies just beyond those limits. We have seen that this strategy runs through Levinas's reading of Husserl on sensation and points him toward the notion of sensibility. We have also seen at another level that a subject's intention can carry it toward a limit where that intention breaks down and effects a transformation in which the alterity of the Other is sensed in an approach.

116

Notes

1. Emmanuel Levinas, *Autrement qu'être, ou au-delà de l'essence* (The Hague: Martinus Nijhoff, 1978); *Otherwise Than Being, or Beyond Essence*, trans. Alphonso Lingis (The Hague: Martinus Nijhoff, 1981). Hereafter cited in the text as *OB*. Page references to all works cited in these notes refer to the English editions cited.

2. Emmanuel Levinas, *Totalité et infini* (The Hague: Martinus Nijhoff, 1971); *Totality and Infinity*, trans. Alphonso Lingis (Pittsburgh: Duquesne University Press, 1969). Hereafter cited in the text as *TI*.

3. Passages to this effect abound in *Totality and Infinity* and *Otherwise Than Being*. Craig Vasey suggests that Levinas rejects the notion of intentionality only in *Otherwise Than Being* and not in *Totality and Infinity*, citing Levinas's discussion of the intentionality of enjoyment in that text. See Craig Vasey, "Emmanuel Levinas: From Intentionality to Proximity," *Philosophy Today* 25 (Fall 1981): 178–95. While it is true that Levinas does distinguish between the intentionality of representation and that of enjoyment in *Totality and Infinity*, he further distinguishes between enjoyment and metaphysical desire. Insofar as enjoyment involves the contentment and satisfaction of the ego, it resembles the "filling of a lack" which is characteristic of need. Desire involves an infinite movement toward the other which is missing in enjoyment. In *Totality and Infinity* desire plays the other to intentionality that proximity seems to play in *Otherwise Than Being*.

4. See, for example, Emmanuel Levinas, "Enigme et phénomène," in *En découvrant l'existence chez Husserl et Heidegger* (Paris: J. Vrin, 1982), 203–16; "Enigma and Phenomenon," in *Emmanuel Levinas: Basic Philosophical Writings*, ed. Adriaan T. Peperzak, Simon Critchley, and Robert Bernasconi (Bloomington: Indiana University Press, 1996), 65–77.

5. See Edmund Husserl, *The Phenomenology of Internal Time-Consciousness*, ed. Martin Heidegger, trans. James S. Churchill (Bloomington: Indiana University Press, 1964), esp. 50–71. For Levinas's interpretation, see especially Emmanuel Levinas, "Intentionalité et sensation," in *En découvrant l'existence*, 145–62; "Intentionality and Sensation," in Emmanuel Levinas, *Discovering Existence with Husserl*, trans. and ed. Richard Cohen and Michael Smith (Evanston: Northwestern University Press, 1998), 135–50. See also Levinas, *Otherwise Than Being*, esp. 31–34 and 61–64. "Intentionality and Sensation" hereafter cited in the text as "IS."

6. "Even though the novelty of the notion of an intuitive act seemed to result from its intention or its 'claim' to present being 'in the original' (from its *Meinung*), it now turns out that a sensible content is necessary in order for such a meaning to be thought. The presence of the object is not thought as such; it results from the materiality of sensations, from the nonthought that is lived" (Levinas, "Intentionality and Sensation," 139). And, "intention transcends life in order to intend an object, but the object is only represented owing to a lived content that is *similar* to the object" (140).

7. "But each intention—which starting out from each instant retains or anticipates (protains) the identity of the sensation already in part elapsed and in part

still to come—is for Husserl just the very consciousness of time. Time . . . is the sensing of sensation, which is not a simple coincidence of sensing with the sensed, but an intentionality and consequently a minimal distance between the sensing and the sensed—precisely a temporal distance" (Levinas, "Intentionality and Sensation," 142).

8. See also Emmanuel Levinas, "Intentionality and Metaphysics," in *Discovering Existence*, 125–27; "Intentionalité et métaphysique," in *En découvrant l'existence*, 137–44.

9. Levinas, *Otherwise Than Being*, 31–34; on Levinas's reading (minus the critique) of *Urimpression* in Husserl, see also "Intentionality and Sensation," 140–43.

10. Must we use a temporal image here? In a sense this is consistent with Levinas's view that he is describing a sensation which is anterior to time, which is itself a temporal expression for extra-temporality.

11. As opposed to preserving the distance implied by intentionality.

12. "An analysis that starts with proximity, irreducible to consciousness of . . . , and describable, if possible, as an inversion of intentionality, will recognize this responsibility to be a substitution" (Levinas, *Otherwise Than Being*, 47). "The act of saying will turn out to have been introduced here from the start as the supreme passivity of exposure to another, which is responsibility for the free initiatives of the other. Whence there is an 'inversion' of intentionality which, for its part, always preserves before deeds accomplished enough 'presence of mind' to assume them" (47). In the second passage, I attribute the use of scare quotes to indicate the eventuality in which it may not truly be possible to describe proximity as an inversion of intentionality. In any case, it is clear that it is an inversion which Levinas is striving toward, even if he thinks he may fall somewhat short of it.

13. Emmanuel Levinas, "Langage et proximité," in *En découvrant l'existence*, 217–36; "Language and Proximity," in *Collected Philosophical Papers*, trans. Alphonso Lingis et al. (The Hague: Martinus Nijhoff, 1987), 109–26. Hereafter cited in the text as "LP."

14. This ethical subjectivity will ultimately be characterized in *Otherwise Than Being* as substitution.

15. The idea that Levinas is pursuing a reversal of intentionality is also noted by Jeffrey Powell. However, Powell is primarily concerned with whether Levinas represents Husserl fairly and whether there are not indeed adequate resources in Husserl to accomplish Levinas's goals. He does not discuss in any detail what is meant by this reversal. See Jeffrey Powell, "Levinas Representing Husserl on Representation: An Ethics beyond Representation," *Philosophy Today* 39, no. 2 (Summer 1995): 185–97.

16. Emmanuel Levinas, "Meaning and Sense," in *Basic Philosophical Writings*, 33–64. Hereafter cited in the text as "MS."

17. What I am trying to stress here is that it is never a question of an intentional relation not being initiated, but always of its being overwhelmed. To the extent, however, that average comportment is intentional, it is never really a question of initiating this movement; the movement is always already underway.

18. See Levinas, *Totality and Infinity*, 82–90.

19. On this, see also Levinas, "Language and Proximity," 124–25.

20. Similarly, one might say that the transformation of intentionality transports it back to the sensibility which it is primordially and that in this sense the self returns to itself. But there is an ambiguity here, for Levinas does not really suggest that one returns to sensibility so much as one moves on to proximity. Although this is understood to be grounded in something which is anterior, it is not an anteriority which is continuous with the time of the subject and so is not a time to which one can return.

Face and Revelation: Levinas on Teaching as Way-Faring

Anthony J. Steinbock

> Discourse is discourse with God and not with equals, according
> to the distinction established by Plato in the *Phaedrus*.
> Metaphysics is the essence of this language with God; it leads
> above being.
> —Levinas, *Totalité et infini*

"This most banal incident of human history corresponds to an exceptional possibility—since it claims the total negation of a being" (*TeI* 173,
TI 198–99). This most banal incident of human history—murder—is the
experiential point of departure for Levinas's philosophical reflections. Or
so it seems. For *reflection* on murder, murder incarnate in the Jewish Holocaust, but also in other genocides and acts of hatred directed toward even
one single being, immediately shows up a contradiction: the negation of
person presupposes something even deeper than murder that would
found it as a point of departure. More original than the originality of murder, pre-original, as it were, is Discourse from God. This language with the
Infinite does not start from me, but goes out from God *to me* before I could
instigate a conversation, before I could hear it, want it, or believe in it.
This discourse directed uniquely to me is not only my pre-original Desire
for the Infinite, but also my moral responsibility for the absolute human
presence of the Other *as* welcoming this Other in acts of hospitality and
generosity.

   Violence is an exceptional possibility because it is not anywhere preordained in personal gestures, exceptional because it takes place only on
the basis of the given personal presence of an Other, in the face-to-face
relation. "Violence can aim only at a face" (*TeI* 200, *TI* 225), but it does so
exceptionally, in a contradictory fashion, for it must presuppose what it

makes pretensions to negate and bears upon an Other who both falls within violence's hold and eludes its very grasp. This reveals the interpersonal or *moral* impossibility of murder, and alone, writes Levinas, makes violence endurable in patience and hope: "Violence does not stop Discourse" (*TeI* 209, *TI* 232–33; *TeI* 216–17, *TI* 239; and *TeI* 173–74, *TI* 199). Violence cannot be presupposed as a starting point, but rather as a reversal of a "pre-original" giving or "saying": murder starts by reversing.

It is commonplace today to hear the expression "the Other" invoked at every turn in a variety of academic circles, in discussions on epistemology, ethics, politics, religion, gender, race, and ecology. This expression, "the Other," takes on just about as many meanings as there are concerns: as something to be honored and revered, as something wild, as the person persecuted, as a quality or trait that is excluded from a canonical discourse, etc. But within the framework of ethics as it has been inspired by the works of Levinas, the Other is generally understood merely, or at least primarily, as an *interruptive* or *disruptive* force. The Other calls into question my autonomy and caprice, my ability to kill. And while this would already be a lot, the Other cannot merely be understood as an interruptive force. The disruptive force is itself grounded in a revelatory, invitational force of the Other, a force that is presented in teaching as "way-faring."

To articulate the Other as teacher, which is essentially distinct from the interruptive force of the Other, is the task of this paper. I address this issue by (1) discussing the problem of the Other and characterizing the interruptive force of the Other in relation to givenness as disclosure, (2) giving an exposition of revelation and revelatory giving, (3) specifying and expounding upon implications of teaching as way-faring, and (4) concluding with remarks on the face as a moral revelatory force in relation to other revelatory forces.

Interruption and Disclosure

In this section, I explain the motivation of speaking of the Other as an interruptive or disruptive force. It is well known that, in *Totality and Infinity*, Levinas distinguishes *metaphysics* from *ontology*. Metaphysics is characterized as the individual's possession of the idea of infinity—the Desire of Transcendence—a movement toward the Infinite that begins not with me, but with the Infinite inciting me in particular. In the metaphysical relation, I am revealed as fundamentally passive, on the hither side of the correlation, active and passive. Ontology is characterized generally as my active comprehension of being, resulting in my subsumption of the particular being under a concept. Strictly speaking, ontology is not problematic as long as the "particular" in question is not the Other person. If the Other person is at issue, ontology has the effect of depriving the person of his or her alterity (*TeI* 13, *TI* 42). This is why Levinas remarks that ontology ultimately reduces the Other to the Same, which is to say, promotes my spontaneity or autonomy *to the point of* internalizing or comprehending exteriority, placing the Other in a closed context of meaning: in short, ontology extended to the Other issues in "totality."

One should caution, however, that "totality" is not equivalent to the "Same," to my identity as an ego. The Same as such is not a problem, quite the contrary. The Same must be the Same in order to have a hospitable asymmetrical relation with the person who is absolutely Other. In this regard, even the Same is resistant to totality (*TeI* 24, *TI* 54). The problem is *totality*. Totality is a particular kind of *relation*, a relation of the Same to the Other where the Other is overpowered by or equated with the Same.

The Same is produced or constituted through various primordial modes of experience. These modes of experience integrate the "outside" world (the air one breathes, the apple one eats, the matter one works on, the thoughts one thinks) into the Same, giving the latter a subjective density or materiality. These modes of experience range from enjoyment to labor, from nourishment to ideation. In general, these modes of experience share the structure of intentionality.

Associating the phenomenological term of intentionality with other related ones, Levinas will characterize the structure of the Same as "experience," as "relation," as "teleology," as "history," etc. On the one hand, this means that it is I who gives sense to the world, not just as a consciousness endowing meaning, but as a body that is steeped in its elements, inhabiting my environing-world, initiating the appearance of things (*TeI* 111, *TI* 137). On the other hand, the intentional structure means that objects or aspects of objects can solicit my response to them, can exert an affective force upon me.[1] The world's affection on me is as much a player in the constitution of sense as my power of disposition. Though both the ego and the world can be the instigators of sense, in the final analysis, there is a *correlation* or *synchrony* between my powers of sense-giving and the world's disclosure, or the world's provocations and my compelled attentiveness to them. What Levinas has in mind by this active-active structure that gets called "intentionality" is the entire sphere of *disclosure* (*dévoilement*). Disclosure, be it instigated from the "side" of the subject or the "side" of the object, is the exercise of the Same.

Levinas understands the Other as radically different from the intentionality of disclosure. If one *starts* from *this* sphere of disclosive experience, as Levinas *seems* to do, then the Other can only be that which *interrupts disclosure,* that is, *calls into question my spontaneity,* or *calls into question the exercise of the Same* (*TeI* 13, *TI* 43). The Other limits my freedom, alienates me from myself, shatters context. "To welcome the Other is to put in question my freedom" (*TeI* 58, *TI* 85). Since the Other cannot be comprehended in terms of *being-disclosed,* the Other is interruptive of what is primarily a relation of disposal, correlation, reversibility, knowing, generalizing the individuality of another person, etc.

Since the Other as transcendence does not fit into correlation, I cannot exist in an intentional relation with an Other. The Other is characterized as *absolved* from the relation (of disclosure), and hence as "absolute," that is, as "separate" from a relation; I cannot have an "experience" of an Other if what we mean by experience is a subject objectifying an object, be it a sense-datum or an idea.

To remain with this negative characterization of the Other, however, is to go no further than, say, Husserl has gone. When, for example, Husserl writes that the Other or the Alien cannot be given in the manner of a spatial object, like the thing's "absent" back side that is apperceived as co-present, or be given in the manner of a temporal object, like a past event that was present at one time, or a future event that may *be* (present), he defines alienness in a paradoxical manner: Alienness can never be re-presented; rather, alienness is accessibility in the mode of inaccessibility and incomprehensibility, given as not being able to be given.[2] For Husserl, the experience of the Other is not an experience of a subject-object correlation; the relation with the Alien is not, initially at least, an epistemological relation. The Alien is a surplus over disclosure.

The question for us, however, is whether the Other can be limited only to this paradox, whether the Other is merely a surplus over disclosure and is to be characterized merely negatively as an interruptive force, even though such descriptions certainly make sense from the perspective of disclosure.

But if the Other is only addressed from the perspective of disclosive givenness, and if there is no description of another mode of givenness with its own integrity, if one merely expresses the Other *as interruptive,* one is implicitly confined to disclosure. To be confined to disclosure *in this way* is to equate all other modes of givenness to it; it is—perhaps unwittingly—to equate signification with essence, to exhaust the saying in the said, to reduce Desire to need, to entrap the Other by the Self, to relativize the absolute Other, to justify murder. In terms I have used in a different context, *it is to commit idolatry.*[3] Though one wants to emphasize the ethical bearing of the Other by insisting that the Other is interruptive, *to equate* the Other with a disruptive force is to be entrapped by idolatry: first because one ignores another mode of giving peculiar to the Other that is not disclosure, and intimately related to this, because one does not bring into play the religious armature of the ethical encounter. This is to say, the characterization of the Other as interruptive within disclosure does not point the way back to a pre-original generosity on the hither side of acts that get thematized as murder.

Revelation and Revelatory Giving

Must givenness, relation, experience, etc., be confined to the realm of disclosure? Must the ethical relation be restricted to interruption? Must the Other be characterized merely in a negative fashion? Levinas himself does not think so: "The incomprehensible nature of the presence of the Other, which we spoke of above, is not to be described negatively" (*TeI* 169, *TI* 195); and again, "This 'beyond' the totality and objective experience is, however, not to be described in a purely negative fashion" (*TeI* xi, *TI* 23).

Levinas could only make such statements because he has a different type of givenness already operative in his depiction of disclosive givenness, one that is at least as vast: revelatory givenness. "*The absolute experience is not disclosure but revelation*" (*TeI* 37, *TI* 65–66; compare *TeI* 39, *TI* 67). Revelatory givenness concerns the saying of the Infinite, as well as the Other person who remains absolute in the giving. Discourse is not derived from disclosure but has its own source as a relation with exteriority.

Since revelation has its own source in the Infinite saying pointing me to the Other before I could have a choice about it, and since it has its own source in the self-presentation of the Other in expression, Levinas need not confine intentionality to a subject-object structure, but can recognize a "very different intentionality" (*TeI* 98, *TI* 126), a "relation or an intentionality of a wholly different type," an "intentionality of transcendence" (*TeI* 20, *TI* 49) that Levinas from the start attempts to describe and to evoke in *Totality and Infinity*.[4] He can speak of an "*experience* par excellence" or a "privileged *experience*" with respect to the epiphany of the Infinite, or again, a "pure *experience*" as experience of absolute other as absolute experience (*TeI* 170, *TI* 196; compare *TeI* 81, *TI* 109; *TeI* 45, *TI* 73). It is not I who absolutize the other, the Other is "experienced" as absolute.

My point here is not to insist that Levinas does or even should stick to traditional phenomenological language in his writings, but only that he also uses it at times *from the perspective of revelation,* and here it corresponds to a positivity in the ethical relation that is grounded in a distinctive mode of givenness that cannot be restricted to disclosure. He does not maintain that there is nothing beyond disclosure, but only that *revelation* constitutes an inversion of disclosive, of *objectifying cognition* (*TeI* 39, *TI* 67), and in such a way that the relation of disclosure has to be seen as founded in revelation. That disclosure is rooted in revelation could not be recognized if the ethical Other were only an interruptive force. I do not get around the Other through "ruse and ambush," or even murder, which constitute the essence of war, but I respond to the Other's expression, which is "first revelation" and which is presupposed in all other relations with the Other (*TeI* 171, *TI* 197).

Asserting that the Other is not merely a negative force but a moral one does not yet respond to the question concerning *the mode of this revelation*. How can it be evoked beyond the disruptive power of the Other in the Same that calls into question my freedom?

Teaching as Way-Faring

Although it is frequently maintained that Levinas's work in *Totality and Infinity* either is not phenomenological because he explicitly criticizes certain notions unique to phenomenology belonging to the sphere of disclosure, or is quasi-phenomenological because he employs these same terms in a different sense or seeks certain conditions of possibility, the *style* of Levinas's approach can be understood to be at root phenomenological. The phenomenological character of his philosophical work is rooted in a shift in perspective from the "what" of being to the "how," "manner," "mode," or "way" in which being gets produced, constituted, or said—a shift already described by Husserl in his Fifth Logical Investigation.[5]

Though Levinas will give definitions of various terms he uses, underlying these essential distinctions are modes of approach that characterize the matters at hand. For example, psychism is described as a "manner" or "way" (*manière*) for the real to exist as plurality of being (*TeI* 24, *TI* 54; *TeI* 29, *TI* 58); the *way* of metaphysics is portrayed not as action, but as the social relation (*TeI* 81, *TI* 109); enjoyment is the way (*façon*) that life relates to its contents, and sensibility is the way (*façon*) of enjoyment (*TeI* 94, *TI* 122; *TeI* 108, *TI* 135); the intentionality of living from . . . is the *way* in which the same is determined by the other (*TeI* 101, *TI* 128); vulnerability is approached as the *way* (*manière*) of the tender (*TeI* 233, *TI* 256; *TeI* 236, *TI* 259); apophansis is characterized as a "way" ("*façon*") of essence, as the *how* or modality (*comment*) of this essence or this temporalization;[6] the face is portrayed as the *way* of the neighbor, and *way* of the neighbor or interlocutor is understood as the manner of starting from him- or herself as foreign, yet presenting him- or herself to me (*AE* 112, *OB* 88; *TeI* 39, *TI* 67).

This phenomenological attentiveness to the modes or manners of givenness allows Levinas to distinguish between two different "ways" of givenness: disclosure and revelation. Before going on to Levinas's notion of teaching as peculiar to revelation, let me expound upon revelation as a "way" of givenness, as well as upon the relation between disclosure and revelation.

Of course, one could object to the use of "givenness" here in the same way that one could object to the use of "relation" or "experience" in describing the face to face. Levinas, working within a tradition and attempting to reformulate it, both disappropriates and appropriates such expressions to convey a fundamentally different (personal, moral) kind of "experience," i.e., absolute experience, absolute relation, absolute givenness. Further, in the case of revelation, we no longer speak of the givenness of sense, but of "significance," and in particular, as I will point out below, "first significance," which is peculiar only to revelatory givenness.

To speak of revelation in this way, however, does not posit this mode of givenness as "above" disclosure, as if to a dualism. Revelation is not the opening up of the skies, with all the mysteries of the world displayed, but the way in which the Other gives him- or herself in a mode radically different from a thing, object, past event, etc., but who gives him- or herself nonetheless, where the givenness is one of "first significance," as solicitation and as "enigma." There would only be a dualism of modes of givenness if disclosure and revelation were parallel modes of givenness. They are not parallel, however, since disclosure has to be understood as founded in revelation. This implies a direct critique of secularism and secularist thought (an overcoming that is resisted precisely within the context of secularism, in the same way—though more perniciously—that the scientific worldview resists seeing itself as founded in the life-world).

In fact, I would argue that there is no justification for restricting givenness to only one mode of givenness, namely, disclosure.[7] This would be an arbitrary restriction, one which is shown up as arbitrary precisely because there is experientially a "givenness" of the Other as a non-postponable urgency, as a moral invitational force, as "teacher," to use Levinas's language, which *then* has the effect of disrupting my freedom. There is no way of arguing this theoretically, however, because the distinction is grounded in the "givenness" itself, even if this givenness does not meet our expectations of disclosive givenness. And if we rule out this possibility of the "givenness" itself, how could we ever depict disclosure as a mode of givenness in which the Other is given as "interrruptive," and as the very model of givenness to which givenness is restricted in the first place? When someone faces me, it interrupts me. But it interrupts me and my relation to the world in the economy of disclosure because the face is not disclosed; the face is revealed as an evocative, imperative force.

It is here that teaching as the face of the Other takes one beyond its depiction as merely a disruption of the Same. Teaching is described positively and as a revelatory *way* in which the Infinite is revealed in the face of the Other. Far from being merely interruptive, seen from the way of revelation, teaching *continues placing in me the idea of the Infinite* (*TeI* 155, *TI* 180), which is the very relation of metaphysics; that is, teaching—which occurs through the face of the Other—deepens the revelation of the Infinite to me, a revelation that is beyond my efforts either to produce it or recall it in the manner of Socratic maieutics. The teacher, then, is not anything, but a "point" that points; the teacher is a pointer, as it were, where what is functional is not what the teacher is saying, or what the teacher tries to do. In fact, the teacher is not the issue, but a movement to the Infinite, which is to say for Levinas, *service*, a turning toward Others.[8] In this sense, one need not try to be provocative, since this is the way the face is revealed. What this revelation means in terms of my relation with Others will have to be explained below. What is important here is to note that in teaching the revealer and revealed coincide. And this modal coinciding for Levinas is the essence of language (*TeI* 38, *TI* 67).[9]

Teaching takes place in language as expression or speech. By calling attention to the coincidence of expressing and expressed, Levinas is attempting to liberate a peculiar mode of signification and rationality from its traditional identification with ontological intelligibility. Expression or the presence of the face is not one signification ranked among other significations, but is "first" signification, "first" expression, "first" intelligible, the very upsurge of rationality or truth (*TeI* 194, *TI* 218; compare *TeI* 183–84, *TI* 208–9). The "first" here attributes a primordiality to a signifying saying that thematizes in propositions, where propositions are literally that, proposals or lures: "Speech first founds community by *giving*, by presenting the phenomenon as given; and it gives by thematizing" (*TeI* 72, *TI* 98; compare *TeI* 69, *TI* 96).

Yet the significant expression, while giving the said, is not correlative to what is said; it precedes or succeeds what is said as if coming irrecuperably from a different time (diachrony) or a different plane (asymmetry, "height"). First signification does not arise from me: "In this relation we have recognized language, produced only in the face to face; and in language we have recognized teaching. Teaching is a way [*façon*] for truth to be produced such that it is not my work, such that I could not derive it from my own interiority" (*TeI* 271, *TI* 295). First signification arises from the Other who implores me to go the way of Infinity, which is to assume responsibility for all the Other does. As first signification, teaching is the revelation of the Infinite. The revelation of the Infinite is my witnessing this way as service toward others.[10]

In teaching, the content of instruction is the expressing itself. Accordingly, the so-called first "signifier" is not a sign but the personal signifier, the face of the Other who gives signs. "The first intelligible is intelligence" (*TeI* 194, *TI* 218). Moreover, the face of the Other is not reducible to works, which are meaningful in a derivative sense. On the one hand, works do not attend their own manifestation in the way that the face attends its own revelation. The work is disclosed, its meaning is subject to the interplay of dissimulation and appearance, its meaning can change from one historical context to another, and is interchangeable with other goods. A work is a type of (subsequent) signification that can and must be open to interpretation (*TeI* 202–3, *TI* 227–28).

On the other hand, the face is so integrally revealing-revealed that it is not subject to the economy of appearances (*TeI* 37, *TI* 66; *TeI* 71, *TI* 98). There is leeway for hesitation. The face does not derive its signification from a context, from its relatively perfunctory role in history; its meaning is not mediated by politics or economics. The face is *first, absolute, unique* signification. There is no hermeneutics of the face, since the revealed personal presence of the Other is not open to critique, analysis, or debate (*AE* 21, *OB* 166); as witnessed in the uniqueness of this particular person, I already receive the vocation to substitute myself for the Other. Being a subject (which means being subjected to the Other), I am from the very start within the sphere of morality. The attempt to debate this moral responsibility (to undertake a hermeneutics of the face, to attempt to adjudicate who is worthy of my love and who is not, to make a choice about a commitment, etc.) would be precisely totality—or idolatry—since it would feign to relativize the absolute.

Revelatory teaching teaches transcendence: "The first teaching teaches this very height, tantamount to its exteriority, the ethical" (*TeI* 146, *TI* 171). Teaching does not fix on a teacher or some *thing* taught, since the Infinite is not a theme to be disseminated; but as revelatory, teaching is the very revealing of the Infinite itself. Likewise conversation means receiving the revelation which could in no way proceed from me; for the subject this means welcoming the idea of infinity through expression, "to be taught" (*TeI* 22, *TI* 51). Desire, which is the movement toward the Infinite as inspired in me as coming from the Infinite, is teaching received (*TeI* 171, *TI* 197).

I have explicated teaching as a process of "pointing the way" or "way-faring." The content of teaching is the revealing itself, not the learning of facts but the turning of the individual to the Holy, in the way of the Infinite, which is to say, the recovering of who we are in the deepest core of our subjectivity, as a turning toward Others.

Of course, the question can be asked, just who teaches, who points the way, and further, just how does one point? Initially we can respond by saying that since every face reveals, every face, every *human* face teaches. But this raises a host of questions: Are there not gradations of teaching where some manners are deeper, more revealing than others? Are some by virtue of the way they way-fare more forceful teachers than Others? Though the teacher is Master in height, are some more "masterful"? Are there not different kinds of teaching?

Levinas's responses to these questions are sparse. Still, these are legitimate questions, and I will attempt to address them by risking interpretation under the following six points of clarification.

First, *teaching is the way the face way-fares.* For Levinas, the very "presence" of the face—the absolute irreducibility of the person of the proper name—bears the trace of the Infinite, for the face of the neighbor is the trace of the reclusion of God. In this way, the face already teaches the Holy, revealing the very inordinateness of Infinity: the face resembles God and teaches transcendence itself (*TeI* 269, *TI* 293; *TeI* 146, *TI* 171). This does not mean that the Other plays the role of a mediator, for "the Other is the very locus of metaphysical truth, and indispensable for my relation with God" (*TeI* 51, *TI* 78). Precisely through the face of the Other, the Other is the revelation of the height where God is revealed: "The dimension of the divine opens forth from the human face" (*TeI* 50–51, *TI* 78–79). By employing these kinds of formulations, Levinas suggests that he is already articulating the face from the perspective of revelatory givenness, from the saying prior to and revealed in the said.

Second, there is still a question whether one could creatively and inventively live this "first signification" of the face, and in this manner most profoundly reverse the reversal. It is no coincidence that Levinas does not articulate this kind of clarification of teaching, since he wants to stay focused on the pre-original, receptive moment of the vocation ("Discourse," "saying"), and not on active origination. Moreover, because the Other is characterized as *absolute,* and because the revelation is precisely absolute, I do not think Levinas's portrayal of teaching would be susceptible to other modes of teaching that could admit of various degrees of "slippage" between the expressing and the expressed.[11]

Third, *one relates to the teacher as a way-farer.* To take the teacher as a resting point and not as a way-farer, to take the teacher as disseminating information in the manner of disclosure, would be to equate the signifier (person) with what is said and to take the Other in the sphere of disclosure merely in terms of acts that can be thematized. Teaching or wayfaring, however, is itself the "content" of the teacher—teaching and teacher coincide. Otherwise, one would grasp the Other as *exhausted in* acts that are thematized, reducing revelation to disclosure, and in this way constituting what Levinas calls totality. There would be no "trace" of the reclusion of God as the face of the neighbor.

Fourth, *revelatory teaching is essentially ambiguous.* By this I mean that the teacher (1) reveals the Infinite to us as being a way of the Infinite, presenting the Infinite in his or her "face"; (2) offers to us possible manners of living that are ultimately holy; and (3) is him- or herself revealed to us by revealing in this way.

Fifth, teaching is not neutral, but is ultimately a *moral force of invitation.* It is true that Levinas understands Infinity to be stronger than murder; its resistance to violence is revealed in the "primordial expression," the interdiction "you shall not commit murder" (*TeI* 173, *TI* 199). But what Levinas's analyses also show is that the Other is not merely an interruptive force that embodies the commandment "thou shalt not kill." The latter is itself rooted in the revelation of the Other, the Other in his or her "nudity," that is, his or her sheer, immediate presence as absolutely unique in an absolute relation to an absolute, beyond form, predication, and image, revealing-revealed, and in this way as "destitution," "hunger" (compare *TeI* 174, *TI* 200). The Other as teacher is an invitation to be living in the way of the Infinite; he or she is an invitation to goodness as giving in the manner of the Infinite. The commandment "thou shalt not kill" has to be rooted in generosity, in "saying," as it is revealed in the face of the Other as teaching; it cannot be grounded on itself as mere inter-diction.

This moral invitational force for one reason or another gets overlooked in Levinas's works. Nevertheless, the invitational force of the teacher that founds the inter-diction as expressive of a contra-diction is suggested by many of Levinas's own formulations of the face: as invitation, solicitation, imposition, invocation, arousal; further, as exhortation, sermon, and prophetic word; even as obligating, commanding, and as implied in expressions like "height," "master," etc.[12]

There are two issues here. First, to understand teaching as neutral would be to understand the Other as an image, as idol, as a work that would be mediated by form; it would be to understand the relation with the Other as idolatrous. Levinas of course does not do this, and already the interruptive force of the face imposes itself above form and escapes this threat of idolatry. But, second, as teaching the moral force of the Other is a surplus even over that, it is an *invitational force.* Accordingly, Levinas himself writes that in expression, the Other's imposition "*does not [merely] limit* but promotes my freedom, *arousing my goodness*" (*TeI* 174, *TI* 200, my emphasis), and similarly, that "the relation with the Other, discourse, is not only the putting in question of my freedom, the appeal coming from the other to call me to responsibility, is not only the speech by which I divest myself of the possession that encircles me by setting forth an objective and common world, *but is also sermon, exhortation, the prophetic word*" (*TeI* 188, *TI* 213, my emphasis).

The teacher or master is so much an exhortational and *invitational force* that Levinas distinguishes the teacher as solicitation from a mere "letting be" (*TeI* 169, *TI* 195). Something is at stake here, is urgent: the face is not neutral, but neither is it merely disruptive; the epiphany of the face signals a "non-postponable urgency" to goodness. Certainly, "letting be" may be seen as an alternative to forcing another to go my way; and the invitational force of the face is not an activity that takes me somewhere for me; it does not "force" me to the Infinite, but points me to Infinity with urgency. The moral invitational force is a revelatory force. Nevertheless, the face teaches as an urgency that is not neutral and in this sense can only take us to the brink. It only "lets be" (if we wish to use that expression) at the brink, but as teaching the face remains a moral lure.

Sixth, as a moral invitational force signaling a non-postponable urgency, the Other as teacher makes "conversion" both a possibility and a necessity. At stake is a fostering of the idea of Infinity within us, a deeper revelation of the Holy who points us to goodness and justice, allowing hospitality to (try to) catch up with generosity, and *as a consequence* making the interdiction of murder louder and stronger. Infinity as absolute, separate, or Holy constitutes in the subject what Levinas calls "atheism" (in the realm of disclosure) such that in and through its very Holiness, Infinity can (but need not) be "forgotten"; the generosity of transcendence can be reversed. This reversal is not produced as an accident in a separated being, for according to Levinas, the possibility of reversal is rooted in the absoluteness of the Other, in separation (being absolved from a relation of disclosure).

The teacher, however, as the epiphany of the idea of Infinity and as forcefully continuing this absolute giving, is a way of conversion or reversing the reversal of murder. As a "way" the teaching is not a new (original) teaching, but a cultivation of a prior, anarchical giving. Taking us to the brink, the teacher is a lure to turn in the *manner* of the Holy. The turn toward the Infinite is itself a conversion toward the neighbor (*AE* 15–17, *OB* 12–13).

It is only by going the way of the way-farer, as living from a religious and ethical dimension, that one *then* sees that one's freedom is called into question *as* arbitrary. Calling into question my freedom, critique already presupposes conversion. In my commerce with the teacher, I *discover myself as violent, as guilty, as accused,* even if I am "faultless"; this means for Levinas that one is given to oneself *as* fundamentally passive, *as* able to respond to the saying (vocation) before being able to affirm or reject it; I am given to myself as already subjected to the other, and this is the very meaning of subjectivity. In the core of my subjectivity, I am pitched toward the Other such that the "more" I approach the neighbor, the deeper I recur to myself as subjectivity. One cannot justify one's own freedom, but in apology for arbitrary freedom one can seek justification in and by the Other (*TeI* 230, *TI* 252). Only now is there a call for humility, for one cannot circumvent pride by oneself; only now can the sphere of enjoyment become meaningful, significant; only in relation to Infinity through the face as teacher is one revealed to oneself as violent. This conversion is the origin of morality: "Morality begins when freedom, instead of being justified by itself, feels itself to be arbitrary and violent" (*TeI* 56, *TI* 84).

The Face That Teaches and Revelation

Teaching has been explicated as "first teaching" such that the teacher is essentially the way-farer who is most profoundly not merely a disruptive force, but a moral revelatory invitational force that is a locus of conversion and service. The face of the Other teaches.

Granted that the dimension of the divine opens forth from the human face in the manner of teaching, is it the case that *only* the *face,* only the *human* face, can teach? Or perhaps we should put the question differently: Granted that the human face teaches and in this way reveals, does only the face reveal? Are teaching and revelation to be strictly identified? I think that Levinas too hastily limits revelation to the face, and that when revelation is seen in its expanded form, there are new possibilities of relation with life other than human: birds, the boulders we climb, the blades of grass, the air we breathe, and spiritual manifestations too, like works of art, objects of labor, etc. I suggest, then, it is not only the face that reveals; however, the face has a unique place in revelation: precisely as the face to face, we have the institution of the moral encounter. To make this point, I will address all too briefly Levinas's position on "elements" and "spiritual works."

On various scores only the human face teaches for Levinas, and in this sense functions as a revelatory, invitational force capable of promoting conversion. For Levinas, the human face as teaching is essentially distinct from natural elements, animal life, and from all spiritual formations.[13]

First, far from denigrating the earth and terrestrial elements, Levinas sees in them a positive function. In a way that is not dissimilar to Husserl's later reflections on the constitutive role of the earth as absolute *Erdboden*,[14] Levinas understands the earth itself to be the nourishing constitutive condition of the constituting subject; I stand upon it as absolutely presupposed, and it enables me to enjoy sensible objects without it having to become an object of reflection (*TeI* 101, *TI* 128; *TeI* 111, *TI* 138).

That which cannot become an object of possession correlative to me, and is the basis for which I can have something in an intentional relation of possession, Levinas calls the "elemental" (*TeI* 105, *TI* 131); in enjoyment things revert to their elemental qualities. The element is like the thing insofar as it too has no face (*visage*), but the element is different from the thing (and in this respect only, similar to the Other) because the thing has a facet (*face*), whereas the element has no facet at all; it has anonymously and indeterminately no end; the element has no face or facet; it is endless but not Infinite (compare *TeI* 104–5, *TI* 131–32).

This endless spatiotemporal prolongation of the element is not the dimension of radical exteriority, Infinity, but the province of mythical gods; the mythical is the *way* of existing *without revelation,* according to Levinas: "The future of the element as insecurity is lived concretely as the mythical divinity of the element. Faceless gods, impersonal gods to whom one does not speak, mark the nothingness that bounds the egoism of enjoyment in the midst of its familiarity with the element. But it is thus that enjoyment accomplishes separation" (*TeI* 116, *TI* 142). It is labor, not the religious or ethical life, that recovers the gap between the elemental insecurity of the future and what comes under my control as objects of enjoyment and knowledge.

Moreover, like the elemental, even animals and plants do not reveal in the sense of teaching because they do not face us with discourse: for Levinas, the very meaning "thou shalt not kill" is not expressed here, whereas this is what the human face *means.*

Second, there is another issue regarding manifold spiritual formations like aesthetic objects ranging from literary to plastic art, not to mention socially and politically produced goods. As mentioned above, produced works of any kind do not transcend in the way the discursive expression of the human face does. Whereas the produced work attests the producer in the latter's absence, the face attends its own revelation completely and anterior to any image. The inexpressive character of the product is reflected in the separation between content and form, the separation between the produced work and the producer, in its interchangeability with other goods (its "market value"), and its accessibility to interpretation; it can assume a meaning other people give it which can change from one historical context to another (*TeI* 203, *TI* 227). An object could become an icon, and an icon could be transmuted into a mere art object. But for Levinas, it is impossible for the face not to teach, since it attends its own revelation. Of course, one can enslave the Other and deny implicitly or explicitly the teaching quality of the Other. But even through this, the face still teaches.

Whereas there can be an interchangeability and a hermeneutics of works, there cannot be an interchangeability and hermeneutics of the face. The face and teaching coincide; the face is absolute, irreplaceably unique, immediate, and imperative anterior to my consideration, my willingness to accept or to "believe," and in this respect has a meaning outside of any historical context. In relation to the face, I am ultimately passive, receptive; I do not stand before the Other contemplating him or her, but am inclined in responsibility toward the Other.

In *Totality and Infinity* it is the face that teaches and reveals the Infinite. Everything else (perhaps with the exception of the elemental earth) belongs to the sphere of disclosure and does not reveal. At least this seems to be the overwhelming drift.

But in his *Otherwise Than Being* there are hints in another direction. While revelation and disclosure are distinguished like they are in *Totality and Infinity,* there seems to be less of a "dualism," as it were. Now Levinas is more explicit that the Infinite is revealed even in what is disclosively thematic: not only the face, but the "said" in all its forms bears the *trace* of "saying." Not only does the saying become fixed in a said, in books, in works, in science, in Western history, or in the Holocaust, but the said, which is said in many ways, bears a trace of the saying. One could extrapolate: Would it not also be a type of violence to assign an exchange value not only to persons, but also to works?

True, God, the Infinite, does overflow both cognition and the enigma of the face through which the Infinite leaves a trace in cognition. "Its distance from a theme, its reclusion, its holiness, is not its way to effect its being . . . , but is its glory, quite different from being and knowing" (*AE* 206, *OB* 162). The trace of the reclusion of God is the face of the neighbor. But Levinas also writes that even the said contests the absenting of the saying, and thus bears the diachronous trace of the Infinite beyond being: "The said, contesting the abdication of the saying that everywhere occurs in this said, thus maintains the diachrony in which, holding its breath, the spirit hears the echo of the *otherwise*" (*AE* 57, *OB* 44). Because of this very contestation of this signification, the ontological form of the said ultimately could not alter the signification of the beyond being which shows itself in the said (*AE* 198, *OB* 156). Can, then, the trace of the reclusion of God be confined to the face?

The said itself is not flat, not mere diction, but inherently a contradiction, since it harbors a trace of the saying; Transcendence, other than
being, is signaled in ontology, in the tumultuous and sometimes tragic history of the West. Levinas writes:

> And we would not here have ventured to recall the *beyond essence* if this
> *history of the West* did not bear, in its margins, the trace of events carrying
> *another signification,* and if the *victims of the triumphs which entitle the eras of
> history* could be separate from its meaning. Here we have the boldness to
> think that even the Stoic nobility of resignation to the logos already owes
> its energy to the [revelatory] openness to the *beyond essence.* (*AE* 224–25,
> *OB* 178, my emphasis; compare *AE* 224–25, *OB* 178–79)

Levinas's works suggest obliquely that revelation need not be re-
strictively confined to human teaching; beings otherwise than the face,
such as spiritual formations, do maintain the saying. This already decisively roots disclosure in revelation without equating one with the other;
this implies that revelation is not merely a surplus over disclosure, since
disclosive being would ultimately be given within revelatory giving. One
might even go so far as to say that elements and living beings, precisely as
"said," also bear a trace, though Levinas himself does not explicitly give
this indication in the works dealt with here. At all events, all modes of the
said echoing the otherwise than being can function as "icon," being the
visible of the Invisible. As such one would also have a unique responsibility toward them; the turning toward the Infinite would be a responsibility
toward the manifold ways the Infinite gets said.

But I must also hasten to add that if one cares to use the term "responsibility" in the former context, it is still qualitatively different from
moral responsibility. The Divine does not only open up *from* a human face,
but it does only open up *to* a human face. This opening up to the face institutes the sphere of morality (which Levinas expresses with the terms
"pre-original responsibility," "substitution," "proximity," "diachronous
saying," etc.). And this is why Levinas seems to reserve the term "revelation" for the human face: the revelation of the Infinite is not revealed except through the subject that confesses it or contests it. Revelation is made
by him who receives it (*AE* 199, *OB* 156). Revelation is a mode of giving
that belongs distinctively to the moral sphere.

For my part, I would be tempted to say that aesthetic works or spiritual formations do reveal, but that their mode of revealing is fundamentally different. They reveal in a *way* that differentiates them from the
human face. The same would hold for elements and life other than
human. I would initially want to use this language of revelation here be-

cause it would indicate that even the "said" or what is "thematic" is not flat, without a trace, and that even though it operates within the sphere of disclosure as a distinct mode of givenness, it is not *merely* disclosive. They would still be modes of revelation because the revelation is made in relation to a human face.

But then the challenge would be to differentiate these other so-called modes of revelation from a revelation that is distinctively *moral.* The moral qualification of this revelation would issue not only from a revelation that is made *to the face, but also one that comes from the face.* Morality would be the relation of the face to face. This would be teaching.

On this score I would like to distinguish three modes of givenness, each designated by a different name. (1) A type of "horizontal" (synchronic?) givenness called *disclosure.* This would be a type of givenness that would be *merely* aesthetic (taken in the original broad sense of that term). (2) A mode of "vertical" givenness called *manifestation* that could account for the "depth" of the trace of the Infinite in the manifold modes of the said, but that properly speaking would not be revelation that institutes the moral dimension. And (3) a mode of "vertical" givenness called *revelation* that would concern the person-to-person or face-to-face revelation and that would be properly "moral."

At least such distinctions might remain conversant with Levinas's own expositions. For Levinas, the positivity of this ethical language instigated by the face is my profound passivity in revelation. Revelation here is a "non-thematizable provocation," demanding a response that can only be radically subsequent to it, but equally radically prior to my volition to heed the call. The moral dimension is opened up by the face that teaches; it is not merely the resistance of the face to the violence of murder, but the constitution of the very core of my "being" as capable of substituting myself for the teacher; it is an invitation to reverse the reversal, or as Levinas might say, an invitation to glory.

Notes

The epigraph is from Emmanuel Levinas, *Totalité et infini* (The Hague: Martinus Nijhoff, 1961), 273; *Totality and Infinity,* trans. Alphonso Lingis (Pittsburgh: Duquesne University Press, 1969), 297. Hereafter cited in the text as *TeI.* and *TI,* respectively.

1. See Levinas, *Totalité et infini,* 163, 166, 169; *Totality and Infinity,* 51, 189, 191, 194. And see Edmund Husserl, *Analysen zur passiven Synthesis,* ed. Margot Fleischer, in *Husserliana,* vol. 11 (The Hague: Martinus Nijhoff, 1966), esp. division 2.

2. Edmund Husserl, *Phänomenologie der Intersubjektivität: Dritter Band,* ed. Iso Kern, in *Husserliana,* vol. 15 (The Hague: Martinus Nijhoff, 1973), 631.

3. See my "Idolatry and the Phenomenology of the Holy: Reversing the Reversal," in *Interkulturelle Philosophie und Phänomenologie in Japan: Beiträge zum Gespräch über Grenzen hinweg,* ed. T. Ogawa, M. Lazarin, and G. Rappe (Munich: Iudicium, 1998), 385–407.

4. Levinas even goes so far as to say that he "reserved the term *intentionality*" for "metaphysical thought, where a finite has the idea of infinity" (*Totalité et infini,* 276; *Totality and Infinity,* 299).

5. Edmund Husserl, *Logische Untersuchungen,* vol. 2 (Tübingen: Niemeyer, 1968), §17.

6. Emmanuel Levinas, *Autrement qu'être, ou au-delà de l'essence* (The Hague: Martinus Nijhoff, 1978), 49; *Otherwise Than Being, or Beyond Essence,* trans. Alphonso Lingis (Dordrecht: Kluwer Academic Publishers, 1991), 38. Hereafter cited in the text as *AE* and *OB,* respectively.

7. This is a point made forcefully by Michel Henry and which he calls "ontological monism" in his *L'essence de la manifestation,* 2nd ed. (Paris: Presses Universitaires de France, 1990). See my "The Problem of Forgetfulness in Michel Henry," in "The Philosophy of Michel Henry," ed. Anthony J. Steinbock, special issue, *Continental Philosophy Review* 32, no. 3 (1999): 271–302.

8. Emmanuel Levinas, "God and Philosophy," in *Collected Philosophical Papers,* trans. Alphonso Lingis et al. (The Hague: Martinus Nijhoff, 1987).

9. Given what I have noted above concerning the reduction of revelation to disclosure, and further, the reduction of the Other to merely an interruptive force, it is perhaps no coincidence that very little work on Levinas has highlighted the notion of teaching in his thought. I can direct the reader's attention to only two articles (both by the same person): Norman Wirzba, "From Maieutics to Metanoia: Levinas's Understanding of the Philosophical Task," *Man and World* 28 (1995): 129–44; and Norman Wirzba, "Teaching as Propaedeutic to Religion: The Contribution of Levinas and Kierkegaard," *International Journal for Philosophy of Religion* 39 (April 1996): 77–94.

10. See Levinas, "God and Philosophy," 165: "We have designated this way for the Infinite, or for God, to refer, from the heart of its very desirability, to the non-desirable proximity of others, by the term 'illeity.'"

11. We do in fact creatively live this relation. For example, there is a qualitative difference between the "accused" who is "faultless" and the "accused" who has committed crimes against humanity, and this difference is a constitutive, historical one. There are at least two ways of taking up this issue further. One way would be to approach it via Max Scheler's notion of exemplarity, which could address essentially distinct modes of being guided by and pointing to that range from the saint to the connoisseur. All of these modes would be grounded in the absolute value of person. Here, the "slippage" between the expressing and the expressed would be a creative elaboration of personhood. It would be an expression of our "finitude." David Michael Kleinberg-Levin has indicated another possibility in his "Persecution" which articulates several ways of "transformative recuperation" of a

pre-originary substitution for the Other. See Kleinberg-Levin's essay on "Persecution" in this volume.

12. For example: "le visage me parle et par là *m'invite* à une relation sans commune mesure" (Levinas, *Totalité et infini*, 172, my emphasis; *Totality and Infinity*, 198); "Cette assistance, n'est pas le *neutre* d'une image, mais *une sollicitation* que me concerne de sa misère et de sa Hauteur" (174, my emphasis; 200); Se manifester [*sic*] comme visage, c'est *s'imposer* par delà la forme" (174; 200); "Se manifester [*sic*] en assistant à sa manifestation revient à *invoquer* l'interlocuteur" (174, my emphasis; 200); "De sorte que, dans l' expression, l'être qui *s'impose* ne limite pas *mais promeut ma liberté, en suscitant ma bonté*" (175, my emphasis; 200); "C'est pourquoi la relation avec autrui . . . est . . . aussi la prédication, l'exhortation, la parole prophétique" (188; 213). See also *Totalité*, 229, 266–67; *Totality*, 251, 291.

13. There is a question within many of Levinas's texts concerning the extent to which the face is only a masculine face. This is not unproblematic. For example, Levinas writes that the primary hospitable welcome that describes the field of "intimacy" and "discretion" is the Woman; *this* "Other," feminine alterity, is "not the *you* [*vous*] of the face that reveals itself in a dimension of height, but precisely the *thou* [*tu*] of familiarity: *a language without teaching*" (*Totalité* 28–29; *Totality* 155, my emphasis). Situating the feminine and the face is complicated by the fact that Levinas also attributes to the judgment of God a fundamental "discretion" (221; 244) and therefore at least implies a deep connection between the divine and the feminine. Levinas for his part says that instead of speaking of the archaic differences between the masculine and the feminine as if they were ontological species or gender differences, one could say that these differences are shared by every human being—a response that is unsatisfactory in many respects. See Emmanuel Levinas, *Ethique et infini: Dialogues avec Philippe Nemo* (Paris: Fayard, 1982), 61. The best I can do here is to point to others who have taken up these issues in a more forceful manner. See Luce Irigaray, *Ethique de la différence sexuelle* (Paris: Minuit, 1984), esp. 173–99; Grace M. Jantzen, *Becoming Divine: Towards a Feminist Philosophy of Religion* (Bloomington: Indiana University Press, 1999); Kate Ince, "Questions to Luce Irigaray," *Hypatia* 11, no. 2 (1996): 122–40; and Tina Chanter, "Feminism and the Other," in *The Provocation of Levinas: Rethinking the Other*, ed. Robert Bernasconi and David Wood (London: Routledge, 1988), 32–56.

14. See Edmund Husserl, "Grundlegende Untersuchungen zum phänomenologischen Ursprung der Räumlichkeit der Natur" (1934), in *Philosophical Essays in Memory of Edmund Husserl*, ed. M. Garber (Cambridge: Harvard University Press, 1940), 307–25; and Edmund Husserl, "Notizen zur Raumkonstitution" (1934), ed. A. Schütz, in *Philosophy and Phenomenological Research* 1, no. 1 (1941): 21–37. And see Anthony J. Steinbock, *Home and Beyond: Generative Phenomenology after Husserl* (Evanston: Northwestern University Press, 1995), 109–22.

Being and the Other: Ethics and Ontology in Levinas and Heidegger

François Raffoul

Introduction

There is a tendency nowadays, in the wake of a certain reading of Levinas, to oppose ethics to ontology, the thought of the other to the thought of Being. I would like in this paper to question the pertinence of this opposition, the accuracy or the justice of Levinas's critique of Heidegger. Should we accept without question the equivalence that Levinas posits between Being and the Same? Can the question of the other and there-fore—for Levinas—of ethics only be posed "beyond being," beyond ontology? And in that respect, what can the "primacy of ethics over ontology" mean if the thought of Being, as Heidegger explains in the "Letter on Humanism," is an "originary ethics" (*ursprüngliche Ethik*)?[1] What is the relation between Being and the Other? Does fundamental ontology represent the obliteration of ethical concern? Is there a possibility, despite Levinas's claims, of developing an *ontological* sense of ethics and praxis? These are some of the questions that I will pursue here, by focusing on Levinas's interpretation of Heidegger.

The Ethical Trial of Ontology

Ontology as a Thinking of the Same

Levinas's critique of Heidegger begins, as we know, by putting the "primacy of ontology" into question; that is to say, to be precise, the primacy of ontology *over ethics*. At the outset, with Levinas, everything revolves around the meaning to be given to ontology. It is thus important to dwell

on this question for a moment. Levinas's thesis, which appears throughout his work and is introduced very early on, can be summarily presented
as follows. Ontology, the thinking of Being, as it has defined the entirety
of Western philosophy from Parmenides *to Heidegger,* is a thinking of the
Same, a thinking which reduces otherness to the Same by the very power
of its theoretical comprehensiveness. Levinas states: "Theory also means
intelligence—logos of being—that is to say, a manner of approaching the
known being in such a way that its otherness in relation to the knowing
being vanishes."[2] In the traditional philosophical correlation between
Knowledge and Being, knowledge represents, as Levinas explained in the
1982 lecture "Ethics as First Philosophy," "an activity which *appropriates*
and *comprehends* the alterity of the known."[3] Consequently, Western philosophy has most often been an ontology, "*that is to say, a reduction of the
Other to the Same*" (*TeI* 33–34). *Ontology is understood, then, as a reduction of
alterity.* In opposition to the tradition of Western thought, defined as we
just saw, Levinas, as early as 1947 in *Time and the Other,* attempts to go
"beyond the eleatic notion of Being," to overcome ontology, and to move
beyond Being, toward what he calls "the absolute other."[4] The "absolute
other" is for him the other *human* (*l'autre homme*). One should note here
the crucial importance of this movement, the constitutive motif of "evasion beyond Being," in Levinas's thought. From the essay *On Evasion*
(1935) until *Otherwise Than Being* (1974), one finds this motif of a need to
escape, to exit what Levinas calls the suffocating nauseating presence of
being, the *il y a,* the suffocating presence of a Same. One could in fact approach Levinas's thought as a whole from this effort to exit, or go beyond,
and toward an other that does not return to a same, that does not come
back, and in that sense is Absolute.

There would indeed be much to say, or question, concerning this
broad definition of the entire Western tradition as a "thought of the
Same." But what of Heidegger's place in this history? Wasn't he the one
who subjected Western metaphysics to an unprecedented phenomenological destruction? Most important, wasn't he the one who *destroyed* Western ontology by bringing out the difference between Being and beings,
a difference ignored by metaphysics in its enterprise of substantialization
of Being? In short, wasn't it precisely Heidegger who undertook the overcoming or abandonment of "Western onto-theo-logy"?

For Levinas, the answer to these questions is no. Precisely to the contrary—*at least for Levinas*—the phenomenological thought of Heidegger
would in fact be the "imperialist" culmination of the dictatorship of the
Same (*TeI* 35). By positing the anteriority of Being over beings, Heidegger
would have only accentuated the all-encompassing character of Being,
and thereby the reduction of the entity, which is other, to the Sameness of

Being. Levinas's tone in the opening pages of *Totality and Infinity* is quite harsh. For example:

> As a philosophy of *power,* ontology, as first philosophy, which does not put the Same into question, is a philosophy of *injustice.* Heideggerian ontology, which subordinates the relation with the Other to the relation with Being in general . . . leads fatally to . . . *imperialist domination,* to *tyranny.* . . . Being before beings, is . . . a movement within the Same, without regard for any obligation to the Other. (*TeI* 38, emphases mine)

What could be the basis for these virulent charges? The answer to this question can be found in a seminal text of Levinas, the 1951 article "Is Ontology Fundamental?" In this essay, Levinas defines fundamental ontology as "the knowledge of Being *in general.*"[5] This is a first decisive interpretation on Levinas's part, one which will prove crucial to his interpretation. On the basis of this identification of Being with the *generality* of beings, Levinas draws the consequences, writing: "Ontology is the essence of any relation with beings and even any relation within Being. Being is thus the *horizon* of beings and of any relation to beings." Horizon, Levinas continues, plays "a role that is equivalent to that of the *concept* in classical idealism." Being then becomes analogically identified with a concept: "Beings emerge against a background that exceeds them, as the individual cases against the background of the *concept*" (*EN* 12, emphasis mine). This is a second crucial interpretative decision on Levinas's part: Being is understood as *conceptual* generality. One must therefore say that just as individual cases fall under their concept, all beings and relations to beings fall within Being. All relations to beings fall under Being: and in particular relations to the *other* entity fall under Being. But the other entity par excellence is the other person, the "other human." If the relation to beings takes place within the horizon of Being, then the relation to the other person is *included within* Being, that is to say, subjected to Being as a neutral essence. Being as conceptual generality *neutralizes* the alterity of the entity. The other is included in Being. Levinas specifies: "Being-with-one-another—*Miteinandersein*—thus rests for Heidegger on the ontological relation" (*TeI* 17). It is this dependency or subjection that Levinas vehemently rejects: all entities fall within Being, *except for the other.* The other is not a possible case of a relation to entities, escapes the ontological horizon, does not let itself be circumscribed by a thinking of the Same. The relation with the other does not occur against the *background* of the ontological relation. The relation to the other is not ontology: it escapes ontology, it precedes ontology. In fact, Heideggerian ontology cannot do justice to the other because "as soon as I have grasped the other within the opening of Being in general, as an element of the world where I stand, I have apprehended it at the horizon. I have not looked it in the face, I have not encountered its face" (*Tel* 21). The comprehension of Being cannot comprehend the relation to the other, it "cannot *dominate* the relation with the other" (*Tel* 39). One must in fact invert the hierarchy, one must "invert the terms" (*Tel* 38). It is the relation with the entity—with the other—that commands and precedes the relation with Being. And since for Levinas the relation with the other is what rigorously defines "ethics," then we must say that ethics precedes ontology, and not the inverse.

Authenticity as Egoistic Thought

This radical critique of Heideggerian ontology, as a thinking of Being *in general*, is accompanied by a questioning of what Levinas considers to be the *solipsism* of Heidegger's thought. This solipsism would appear in what Heidegger calls the "mineness" (*Jemeinigkeit*) of *Dasein*. Ontology as the thinking of the Same would culminate in a solipsistic egology, in the form of mineness. We could here in passing note a tension, if not a contradiction: for how can one affirm on the one hand, in order to reproach Heidegger, the generality or neutrality of ontology, and on the other hand, speak of the irreducible mineness of that same ontology? However, the contradiction is perhaps only apparent, for it is precisely because ontology is a thinking of the Same, that is a negation of otherness, that it takes the form of an egoistic and solipsistic thought. Here sameness and mineness are one and the same; Levinas writes: "*The Other becomes the same by becoming mine*" (*Tel* 37). In a 1962 lecture to the *Société française de philosophie*, Levinas goes so far as to claim that the "knowing ego is . . . the Same par excellence."[6] We know that for Heidegger, Being is "each time mine" (*je meines*), that "mineness" belongs constitutively to *Dasein*. And we also know that it is Heidegger himself who speaks of an "existential solipsism" in order to characterize the analytic of *Dasein*. Levinas will thus interpret, with some justification it seems, the fundamental character of mineness as the sign of an enclosure upon oneself of a "mine," if not of an ego, as the closure of ontology in an egology that reduces alterity. For if Being is each time delivered over to *Dasein*, such that it takes it on authentically by projecting itself toward death as its most extreme and proper possibility, that would be at the price, it seems, of a radical exclusion of the other. Isn't the other irrelevant in my authentic assumption of death? To be convinced of this, one only needs to read side by side, as it were, the deprecating analyses of being-together in the world, the inauthentic relation of *Dasein* to its being, on the one hand, and on the other hand the interpretation of authentic existence which seems only capable of occurring in a radically solitary *metaphysical* individuation. My death is mine alone, I am alone in being faced irrevocably with death, which is never just death in general and neither that of the others, but above all only mine, "my" death. The verb "to die," which for Heidegger defines the being of human beings, is declined exclusively in the first-person singular. In this primacy of my death, all relations to other *Dasein* fade. Levinas states: "The authenticity of the most authentic potentiality-of-Being dissolves any relation to the other" (*EN* 211). Levinas thus understands mineness as a "primordial contraction of the ego . . . on the basis of a *to-oneself* and a *for-oneself* in their inalienable co-belonging" (*EN* 238). What is important in this reading is Levinas's understanding of mineness as the reduction of the other to the ego, or to the same—the terms are now practically synonymous. This allows Levinas to explicitly associate Heidegger with the modern egoistic and subjectivistic tradition. In "Diachrony and Representation" (1985), he thus writes of "the egology of presence affirmed from Descartes to Husserl, and *even all the way to Heidegger,* where in paragraph 9 of *Being and Time* the 'to be' of Dasein is the source of *Jemeinigkeit* and hence of the ego" (*EN* 167, emphasis mine).

We will have to interrogate this identification of mineness with egohood and the alleged solipsism of mineness. But Levinas follows this interpretation further yet, and on the basis of it, opposes to "solitary mineness" a being-*for*-the-other that would be more authentic. He explains in the lecture "Dying for . . ." that for him it is a matter of a genuine "*alternative* between the identical in its authenticity, in its inalterable *proper* or *mine* of human beings, in its authenticity, independence and freedom, and being as human devotion to the other" (*EN* 208, emphasis mine). To be sure, one could object that for Heidegger *Dasein* is essentially *Mit-sein,* "being-with." "*Dasein* is essentially being-with" (*wesenhaft an ihm selbst mit Sein*), he emphasized, the "with" being an existential and not an accident (*GA* 2:120). But for Levinas it makes no difference. Why? On the one hand, because it is precisely in that same being-with that Dasein "begins to identify with the Being of all others and understand itself from the impersonal anonymity of the They, to lose itself in averageness or to fall under the dictatorship of the They" (*EN* 210); in sum, to be inauthentic. And is it an accident if, when he wants to describe the inauthenticity of *Dasein,* Heidegger does so in an analysis of Being-with? For Levinas it is no accident: it springs from "Heidegger's very philosophical project" (*EN* 211), a project in which "the relation to the other is conditioned by being in the world, and thus by ontology" (*EN* 211). But on the other hand, and more radically, it is the very conception of the other in Heidegger's thought which is problematic: he indeed understands the other as being-with. But this "with," with its meaning of "a reciprocal being with one another" (*TA* 19), is still for Levinas in one sense neutral, a middle term. Being-together "is a collectivity around something in common."[7] Now the relation to the other, that is to say, for Levinas, necessarily, the *absolute* other (escaping absolutely from the Same), is "not a communion." A communion would reproduce a logic of the same, and it is this logic that Heidegger maintained when he treated of the other, or rather we should say, of being-with. Levinas writes: "We hope to show, for our part, that the proposition with [*mit*] is unable and inapt to express the original relation with the other" (*TA* 19). The true relation to the other is not a being-together in a shared world, but lies in an encounter in the "redoubtable face to face of a relation without intermediary and without mediation" (*EE* 162). Here, too, we would have to question: what of this relation to an absolute, "taking place" (but does it only have any *place?*) outside of the world, outside mediation, and as we already know, outside or beyond being? It remains that Levinas, in his effort to give thought to an experience of alterity that cannot be reduced to the Same, rejects the Heideggerian primacy of mineness. It is a matter of leaving "the *Jemeinigkeit* of the *cogito* and its immanence, mistakenly understood for authenticity" (*EN* 229).

Responsibility for the Other

This departure takes place, we know, in the notion of a responsibility *for the other*, which is the experience of "being devoted to the other" in the guise of being a hostage of the other. "It is a relation to the other as other and not a reduction of the other to the same. It is a transcendence" (*EN* 180). Responsibility to the other is opposed to what Levinas calls "the immanence of the *Jemeinigkeit* of Dasein who has to be" (*EN* 180). It is that experience that permits the departure from ontology and from the rule of the Same, it is that experience that gives access to the absolute alterity of the other. Therein lie both the break with ontology and the primacy of ethics. Such a responsibility, Levinas explains in *Humanisme de l'autre homme,* "is prior to Being and to beings, is not said in the ontological categories" (*HH* 91).[8] In *Ethics and Infinity,* Levinas clarifies the meaning of this responsibility. "I speak of responsibility as the essential primary and fundamental structure of subjectivity. For it is in ethical terms that I describe subjectivity. Ethics here does not supplement a prior existential basis, it is in ethics understood as responsibility that subjectivity is constituted." And he adds immediately, as if to avoid a possible misunderstanding: "I understand responsibility to mean responsibility *for the other.*"[9] It is

FRANÇOIS RAFFOUL

equivalent to an originary passivity before the infinite obligation to the other. I am, as Levinas says, "hostage of the other." This being-hostage, this infinite responsibility for the other, testifies, as Derrida shows in his recent book on Levinas, *Adieu to Emmanuel Levinas,* to the radical dispossession or expropriation of the subject in Levinas's work. The subject is no longer a self-identity, an ego, a self-consciousness, even an authentic self or *Dasein;* it is an openness to the other, it is a welcome of the other, in the subjective genitive sense (the other's welcome).[10] We are miles away, it seems, from Heideggerian ontology with its *Dasein* closed on itself in a solitary and solipsistic authenticity . . . And yet, do these characterizations stand the test of the only thing which in the final analysis we can rely on, namely reading the texts themselves?

Being and the Other

We must indeed admit that a number of the analyses offered by Levinas are not devoid of a certain interpretative violence, and perhaps don't do complete justice to the philosophical advances that one can find in Heidegger, in particular his thinking of the other, of responsibility, and of selfhood. And I would like to devote this second part of my paper to taking up a number of these "injustices," not with the intention of simply refuting them, but with the aim of deepening our understanding of the relation between ethics and ontology.

I will therefore take up the main points of the Levinasian critique of Heidegger that I have all too briefly summarized. The first, we remember, characterized ontology as a thinking of the Same. Levinas has a tendency to conflate, if not identify, what he calls "Heideggerian ontology" with classical ontology. Now let us be quite clear: this identification simply *does not hold.* It does not hold, not because ontology in Heidegger's work would differ from traditional ontology, but quite simply because *there is no* Heideggerian ontology: Heidegger's thought of Being is *not* an ontology. Indeed, what is ontology? Ontology is the science of beings as beings; it is therefore the science of what Heidegger calls "beingness" (*Seiendheit*). Now, Heidegger's entire thinking, on the contrary, consists in putting into question the meaning and the truth of *Being* itself, and not simply of beings. This is why, as we know, Heidegger subjected ontology to a radical destruction or deconstruction, and decisively transformed the manner in which the thinking of Being is to be conceived. For to bring out Being *as Being* is to manifest it in its *difference* from beings. It is in this sense that one could say, following Heidegger, that Being is the *Other* of all beings. Now if Being is the *Other* of beings, how then could it still be characterized, as by Levinas, as a universal genre of beings? If that were the case, Being would once again be conflated with the whole of entities, with beingness. Being is thus not the Same in the sense of the universal concept of beings. In fact, one only needs to open the first page of *Being and Time* in order to realize this.

In that book Heidegger reviews three traditional interpretations of the concept of Being. The first states that Being is "the most universal concept" (*GA* 2:3). And admittedly Being possesses some sort of universality, since it determines *all* beings, everything that is: Being is that by which a being (entity) is a being. Yet Heidegger strongly insists on the fact that this universality of Being is not generic. He writes: "But the 'universality' of Being is not that of a *genre*" (ibid.). Indeed, if that was the case, it would mean that Being is the generalized abstraction of beings. Now this is not possible, since beings suppose Being as a true a priori. This is why Being cannot be understood as a genre of beings. So when Levinas interprets fundamental ontology as "knowledge of Being *in general*" (*EN* 12, my emphasis), and when he understands that *in general* as a unifying concept of beings, as a conceptual generality, he is in defiance of both *the spirit and the letter* of Heidegger's thinking with respect to the meaning of Being. The meaning of Being, for Heidegger, is not to be the genre of beings, but the *openness* of beings, that is to say, the event of presence in which beings come forth. What does this mean? Quite simply, that Being is the exposure and the disclosure of entities as a whole, *the disclosure of beings and nothing more.* It is not situated above or below, it doesn't unify anything, it is only the *es gibt* (there is) of entities. This is why the entity which possesses the meaning of Being, namely *Dasein,* is essentially characterized by Heidegger as a disclosure of Being unveiling the whole of what is. Heidegger often specifies this exposure to all things in the following manner: *Dasein* is disclosed (exposed) to intraworldly entities, it is exposed to other *Dasein;* it is exposed, finally, to the entity that it itself is. As we can see, the very concept of *Dasein* includes a primordial relation to the other: to the other entity, to the other *Dasein,* and to oneself *as an other.* How, then, can Being be opposed to the other? Wouldn't Being rather be the very disclosure of alterity, that is, of a *relation to* an alterity? Isn't Being thought in Heidegger as transcendence, on the basis of the ek-static, that is to say, as a boundless expropriating exposure to the other? On this account, what can it mean to go beyond Being, if Being *is* already the beyond?

To this extent, Levinas is wrong to claim that for Heidegger the other is only a "possible case" of the relation to entities, that "Being with-one-another—*Miteinandersein*—depends . . . on the ontological relation" (*TI* 17). First, because the relation to entities depends on *nothing*, as Being is not the ground of entities. Being gives itself on the same level as entities, and does not give anything other than the entity itself. But more precisely here, because Being is from the outset defined as a relation to an alterity, and from the outset a *being-with, Sein* is constitutively *Mit-Sein*. The "with" is coextensive with Being. Jean-Luc Nancy emphasizes this point in *Being Singular Plural* by insisting on the indissociability of Being and the other. He writes, in opposition to Levinas: "But what he understands as 'otherwise than Being' is to be understood as what is 'most proper to Being,' precisely because *it is a matter of thinking being-with rather than the opposition between the other and Being*" (ESP 52n1, my emphasis).[11] The other, far from being opposed to Being, becomes "the very problem of Being," "*the most proper problem of Being*" (ESP 52n1, my emphasis).

In this regard, we must return to the second axis of the Levinasian critique, that which pertains to the "mineness" of *Dasein*. Levinas understood this as a solipsistic closure on the self. But what is at stake in the theme of mineness? It is precisely a question of showing that Being is not a substance or an essence, but that it "is" each time at issue in the entity that I am, that it is a "task of Being." The intent is thus from the outset a departure from the subjectivist tradition: mineness is determined as early as *Being and Time* on the basis of Being itself and no longer as a form of the ego.[12] One need only read the first lines of paragraph 9 of *Being and Time*. After having posited that the Being of entity that we are is each time mine, Heidegger explains, "it is Being that, for that very entity, is always at issue" (*Das Sein ist es, darum es diesem Seienden je selbst geht; GA* 2:41). Being mine means then Being itself, in the sense that it is each time at issue in the entity that I am. Mineness is that event of Being that I have to be authentically. Mineness is not ontical individuality, worldless egohood, or a self-consciousness closed on its *cogitationes*, but is to be understood in its meaning of Being, that is, as the meaning of Being. Since *Dasein* is understood as an openness to the other entity (being-in-the-world, Being-with-others), its individuation cannot be understood to mean the exclusion of the other. The so-called "existential solipsism" does not indicate *Dasein*'s closure on itself, but designates instead the solitude, isolation, or individuation of the *existent*. Now the existent is defined by the *openness* to beings. It is necessary, then, to think of the individuation of the self and the openness to the other being—and to the other—*at the same time*. Existential solipsism posits that *Dasein*, in its Being-singular and in this very solitude, is Being-with. It is as that singular entity that I am with the other. Heidegger writes: "Being-together is part of the essence of human existence, that is to say *of an always singular entity*" (*GA* 29/30:301). It is as if it was in the very separation of metaphysical solitude that the relation to others opens.

Dying For . . .

This is the point, which Levinas completely fails to take into account, of Heidegger's thinking of death, of being-toward-death. We remember that Levinas opposed to the dying for oneself in Heidegger, a dying for the other that would be more primordial. In *Ethics and Infinity* he writes: "The fundamental relation of Being, in Heidegger, is not the relation with the other, but with death, where everything inauthentic in the relation with the other is denounced, since one dies alone" (*EI* 51). Levinas challenges that privilege of dying for oneself in Heidegger over the concern for the other, and he attempts to imagine a dying of the other that could "concern me before and more that my own death" (*EN* 240). In the lecture "Dying for . . . ," he also appeals to a sense of sacrifice which "would not fall within the opposition between the authentic and inauthentic," and where "the death of the other preoccupies human Dasein before its own death" and which, once again, would indicate "a beyond ontology" (*EN* 214). As Levinas stated in *God, Death and Time* (lecture of January 9, 1976): "The death of the other: therein lies the first death" (ibid 48).[13] Here again one could express a certain befuddlement, for to only be able to sacrifice myself for the other, to die for the other, I must already be able to die, *myself.* Death must already be, as Heidegger defines it, a possibility of *my* Being. Furthermore, dying *for* the other does not mean dying *in its place,* if one understands this expression to mean "to die the other's death." I cannot take away the other's death, at most I can just delay it . . . "No one can take the other's dying" (*GA* 2:240), writes Heidegger. In the sacrifice, *I* die *for* the other but I do not die *in place* of the other. Death only takes place in the first person singular: "death" "in general" does not exist: there is only *my* death. It is in this sense that death is the supreme principle of individuation for Heidegger. He writes: "death, in so far as it 'is,' is each time essentially mine" (*GA* 2:240). All shared death in a common fate, or all death for the other, in sacrifice, already supposes the unsubstitutable "mineness" of my death. Jacques Derrida stresses this in *The Gift of Death*: "Giving one's life *for* the other, dying *for* the other, Heidegger insists, does not mean dying in the place of the other. On the contrary, it is only to the extent that dying—insofar as it 'is'—remains mine, that I can die for another or *give* my life to the other. There is no gift of self, it cannot be thought of, except in terms of this irreplaceability."[14]

To avoid this opposition between a dying for oneself and a dying for the other, one could follow here the recent work of the young French phenomenologist Claude Romano, and advance the notion of a *primordial mourning* in which the death of others concerns me to the extent that I exist as a self-for-the-other. The loss or death of the other is in that sense my loss, and my own death. Mourning is the "dying to the other undergone by those who remain," and such a dying to the one who is dead is essentially a dying to oneself.[15] With the death of others, I die too. In that sense, the dying to oneself is indissociable from the dying of others: what dies for me in the death of others is my very self-for-the-other. This last representation would require thinking the singular self as constituted by its being-with. One thinks here of Nancy's remarks on death in its relation to being-with. "Death," he wrote in *The Inoperative Community*, "is indissociable from community, for it is through death that the community reveals itself" (14).[16] Death essentially exposes the with of existence. One always dies *to,* to the world, to life, to others. In fact, still drawing the consequences from Heidegger's claim according to which Being-with belongs to *Dasein,* and following Nancy's gesture of understanding the "with" as what is most proper to Being, death—as the most proper possibility of existence—should be taken "as a possibility of the with and as the with" (*ESP* 114). It follows that nobody ever dies "alone," because "we are born and we die to one another" (*ESP* 113), because death is "my" possibility to the extent that "this mineness is delivered over to the singular plural of the always-other-mineness" (*ESP* 114–15). Nancy suggested in *The Inoperative Community* that "Dasein's 'being-toward-death' was never radically implicated in being-with- in *Mitsein,*" and that *"it is this implication that remains to be thought."*[17]

But doesn't this precisely confirm Levinas's concern and diagnosis, namely, that the thinking of Being is a solipsistic thinking which negates the other, that is, a thinking of the Same? And doesn't Heidegger himself explain that in the authentic relation to my death, "all relations to other Dasein are dissolved" (*GA* 2:250)? Things are in fact more complex. For it is not so much the relation to the other *as other* that is dissolved in the authentic assumption of my death, but a certain mode of relation to the other, that of substitution, which is an *inauthentic* mode of being with others. It is in opposition to this model of substitution—"substitution," let us say in passing, is the fundamental word used by Levinas in *Otherwise Than Being, or Beyond Essence* (1974) to designate the relation of the I to the other—that Heidegger explains that authentic Being-with cannot be understood on the basis of an identification between the self and others in a common being. One must think Being-together in a way that accommodates the fundamental solitude and singularity of existence. In this sense it is death, insofar as it is always my death, insofar as it marks the interruption or absence of any relation to the other (*unbezüglichkeit*) by which the singularity of *Dasein* is revealed, which will prove paradoxically to be the very basis of any relation to the other. Everything happens as if it was on the basis of a certain *interruption* of being-in-common that the other can give itself *as other.* The other gives itself here on the basis of the unique, singular, non-substitutable character of *Dasein;* the other, the very experience of otherness, gives itself on the basis of what cannot be shared. The isolation (*Vereinzelung*) of *Dasein* is granted by death insofar as it can only be *my* death. However, it is precisely this interruption of any relation which is that by which all relation can be opened. The relation to the other opens in the relation to death. Without this interruption it is the dictatorship of the Same. Hence, despite what Levinas maintains (namely, that the thinking of death in Heidegger is extreme individualism and solipsism, that it excludes the possibility of an authentic opening to the other), we must on the contrary recognize the constitutive character of Being-toward-death for Being-with. For authentic Being-toward-death does not dissolve being-with but only the possibility of substitution, which, we must insist, is an *inauthentic* mode of Being-with. In its singularity and in this very solitude, *Dasein* is open to others. It is as this singular entity that I am with, and for the other.

Conclusion

It would be appropriate at this stage to inquire about the reasons for this *differend* between Levinas and Heidegger, a task which obviously is beyond us in these pages. I will simply conclude by suggesting what in my view might be some of the underlying reasons for such a situation. It may reside in part in the presence in Levinas's work of a number of implicit assumptions that secretly govern his thought. One, as we already saw, lies in the identification of Being with the Same, ontology with knowledge of beings in general, an identification that I have tried to qualify. The other, on which I will conclude, has to do with the motif of subjectivity as it operates in Levinas's approach.

As we know, with Heidegger the question of the other is not raised in an egological or anthropological frame. It is approached ontologically through and through. It can only take the form of a question on the *Being* of the other, on *Being-other* as such. This is why the other in Heidegger's work will never appear in the form of what is other for the ego. *Here the issue is with the Being of the other, not with the other to the ego.* Whereas for Heidegger the motif of subjectivity is phenomenologically destroyed, Levinas himself states in *Totality and Infinity* that this work is "a defense of subjectivity" (*TeI* 11), one which takes the paradoxical form of a subjection of the subject to the other. But precisely *as* destituted, expropriated, the subject is maintained and becomes the "elected one," who, writes Levinas in *Of God Who Comes to Mind,* is the true *sub-jectum:* "The ego is no longer taken as a particular case of the Ego in general, it is the unique point which supports the universe ['supports' in both senses of bearing the unbearable and supporting it]" (135).[18] Ultimately, this is perhaps still the Cartesian-Husserlian point of departure taken by Levinas. Being is put in brackets, "reduced" (since ontology represents the thinking of the Same), so that the analysis can begin with the I, with the subject (hence the "defense" of subjectivity). On the basis of this point of departure, Levinas *then* attempts to exceed the subject toward its outside, to "subject" the subject to the other. We know that Levinas understands the other as *exteriority.* Exteriority to what, if not, of course, to the ego, the self-enclosed ego of the Cartesian tradition? It is striking in this respect to note that Levinas's constant reference throughout his work to designate the irruption or emergence of the other in its authentic sense is, of all possible examples, Descartes' idea of the infinite in the Third Meditation, that is, a context of absolute solipsism for the *ego cogito.* My hypothesis is that Levinas remains dependent on egological thinking, that he merely *reverses* it. Levinas constantly describes his thought as a reversal of the tradition of willful intentionality. In a particularly revealing passage of *Otherwise Than Being,* for example, Levinas writes that the responsibility for the other "*goes against the grain* of intentionality and the will" (*AE* 221). This is, we know, Ricoeur's point: Levinas's thought, he explains, is a *reactive* thought, a thought "of rupture," of "excess," of "hyperbole," a kind of symmetrical reversal of the Cartesian and Husserlian tradition in philosophy, opposing it but never really questioning its foundations.[19] For it is one thing to reverse this tradition, and quite another to no longer use it as a point of departure: precisely by beginning no longer from the ego *but from Dasein, that is, from Being as Being-with.* Rather than begin from the ego, in order to then attempt to leave it by appealing to the only concept that remains, namely, that of exteriority, of the outside, it would be a question, then, not of opposing Being and the Other, ethics to ontology, but of thinking the ethical resources of ontology, and the ontological senses of ethics. A question, then, of thinking the Other *as the most proper problem of being.*

Notes

1. I wish to thank David Pettigrew for translating an earlier version of this paper into English. Martin Heidegger, *Wegmarken,* in *Gesamtausgabe,* vol. 9 (Frankfurt am Main: Klostermann, 1976), 353. English translation in Martin Heidegger,

Basic Writings, ed. D. F. Krell (New York: Harper and Row, 1977), 235. *Gesamtausgabe* hereafter cited as *GA.*

2. Emmanuel Levinas, *Totalité et infini* (Paris: Livre de Poche, 1994), 32. Hereafter cited in the text as *TeI.* All translations of Levinas are my own.

3. Emmanuel Levinas, *Éthique comme philosophie première* (Paris: Payot et Rivages, 1998), p.69, my translation.

4. Emmanuel Levinas, *Le temps et l'autre* (Paris: Presses Universitaires de France, 1983), 88. Hereafter cited in the text as *TA.*

5. Emmanuel Levinas, "L'ontologie est-elle fondamentale?" in *Entre nous: Essais sur le penser-à-l'autre* (Paris: Livre de Poche, 1993), 12, my emphasis. Hereafter cited in the text as *EN.*

6. Emmanuel Levinas, *Liberté et commandement (Fata Morgana, 1994), p. 61.*

7. Emmanuel Levinas, *De l'existence à l'existant* (Paris: Vrin, 1993), 162. Hereafter cited in the text as *EE.*

8. Emmanuel Levinas, *Humanisme de l'autre homme* (Paris: Livre de Poche, 1987), p. 91.

9. Emmanuel Levinas, *Ethique et infini* (Paris: Livre de Poche, 1996), 91. Hereafter cited in the text as *EI.*

10. Jacques Derrida. *Adieu à Emmanuel Levinas* (Paris: Galilée, 1997), 51. On this point, see my "The Subject of the Welcome," *Symposium* 2, no. 2 (1988): 211–22.

11. Jean-Luc Nancy, *Being Singular Plural* (Stanford, CA: Stanford University Press, 2000), p.199, note 37, translation modified. Hereafter cited as ESP.

12. On this point, see my *Heidegger and the Subject* (Amherst: Prometheus Books, 1999).

13. Emmanuel Levinas, *God, Death, and Time* (Stanford, CA: Stanford University Press, 2000), p.43.

14. Jacques Derrida, *The Gift of Death,* trans. David Willis (Chicago: University of Chicago Press, 1995), 42.

15. Claude Romano, *L'événement et le monde* (Paris: Presses Universitaires de France, 1998), 156–58.

16. Jean-Luc Nancy, *The Inoperative Community* (Minneapolis, MN: University of Minnesota Press, 1991), p.14.

17. Nancy, *Inoperative Community,* 14.

18. Emmanuel Levinas, *De Dieu qui vient à l'idée* (Paris: Vrin, 1982), p. 135.

19. Paul Ricoeur, *Oneself as Another* (Chicago: University of Chicago Press, 1992).

Some Questions for My Levinasian Friends

David Wood

Those of us disappointed with Levinas's position on animals might conclude in a moment of exasperation that it shows clearly that ethics is *not* first philosophy for Levinas; that what comes first is a commitment to other humans, especially those in need, and that this discrimination is framed in terms that are philosophically unremarkable—the capacity to speak, for example. We might add that his view of the feminine makes it equally clear that Levinas's ethics disguises a further quite specific ontological commitment, even virility. We might conclude that for all Levinas's opposition of ethics to "ontology," that his ethical opening precisely rests on an ontology.

I want to pursue precisely this thought, suggesting that (1) Levinas's ethics rests on an ontology, one which is importantly flawed; (2) his relation to Heidegger is at least symptomatic of his blindness to his own ontological commitments; (3) if the climate of Levinas's thought is marked by the asymmetry of the ethical relation, we need to move on; and (4) we need to open ourselves to an other event, one in which the event of otherness explodes in many directions.

Levinas writes that I am infinitely obliged, I more than others, that I am even responsible for the other's responsibility. And that the face of the other is the command "Don't kill me." This seems like a specific formulation of the ethical. And it is surely essential to ask whether there is concealed in these formulations a response to the particular circumstances of imprisonment, degradation, and genocide.[1]

What if the very formulation of the ethical provided by Levinas, and the implicit proposal that vigilance is the only answer, are as much symptoms of the problem as responses to it? In particular, what if the hyperbole in Levinas's formulations were a sign of the impotence of the stance rather than of its significance?

Levinas's formulation of ethics as first philosophy seems, in part, to rest on his reading of Heidegger. I would not be the first to wonder whether his readings of Heidegger can be seriously defended. But I would like to ask a more complex question: whether his opposition to Heidegger, and the formulation he gives of his own position, would not profit from a better understanding of what is involved in reading another philosopher, an issue on which Heidegger himself offers valuable guidance. This has consequences on two levels: by supplying a better model of how to read than Levinas perhaps practices, but also by opening up, through reflection on that relationship, an ethical dimension that may have escaped Levinas.

In *What Is Called Thinking?* Heidegger distinguishes between two ways of reading another thinker: going counter to them (through critique, polemic), and "going to their encounter."[2] What does it mean to go to the other's encounter? I understand this to mean entering, or trying to approach, the space of the other's relation to alterity. This requires a certain generosity, and not just for the other's sake, but for the sake of the encounter itself, the space into which one has entered. By generosity I mean foregoing the temptation to oppositional thinking, trying to see where the other person may have already addressed the question you are raising, not just to do justice to him, but also to thinking itself, and to the very idea of respect.

Let me take just one example to begin with. Levinas writes: "What seems to have escaped Heidegger—if it is true that in these matters something might have escaped Heidegger—is that prior to being a system of tools, the world is an ensemble of nourishments."[3] Levinas presents this as an objection to Heidegger's totality system (almost as Kierkegaard would have referred to Hegel). There are three responses to be made to this. First, it would be interesting to ask whether Heidegger had simply failed to grasp that the world was an ensemble of nourishments, or had perhaps recognized the significance of this in a different way. Second, it is important to grasp the status of Heidegger's account of the "world of tools" in *Being and Time*, and as it takes its place in his subsequent path of thinking. Third, we might want to ask whether understanding the world as an ensemble of nourishments can really be sustained in the way Levinas suggests.

In *What Is Called Thinking?* it is precisely through the theme of nourishment that Heidegger attempts to expand and displace Descartes' image of the "tree of knowledge" with a detailed focus on the question of the relation between the roots and the soil. Indeed, one could say that the entire language of the "gift" as Heidegger introduces it is a recognition of the being itself as nourishment. Second, while there is no doubt that in

Being and Time the world is first described as a referential complex of in-strumentalities, Heidegger has a very specific target here—that of dis-placing the Cartesian sense of the world as a kind of "extended stuff." For that he needs to be able to demonstrate our participation in a space which has a kind of non-constructed wholeness. For this our instrumentally in-terconnected world, in which we engage whenever we pick up a pen to write, without explicitly positing that world, works very well. Elsewhere in *Being and Time,* Heidegger speaks of the world of public interpretation, the ways in which historical triumphs of world understanding get threat-ened and lost, and so on. Here, at least, Levinas seems to be siding with the pragmatist reading of Heidegger, losing sight of the specific strategic significance of those formulations. In subsequent writings, Heidegger will discuss the ways in which art and poetry open worlds, and how technology enframes it. The world could not, in an important sense, be an ensemble of nourishments, because an ensemble is not a world. Third, and last, there is something strangely one-sided about the very idea of nourish-ment. We may imagine everywhere mothers feeding their children, where nourishment is an act of love. But the truth of the matter is otherwise. The world of nourishment, if we want to call it that, is just as much the world of death and violence, the jungle, the Discovery Channel (mostly sharks, lions, and packs of hyenas), and the meat industry, which in the United States alone accounts for hundreds of millions of animals fattened (nour-ished) for food, then killed and eaten every year.[4] Here, perhaps, we find a "world of nourishment." If Levinas objects to the idea that Heidegger is talking about nourishment when he speaks of the gift, because it is, what, too ontological, let us talk ontically. Not only do we find that nourishment is not neutral, but it has victims. And for all its own limitations, we should look again at Derrida's interview with Jean-Luc Nancy, "Eating Well," where he introduces the idea of carnophallogocentrism.[5] My nourish-ment may be the other's death (as, to be fair, Levinas acknowledges when he speaks of Nicaraguan coffee). To the extent that nourishment is a sys-tem, or a world, and even if we prefer to think of more primitive forms of rural agriculture—grazing, farming crops—we are tied up with the very world of tools (from plows to tractors) that Levinas wants to make sec-ondary.

Anyway, when Levinas says that Heidegger's position is a philosophy of being, and contrasts this with a search for the good beyond being (and having praised *Being and Time* for its "intellectual vigor, and . . . steadfast-ness"), Levinas asks nonetheless, "Can we be assured, however, that there was never any echo of evil in it?" He goes on to speak of the diabolical as "endowed with intelligence." Such a question, I have to say, betrays the logic of the Inquisition and worse. "Can we be assured that . . . never . . ."

Of course not! But the charge works by insinuation. It is not without a certain sense of strong irony too, when we think that this distinction—between mere intelligence and something deeper or more responsible—is one deployed regularly by both Hegel and Heidegger.

Levinas claims Heidegger's is an ontology of Being. But how does this correspond to what Heidegger himself thinks he's doing? In *Being and Time* Heidegger says he is trying to ask the question of the meaning of Being. Why? Because he claims we have lost contact with the question in the very process of trying to come to terms with Being. He describes metaphysics as modeled, unhelpfully and misleadingly, on the particular kind of beings we come across in the world. And Heidegger believes we can come to some understanding of the meaning of Being by opening up the horizon of time. It is by this move, as I see it, that Heidegger claims precisely *not* to be just offering a philosophy of Being in the traditional metaphysical fashion. So, I suggest, the question of whether Heidegger's philosophy of Being is susceptible to Levinas's charge will depend on what Heidegger can eventually do with the horizon of time and temporality.

Perhaps the salient question raised by Heidegger's account of time in *Being and Time* is the significance of being-toward-death. Why is this such a big issue? Because here each man faces his mortal condition and has the possibility of realizing himself. What is wrong with genocide? With gas chambers? With war? We are horrified that our fellow human beings can engage in these practices. But what is it that horrifies us? The desensitized camp guards. The technological rationality with which the rounding up and killing took place. It is not just the outcome, the numbers of dead, the selection of the Jews and other marginal groups. We are horrified at the thought that the perpetrators might not be so different from us, as we too have largely embraced lives of limited ambition within desensitizing techno-instrumental complexes. But we must not lose sight of the fact that these innocent people were degraded, imprisoned, worked to death, tortured and killed. The many layers of evil here—and the point, I take it, of Heidegger's unhappy comparison with factory farms—center on the fact that humans are *not* just animals, but are here being treated in the way we do treat animals. Now I believe it is also a crime to treat animals in this way.[6] But the particular reason it is evil to treat humans like this has to do with the kinds of lives it is taking away. It is precisely because we are not just biologically alive, but place a value on our own lives, and that we typically do value life, liberty, and the pursuit of happiness, which makes mass killing so horrific. What was cut short was in each case human hope and fulfillment. (In this sense, being stripped of rights, jobs, property, is a full part of this terrible process.) The Other, whom we fear for, whom we protect, whom we may harm, is always a being capable of pain and suffering, of joy, and of a certain fulfillment. Each time we leave something off the list, we do violence to the Other. If, as with Mill, we think of the other simply in terms of the capacity for pleasure and pain, we do violence to them at the very point at which we seem to take account of them. How we understand the other is essential to our capacity to honor, respect, and protect them. When Descartes, after la Mettrie, compares the cry of a cat to the squeak of a carriage wheel, the only reason not to step on its tail would be to protect our ears from sharp sounds. The implication of all this, of course, is that we cannot separate ontology from ethics. If so, ethics cannot be first philosophy. Or if it were, ontology would have to be equiprimordial.

Suppose someone says to me that each I is infinitely obliged to the other. I reply that I agree, which is why I leave the bats undisturbed in my roof, why we should ban hunting, why I gently remove the daddy longlegs from the bathtub, and why stands of ancient oaks should be preserved.[7] I am then corrected, and I am told that it is only humans that infinitely oblige me. If I then scratch my head, I may be told that of course I can extend this sense of obligation to nonhumans if I wish. But it would be an analogy. Which puzzles me, because I thought part of the point of the account of the face-to-face relation was to circumvent the analogical transfer Husserl needed in the Fifth of his *Cartesian Meditations*.[8] How strange that it should turn up again a little further down the line. Now, of course, we can give an *account* of why the other is first and foremost human. That's what metaphysical principles are for. We no longer say that man is rational. Somehow that doesn't seem so convincing. Now we say that the human other can speak. Or that the human other is aware of his mortality. Or belongs to a species, many members of which can speak or "die" in the full sense.[9] But it is hard not to conclude that what all this comes down to is "beings like us." That would not make Levinas's position ontological in any explicit sense. But it does suggest that it operates on implicit humanistic premises, premises from which Buddhism's generalized respect for sentience, for example, seems free. And the strangest thing is that the principle of my fundamental exposure to the other is precisely the kind of principle that we need in order to breach the repeated roadblocks in the way of our respecting the various modes of otherness of the other. What does this tell us about the significance of ontology for ethics? I am tempted to say that ontology without ethics is empty, and ethics without ontology is blind. I suspect that it could be shown that ontology is not possible without at least such protoethical concepts as openness, relation, and other. But just having an ontology does not alleviate blindness. We need to recognize the ways in which one's ontological commitments and prejudices can inform the kind of respect and response proper to different

kinds of beings, and, where missing, can limit one's capacity for responsiveness.

And what is true of the various species of otherness is quite as much
true of oneself. My capacity for response to the other's needs will depend
to a considerable extent on the health and expansiveness of my understanding of myself, and what it is to be human. It has been said that Levinas's aversion to psychoanalysis is based on the fear that a divided self
would have alibis for non-responsiveness. Perhaps too, it might under-
mine the distinctively ethical character of any self-constitutive opening to
the other. Yet again, it might cast a troubling light on the images of height,
command, face, and obligation with which my relation to the other is
articulated. And finally, it might be thought that psychoanalysis is to be
thought of as a moment of self-absorption, deflecting us from our primary
obligation to the other. But surely a better response would be this: my
obligation to the other is inseparable from my acquiring the insight (and
even knowledge) that would enable me to reach out and help the other.
Ethical commitment is no substitute for medical training when you're
faced with a road accident victim. And it is essential to have grasped some
of the complexities (projection, identification, etc.) involved in therapeutic assistance to the other. Now these claims might be thought to be
uncontentious. But if they entail that the quality of my response, even my
capacity to respond at all to the other, may depend on the way I understand and relate to myself, and on my sense of what it is to be human (or,
more complicatedly, what it might be like to imagine being a horse, or
a herring, or to recognize important limits to my imagination in these
cases), then ontology is central to ethics. When Heidegger distinguishes
between that mode of concern that involves "leaping in" and taking over
the other's project, and "leaping ahead of" the other, the key to the second response being superior is that it addresses the other in their freedom.[10] And that is an ontological discrimination. A common everyday example of this, one which touches again on the problematic question of
nourishment, is from Mao: that if you give a man a fish you feed him for a
day, but if you teach him to fish, he will feed himself forever. These may
just seem like two practical options. But they can be seen to address the
other in qualitatively different ways. In the first, the other is a passive victim in immediate need. In the second, the other is acknowledged as a
being with powers that can be cultivated and encouraged. If this distinction is indeed ontological, then it might seem from Levinas's examples
that he made quite distinctive ontological choices in this area too. And the
apparent opposition to ontology would seem to disguise this.

It may be that I am oversimplifying the purported relation between
ethics and ontology. Perhaps Levinas should be read not as claiming that

DAVID WOOD

ethics is free from ontology, but that it somehow supersedes it. This would involve reading his account of my solitude, my suffering, my recognition of my mortality as making possible an opening onto the other (or the Other) which would transcend any such ontological determinations. I don't know that he can be read in this way, but it would surely not work. Because the motivation and formulation of this ethical opening rest on the ontological formulations that it then supersedes. If we were to contest those formulations, the sense of and the incentive for such an opening would disappear.

Another approach would be to argue that ontology means something rather special to Levinas—the philosophy of light, or the reducibility of being to knowledge, the triumph of a certain positivity. But on this reading, Heidegger would not be doing ontology, and Levinas would have to formulate his position differently, and would have to engage in dialogue about the ontological grounds of ethics. I do not see him willing to do this.

Let us take one or two examples. In the formulations of the 1940s, in *Time and the Other,* and in *Existence and Existents, Levinas begins with the relation between a solitary existent and being, he begins with solitude, and witnesses the dawning of a consciousness that tears itself away from the vigilance of the il y a.*[11] In *Time and the Other,* this will start him on the long march through the experience of suffering, death, otherness, the other person, eros, and fecundity. But these "primal scene" stories somehow do not have the allure they once did. It has seemed to many that these stories are little more than retrospective reconstructions whose artificiality is testified to by the kind of language used in their formulation, language which knows too much, which has already been to the end of the trail and come back to guide the way. The child's experience of solitude, for example, is unthinkable without it being the experience of the absence of its parents. And I for one would need convincing that Levinas does not betray more of his hand than he might have intended, when he compares my already being hollowed out by my obligation to the other, to Descartes' sense of the presence of God in me in the shape of the idea of perfection. The question opened up for me by such a Cartesian filiation can best be phrased along Heideggerian lines: if the Cartesian conception of the subject has indeed inherited the medieval conception of substance—namely, something which needs nothing else in order to be itself—do we not have a most powerful ontological prejudice right at the heart of Levinas's thought? God would be the wholly independent substance, and man would be a dependent substance, having no essential relations to other men, but an essential dependence on God. What Levinas helps us navigate, in effect, is his transposition of this relation to God onto my relation to the other. If this reading were correct, however, it would not just make the ethical bound up with ontology. The ethical relation would be an essentially ontological one, indeed onto-theological, as Heidegger would put it.

Now there is a certain genius in setting oneself the task of thinking God in and as the relation to the other. Without some such immanence, theology becomes a branch of stargazing. But two further questions are raised by Levinas's version of this move: first, the sense that this relation to the other is essentially a relation to the other human; and second, that it is essentially characterized by an infinite *obligation,* that I am responsible, more than others, and even for everyone else's responsibility, that the other addresses me from a height, with "a commandment which comes from one knows not where," etc. (*TO* 136). It is hard not to conclude that in both of these dimensions, Levinas leaves his always problematic phenomenology behind, and follows the lines already laid out by the Judaic or Judeo-Christian tradition. The task that he sets himself, then, would be that of transferring the properties of my relation to God understood within that tradition back onto my relation to man. Of course, if we thought, like Feuerbach for example, that God had originally been created in the image of man, then we might expect this humanistic reclamation to proceed smoothly. I am indeed tempted by a quasi-Feuerbachian story here. But the question it (helpfully) raises for us is whether the characteristics of God were not in fact *generated* by his original alienation from the interhuman space, and yet others subsequently acquired in exile. As I see it, these kinds of questions are hard to avoid when we struggle to make sense of what Levinas says about my relation to the other. For example, we can see "height" as a marker of a kind of relationship beyond mundane everyday human activity, reflecting both the relative position of the sun and the sky, and also of a parent to a child. But the idea that the other person addresses me from a "height"? Is it not possible that the theological transfer of epithets is taking place too swiftly? And the "commandment that comes from one knows not where"? This is surely a piece of the Old Testament looking for somewhere new to land, once it has heard that "the moral law within" is wearing thin.

I pursued this issue out of a conviction that Levinas's reference to Descartes told us all too much about his ontological commitments. I will shortly spell out what I think are the real dangers of the hidden ontological commitments Levinas does have. But before then, I would like to draw attention to another dimension of his fundamental solipsism. This time, the reference would be back to Hobbes rather than Descartes, although in the place I am referring to (his "Dialogue" with Richard Kearney), Levinas alludes to Spinoza, Pascal, Darwin, and Freud.[12] Levinas asserts:

DAVID WOOD

"Ethics is, therefore, *against nature* because it forbids the murderousness of my natural will to put my own existence first."[13] This is both astonishing and yet not astonishing. It is astonishing in that it reveals in the starkest terms Levinas's commitment to a particular view of the state of nature, and even a particular way of understanding that view. And here, I suggest, Levinas's relation to social Darwinism is most unfortunate—that he treats it as articulating in a developed form the biblical truth of the story of Cain and Abel, that he takes it to be the truth, but not the whole truth. And yet it is not astonishing, because it makes so much more sense of his general position. But what if his ethical position was not so much a vital corrective to our natural murderousness, but a supplement to a particular, strongly contested view of human nature with its own history, its own ideological background, etc. I would refer again to Robert Bernasconi's reference to Marx, comparing social Darwinism to the structure of bourgeois society in nineteenth-century England.[14] And if we reject this account of the state of nature, doesn't the appeal of Levinas's ethical philosophy wane too? I cannot here mount a full-scale critique of this account of the state of nature, but I would make four comments here:

1. There are plenty of studies that suggest that even in the animal world, individual survival is not an overriding instinct.

2. The same is true of human beings. One only has to think of the many examples of heroism and altruism, in which people sacrifice their lives for others and for ideas they care about. Even Nietzsche's account of the will-to-power, which Levinas would not approve of, is a critique of the will to exist.

3. It is not hard to argue that much human violence is not the eruption of some natural condition, but the developed response to particular social conditions, of threat, fear, scarcity, and so on.

4. Even if we were to accept the idea of a primitive "natural will to put my own existence first," it is an extraordinary thing to call this "murderous." This would make no distinction between defending one's family against Charles Manson and being a serial killer oneself.

Levinas's view of human nature as "naturally murderous" is perhaps understandable, even "natural" given what he went through, what he suffered, what he saw. But the fact that other humans who may seem so normal in other ways can do unbelievably horrific things is not an argument for man's naturally murderous condition. Indeed, the many ways in which what has too often happened this century has gone *beyond* murder (extermination, torture, psychological brutality and traumatization, etc.) is strangely further evidence for the thought that we are not dealing with some deep facet of human nature but with social pathology.

What alternative account could be given of the human propensity to violence?

I suggest that it would be a considerable shift in our thinking if we began from the thought that the capacity for the worst violence, the transformation of multicultural toleration into ethnic cleansing, the willingness when provoked to kill, either in defense or in preemptive defense called aggression, is, at least in many cases, the predictable outcome of people finding themselves in or believing themselves to be in a desperate situation. If this is so, it suggests a different line of remedies. Allow me to present an analogy.

In England, most Victorian houses are plagued by the actuality or the reality of dry rot, a particularly vigorous fungus that turns healthy structural timber into dry frangible cubes. It thrives wherever there is wood in a house combined with a source of water, or even dampness. Chemical companies mushroomed in the 1970s that would spray, inject, and otherwise poison your house to kill off this fungus. In fact this fungus is always present, its spores are airborne, and it is impossible to eradicate it. One all-too-honest contractor told me that you can, however, completely eradicate the development of dry rot just by preventing any contact of any wood with any source of damp. What if violence were often to be understood in the same way?

To describe a response to extreme conditions as predictable is not to condone it. But there are and always have been conditions under which humans do not act or feel in ways that reflect anything we commonly value. Wild animals in traps will chew off their legs to escape. Humans in conditions of extreme hunger turn cannibalistic, even if it is only to eat the dead flesh of their companions. And in conditions of extreme fear, even rational humans are driven by what Freud would call "primary processes." When we fear for our lives, or those of our loved ones, and we believe or imagine that others really are hunting us, poisoning us, or sucking our blood, it is hard to see what we can learn from the things that people will do in those circumstances. It would be crazy to formulate principles like: killing your neighbors tonight is okay when they are planning to kill you tomorrow. And yet I take it that countless ordinary people have found themselves in just this position. The true criminals are not these unfortunate people, but those who fan such fears, pouring gasoline on the flames, or water into the foundations of Victorian houses.

The implications of these claims are at odds with Levinasian ethics in the following ways. We cannot exercise the vigilance captured by the demand that we *not forget* (the Holocaust) unless we know what it is we are remembering. What if thinking of it in primarily ethical terms were a way of forgetting, that is, *not* understanding what happened. What if our ethical response were a *symptom* of our utter revulsion at these events, rather than any kind of prophylactic?

Suppose what happened would not have occurred without the concurrence of a range of factors, such as unemployment and economic hardship in Germany in the 1930s (with its own causes); the concomitant real economic fear and despair of the German people; the desire for power on the part of Hitler and his friends; the actual or perceived bankruptcy of the Weimar Republic; the historic exclusion and marginalization of the Jews in Europe; the susceptibility of even educated people to believe simple scapegoating stories about how this situation can be rectified; a mechanism (SS, Gestapo) for selecting and mobilizing psychopaths to commit horrific acts in the service of the Reich; and a technological capacity for mass killing (gas chambers, railway system).

The articulation of these "factors" is not meant to hide or attenuate in any way the horror of what happened, or the responsibility of those involved. If I am right, however, there are important causal preconditions that had to be in place for it to occur, and my claim is that it is these that should be the focus of our attention. And here we find a real hard case of "responsibility." For it has not to do with "my" infinite responsibility, and I more than others. It has everything to do with getting away from delusional thinking of every sort. True responsibility here consists in accepting that it precisely is *not* "my" responsibility, but ours. And this is not to spread the risk, as they say, not to avoid a responsibility that is properly mine, but to locate it in the only way that will make a difference.

As an example, there are many factors that need to be worked on: new practices of negotiation (if the Vietnam War was unwinnable and so too, in some ways, Kosovo, what strategies and practices would allow for nonviolent resolutions?), the development of new political institutions (educating politicians), changes in our educational practices, the development of new financial and even military institutions. But also developing powerful forms of nonlethal intervention in such conflicts. The bottom line here is that we need a different account of our ethical stance toward others for this to go ahead. That is, we need an account that abandons the purity of asymmetry. Asymmetry is an unstable and transformable structure—and includes torturer/tortured, rapist/victim, as well as the relation of forgiver to the forgiven.

The utter repudiation of the whole space of negotiation, by associating it with a certain ideal reciprocity and community, and contrasting this with the ethical relation of asymmetry, might plausibly be thought to reflect the trauma of being subjected absolutely to the power of another. I doubt that anyone who has not experienced this can begin to imagine what it is like. But it is important to ask whether the lesson it teaches us is the right one.

The asymmetry of the face-to-face relation seems blind to contemporary threats to our capacities for self-determination—through cultural imperialism, through the invasive deterritorializing infantilization of an economic system that demands our participation at any cost. The need for some sort of workable identity, the struggle for recognition—these do not dissolve in the experience of the face of the other. The danger of Levinas's position is that the substitution that becomes important is not my willingness to substitute myself for the other, but the substitution of these traumatized relations to the other for ones in which the ethical complexity of the self-other relation is allowed to appear.

Levinas believes morality is founded on ethics as responsiveness to the other. But is not the character of our grasp of that responsiveness itself dependent both on knowledge and on ontological commitments?

Levinas says that it was first Bergson and then Heidegger who showed him that "the phenomenological search for eternal truths and essences originates in time, in our temporal and historical existence." Levinas's innovation is to have claimed that the central meaning of the break in totalizable self-presence implied by time is to be found in my relation to the other. "The relation to the other is *time*," "Time means that the other is forever beyond me, irreducible to the synchrony of the same."[15] Of course, I have a great deal of sympathy with the tradition of temporalization which Levinas is radicalizing. But how does he make the move in which the relation to the other is not merely an important example of the alterity of time, but is time itself? We have to look back to what Levinas says about death. Eventually he will want to say, against Heidegger, that what is central is the death of the other, not *my* death. But in *Time and the Other*, the critical role that death plays is as my death, where it announces the end of the subject's mastery. And the end of mastery "indicates that we have assumed existing in such a way that an event has happened to us that we can no longer assume." Death is "the impossibility of having a project" (*TO* 75).

I would like to scrutinize more carefully here the move that Levinas will now make of identifying the alterity, the otherness announced in death, with the other person. But first, it is important to remind ourselves that Levinas is explicitly reworking Heidegger's account of *being toward death*. His basic line of argument seems to me reminiscent of Sartre's objection to this same analysis; i.e., that Heidegger appropriates death, makes death work for him, generating "a supreme lucidity and hence a supreme virility."[16] While Levinas's discussion of death places it at the end of a spectrum of suffering. As I see it, Levinas is offering us, once more, a somewhat one-dimensional view of Heidegger. He operates here (and when he comes to describe femininity) with what seems to be a rigid opposition between virility, mastery, lucidity, power on the one hand and femininity, ungraspability, passivity on the other. But to the extent that being-toward-death produces lucidity in Heidegger, it is the lucidity of one who has recognized his mortality, his limits, and resolves not to lose sight of this. As with Levinas, Heidegger's account is not a phenomenology of the experience of dying, but an account of the impact on my self-understanding of recognizing my mortality. As with Heidegger's account of the experience of *Angst*, being-toward-death seems to me to bring him closer to Levinas's position than Levinas is comfortable with. We know with *Gelassenheit*, with the growing importance of the *es gibt*, and with Heidegger's subsequent account of man's relation to language, that Heidegger's position becomes ever more clearly a many-fronted critique of the very mastery which Levinas attributes to him. But the point of these remarks here is not just to rub in the extent to which Levinas makes Heidegger into a straw man, or what Robert Bernasconi has called a surrogate. Rather, I think that in this case it is particularly important for Levinas to accentuate his distance from Heidegger—however much they agree on a critique of the "now"—because of the strikingly different, and in my view, deeply problematic way, he wishes to develop the significance of my becoming aware of my mortality.

Levinas writes that "the end of mastery indicates that we have assumed existing in such a way that an event can happen to us that we no longer assume" and "This approach of death indicates that we are in relation with something that is absolutely other . . . something whose very existence is made of alterity" (*TO* 74). What does he mean by this other here? Is it another person? Is it my non-existence? Levinas writes that "the other does not possess existing as the subject possesses it; its hold over my existing is mysterious. It is not unknown but unknowable" (*TO* 75). At this exact point Levinas makes the following argument. He says that all this shows that "the other is in no way another myself, participating with me in a common existence" (ibid.). This claim, which is completely indeterminate as to whether it refers to a god, a rock, a cloud, nothingness . . . is immediately treated as capturing the distinctive characteristics of the other person (alterity, exteriority).

There is, of course, a whole cluster of argument fragments in the vicinity working somewhat rhizomally toward the same end. Let me just rehearse one more before explaining my resistance to them.

In part 4 of *Time and the Other*, Levinas begins by reaffirming the

Bergsonian sense of time as creative. "Time," he writes, "is essentially a new birth" (*TO* 82)—a phrase which of course anticipates its literal accomplishment in his later account of fecundity in *Totality and Infinity*. However, he claims, "The strangeness of the future of death does not leave the subject any initiative." The problem this poses us is that of vanquishing death in such a way as to "maintain, with the alterity of the event, a relationship that must still be personal" (ibid.). Two pages later, this question will have been answered by my relation to the other person, in his or her alterity. And with the examples of the "widow" and the "orphan," this relation is claimed to be essentially asymmetrical. Obviously, these matters get revisited in later texts. But let us just focus on the argument at hand. His problem is to work out how there can be creative time after an experience of mortality that "leaves the subject with no initiative." But the strangeness here lies not in the experience of death, but in Levinas's account of its consequence, an account tied up with his outright rejection of Heidegger's account of being toward death as virility. But surely Heidegger shows us a much more nuanced account of just how a "subject" can retain initiative in the face of mortality. (Just as Kierkegaard does in his account of how love and the eternal are embodied in marriage in *Either/Or.*) In other words, Levinas seems at least here to be offering a solution to a problem, when the real problem lies in his formulation of the problem in the first place. It is difficult here to follow how the other comes to be specified in terms of the widow and the orphan. I assume it is because my sense of my own mortality brings to my special attention those living close to the limit. But what this shows, importantly, is just how far my own self-understanding is vital in focusing my obligation to the other. And how difficult it is for Levinas to maintain the claim that "man's ethical relation to the other is ultimately prior to his ontological relation to himself."[17] As I see it, everything points to an unavoidable dialectic between the two.

However, it is by these arguments that the path is established that will allow the face-to-face relation with the other person to *be time*. There is no doubt at all that time is inseparable from my relation to the other, but this is not because time is some one thing that can be identified with the other person. But rather because time, even when thought of as event—with which I have much sympathy—is a multifaceted phenomenon that cannot be reduced to any one dimension. Let me try to explain what I mean. For Levinas, the identification of the *event* with the *other* seems to take place, at least on one occasion, through the sense that my own death-induced lack of initiative in the face of alterity is redeemed by this alterity taking a human form. The idea of event is tied up both with the human other and with the idea that it is something that happens to me, rather than something I do. Clearly this sets the stage for hearing the command of the other. But the deep acknowledgment of the limits to my active powers can and does take many other forms, some of which importantly complicate the account Levinas gives of my relation to the other person and some which supplement it with strange new dimensions. But all of them are ways of making good on Bergson's sense of time as essentially the birth of the new.

As time is running short, I apologize for not presenting some of these suggestions more systematically or poetically. I present them as questions for Levinas, and for us trying to read and interpret him.

If I experience the erotic relation in terms of a relation to an absolute, recessive, modest, feminine, what would it be for the oppositional frame within which this account is set up to fall away? It would be an event, an opening onto a brave new world of eroticism, in which the putting into play of this very polarization brings its own delights. Or perhaps the event would be to recognize that it has always been so.

1. If I find myself in the mountains, climbing rocks almost as old as the earth, walking among specimens of the bristlecone pine dating from before the rise of the Roman Empire, and at night I gaze into the starry sky at points of light so old they no longer exist, the ungraspable other appears at every step—never human—and yet sometimes speaking a strange language, hard to decipher.

2. I am reading a philosophy book. I notice the way in which the thinker proceeds by one sharp opposition after the other—ontology and ethics, morality and ethics. I notice something glinting through the cracks. What is it? Could it be the real? The complexity of the real? I wonder what happened to that man who knew a thing or two about thinking, who described his style as a dance, an overleaping mockery of symmetries? Was that thought not also an event? I wonder what happened to that other man who suggested we might not be speaking unless we listened to the speaking of language.

3. I am watching a lizard on a rock in the heat of the day. I can see the pulsing of its heart. I watch a spider for hours, spinning its web, waiting for flying food to entangle itself. I watch a snake at the water hole. The panther in its cage. The snail eating my tomato plants. First event—I notice them in their "world," not just in mine. Second event—I realize, shatteringly, that while I have some measure of access to what they might be, and are up to, in other ways, they are utterly incomparable.

I will not multiply examples indefinitely. I hope the point is clear. There is a structure to the event, an unexpected transgression of limits that opens onto an unknown future, one that exceeds any attempt to shackle it to the human other. What I am calling for is the event of the event, the explosion of eventuation beyond the boundaries to which Levinas confines it. Is this unsettling? Of course. Does it help us resolve conflicts? No, sometimes it produces conflicts where none were in view.

And my other conclusion? I do think that Levinas is right to pursue the question of time in relation to the other, and to show the intimacy with which this relation is worked through. But I wonder if it is not what Husserl would call a regional ontology, with the word "ethical" functioning as a marking of the intimacy of the relation being explored. And even in relation to the other, even when one understands that relation ethically, I claim that we cannot merely eliminate the ontological dimension, as occasionally Levinas admits. We cannot ignore the fact that the positions Levinas takes up are grounded on analyses of the human condition which are both ontological and, if not plain disputable, at least of limited validity.

I will just indicate what I mean here. I have tried to give some sort of explanation of how Levinas comes to treat my relation to the other in terms of height, transcendence, etc. But his further claim is that ethics so understood, as an infinite obligation to the other, is quite distinct from everyday morality, and yet supplies the basis for that everyday morality. To be very quick, it seems to me that he makes the same mistake as Kant in supposing that any trace of self-interest is proof that what we are dealing with are those social arrangements for mutual benefit that masquerade under the name of morality, and not ethics. The former are characterized by some sort of symmetrical interaction, the latter by a fundamental asymmetry. Can this distinction be sustained? It is not hard to see something of what lies behind this thought. The widow and orphan seem to lie outside any obvious system of exchange. Our response to them must be motivated by something other than the thought that they are "part of the community," part of the extended "same" with which I can identify myself. The stranger comes precisely from outside. But the opposition between asymmetrical and symmetrical is a dangerous one. If we understand the ethical relation to the other as purely asymmetrical, we are establishing this relation on the same grounds, with a reversed valence, as those that allow the greatest violence. Asymmetry is just what characterizes the relation between overwhelming power and victimhood. And what worries me here is that focusing on the relation of asymmetry will distract us from thinking about those *complex forms of mutual dependency and interaction* which would block a simple reversal of the valency of the relation. The idea that the obligation is all mine (and mine more than others) is clearly meant to define the nature and purity of obligation. But can this not be taken to deprive the other of all capacity for moral agency? Or magnanimity? Or generosity? I am sure Levinas's position can be explained in such a way that it does do this. But the deeper point is that if "never forget" means

DAVID WOOD

"find constructive ways of making it less likely that genocide and every other form of violence will happen again," then I for one want to spend much more time thinking about those impure forms of human relation that do not absolutize the other's alterity, but bring the other in all kinds of ways into relation with us.

Two brief indicators: the principle of hospitality often found in undeveloped countries need not be understood as one of pure generosity, for it to be cultivated. There is no reason to think that it does not have a practical value, *as well as* giving expression to a capacity to imagine being in the same situation oneself. And interestingly, when the stranger you have helped wants to help you, one is not suddenly stepping out of the ethical when one accepts his offer. Second, the other to whom one has an infinite asymmetrical obligation *must* be thought of in whatever ontological terms are appropriate (bird, fox, plant, man), and *hence in terms of the kinds of further relation that might be possible with that being*, or else it becomes a purely abstract relation. A guilty monad scurrying out to carry his infinite obligations, then scurrying back. These are meant as examples of how the asymmetrical relation of obligation can be productively conjoined with symmetrical relations (of friendship, cooperation, negotiation, etc.). The ethical cannot and must not be reserved for relations of pure asymmetry. If it is said that the ethical, as Levinas develops it, is not really a relationship at all, but a certain vigilance with respect to any relationship, I would be much happier. This does not, however, fit with much of what he says. And what it demands of us is that we focus on the practical and theoretical tasks of developing those models of interpersonal, social, and political relations that open up ever more complex symmetries, and mixed forms of symmetry and asymmetry. Now that would be an event!

Notes

This paper was originally presented at the "Addressing Levinas" conference at Emory University, Atlanta, on October 16, 1999. I am grateful to the organizers, Antje Kapust and Eric Nelson, for inviting me before they knew what I would say.

1. This should not be interpreted as an attempt to *reduce* Levinasian ethics to the conditions that may have prompted its formulation. It may be that *all* significant ethical beginnings are particular, and that what is distinctive about a philosophical elaboration or articulation is the way in which it generalizes from that particular beginning. Our question could be formulated as: what shape has the elaborative generalization taken in this case? What does it close down as it opens up?

2. Martin Heidegger, *What Is Called Thinking?* trans. Fred Wieck and J. Glenn Gray (New York: Harper and Row, 1968), 77. Heidegger's words are "einmal das Entgegengehen und dann das Dagegenangehen."

3. Emmanuel Levinas, *Time and the Other,* trans. Richard Cohen (Pittsburgh: Duquesne University Press, 1987), 63. Hereafter cited in the text as *TO.*

4. "The Discovery Channel" is a reference to an American television channel devoted to wildlife, etc.

5. This interview can be found in Jacques Derrida, *Points . . . : Interviews, 1974–1994* (Stanford: Stanford University Press, 1995).

6. See my "Comment ne pas manger: Heidegger and Humanism," in *Animal Others: On Ethics, Ontology, and Animal Life,* ed. H. Peter Steeves (Binghamton: State University of New York Press, 1999).

7. The classic contemporary paper on this matter is Christopher D. Stone, "Do Trees Have Standing: Towards Legal Rights for Natural Objects," in Joseph Des-Jardins, *Environmental Ethics* (Mountain View: Mayfield, 1999). See also John Llewelyn, *The Middle Voice of Ecological Conscience* (London: Macmillan, 1991), 148–50.

8. Edmund Husserl, *Cartesian Meditations* (The Hague: Martinus Nijhoff, 1960).

9. See Derrida's *Aporias,* trans. Thomas Dutoit (Stanford: Stanford University Press, 1993), for the argument that if being able to die in the full sense ("as such") is definitive for the distinction between humans and animals, and if that involves our grasp of the meaning of what it is to die, the distinction may be in trouble.

10. See Martin Heidegger, *Being and Time,* trans. Joan Stambaugh (Binghamton: State University of New York Press, 1996), sec. 26, H122.

11. Emmanuel Levinas, *Existence and Existents,* trans. Alphonso Lingis (The Hague: Martinus Nijhoff, 1978).

12. Richard Kearney's "Dialogue with Emmanuel Levinas" can be found in *Face to Face with Levinas,* ed. Richard A. Cohen (Binghamton: State University of New York Press, 1986).

13. Kearney, "Dialogue," 24.

14. See Robert Bernasconi's paper in this collection.

15. Kearney, "Dialogue," 21.

16. Jean-Paul Sartre, *Being and Nothingness* (London: Methuen, 1958), 564.

17. Kearney, "Dialogue," 21.

Levinas and the Struggle for Existence

Robert Bernasconi

It is often said that there is little or no political philosophy in Levinas. I have challenged this claim elsewhere, but it is easy to understand why some readers might not recognize the full extent of his political philosophy.[1] In his major philosophical works, at least, Levinas mentions very few works of political philosophy by name. Although there are references to Hobbes, Hegel, and Marx, the title of only one work of political philosophy, other than Plato's *Republic*, is given in either *Totality and Infinity* or *Otherwise Than Being*. It is Kurt Schilling's *Einführung in die Staats- und Rechts-philosophie* (*Introduction to the Philosophy of Right and the State*). This was one of three books of political philosophy Schilling wrote during the 1930s.[2] Kurt Schilling is virtually forgotten today. He is not discussed except in the most encyclopedic surveys of philosophy in Nazi Germany.[3] In 1929, under the name Kurt Schilling-Wollny, he wrote a scholarly and still-valuable book on the sources of Hegel's account of actuality.[4] He joined the Nazi Party—like so many others, including Heidegger—on May 1, 1933. In November 1939 he was called to teach in Prague, subsequently returning to Munich. A short book on Kant written in 1942 shows the impact of Heidegger.[5] Why did Levinas single out Schilling for attention?

It was not for Schilling's own sake. Levinas describes Schilling's book as "typical of racist philosophy," and it is striking to find, given how much there is to object to in Schilling's book, that Levinas focuses on features in the book that parallel points he had already made about Heidegger.[6] Part of Levinas's objection to Schilling is that in his work the happiness of individuals is bypassed for a focus on want or distress (*Not*) and its threat to life (*TeI* 93n, *TI* 120n). *Not* was also a central concept in Heidegger's writings in the late 1930s and early 1940s, but more significantly, Levinas had frequently directed the same complaint against Heidegger's ontology of

Dasein. In *Existence and Existents* Levinas insisted that we eat because we are hungry and not in order to live.[7] The same point is made in *Totality and Infinity*, where it is said that Heidegger's *Sorge*, which Levinas somewhat tendentiously equates with the naked will to be, forgets love of life: "being is risked for happiness" (*TeI* 84, *TI* 112). A second point of contact between Levinas's treatment of Schilling and his discussion of Heidegger lies in Levinas's reference to "participation" in the course of his explication of "the philosophy of life or of race" (*TeI* 93, *TI* 120). Levinas had already earlier in the book associated "participation" with Heidegger's concept of enrootedness (*TeI* 32, *TI* 60). However, it is a third point that Levinas makes about Schilling that is of particular interest to me here. Schilling's discussion of race is conducted in terms of *der Kampf ums Dasein*, "the struggle for existence." *Einführung in die Staats- und Rechts-philosophie* represents the direct application of Darwin's ideas of adaptation and natural selection to political philosophy.[8] Levinas highlights Schilling's Darwinism when he explains that, according to Schilling, "individuality and sociality would be events of life that precede individuals and create them for better adaptation, in order to ensure life" (*TeI* 93n, *TI* 120n). The question is whether Levinas tries to establish a connection between the Darwinian *Kampf ums Dasein* and Heidegger's *Dasein*.

In this paper I show not only that Levinas makes such a connection, but also that he formulates his thought as a radical alternative to social Darwinism and to all philosophies based on the struggle for existence. In other words, he opposes one of the most dominant tendencies of modern political thought. It was, for example, in the name of social Darwinism that eugenics prospered throughout the Northern Hemisphere in the first half of the twentieth century. Furthermore, social Darwinism continues to dominate political debate, for example, in attacks on the idea of a welfare state. That Levinas *should* be against social Darwinism is obvious. The extent to which it animates his work has hitherto largely gone unnoticed.[9]

Although the phrase "struggle for existence" is now virtually synonymous with social Darwinism, much as Herbert Spencer's phrase "survival of the fittest" is, it is not confined to social Darwinism. It can already be found in Thomas Malthus and Charles Lyell prior to its use by Darwin in *The Origin of Species*.[10] Karl Marx recognized that the idea of a "struggle for existence" was common sense for the English. Marx wrote to Engels:

> It is remarkable how Darwin rediscovers, among the beasts and plants, the society of England with its division of labor, competition, opening up of new markets, "inventions," and Malthusian "struggle for existence." It

is Hobbes's *bellum ommium contra omnes* and is reminiscent of Hegel's *Phenomenology* in which civil society figures as an "intellectual animal kingdom," whereas, in Darwin, the animal kingdom figures as society.[11]

Marx's recognition that Hobbes's description of the state of nature as the "war of all against all" was the intellectual ancestor of the Darwinian struggle for existence shows that it was not by any means a recent idea.[12] I will show later that Levinas finds its roots much earlier in the *polemos* of Heraclitus, indeed in what might be called human nature. But perhaps the most provocative aspect of Levinas's contestation of social Darwinism is his attempt to associate Heidegger with social Darwinism. My claim is that without addressing Darwin directly, Levinas uses Heidegger's ontology as a surrogate for Darwinism, social Darwinism, and related ideas. By doing so, he finds a way of confronting the idea of a struggle for existence on terms of his own choosing.

Perhaps the most quoted sentence in all of Levinas's work is from the early text *Existence and Existents,* where Levinas acknowledges that, although his reflections were initially inspired by the philosophy of Heidegger, they are also governed by a profound need to leave "the climate" of that philosophy, albeit not for a philosophy that would be pre-Heideggerian (*DE* 19, *EE* 19). Because of the depth of Levinas's personal suffering during the Second World War, which included the loss of all his family members with the sole exception of his wife and daughter, commentators tend to quote the sentence without pausing to specify what it means for a philosophy to be post-Heideggerian and not pre-Heideggerian. But insofar as we have not made explicit what exactly it is in Heidegger's thought that necessitates a move beyond it, we have not only failed to identify the inspiration beyond Levinas's thought, we are also in danger of betraying it. Discussions of Levinas's critique of Heidegger tend to focus on his criticisms of specific issues in Heidegger, while leaving the question of the climate of Heidegger's thought shrouded in vagueness. My claim is that the crucial elaboration of the climate of Heidegger's thought is not ultimately to be found in the reference to Heidegger's ecstatic conception of existence which provides the immediate context (*DE* 19–20, *EE* 19). Rather, it is to be found only a few pages after these remarks, when Levinas introduces a discussion of "the struggle for life" and "the struggle for existence."

At the beginning of the second chapter of *Existence and Existents,* Levinas introduces a discussion of the concrete forms of an existent's adherence to existence with reference to "the struggle for life." According to Levinas, this concept, with the support of the biological sciences, has come to have a decisive impact on contemporary philosophy. Indeed, he claims that life has come to figure as the prototype of the relationship between an existent and existence. The struggle for life as a struggle for existence is a struggle for a future and "the care that a being takes for its endurance and conservation" (*DE* 29, *EE* 23). Even with the reference to care and the focus on the human being taking up an attitude toward its existence, ideas which suggest Heidegger, it would not be unreasonable to continue to read the discussion of a struggle for existence without reference to Heidegger. This is because there is much in Heidegger's texts that resists any attempt to connect his thought with Darwinism.

So far as I am aware, Levinas makes explicit the connection between Heidegger and Darwin in only two places. One is found in an interview with Richard Kearney. Levinas says: "In *The Letter on Humanism* Heidegger defines *Dasein* in almost Darwinian fashion as 'a being which is concerned for its own being.'"[13] Because *Letter on Humanism* does not in fact discuss this phrase, one might be tempted to dismiss Levinas's comment as an off-hand remark, even while one notes the studied caution that is evident when he insists that Heidegger is only *almost* Darwinian. Nevertheless, Levinas repeats the same point without any reservations in another interview, when he says the following: "Heidegger says at the beginning of *Being and Time* that *Dasein* is a being who in his being is concerned for this being itself. That's Darwin's idea: the living being struggles for life. The aim of being is being itself."[14] That a note of caution might have been advised before equating Heidegger's formulation with Darwinism is clear, if one returns Levinas's quotation from Heidegger to its true source in the first paragraph of section 9 of *Being and Time*. After saying that we are the beings to be analyzed and that the Being of any such being is in each case mine, Heidegger writes: "Das Sein ist es, darum es diesen Seienden je selbst geht."[15] Macquarrie and Robinson translate it thus: "Being is that which is an issue for every such entity."[16] Joan Stambaugh renders it as "It is being about which this being is concerned."[17] Heidegger is clear that the "es geht um . . ." is essential (*SZ* 192). It is *Dasein*'s Being that is an issue (*SZ* 33). Heidegger will also say that *Dasein* as Being-in-the-world is an issue for itself (*es als In-der-Welt-sein um es selbst geht; SZ* 143). This is confirmed by *The History of the Concept of Time:* "Dasein is an entity for which in its being, in its being-in-the-world, its very being is at issue [*um sein Sein selbst geht*]."[18] But does this sentence mean that *Dasein* is concerned about its existence in the sense of its longevity, its preservation?

One would be hard-pressed to find a Heidegger scholar who thinks so today, but on the basis of his essay "Martin Heidegger and Ontology," it is clear that Levinas thought so in 1932.[19] In this early essay Levinas juxtaposes two sentences of Heidegger's. The first concerns man's understanding of Being. In Levinas's version it reads: "Man exists in such a manner that he understands being." The second sentence reads in Levinas's translation: "Man exists in such a way that his own existence is always at stake for him" (*L'homme existe de telle manière qu'il y va toujours pour lui de sa propre existence;* "MH" 406, "MHO" 17). Levinas concedes that the second sentence seems to say more than the first, but he insists that they must come to the same thing, because if one were to separate *Dasein*'s understanding of Being and *Dasein*'s mode of existence, one would maintain a separation between contemplation or knowledge, on the one hand, and existence, on the other, that would be foreign to Heidegger. The two sentences come together in Levinas's summary: "To understand being is to exist in such a way that one takes care of one's own existence" ("MH" 408, "MHO" 18). With this paraphrase Levinas already moves Heidegger in the direction of the social Darwinism that in *Existence and Existents* is articulated as a care for endurance and conservation.

That is why it is comes as a surprise to find that in 1934, in "Reflections on the Philosophy of Hitlerism," when Levinas issues a warning about the philosophical climate in Germany, Heidegger is not named. It is Nietzsche, not Heidegger, who is identified by Levinas as the thinker who represents the ideas behind National Socialism.[20] So it seems that it was only in retrospect that Levinas saw the danger in Heidegger's formulation. In his 1990 introduction to "Reflections on the Philosophy of Hitlerism," Levinas evokes Heidegger's idea of a being that in its Being is concerned with this Being and in that context comments that Western philosophy has not sufficiently insured itself against the essential possibility of elemental Evil ("RPH" 62–63). The possibility of elemental Evil is "inscribed within the ontology of being concerned with being—a being, to use the Heideggerian expression, *dem es in seinem Sein um dieses Sein selbst geht*" (ibid.). This would seem, therefore, to be Levinas's answer to his own question in "As if Consenting to Horror," when he asks of *Being and Time:* "Can we be assured, however, that there was never any echo of Evil in it?"[21] Earlier in the essay Levinas acknowledged that *Being and Time,* a book he continued to admire, looks innocent enough: "Nothing in this new phenomenology, as it is elaborated in the magnificent opening pages of *Sein und Zeit,* portends any political or ulterior motive" ("CCH" 48, "ACH" 486). That is why Levinas concedes that there is always some difficulty recognizing the diabolical, given that it is endowed with intelligence ("CCH" 49, "ACH" 488). He readily acknowledges that at first he did not see the possibility of the evil inscribed in this ontology, even though it is apparent that in 1932 he already saw what he would later identify as evil.[22]

At a scholarly level it is not difficult to distance Heidegger from Darwin, especially if we are ready to use texts Levinas was not aware of while formulating his philosophy. Heidegger's rejection of Darwin was already explicit in the 1929 lectures, *The Fundamental Concepts of Metaphysics*. To be sure, by objecting to Darwinism on the grounds that it introduced certain misleading questions into biology, Heidegger objected not to its focus on self-preservation and the maintenance of the species, which he acknowledged was familiar from "vulgar experience," but to the fact that it interpreted self-preservation from an economic perspective.[23] Heidegger's counterclaim was that self-preservation should be understood with reference to captivation (*Benommenheit*), in terms of which he understood the essence of the organism (*GA* 29/30:376–77, *FCM* 258–59). Focusing on the Darwinian notion of adaptation, Heidegger complained that instead of exploring the relational structure between the animal and its environment in terms of openness, Darwinism treated the animal as if it was first independent and only subsequently adapted itself to an independent world such that the fittest is selected (*GA* 29/30:382, *FCM* 263). Heidegger does not underwrite the idea of natural selection in these lectures, but it is worth bearing in mind that *The Fundamental Concepts of Metaphysics* was not published until 1983. Similarly in his Nietzsche lectures of 1939, Heidegger opposes talk of Nietzsche's Darwinism in terms that make clear his own opposition to the ideas of "self-preservation" and "struggle for existence."[24] However, the Nietzsche lectures were not published until 1960, although we know that Levinas had read them, at least in part, by 1962.[25] That is why it is significant that in the Rectoral Address of 1933, in the context of a discussion of the elevation of certain university teachers to a leadership role, in a text that was available to Levinas, Heidegger underwrites the idea of natural selection.[26]

Nevertheless, Levinas would not have been disarmed by this new evidence distancing Heidegger from social Darwinism. The association of Heidegger with social Darwinism, which runs contrary to Heidegger's intentions, is not defensible on strictly scholarly grounds. It might seem at times like a witch hunt, but Levinas's confrontation with Heidegger is no more confined to the philological level than Heidegger's own "thoughtful dialogue between thinkers" in *Kant and the Problem of Metaphysics:* it has its own agenda, but the violence of the interpretation does not mean it is arbitrary. It is "bound by other laws."[27] This does not mean that Levinas is always committed to presenting a one-sided picture of Heidegger. In "Diachrony and Representation," in the context of a discussion of the putting in question of the existential insistence on the perseverance of the *I*, the *conatus essendi*, Levinas evokes Heidegger's discussion of *Unfug* in "The Anaximander Fragment" and finds there—in Anaximander and it also seems in Heidegger—"a putting into question of that 'positivity' of the *esse*."[28] He asks: "Did not Heidegger, despite all he wants to, teach about the priority of the 'thought of being'—here run up against the original

ROBERT BERNASCONI

significance of ethics?" (*EN* 187, *ENT* 168). Given the textual liberties that Levinas often takes in his polemic against Heidegger, it is striking to find that they are not always negative.[29]

The decisive point is that Levinas ultimately does not treat Heidegger on his own terms, but as the most recent representative of a tradition of thought that extends far beyond Heidegger, back past Hobbes and Spinoza, who are also frequently the targets of Levinas's polemic, to Heraclitus. Although in *Existence and Existents* Levinas emphasized the novelty of the idea of the struggle for existence (*DE* 29, *EE* 23), subsequently, as Levinas turned his attention to the need to give an account of the tradition, he came to place it in a broader context. For example, in *God, Death and Time*, lectures from 1975, he explicitly relates Heidegger to the *conatus essendi:*

"The formula 'Dasein is a being for whom in its being being is at issue' was seductive in *Being and Time* where it signifies the *conatus*. But the conatus is in fact deduced from the degree of astriction of this being to being."[30] This is the *conatus* of Hobbes, but especially the *conatus essendi* of Spinoza (*EN* 10, *ENT* xii). Proposition 7 of the Third Part of Spinoza's *Ethics* reads: "The striving [*conatus*] by which each thing strives to persevere in its being is nothing but the actual essence of the thing."[31] And so Levinas brings together Spinoza and Heidegger, even if Heidegger himself was never entirely sure where to locate Spinoza.[32] Indeed, in later essays, Levinas prefers to evoke the *conatus essendi* at least as often as the struggle for existence or perseverance in being. He makes an effort to rewrite the history of philosophy from his own perspective much as Heidegger does when he reconstitutes it in terms of the history of Being as presence. It is as if Levinas cannot ultimately leave the climate of Heidegger's philosophy for a philosophy that is post-Heideggerian without showing on his own terms that Western philosophy culminates in Heidegger.

But it is not only philosophy that is at issue. Levinas refers to Heidegger's involvement with National Socialism as the echo of "a deeper and older crisis" (*EN* 219, *ENT* 207), that of Cain and Abel. That is to say, Levinas ultimately relates the struggle for existence to the history of humanity at large. Readers of Levinas have too often tended to focus on his polemic against certain philosophical opponents without acknowledging that his thought fails to reach its target if his discourse remains exclusively philosophical. His real target is the suffering human beings cause each other and, in the context of the twentieth century, totalitarianism, not Heidegger, or Heraclitus. But Levinas believes there is a connection between philosophy and this suffering. He says it very well in "From the Carefree Deficiency to the New Meaning," in which Levinas returns to his ongoing polemic against teleological philosophies of history that promise "the universal integration of Being within the Idea."[33] That is not Heidegger. That is Kant and Hegel. In this context he characterizes the division that such philosophies of history promote within humanity: "deficient humanity—criminal, immoral, diseased, arrested or retarded in its development—should have to be separated—whether incarcerated, interned, colonized, or educated—from the true humanity—good, healthy, and mature" (*DVI* 80, *GCM* 45). One can scarcely imagine a better summary of what the impact of the application of social Darwinism in politics during the twentieth century has meant. But what does Levinas offer in its place?

When Levinas shifts the question of philosophy from existence—"to be or not to be"—and instead poses the question of my right to exist, when he asks not about my fear for myself but my fear for the Other, he is not only expressing the guilt of a survivor, he is also offering an ethical challenge to the idea of life as a struggle for existence.[34] He is questioning the right to exist.[35] Levinas does not deny that there is, as he puts it, a "conservation instinct" (*EN* 10, *ENT* xii). This survival instinct is to be respected, much as the ontological remains essential in relation to the ethical. For Levinas, there is no ethics without ontology. One cannot approach the Other with empty hands.[36] As he writes in "Uniqueness," "Through the hidden violence of perseverance in being—a beyond" (*EN* 215, *ENT* 194). Not in spite of it, but *through* it. Nevertheless, reverting to one of those assertions of priority that Levinas sometimes employs in spite of the fact that they leave unclear the precise nature of the relation, he writes in "Dying for . . ." that the call to holiness precedes the concern for existing (*EN* 228, *ENT* 216). And yet in the preface to *Entre Nous,* the collection in which "Dying for . . ." is reprinted, Levinas identifies the "survival instinct" evident in the struggle for life as the origin of all violence (*EN* 10, *ENT* xii). In spite of everything that the struggle for existence means to Levinas in terms of its relation to evil, or perhaps because of it, it retains a prominent structural role in his thought. But this makes it seem that Levinas is not denying the truth of Darwinism altogether, only its completeness. And yet completeness cannot be what Levinas aims at. It must be rather that the struggle for existence is disturbed, interrupted. Other texts confirm this.

In a crucial, but far from transparent, passage toward the end of *Otherwise Than Being,* Levinas asks if subjectivity draws its sense and direction from essence. The implication is that if this were the case, then subjectivity would be unable to accuse itself for engaging in the struggle for existence and for letting itself be seduced by the force of power in the guise of the violences of nationalism.[37] In other words, it is the bad conscience that arises from the struggle for existence which establishes that subjectivity is not reduced to being, but opens to the otherwise than being. Levinas continues:

> The true problem for us Westerners is not so much to refuse violence
> as to question ourselves about a struggle against violence which without
> blanching in non-resistance to evil, could avoid the institution of vio-
> lence out of this very struggle. Does not war perpetuate that which it is
> called on to make disappear, and consecrate war and its virile virtues in
> good conscience? (*AE* 223, *OB* 177)

In fact, Levinas had already given his answer twenty pages earlier: "It is not
without importance to know that war does not become the instauration of
a war in good conscience" (*AE* 203, *OB* 160). But Levinas cannot avoid the
problems posed by the violent struggle against violence, the choice between violences, the choice of sides. These are political problems.

Levinas apparently supported the view he attributed in "Judaism
and Revolution" to Rabbi Eleazar ben Rabbi Simeon: "violence is needed
to put an end to violence."[38] But how does one make the determination of
when to use violence? How does one differentiate between, to use Levinas's own categories, revolutionary violence and state violence? To address this question one needs to pass beyond politics to a knowledge of
evil, as he had done in "As if Consenting to Horror." He asks: "How can
you act politically while ignorant of the nature of Evil, while ignorant of
its metaphysical and spiritual reason?" (*SS* 38, *NTR* 110).[39] It is not a question of seeking a justification for violence, because justification would establish good conscience, which Levinas consistently opposes. Hence the
problem of violence gives way to an aporia: the only violence one could engage in with a good conscience is a violence that arises from the agony of
a bad conscience, fearful of making the innocent suffer. The aporia arises
from the ambiguity of the face. To be sure, in a world of scarcity not all
wars are unreasonable. But beyond reason, *through* the struggle for existence, the Other is not only hungry or homeless, but also the site of hatred and persecution: the Other's hatred for me and my hatred for the
Other. The Other says "You shall not kill," but says that only because, as
Levinas also insists, the Other is the sole being I can want to kill (*EN* 22,
ENT 9; *DL* 28, *DF* 8).[40] Thus, when Levinas declares that "the true problem
for us Westerners is not so much to refuse violence as to question ourselves
about a struggle against violence" (*AE* 223, *OB* 177), when he asks if war
does not consecrate the virile virtues of war in good conscience, his questioning is specifically directed against state violence, as the reference to
"virile virtues" makes clear (compare *TeI* 284, *TI* 306).[41] Levinas also associates virility with Heidegger, presumably in a further effort to associate
Heidegger with National Socialism. Levinas writes of the adventure of
Being as *Da-sein* as it takes shape in "the virility of a free ability-to-be, like
a will of race and sword" (*EN* 219, *ENT* 207).[42] But it is also because the is-

sue is state violence that Levinas addresses the problem to "us Western-ers." The question is whether that phrase is not itself violent.

If Levinas addresses "us Westerners" at that point in *Otherwise Than Being*, it is not because he thinks that only Westerners will read his book. Still less is it because he writes only for Westerners, as Hegel did.[43] It is be-cause Levinas believes that the problem he is posing is a peculiarly West-ern problem, which is in turn because he thinks of the State as a peculiarly Western institution. But if this is so, it returns us to the fact that it is in the West and for us Westerners that the struggle for existence has given rise to a philosophy which diverts politics further from the path of justice. It is, in Levinas's view, philosophy that has promoted within humanity the divi-sion between "deficient humanity" and "true humanity" (*DVI* 80, *GCM* 45). But the question then becomes how Levinas, who can hardly be ex-pected to promote a tradition that culminates in the Holocaust (*DL* 211, *DF* 161), any more than he can be expected to privilege culture over ethics, nevertheless exalts European civilization in the face of the savagery committed by Europeans against those they called savages, not to men-tion the savagery Europeans committed against each other. He does so be-cause he also thinks that bad conscience has played a particularly promi-nent role in Europe, albeit through its Hebraic component rather than its Hellenic component.[44] Levinas suspects that the tendency within Europe's universities to affirm particular cultures at all ends of the earth has its source in remorse at the memory of colonial wars that Europe has waged (*AT* 140, *ATT* 133). In other words, multiculturalism arises from Europe's bad conscience over how it has treated other peoples. But it was not a move Levinas would follow.

Although Levinas cites "de-Europeanization" as evidence of Euro-pean generosity, he insists that Europe's cultural dominance was justi-fied.[45] Levinas, the philosopher of bad conscience par excellence, seems to have no sympathy for those European intellectuals who in his eyes de-mean Western civilization by exercising that bad conscience on Europe it-self. It seems that Levinas celebrates bad conscience among individuals, but does not identify it as a political virtue. Furthermore, Levinas does not acknowledge a connection between European culture and European poli-tics, although he insists on drawing a connection between political move-ments and the philosophies that sustain them, as in the opening pages of *Totality and Infinity* or when he declares that "political totalitarianism rests on an ontological totalitarianism" (*DL* 267, *DF* 206). Nor does he acknowl-edge a material basis to philosophy, to society, or to political movements within those societies. This is perhaps why, contrary to the evidence, he can proclaim the European accomplishment of the egalitarian and just state (*AT* 150, *ATT* 144) and does so without asking whether its existence is predicated on a level of material well-being that is founded on and preserved by the systemic oppression of the Third World.

I do not pretend to have exhausted the complex question of Levinas's relation to the idea of Europe.[46] Nor have I tried to pass judgment on the resources that Levinas develops as an alternative to social Darwinism and the tradition that precedes it. My aim has been to reorient the study of Levinas so that his challenge to the intellectual and political currents of our time is not overlooked. Levinas's reading of Heidegger needs to be understood as a response to the traumatic events of the twentieth century, which means that one must hear those events reverberating through Heidegger's texts, just as one must hear in Levinas's philosophy a response to the predominance of the struggle for existence in Western thought. There is therefore a form of political philosophy in Levinas. But precisely because Levinas does not deny a prominent role to the struggle for existence, one would expect him to pay more attention to the institutions that are designed to limit it (compare *EN* 210, *ENT* 190). If it is legitimate to hold Levinas to the standards that he himself imposes on certain other philosophers, his failure to take his political philosophy to the point of a philosophy of institutions is a serious omission, just as his Eurocentrism is irresponsible and perhaps, when one associates it with the traumatic violence of Western imperialism, even diabolical.

Notes

1. Robert Bernasconi, "The Third Party," *Journal of the British Society for Phenomenology* 30, no. 1 (January 1999): 76–87. The full version of this lecture is available only in German, translated by Antje Kapust, "Wer ist der Dritte?" in *Der Anspruch des Anderen,* ed. B. Waldenfels and I. Därmann (Munich: Wilhelm Fink, 1998), 87–110.

2. Kurt Schilling, *Einführung in die Staats- und Rechts-philosophie* (Berlin: Junker und Dünnhaupt, 1939). The other two works by Schilling are *Der Staat, seine geistigen Grundlagen, seine Entstehung und Entwicklung* (Munich: Ernst Reinhardt, 1935) and *Geschichte der Staats- und Rechtsphilosophie im Überblick von den Griechen bis zur Gegegenwart* (Berlin: Junker und Dünnhaupt, 1937). There is no evidence that Levinas read the two earlier works, but in any case he selected the one that best served his purpose.

3. See George Leaman, ed., *Heidegger im Kontext: Gesamtüberblick zum NS-Engagement der Universitätsphilosophen* (Hamburg: Argument, 1993), 75.

4. Kurt Schilling-Wollny, *Hegels Wissenschaft von der Wirklichkeit und ihre Quellen,* vol. 1 (Munich: Ernst Reinhardt, 1929).

5. Kurt Schilling, *Kant: Persönlichkeit und Werk* (Munich: Ernst Reinhardt, 1942), 69–70. Schilling's interest in Heidegger is confirmed by *Einführung in die Geschichte der Philosophie* (Heidelberg: Carl Winter, 1949), 12–18

6. Emmanuel Levinas, *Totalité et infini* (The Hague: Martinus Nijhoff, 1974), 93n; *Totality and Infinity*, trans. Alphonso Lingis (Pittsburgh: Duquesne University Press, 1969), 120n. Hereafter cited in the text as *TeI* and *TI*, respectively.

7. Emmanuel Levinas, *De l'existence à l'existant* (Paris: Vrin, 1947), 56; *Existence and Existents*, trans. Alphonso Lingis (The Hague: Martinus Nijhoff, 1978), 37. Hereafter cited in the text as *DE* and *EE*, respectively. See also Levinas, *Totalité et infini*, 108; *Totality and Infinity*, 134.

8. Schilling, *Einführung*, 31.

9. A passing reference can, however, be found in Mylène Baum, "Levinas et la bioéthique," in *Emmanuel Lévinas et l'histoire*, ed. Nathalie Frogneux and Françoise Mies (Paris: Éditions du Cerf, 1998), 390. I am grateful to John Drabinski for this reference.

10. See Barry G. Gale, "Darwin and the Concept of a Struggle for Existence," *Isis* 63 (1972): 321–44.

11. Marx to Engels, June 18, 1862, in Karl Marx and Friedrich Engels, *Collected Works*, vol. 41 (New York: International Publishing, 1985), 381.

12. The idea of a war of all against all had already found its way into natural history with Linnaeus. See Knut Hagberg, *Carl Linneaus*, trans. Alan Blair (London: Jonathan Cape, 1952), 193. Ernst Haeckel, Germany's leading social Darwinist, referred explicitly to Hobbes's "war of all against all" in his *Natürliche Schöpfungsgeschichte* (Berlin: George Reimer, 1868), 16.

13. Richard Kearney, *Dialogues with Contemporary Continental Thinkers* (Manchester: Manchester University Press, 1984), 62.

14. Tamra Wright, Peter Hughes, and Alison Ainley, "The Paradox of Morality: An Interview with Emmanuel Levinas," in *The Provocation of Levinas*, ed. Robert Bernasconi and David Wood (London: Routledge, 1988), 172.

15. Martin Heidegger, *Sein und Zeit* (Tübingen: Max Niemeyer, 1967), 42. Hereafter cited in the text as *SZ*.

16. Martin Heidegger, *Being and Time*, trans. J. Macquarrie and E. Robinson (Oxford: Basil Blackwell, 1962), 67.

17. Martin Heidegger, *Being and Time*, trans. Joan Stambaugh (Albany: State University of New York Press, 1996), 39.

18. Martin Heidegger, *Prolegomena zur Geschichte des Zeitbegriffs*, in *Gesamtausgabe*, vol. 20 (Frankfurt am Main: Klostermann, 1979), 405; *The History of the Concept of Time*, trans. T. Kisiel (Bloomington: Indiana University Press, 1985), 292.

19. Emmanuel Levinas, "Martin Heidegger et l'ontologie," *Revue philosophique de la France et de l'étranger* 113, nos. 5–6 (1932): 395–431; "Martin Heidegger and Ontology," trans. Committee of Public Safety, *Diacritics* 26, no. 1 (Spring 1996): 11–32. Hereafter cited in the text as "MH" and "MHO," respectively.

20. Emmanuel Levinas, "Quelques réflexions sur la philosophie de l'hitlérisme," *Esprit* 2, no. 26 (1934): 208; "Reflections on the Philosophy of Hitlerism," trans. Seán Hand, *Critical Inquiry* 17 (Autumn 1990): 71. Hereafter cited

in the text as "RPH." See also Miguel Abensour's extended essay introducing the republication of Levinas's essay, in Emmanuel Levinas, *Quelques réflexions sur la philosophie de l'hitlérisme* (Paris: Payot, 1997).

21. Emmanuel Levinas, "Comme un consentement à l'horrible," *Le nouvel observateur* 22–28 (January 1988): 49; "As If Consenting to Horror," trans. Paula Wissing, *Critical Inquiry* 15 (Winter 1989): 488. Hereafter cited in the text as "CCH" and "ACH," respectively.

22. Sixteen years later, in 1948, in "L'ontologie dans le temporal," when Levinas again gives an exposition of *Being and Time,* he repeats his analysis of section 9. However, the essay on this occasion ends with a clear statement of its tragic accents that "witness to an epoch and a world that it will perhaps be possible to surpass tomorrow" (Emmanuel Levinas, *En découvrant l'existence avec Husserl et Heidegger* [Paris: Vrin, 1974], 80–81 and 89).

23. Martin Heidegger, *Die Grundbegriffe der Metaphysik,* in *Gesamtausgabe,* vol. 29/30 (Frankfurt am Main: Klostermann 1983), 377; *The Fundamental Concepts of Metaphysics,* trans. W. McNeill and N. Walker (Bloomington: Indiana University Press, 1995), 259. Hereafter cited in the text as *GA* 29/30 and *FCM,* respectively.

24. Martin Heidegger, *Nietzsche,* vol. 1 (Pfullingen: Neske, 1961), 488; translated by Joan Stambaugh, F. A. Capuzzi, and D. F. Krell as *The Will to Power as Knowledge* (New York: Harper and Row, 1987), 15. See also Heidegger's attack on the struggle for existence in *Die Geschichte des Seyns,* in *Gesamtausgabe,* vol. 69 (Frankfurt am Main: Klostermann, 1998), 223.

25. Emmanuel Levinas, "Transcendance et hauteur," *Bulletin de la Société française de Philosophie* 54 (1962): 92; "Transcendence and Height," trans. T. Chanter, in *Emmanuel Levinas: Basic Philosophical Writings,* ed. Adriaan Peperzak, Simon Critchley, and Robert Bernasconi (Bloomington: Indiana University Press, 1996), 13.

26. Martin Heidegger, *Die Selbstbehauptung der Deutschen Universität* (Frankfurt am Main: Klostermann, 1983), 14; "The Self-Assertion of the German University," trans. William S. Lewis, in *The Heidegger Controversy,* ed. Richard Wolin (Cambridge: MIT Press, 1993), 34.

27. Martin Heidegger, *Kant und das Problem der Metaphysik,* in *Gesamtausgabe,* vol. 3 (Frankfurt am Main: Klostermann, 1991), xvii; *Kant and the Problem of Metaphysics,* trans. Richard Taft (Bloomington: Indiana University Press, 1990), xix.

28. Emmanuel Levinas, *Entre nous: Essais sur le penser-à-l'autre* (Paris: Grasset, 1991), 187; *Entre Nous: Thinking of the Other,* trans. Michael B. Smith and Barbara Harshav (New York: Columbia University Press, 1998), 168. Hereafter cited in the text as *EN* and *ENT,* respectively. See Martin Heidegger, *Holzwege,* volume 5 of the *Gesamtausgabe* (Frankfurt am Main: Klostermann, 1977), 354–58; translated by D. F. Krell and F. A. Capuzzi as "The Anaximander Fragment," in *Early Greek Thought* (New York: Harper and Row, 1975), 41–45. See also Robert Bernasconi, "Justice and the Twilight Zone of Morality," in *Heidegger in Question* (Atlantic Highlands: Humanities, 1993), 40–55.

29. See also Levinas's inventive analysis of *Fürsorge* as a response to destitution and an access to the alterity of the Other in Emmanuel Levinas, "Martin Buber et

la théorie de la connaissance," in *Noms propres* (Montpellier: Fata Morgana, 1976), 47–48; "Martin Buber and the Theory of Knowledge," *Proper Names,* trans. Michael B. Smith (Stanford: Stanford University Press, 1996), 33.

30. Emmanuel Levinas, *Dieu, la mort et le temps* (Paris: Grasset, 1993), 35.

31. Benedict de Spinoza, *Opera,* ed. J. van Vloten and J. P. N. Land (The Hague: Martinus Nijhoff, 1914), 1:127; *The Collected Works of Spinoza,* trans. Edwin Curley (Princeton: Princeton University Press, 1985), 1:488. On Levinas and Spinoza, see Edith Wyschogrod, "Ethics as First Philosophy: Levinas Reads Spinoza," *The Eighteenth Century* 40, no. 3 (Fall 1999): 202–3; and Jean-François Rey, "Levinas et Spinoza," in *Spinoza au XXe siècle,* ed. Oliver Bloch (Paris: Presses Universitaires de France, 1993), 225–35.

32. See Etienne Balibar, "Heidegger et Spinoza," in *Spinoza au XXe siècle,* 327–43.

33. Emmanuel Levinas, *De Dieu qui vient à l'idée* (Paris: Vrin, 1986), 80; *Of God Who Comes to Mind,* trans. Bettina Bergo (Stanford: Stanford University Press, 1998), 45. Hereafter cited in the text as *DVI* and *GCM,* respectively.

34. Emmanuel Levinas, *Éthique comme philosophie première* (Paris: Payot, 1998), 107; "Ethics as First Philosophy," trans. Seán Hand and Michael Temple, in *The Levinas Reader,* ed. Seán Hand (Oxford: Basil Blackwell, 1989), 86.

35. Emmanuel Levinas, *Éthique et infini* (Paris: Fayard, 1982), 131; *Ethics and Infinity,* trans. Richard Cohen (Pittsburgh: Duquesne University Press, 1985), 121.

36. Emmanuel Levinas, *Difficile liberté,* 2nd ed. (Paris: Albin Michel, 1976), 44; *Difficult Freedom,* trans. Seán Hand (Baltimore: Johns Hopkins University Press, 1990), 26. Hereafter cited in the text as *DL* and *DF,* respectively.

37. Emmanuel Levinas, *Autrement qu'être, ou au-delà de l'essence* (The Hague: Martinus Nijhoff, 1974), 223; *Otherwise Than Being, or Beyond Essence,* trans. Alphonso Lingis (The Hague: Martinus Nijhoff, 1981), 176. Hereafter cited in the text as *AE* and *OB,* respectively.

38. Emmanuel Levinas, *Du sacré au saint* (Paris: Minuit, 1977), 45–46; translated by Annette Aronowicz as *Nine Talmudic Readings* (Bloomington: Indiana University Press, 1990), 114. Hereafter cited in the text as *SS* and *NTR,* respectively.

39. For the important reservations that Levinas puts in place, see Robert Bernasconi, "The Truth That Accuses: Conscience, Shame, and Guilt in Levinas and Augustine," in *The Ethics of Postmodernity,* ed. Gary B. Madison and Marty Fairbairn (Evanston: Northwestern University Press, 1999), 33–34.

40. See Robert Bernasconi, "The Violence of the Face," *Philosophy and Social Criticism* 23, no. 6 (1997): 81–93.

41. In the version of this paper delivered in Atlanta in October 1999, I used this statement as a context for questioning a certain virility left intact by Levinas's strictly masculinist orientation, most evident in the discussions of filiality and fecundity in *Totality and Infinity.* I raised the question as to whether this does not constitute a certain climate of Levinas's philosophy that one needs to leave for a philosophy that would not be pre-Levinasian. In this regard I named Irigaray. If I do not pursue these questions in this version, it is in part because of their complexity, which warrants a lengthier treatment, but it should not be construed as my

backing away from these claims. See Luce Irigaray, "Questions to Emmanuel Levinas," trans. Margaret Whitford, in *Re-Reading Levinas*, ed. Robert Bernasconi and Simon Critchley (Bloomington: Indiana University Press, 1991), 113. As an indication of the complexity, see the final footnote to *Adieu*, where Derrida insists on maintaining Levinas's distinction between paternity and virility. See Jacques Derrida, *Adieu à Emmanuel Levinas* (Paris: Galilée, 1997), 210n; *Adieu to Emmanuel Levinas*, trans. Pascalé Anne Brailed and Michael Naas (Stanford: Stanford University Press, 1999), 152. However, this faithfulness to the letter of Levinas's text cannot be the last word on its climate.

42. See also Emmanuel Levinas, *Le temps et l'autre* (Paris: Presses Universitaires de France, 1983), 57; *Time and the Other*, trans. Richard Cohen (Pittsburgh: Duquesne University Press, 1987), 70.

43. Robert Bernasconi, "'We Philosophers,'" in *Endings*, ed. R. Comay and J. McCumber (Evanston: Northwestern University Press, 1999), 77–96.

44. Emmanuel Levinas, *Altérité et transcendance* (Montpelier: Fata Morgana, 1995), 139–41; *Alterity and Transcendence*, trans. Michael B. Smith (New York: Columbia University Press, 1999), 132–34. Hereafter cited in the text as *AT* and *ATT*, respectively. See also Levinas, *Entre nous*, 211–12; *Entre Nous*, 191–92.

45. Emmanuel Levinas, interview with Christian Descamps, in *Entretiens avec Le Monde. 1. Philosophies* (Paris: Editions La Découverte, 1984), 147; François Poirié, *Emmanuel Levinas: Qui êtes-vous?* (Lyon: La Manufacture, 1987), 131; Emmanuel Levinas, *Humanisme de l'autre homme* (Montpellier: Fata Morgana, 1972), 54–56; translated in Levinas, *Basic Philosophical Writings*, 57–59. See also Robert Bernasconi, "One-Way Traffic: The Ontology of Decolonization and Its Ethics," in *Ontology and Alterity in Merleau-Ponty*, ed. Galen A. Johnson and Michael B. Smith (Evanston: Northwestern University Press, 1990), 67–80.

46. For a more extensive treatment, which is indispensable for understanding my conclusion, see Robert Bernasconi, "Who Is My Neighbor? Who Is the Other?" in *Ethics and Responsibility in the Phenomenological Tradition*, Ninth Annual Symposium of the Simon Silverman Phenomenology Center (Pittsburgh: Simon Silverman Phenomenology Center, Duquesne University, 1991), 1–31. See also Sonia Sikka, "How Not to Read the Other: 'All the Rest Can Be Translated,'" *Philosophy Today* 43, no. 2 (Summer 1999): 195–206.

Wealth and Justice in a U-topian Context

John Drabinski

> in the perspective of saintliness
> —Levinas

Much has been said recently of Levinas's transition from the matters of ethics to those of politics. Those discussions have centered primarily on the question of *le tiers* (the third), the relation of ethics to politics, and the messianic. In what follows, I want to propose a shift in theme by working from two remarks by Levinas. First, a well-known comment from "The *I* and the Totality":

> The quantification of the human—such as the ambiguity of money makes possible—points to a new justice . . . Money lets us catch sight of a justice of redemption, replacing the infernal or vicious circle of vengeance or forgiveness.[1]

Second, a lesser-known remark from "Ideology and Idealism":

> In the social community, the community of clothed beings, *the privileges of rank obstruct justice.*[2]

These two remarks are significant for a couple of reasons. First, they address politics in a *concrete* sense. Both quantification as money and the clothed, living-presence of others pose the political question in terms of the sensible presence of others *and* the sensible conditions of response. Second, and consonant with this notion of a concrete politics, these remarks put the political question in those terms by which I meet the Other "with full hands," so to speak. But the fact that I meet the Other with full hands has, strangely enough, had very little purchase in Levinas's politics—either in his own reflections or in commentary on that work. What would it mean to take these two passages seriously? What would it mean, that is, to begin to think politics in terms of the injustice of privilege, specifically the privilege of wealth? My contention here will be that with these passages in mind, it is not only possible but necessary to alter the terrain of politics in Levinas, moving us away from the *à-venir* of messianism toward the possibility of a politics of generosity—an *ethical* politics.

To begin, I will first consider the significance of Levinas's remarks on utopia as *u-topia*. This consideration is important. It points to a Levinasian phenomenology of social spatiality *as* asymmetrical. This structure of social space modifies the significative origin of law, and so modifies the kind of political responsibilities that emerge from the passage from ethics to politics. This modification initiates another kind of law, a law that binds response quite differently than the law of a politics of peace. We will then be prepared to revisit, by way of conclusion, the question of wealth—that is, how the quantification of the human points to a new justice, a justice of redemption beyond vengeance and forgiveness.

1

The notion of utopia has been something of a quiet constant in Levinas's work. Indeed, it has played a role in his philosophical and confessional writings since the 1950s. Utopia poses an important question, for it promises to provide something missing in much of Levinas's philosophical work: an account of spatiality.

In his various renderings of the ethical relation, the problem of spatiality occasions only oblique mention. The *non-site* of ethics to a certain extent justifies this muted treatment of space. However, the question of social space becomes genuinely urgent when we consider the political question. Because politics involves the intrigue of the interhuman with *all others,* the question of the structure of the space in which "we" meet is particularly acute. Multiplicity in being without totalization is the transition from ethics to politics accomplished; Levinas calls this multiplicity "asymmetrical space."[3] The *mise en question* of the I by the Other serves as the quasi-foundation of this political space. Politics takes ethics as its "model."[4] So the space of politics is marked, albeit programmatically, by the asymmetry of ethics. The fraternal relation takes place in essentially asymmetrical space. How might this spatiality, ethical and political, be rendered? And what help can a notion of utopia offer?

On his first rendering of the issue, utopia seems to hold little promise. In the 1950 essay "Le lieu et l'utopie" ("Place and Utopia"), Levinas writes that the "man of utopia" "wants unjustly. He prefers the cheerfulness of solitary safety to the difficult task of an equitable life. In this way, he refuses the very conditions wherein his bad conscience [*mauvaise conscience*] had set him up as a person [*en personne*]."[5] The term *mauvaise conscience,* of course, will have much currency in Levinas's work. Being in question, the condition of the ethical subject, is this bad conscience. Bad conscience is beyond reconciliation; it admits of neither natural nor teleological good conscience. I cannot wash my hands of obligation. But the desire for utopia dreams of a social space that settles accounts—the space of good conscience. Levinas therefore concludes in 1950 that utopia is both politically and ethically problematic.

An encounter with Celan's 1960 speech "The Meridian" marks Levinas's rethinking of utopia.[6] The 1972 essay "Paul Celan: From Being to the Other" is, to my knowledge, his first positive appropriation of the term "utopia," reclaiming it from the vanity of good conscience.[7] Celan poses the question of social space, which allows Levinas to think of utopia as a kind of "ethical spatiality." Unlike his work on Bloch and Buber, Levinas's reading of Celan treats utopia without reference to the messianic, and so promises us another kind of result.[8] Celan describes social spatiality as concrete, not as a sociality *to come.* Utopia *illuminates* political space. Through Celan, Levinas is able to think the figure of illumination with the Hebraic freed from the Hellenic. What would it mean to illuminate *utopian* space? And further, what would this utopian space illuminate with regard to our political responsibilities?

Let us turn briefly to Celan's speech. "The Meridian" concerns, in part, the fate of the poetic word. The poetic word is utopic. Utopia speaks here not to a dreamed world, but to the otherness of the other in the encounter. Utopia becomes a space of encounter illuminated by what we might call a "Hebraic light," a restless habitation, a movement toward the other. "Habitation justified by the movement toward the other," Levinas writes, "is essentially Jewish" (*NP* 54, *PN* 45). The force of Celan's poetic word lies in its ability to "locate the strangeness, the place where the person was able to set himself free as an—estranged—I" ("DM" 57–58, "TM" 51). The poetic word is always "*en route*" (*unterwegs*) and so places itself, in the estranged voice, "*in the mystery of the encounter*" ("DM" 55, "TM" 49; emphases mine). A topology of this encounter describes *u-topia.* Celan writes:

> And topological research?
>
>   Certainly. But in the light [*Lichte*] of what is still to be searched for: in a u-topian light.

> And the human being? The physical creature?
> In this light. ("DM" 57–58, "TM" 51)

This remark provides a starting point for a notion of asymmetrical spatiality. This spatiality is neither the neutral space of a container nor the abstract space of a transcendental condition. It is, rather, the place of "going beyond what is Human, stepping into a realm which is turned toward the human" ("DM" 47, "TM" 42). This u-topian space, Levinas will say, is "an expulsion outside the *worldliness of the world*" toward the encounter with the "nakedness of him who borrows all he owns" (*NP* 54, *PN* 45). The encounter with the nakedness of the Other, expelled from the world, offers a sense of social space beyond the suffocating nightmare of the world and the dreamy vanity of good conscience. Levinas writes: "This unusual outside is not another landscape . . . Nothing is more strange or foreign than the other man, and it is in the light of utopia that man shows himself. Outside all enrootedness and all dwelling: statelessness as authenticity!" (*NP* 53–54, *PN* 44).

The statelessness of u-topian space, beyond shared, reciprocal landscapes, is the space of obligation. The vanishing of those landscapes is the birth of obligation, the movement into the mystery of the encounter in which the weight of responsibility is first registered. The closing line from Celan's "Vast, Glowing Vault" is instructive here: "The world is gone, I must carry you."[9] U-topia as the disappearance of the world, of rootedness, of dwelling—*this* is the asymmetrical space of obligation. Stateless, I must bear the weight of responsibility. I must carry you.

"In going toward the other man," Levinas writes, "we [transcend] the human, toward utopia"—a notion of utopia that is neither an "accursed wandering" nor a dream, but the "'clearing' in which man shows himself" (*NP* 53, *PN* 44). In this light of utopia, the I "dedicates itself to the other in the non-place" (*NP* 54, *PN* 44). The clearing of u-topian space is the non-place of ethics; the vanishing of the world, which initiates my obligation, leaves no brilliance other than the intrigue of the interhuman. The encounter therefore illuminates, not a shared place, but rather an *out-of-place*—a *u-topos*—in which the vigilant work of obligation is enacted. Levinas underscores the asymmetry of this space in an interview: "This concern for the Other remains utopian in the sense that it is always 'out-of-place' (*u-topos*) in this world, always other than the 'ways of the world.'"[10] The ways of the world impose a light of reciprocity and shared place. The (Hebraic) brilliance of u-topia illuminates the height, mystery, and moral intrigue of asymmetrical spatiality.

2

With Celan, Levinas is able to free the ethical signification of utopia from its traditional anchoring in good conscience. Levinas is also aware that utopia carries the resonance of politics. What would it mean to make our passage from ethics to politics by way of u-topia?

Levinas's work has typically taken the passage to politics by way of *le tiers,* situating the question of justice in the faces of others *in* the face of the Other. His work on utopia focuses primarily on the configuration of the space of moral consciousness. But u-topia points us to the political horizon. Levinas makes this clear in his repeated claims about the intimacy of matters moral with matters political. For example, in the preface to the German translation of *Totality and Infinity,* Levinas writes that ethics is the "absolute interruption of onto-logy, but in the one-for-the-other of saintliness, of proximity, of sociality, of peace. A utopian sociality which still commands the whole of humanity in us and where the Greeks perceived the ethical."[11]

There is much here that warrants consideration, and what follows is something of an extended commentary on this passage. First, a word about the commandment of the whole of humanity. The commandment of humanity—this recalls *le tiers* who looks at me in the face of the Other. The face of the Other is the significative locus of both ethics and politics. Politics begins with the ethical face. This much is clear from the idea that the State takes ethics as its model. The signal of *le tiers,* however, goes further than modeling politics on ethics. The third party is already "there" in moral consciousness; the one-for-the-Other of ethical subjectivity already implicates politics. Political responsibilities are, so to speak, immanent to those issuing from the ethical. Politics begins with the singular face, but not in the sense of a supplement to ethics. Politics is already ethical.

Politics begins with ethics. The passage from ethics to legal justice therefore comes to the fore. The exposition of ethical subjectivity documents the intrigue of singularity, the relation of unicity to unicity, and so documents the infinite responsibility of the I dedicated to the Other. Politics concerns the universality of law, legal justice for all others, and so concerns what Levinas calls the comparison of incomparables. The passage from ethics to politics is one-way traffic: from ethics to politics. What is passed over? Here we must take this question in its double connotation: *what* passes over to politics from ethics and what is *left over* in the passage at its arrival to legal justice? How can law not lose sight of the singular?

Levinas's first answer is simple: law must be *responsible* and thus not represent in the interests of individuals "living for themselves." Ethics must pass the dis-interestedness and non-indifference of ethical responsibility over to political life. Just law, then, is neither interested nor indifferent. To a certain degree, this law gathers the debt owed the Other in ethics and makes that debt political. The human face itself corrects anonymous legality, interrupting the impersonal indifference of law and demanding representation. The passage from ethics to politics demands that the basic feature of the universality of law, representation, function as respect for and protection of the singular. Respectful protection, the function of legal justice, does not settle accounts between "citizens." Rather, protection as respect attends to the singularity of the face by making law just, by making the State ground its politics in the relation of peace. This is what it means for the State to want or wish for peace. Levinas writes:

> The entire life of a nation . . . carries within itself men who, before all loans, have debts, owe their fellow man, are responsible—chosen and unique—and in this responsibility want peace, justice, reason. Utopia! This way of understanding the meaning of the human . . . does not begin by thinking of the care men take of the places where they want to be in-order-to- be.[12]

The passage from ethics to politics therefore marks the State with the irreducibility of responsibility. The utopian space of the encounter, of the obligation and dedication of the oneself to the Other, is preserved in the State by maintaining the debts between citizens. Citizenship, granted under a justice system, does not obscure the face and the weight of responsibilities. Law speaks universally as respect for the Other, not as reconciliation. The debt to and singularity of the Other pass over to politics from ethics.

But more questions remain. What does humanity command in *us*? How does the State bear this mark of the ethical?

Levinas's answer to these questions lies in a politics of peace. The politics of peace recalls law to its origin in justice, which legitimizes law ethically. Thus, Levinas will claim that law "is not a natural and anonymous legality regulating human masses."[13] The egalitarian State, rather, proceeds "from the irreducible responsibility of the one for the Other" ("PeP" 150, "PaP" 144). This is the passage from ethics to politics. Still, as Levinas notes, the passage is not without risk. "Justice," he writes, "inseparable from institutions, and hence from politics, risks preventing the face of the Other from being recognized."[14] Obscuring the face—this danger derives from the problematic contradiction of singularity and universality.

Resistance to this danger comes in two parts. First, Levinas will note the legitimation of peace by the ethical. The ethical puts the first position of the I in question, and so the demand of a peace anchored in the face is that "I seek this peace, not for me, but for the Other" ("IEI" 196). This is an importance nuance. The State introduces freedom and reason into the equation, a result of the comparison of incomparables. But the first word of meeting, the first word of legal justice and sociality, must be peace: "the *wish for peace*—or goodness—is the first language."[15] And, precisely in the manner Celan proposes to speak on behalf of the wholly other, this wish must be spoken *for* the Other, from an estranged I—that is, an I that is disinterested. The first language of peace speaks without returning to the I— the citizen—as the locus of interest. The wish for peace spoken *for* the Other frees the I from the violence of self-sufficiency, of caring only for the places where it wants to be in-order-to-be, accomplished by *answering to and for the rights of the Other.* Levinas writes: "This is a goodness in peace, which is also the exercise of a freedom, and in which the I frees itself from its 'return to self'. . . to *answer for the other,* precisely to defend the rights of the other man" ("DH" 186, "RM" 124–25). The ethical exercise of freedom responds to the political rights of the Other. The incomparability of the Other in the *ethical* passes over to the peace sought for the Other in *politics.*

How can law signal this same passage, this peace for the Other? This is the second part of the resistance to obscuring the face. This problem issues directly from the universality and kind of irreducible impersonality of law. Whatever its configuration and whatever its legitimation, law must still signify for all citizens, and so bears within it a kind of impersonality. So, what is the law of peace? The law of peace must work with nonindifference despite its universality. Levinas's negotiation of this problem underlines how the universality of law accomplishes peace in its *protective function.* Law protects the singularity of the Other in the sense that it shields and defends it from anonymity. Pascal's aphorism, if we play with its words a bit, is instructive here. If the assertion of "my place" usurps the world, then we could say that the law of peace preempts this usurpation by protecting the Other's place in the sun. Protection of singularity defends the Other's place. The face is not obscured. In shielding the Other from anonymity, law carves out the space for singularity. This is how the law of peace no longer stands opposed to singularity. In its universality, law protects the singularity of the unique Other without absorption into an anonymous, general will. A politics of peace must compare incomparables and risk the singular. The law it generates, however, returns not to the interiority of freedom, but to the exteriority of the unique.

Humanity commands in the figure of *le tiers.* This command survives the passage from ethics to politics in the function of law that wants peace for the Other and protects the Other's place in the sun. Utopia, on this account, is accomplished *politically* as legal justice. Peace is utopia made political.

3

Let us return to the question of passage. Passage must be thought in two ways: what passes over and what is passed over. So far we have seen what passes over to politics. What is passed over, however, remains unexamined. The question of u-topia, I believe, bears a forgotten term of passage that, when it passes over, decisively alters the terrain of Levinas's politics.

U-topia puts the question of passage in two distinct terms. U-topia concerns both the uniqueness of the Other and the kind of spatiality in which encounter "happens." The passing over of unicity has already been made clear. But it is altogether unclear how the asymmetrical spatiality of ethics manifests itself to politics. What has happened in Levinas's politics to the irreducible out-of-placeness of u-topian space? The passage from singularity to law necessarily involves risks, the first and foremost of which is confusion of the law that protects singularity with an anonymous legality. Justice answers to singularity with defense and protection. My political freedom is always bound by this singularity; justice forbids usurpation of the Other's place in political space. This is the purchase of a politics of peace. But to close the question of justice here risks obscuring the concrete faces in political space, as well as the concreteness of my political obligations.

Even in politics, there is a debt before all loans. These are Levinas's words. Now, here, Levinas says something more than his own politics can contain. The universality discussed above claims to answer that debt, not by balancing accounts, but by clearing a place in the sun for the Other. This place, it seems, provides something akin to the coexistence (and *not* the interweaving) of debt and the exigencies of legal justice. How well does the law of peace bear this weight of the ethical, of this debt? It is noteworthy that nothing of the out-of-place emerges in politics. Without the passing of u-topian spatiality from ethics to politics, something of the element of the ethical is lost. Is there debt in Levinas's law? Is the politics of peace sufficiently u-topian?

First, a note on what the politics of peace aims to accomplish. The central issue of peace is representation, and so the question of how singularity can be respected in universality. Indeed, Levinas describes the function of law in terms of its ability to represent singularity with a minimum of violence. The focus on representation, however, has limitations.

In the first place, it is unclear how Levinas's law might play in the interaction of response and responsibility. Law protects in its representation, and thus does not simply contradict unicity, but law does not labor from the necessity of *response*. The law of peace stays fixed. This fixity is what makes it unclear how universality of law retains out-of-placeness. In fact, this out-of-placeness is out-of-place in the politics of peace. The rights of the human maintain the place in the sun for the Other and, although that place is sought "for the Other," the implied notion of political spatiality is plainly symmetrical. Law is universal and its space, carved out by the act of comparison, inserts sameness into political life. The nation carries *within* itself the debts between humans. It does not *itself* carry the debt between, for example, classes, races, or genders. Thus, the symmetry of political space in the relation of peace effectively purifies itself of the asymmetry of ethical social spatiality.

Is something else called for? At times Levinas would seem to think so, but often retreats from the implications. The very idea that the political state maintains the debts of the interhuman before all loans points us to a u-topian political space. The debt of the ethical ought to pass over to politics. Levinas does not see this indication. U-topian political space puts special demands on law. An asymmetrical political space reintroduces the interplay of response and responsibility, thereby demanding that law respond to the urgencies of the political Other. This conception of law must issue a responsible response and, because that response must work within the anarchical space of an *ethical* politics, justice cannot rest merely on the protection of singularity. In the transition to politics, Levinas falls back on a rather conservative notion of law, something that his work shares with theorists of the liberal state. Levinas himself recognizes this homology.[16] Although protection of singularity performs an important function, it also must be said that such a conception of justice does not work with the generosity and sacrifice demanded of the ethical. So the fact that law does not reflect the passage of u-topian spatiality to politics reveals the limits in Levinas's notion of legal justice. The limits inhere in the lack of sacrifice and generosity demanded by u-topian space. Even the defense of the rights of the Other leaves my space undiminished. The law of peace demands my respect for the Other. It does not demand that I sacrifice for the Other. There is certainly a generosity in respect, but a *sacrificial* generosity has another kind of character. Still, Levinas neither imposes this limit nor curtails political generosity by mere fiat. It is done for specific reasons and with some justification. Consider the following remarks:

> Utopia, transcendence. Inspired by love of one's fellow man, reasonable justice is bound by legal strictures and cannot equal the kindness that

solicits and inspires it. But kindness, emerging from the infinite
resources of the singular self, responding without reasons or reservations to the call of the face, can divine ways to approach to that suffering
other. ("AUJ" 260–61, "OUJ" 230)

Legal justice is bound by strictures that the responsibly responsive
subject is not; the kindness without reservation of the oneself, solicited by
the face, offers liturgical work. This liturgical work draws on the "full
hands" of the oneself and expends funds at a loss and without return.

What would law look like if we passed over the out-of-placeness of
ethical space to politics? Straightaway, political obligation is decisively
modified. This passage, which initiates a *u-topian* politics and not just a
politics of peace, brings us back to our opening remark from "Ideology
and Idealism"—that privileges of rank obstruct justice. Privileges of rank
manifest asymmetry and so manifest responsibilities of a different order
than simply protection of the singular. Levinas worries about the "permanent exclusion of a minority" in the liberal state, namely, in the case of
democracy, but it remains for him simply a "worry."[17] What does not occur
to Levinas is how this exclusion, and the rank and privilege resultant from
it, change the configuration of political spatiality. When rank and privilege alter political space, they become fecund starting points for thinking
law on the model of generosity. Privileges of rank preserve debt across the
borderline between ethics and politics. Levinas's debt is ethical, and his
conception of the State makes ethical life possible by not interfering with
the debts between unicities. Debt, however, is also political. Debt is owed
not just to the Other as singular, but also to identity formations in asymmetrical political space. If we think debt politically, then all the characteristics of ethics must accompany. Responsibility is concrete, anarchical,
and generous without expectation of return. To make this responsibility
political is to unsettle the work of universal law. Subjection of law to asymmetrical political space shatters the fixity of universality. Subjected to the
anarchy of responsibility, the rights of the human must find the character
of generosity and sacrifice. Law cannot be indifferent. It must *act* responsibly. That is, it must address and redistribute the violence of rank and
privilege that obscures justice.

If privileges of rank outline the figures of u-topian political space,
then we must next ask how law can respond. Law speaks for the rights of
the human. These rights look different in asymmetrical space. How can
law speak responsibly for the rights of the human *and* the rights of the
Other in u-topian political space? That is, how precisely is it that law can
become response-able, able to respond? Here our opening remark from
"The *I* and the Totality" concerning wealth is instructive. The ambiguity

of money makes another kind of justice possible, for it dismantles the abstraction of law. It is an underappreciated feature of Levinas's work, I think, that he affirms money as a philosophical, metaphysical, and moral category. The quantification of the world in money performs a twofold and interwoven function. First, it fills the hands of the privileged *concretely*, renders the Other of political space "orphaned," and marks rank as an ethical problematic. We can *measure* the injustice of privilege in wealth. This measurement, only possible on the basis of a quantification of the world, names, in explicit terms, the Same and Other of political space. Second, and directly consequent from this quantification, wealth makes it possible for law to respond. Quantification sets up both the conditions of obligation—the injustice of rank—and the conditions of response—the hands that are full in quantifiable wealth. Wealth, in a u-topian context, calls for a justice of redistribution and reparation.

But it should be said that Levinas's work alters these categories. Redistribution and reparation must be given without expectation of return, with dis-interestedness, and so must be done without the implicit or explicit language of settling accounts. I think we can divine this in part from Levinas's various mentions of charity as justice. The limit in Levinas's notion of charity, however, lies in his inability to see the demand of charity in the context of legal justice. Charity is merely ethical for him. From the perspective of u-topian political space, we cannot but see charity as the response of a law subjected to the anarchy of an ethical politics. I say an "ethical" politics here because, within quantified political space, extravagant generosity is possible in the name of charity, reparation, and redistribution. Wealth, then, is a moral category, both in terms of the content of political responsibility and the conditions of response to that responsibility. Quantification through wealth concretizes political demands and political giving, and so reintroduces to politics the interplay between response and responsibility.

There is of course much more to this puzzle. From this redistributive, reparative model of wealth, demanded by the law of u-topia, we can further consider two important political concepts: political subjectivity and the character of the work demanded of that subject. I can only offer a sketch of these in this context.

What kind of political subjectivity is proper to this politics? First, this subject must be incarnate. Incarnation makes it possible for the I (*le Moi*) to be accused, that is, accused in its skin. This incarnation, if taken seriously, may provide important clues regarding precisely *how* asymmetrical political space can signify in the ethical. Incarnation also renders me answerable; to be incarnate is to inhabit a social space that is quantifiable by wealth. Incarnation is my participation in the materiality of social space, both in terms of questions of wealth and the cultural-political dynamics of incarnate being. Second, we must describe the kind of work the political subject is subjected to in this space. Levinas's scattered remarks on *sainteté*, "saintliness," are productive in this regard. Consider the closing remarks to the "Avant-Propos" of *Entre Nous:*

> It is as if the emergence of the human in the economy of being upset the meaning and plot and philosophical rank of ontology: the in-itself of being persisting-in-being goes beyond itself in the gratuitousness of the outside-of-itself for-the-other, in sacrifice, or the possibility of sacrifice, *in the perspective of saintliness* [*sainteté*].[18]

In the perspective of saintliness; this is the work, the life, of a political subject subjected to u-topian space and *its* justice. Saintliness is the possibility of sacrifice and that sacrifice is especially significant in the quantified political space outlined by money. The work of this political subjectivity is *liturgical*—the expenditure of funds at a loss and without the expectation of return. Liturgy is then also the character of the law of this subjectivity, the law that determines its work in political space. Law gives in the redistribution of wealth and the payment of reparation. And, in its extravagant generosity, it gives neither with the expectation of return nor with the aim of settling accounts.

A liturgical law, lived by a saintly political subject in u-topian social space, enacts what Levinas calls a "justice of redemption" ("MT" 51, "IT" 37). The term "redemption," of course, here refers us to Franz Rosenzweig. Rosenzweig's redemption does not clear accounts; this is why Levinas says redemption is beyond the justice of forgiveness and vengeance, both of which erase debts between subjects and citizens. Through *The Star of Redemption,* Levinas understands redemption to be the work of *love,* "the transcendence of man-to-man."[19] At the outset of the present reflections I noted my desire to move outside the gestures of messianism. But for Rosenzweig, redemption opens back upon the future, and so may reinscribe traces of messianism back into the scene of a redistributive politics. This is another kind of future, I believe, and one that is not settled by the character of the *à-venir.* Rather, redemption is the relation of "man and world," of love and charity, and therefore "the work of a being absolutely singular—that is, mortal."[20] This singularity and the work of love *must be concrete,* even in the view of its pure future. This concretion of political responsibility is ethical and must be taken up in the perspective of saintliness. Sacrifice is a demand of justice whose future is in the face and faces of injustice, in those subjected to the violence of rank and privilege. That justice is not to come. It is manifest in the very space of our sociality.

Notes

1. Emmanuel Levinas, "Le moi et la totalité," in *Entre nous: Essais sur le penser-à-l'autre* (Paris: Éditions Grasset, 1991), 51; "The *I* and the Totality," in *Entre Nous: Thinking of the Other,* trans. Michael Smith (New York: Columbia University Press, 1999), 37. Hereafter cited in the text as "MT" and "IT," respectively.

2. Emmanuel Levinas, "Ideology and Idealism," in *The Levinas Reader,* trans. Seán Hand (Oxford: Basil Blackwell, 1990), 243–44; emphasis mine.

3. Emmanuel Levinas, *Totalité et infini* (The Hague: Martinus Nijhoff, 1961), 191; *Totality and Infinity,* trans. Alphonso Lingis (Pittsburgh: Duquesne University Press, 1969), 216. Hereafter cited in the text as *TeI* and *TI,* respectively.

4. See, for example, this passage from *Totalité et infini:* "Metaphysics therefore leads us to the accomplishment of the I as unicity by relation to which the work of the State must be situated, and which it must take as a model [*doit se situer et se modeler*]" (*Totalité,* 277; *Totality,* 300).

5. Emmanuel Levinas, "Le Lieu et l'utopie," in *Difficile liberté,* 2nd ed. (Paris: Albin Michel, 1976), 146; "Place and Utopia," in *Difficult Freedom,* trans. Seán Hand (Baltimore: Johns Hopkins University Press, 1997), 101.

6. Paul Celan, "Der Meridian," in *Der Meridian und andere Prosa* (Frankfurt am Main: Suhrkamp, 1994); "The Meridian," in *Paul Celan: Collected Prose,* trans. Rosemarie Waldrop (New York: Sheep Meadow, 1986). Hereafter cited in the text as "DM" and "TM," respectively.

7. Emmanuel Levinas, "Paul Celan: De l'être à l'autre," in *Noms propre* (Paris: Éditions Grasset, 1986); "Paul Celan: From Being to the Other," in *Proper Names,* trans. Michael Smith (Stanford: Stanford University Press, 1997). Hereafter cited in the text as *NP* and *PN,* respectively.

8. Levinas's reading of Celan also points us in a different direction than that taken by Catherine Chalier ("L'utopie messianique," in *Répondre d'autrui,* ed. J.-C. Aeschlimann [Boudry-Neuchâtel: Éditions de la Baconnière, 1989], 53–70) and Miguel Abensour ("Penser utopie autrement," in *Cahiers de l'herne: Emmanuel Levinas,* ed. Catherine Chalier and Miguel Abensour [Paris: Éditions de l'Herne, 1991], 572–602).

9. "Die Welt ist fort, ich muß dich tragen." Paul Celan, "Vast, Glowing Vault," in *Poems of Paul Celan,* trans. Michael Hamburger (New York: Persea, 1988), 224.

10. Emmanuel Levinas, "Interview: Ethics and the Infinite," by Robert Kearney, in *States of Mind,* ed. Richard Kearney (New York: New York University Press, 1995), 197. Hereafter cited in the text as "IEI."

11. Emmanuel Levinas, "Preface a l'édition allemande," in *Entre nous,* 251.

12. Emmanuel Levinas, "L'autre, utopie, et justice," in *Entre nous,* 261; "The Other, Utopia, and Justice," in *Entre Nous,* 231. Hereafter cited in the text as "AUJ" and "OUJ," respectively.

13. Emmanuel Levinas, "Paix et proximité," in *Altérité et transcendance* (Montpellier: Fata Morgana, 1995), 149–50; "Peace and Proximity," in *Alterity and Transcendence,* trans. Michael Smith (New York: Columbia University Press, 1999), 143. Hereafter cited in the text as "PeP" and "PaP," respectively.

14. Emmanuel Levinas, "Violence du visage," in *Alterité et transcendance,* 178; "Violence of the Face," in *Alterity and Transcendence,* 176.

15. Emmanuel Levinas, "Les droits de l'homme et les droits d'autrui," in *Hors sujet* (Montpellier: Fata Morgana, 1987), 186; "The Rights of Man and the Rights of the Other," in *Outside the Subject,* trans. Michael Smith (Stanford: Stanford University Press, 1993), 125. Hereafter cited in the text as "DH" and "RM," respectively.

16. "That is perhaps the very excellence of democracy, whose fundamental liberalism corresponds to the ceaseless deep remorse of justice" (Levinas, "L'autre, utopie," 260; "The Other, Utopia," 229). Levinas will elsewhere link, explicitly, the liberal state with the defense of the rights of the human. Compare Emmanuel Levinas, "Dialogue sur le penser-à-l'autre," in *Entre Nous,* 239; "Dialogue on Thinking of the Other," in *Entre Nous,* 203.

17. Levinas, "Dialogue sur penser," 241; "Dialogue on Thinking," 205.

18. Emmanuel Levinas, "Avant-Propos," in *Entre nous,* 10–11; "Author's Preface," in *Entre Nous,* xii.

19. Emmanuel Levinas, "La philosophie de Franz Rosenzweig," in *A l'heure des nations* (Paris: Éditions de Minuit, 1988), 183; "The Philosophy of Franz Rosenzweig," in *In the Time of Nations,* trans. Michael Smith (Bloomington: Indiana University Press, 1994), 158.

20. Emmanuel Levinas, "Franz Rosenzweig: Une pensée juive moderne," in *Hors sujet,* 82, 84; "Franz Rosenzweig: A Modern Jewish Thinker," in *Outside the Subject,* 56, 58.

Persecution: The Self at the Heart of Metaphysics

David Michael Kleinberg-Levin

> I remember the manifold cord—the thousand or the million stranded cord which my being and every man's being is . . . so that, if everyone should claim his part in me, I should be instantaneously diffused through creation and individually decease. . . . I am an alms of all and live but by the charity of others.
> —Ralph Waldo Emerson

> The difference between the life of the spirit and that of the flesh is itself a spiritual difference.
> —George Santayana, *Platonism and the Spiritual Life*

Project

The reflections that have culminated in the writing of this study were originally provoked by perplexities that I could neither ignore nor dispel regarding Levinas's figure of "persecution." The more I struggled with it, with its implications and equivocations, the more deeply I felt myself hopelessly lost within the darkness invoked by its intrigue. What is offered here is the understanding that eventually emerged from this most demanding struggle. But in the attempt to achieve the lucidity of a certain understanding, I have found that the question of persecution in Levinas's work is much more complicated than he recognizes. Thus, instead of making matters simpler, the process of clarifying has revealed the subject to be much more intricate—and in the final analysis, it has generated even more questions.

As we know, responsibility for the welfare and sufferings of the other constitutes, for Levinas, a fundamental structure of subjectivity. Today I want to show, using figure 1, "The Moral Journey," that Levinas's moral phenomenology implies, and indeed requires, a certain process of moral growth, moral individuation, or self-realization. More specifically, Levinas clearly draws a distinction between the ego and the self, but leaves their relationship, especially their relationship within the temporality of an individual's life-history, in the elusiveness of equivocations. I will show that his distinction implies and requires an interpretation or narrative that registers their relationship within the life-history of an individual, showing how the ego and the self are related, both *diachronically*, in terms of the evolving phases, or faces, of moral self-realization, and *synchronically*, in terms of the dimensions of moral consciousness, moral experience. Without such an interpretation, such a narrative, it is impossible to determine of whom Levinas's phenomenological descriptions of a shared interiority—descriptions in the first person singular—are supposed to be true. Some of his reports would be true of the ego, but not the self; some would be true of the self, but not the ego; others would be true of a pre-originary self, but not true of a morally self-conscious, self-reflective self, or true of the second, but not true of the first. Only such a narrative of moral growth can ultimately make these equivocations instructive.

This narrative requires, first of all, that, in keeping with the quotation from Santayana, we recognize a distinction between the flesh and the body. The flesh is a spiritually appropriated substance; it is the body as traumatized medium, as a substance destined to bear the moral law deeply inscribed within it, a substance shattered by its alterity, radically exposed to the other and summoned to responsibility for the other. Thus Levinas will say that the human "has to be conceived on the basis of the responsibility more ancient than the conatus of a substance or inward identification, a responsibility which . . . disturbs just this inwardness."[1] And also disturbs that representation of the body which reduces it to the prevailing ontology of substances.

I also want to show, using figure 2, "Palimpsest of the Flesh," not only that the difference between ego and self—and the narrative of their relation to the question of moral growth—need to be elaborated in terms of the flesh, but also, more specifically, that Levinas's interpretations of persecution, responsibility, and substitution implicitly recognize that it is, and could only be, first of all, as a claim on my flesh, a claim to my incarnation, that this responsibility takes hold of me, because otherwise it is incomprehensible how an assignment of responsibility for the other could possibly bind me in a time before consciousness, memory, and volition; and that it is as an inscription borne by certain "predispositions" at the very deepest level of the flesh that responsibility as substitution for the other is first assigned to me.[2] How could I be "elected" by the Good to carry the moral law as an assignment—"elected" without at first any realization, any act of the free will, and indeed contrary to certain natural propensities—if not through the medium of my flesh?[3] And since "minds," whether in the Cartesian picture or in the picture of empiricism, are thought to be essentially individual, monadic unities both internally indivisible and externally separate, how could there be, as Levinas's phenomenology asserts, a "shared mind," a shared interiority—the one-for-the-other of substitution, within which, without threatening the other's difference from ourselves, we nevertheless keep, according to Levinas, an "inward place" for the other, taking to heart another's good as distinct but inseparable from our own good—if the "minds" in question were not embodied in a flesh capable of suffering the other's persecution and embracing the other's good? And yet, although only a deep phenomenology of the flesh—a hermeneutical phenomenology able to penetrate the illusions which maintain the skin of prejudice—could give us a compelling account of substitution, the one-for-the-other, Levinas does not articulate the "spiritual," pre-originary dimension of the flesh within his phenomenology of shared interiority.

Moreover, Levinas does not give sufficient articulation to the way that his phenomenology works as a process of moral growth, moral individuation, or self-realization, in which the assignment presumably borne by the flesh would to some extent—if only in the faintest traces of traces— be recuperated for moral life.[4] In discussing what he calls "recurrence to the self" he touches on this recuperation, even using this word, but he does not give sufficient attention to its method—to how it approaches the traces of substitution, of alterity, that are structuring the pre-originary sensibility of our flesh.

I now believe that the difficulties I encountered trying to clarify for myself Levinas's conception of persecution derive not only from the different configurations of meaning into which, without explicit acknowledgment of the differences and equivocations, he casts this term, but also from the fact that (1) although he makes use of a distinction between ego and self which seems to imply a process of moral awakening, he does not explicitly articulate their different positions in the context of such a process. Thus (2) although he speaks of persecution in relation to self and ego, he does not recognize with sufficient explicitness that the self and the ego would experience what he means by "persecution" in radically different ways. Moreover (3) although he locates a certain sense of "persecution" in a pre-originary time before consciousness and emphasizes the importance of sense and sensibility in the "ethical relation," he does not locate this sense of persecution with sufficient explicitness in our experience of embodiment, and, in particular, the intersubjective structure at the very heart of this experience—a structure which I would describe using his words "subjection" and "substitution." And (4) although he speaks of a *récurrence à Soi,* and of a *récuperation du Soi* (*OB* 92, *AE* 117), he does not articulate what they mean in relation to a process of moral growth, moral self-realization; nor does he show what such a recurrence and recuperation would or could mean, in relation to the experience of persecution. Finally (5), although it would seem that moral growth should depend on a recurrence to what I will call the pre-originary self and on a serious attempt to recuperate something of the body's felt sense of its pre-originary experience of persecution, he does not show how the recurrence works as a process engaged in such recuperation; nor does he show how the recuperation could contribute to the ego's moral growth and self-realization—what Levinas describes as "the individuation of the ego in me," *du Moi en moi* (*OB* 126, *AE* 162). In particular, what we need to understand is the phenomenology of this recuperation—how it is related to the emergence, within me, of a bodily felt sense of responsibility for the other, a sensibility sheltering the good of the other, the good-for-the-other, within the very heart of my interiority.

I will argue that, and will show how, Levinas's phenomenology of substitution—and the permutations of substitution in the experience of persecution—involve a shattering deconstruction of the self conceived according to the logic of identity in the discourses of Western ontology, radically opening and exposing the subjectivity of the self to the other— to what, in the language of traditional metaphysics, has been called "transcendence." For substitution is not conceivable within a substance metaphysics that represents subjectivity as the self-determining origin of experience, an absolutely independent, isolated existence with an essential identity that can be neither touched nor moved by the appeal of the other. In the experience of persecution, the subjectivity of the self is recalled to its ethical origin, returned to the suffering of a flesh that is never just its own.

The Anatomy of Persecution

The concept of substitution, in Levinas's later phenomenology, is perhaps his most important contribution to our understanding of moral experience. Substitution is not only the form of an extraordinary responsibility. It is also the very structure of a subjectivity subjected to the other to the point of suffering with others the persecution they suffer, while also at the same time being held in responsibility for their persecution—"accused" of persecution, in Levinas's disruptive and unsettling new sense. All these terms—substitution, subjectivity, persecution, responsibility—have complicated, multiple functions in the plot of Levinas's moral phenomenology. Here, however, I want to concentrate on "persecution," a term which Levinas deploys in ways that require considerable patience and careful thought if one is to penetrate its intricate obscurity and learn from its rigorous lucidity.

In the reading we will be thinking about here, the question of persecution appears in four distinct configurations of meaning.

1. According to one of the configurations, the I (anyone capable of using this first-person singular grammatical form) is responsible for the persecution of others and accordingly stands "accused" of "persecution," because—Levinas says, making his point in the first-person grammar of phenomenological discourse—regardless of my intentions, and even despite myself, I am always, to some extent, and in some way, complicit in the oppression, persecution, violence, and injustice that others have suffered, and I must therefore hold myself responsible, regardless of how others respond to the moral exigencies. (It seems to me that Levinas's phenomenological use of the first-person singular grammar can perhaps avoid the abuse and violence of telling others what they are experiencing only by assuming that it is a question of describing a shared interiority. The phenomenological description of our shared interiority must be at the very heart of his ethics, because, as I have argued elsewhere, to the extent that such description is performative, affectively moving, it would enable us to deepen our bodily felt contact with—or even, for the first time, to discover—the shared dimension of our experience, so that we might realize its promise in the conduct of our lives.) It is not necessary that the I be the immediately causal agent in order to be responsible for the other's persecution, "guilty" as accused. Responsibility for the other's persecution may instead pertain to more indirect involvements: tolerance of discriminatory social practices, tolerance of oppressive legislation, tolerance of economic injustices, tolerance of physical abuse, tolerance of the exploitation of labor in the underdeveloped countries. The responsibility may be that of witness or judge—or it may be that of the indifferent bystander. And I will be pressured into realizing my responsibility in relation to this accusation when, through the other's eyes, the humanity in the other's face, I am made to see and feel the extent to which, even with the best of intentions, I have nevertheless, despite myself, caused or participated in the persecution of others, and must take responsibility for having limited, diminished, neglected, denied, abused, or injured the other. In other

words, all of us are responsible for the sufferings of others and all of us—but some of us, of course, much more than others—stand accused of persecution.[5] In this first configuration, the accusation of persecution is extended far beyond its normal reach—the reach, at least, of juridical law, if not also that of customary moral law; but the meaning of the term is still easily understandable within our prevailing moral mentality.

2. In a second configuration of meaning, there is a *pre-originary* accusation of persecution to which I, as a pre-originary self, am subject. Freud lends support to this interpretation, observing in *The Ego and the Id* that "in many criminals, especially youthful ones, it is possible to detect a very powerful sense of guilt which existed before the crime, and is therefore not its result but its motive. It is as if it were a relief to be able to fasten this unconscious sense of guilt onto something real and immediate."[6] According to Levinas:

> The self, the persecuted one, is accused beyond his fault before [the ego's] freedom, and this in an unavowable innocence. One must not conceive it to be the state of original sin, for it is, on the contrary, the original goodness of creation. . . . Persecution is the precise moment in which the subject is reached or touched without the mediation of the logos. (*OB* 121, 124; *AE* 154–55, 159)

In relation to the ordinary meaning of "persecution," the final assertion *could* be understood as saying simply that persecution does not need language to occur, that it is a violence which occurs when communication breaks down and is no longer possible. But this, of course, would hardly be an interesting observation. What else, then, could these words be taken to mean? Perhaps that the accusation of persecution is to be located, *first of all,* not in words of accusation, or in the discourse of our legal and juridical institutions, but rather, instead, already inscribed in the sensibilities of the flesh, even before the subject, the infant, can speak.

In Jeremiah 31:32 we find this reference to an inscription of the moral law given to the flesh: "I will put my law within them and I will write it on their hearts." This inscription, whereby, prior to processes of socialization, "the subject is already [living] for the other on the level of sensibility" (*CPP* 147, *HH* 94) is for Levinas a gift and a blessing; but it is also a traumatism and an accusation. Now, on my interpretation, what Levinas is calling here "the self" would be the *pre-originary* self. This is the self that is already "accused" of persecution prior to the ego's consciousness, volition, and freedom. And for Levinas, this means—in sharpest difference from the Christian interpretation—that the self is not cursed by an original sin but blessed by "the original goodness of creation," because its flesh has already been endowed with a moral compass, with a sensibility already deeply affected by the other and a capacity to feel the suffering of the other—even to the point of experiencing the other's persecution as its own. Coming into the world already "accused" of persecution, and indeed—as in the fourth configuration—already "persecuted" by a bodily affected, bodily felt responsibility for the other's suffering, the self is not cursed by an original sin but blessed by the moral "knowledge"—the compass of "predispositions"—given through its incarnation in a time beyond time. The mediation of language—and the thematized moral knowledge it makes possible—will come, of course, at a later stage in our moral development and moral relationships.

Thus Levinas is asking us—if only implicitly—to realize that there is a pre-originary assignment of moral responsibility for the other's suffering and welfare, an assignment borne by, and borne in, the very sense and sensibility of our flesh. And, as I can realize only retrospectively in the movement of recurrence, this is an assignment that—in the paradoxical time of the pre-originary self—exposes me to the other, opens me to the claims of the other like a gaping wound opens the flesh, and inscribes an identity-crossing substitution of the myself for the other into the very structure of my subjectivity. In this second configuration of meaning, it is not a question of an accusation of persecution that refers to my comportment in the world; here it is a question, instead, of an accusation that comes from my pre-originary substitution for the other—a substitution that makes me, unbeknown to myself, already responsive to the other and already holds me responsible for the other's suffering and welfare. The accusation against me is visible in the face of the other, soliciting my pre-originary responsibility and recalling me to myself in the grammatically accusative form (*me, se,* in French), an accusative derived, moreover, from no prior nominative form. And it carries within it a summons to responsibility which has already taken hold of me, taking me hostage, claiming the sense and sensibility of my flesh—the flesh of a deep structure of subjectivity, of subjectivity as subjection, a radical, pre-originary heteronomy—in an anachronism before time, before consciousness, before any intentions and actions in the world.

Unlike the responsibility for persecution that accuses me in the first configuration of meaning, confronting the ego with its worldly effects, the responsibility that accuses me in the second configuration touches and marks the *flesh* of the pre-originary self. This is why I am responsible for the other even before consciousness, even before intention, volition, and freedom, even before the time of memory. And this is why there is an accusation of persecution which cannot be denied, cannot be escaped. If I am already responsible for the persecution of the other even before consciousness, then I am also already guilty—despite existing in an "unavowable" innocence—of a failure in responsibility, already guilty, as accused, of persecution. The accusation, which Levinas describes as a "wound," a "trauma," an "obsession," is borne as such by the flesh of the pre-originary self. Its possession of me is a radical dispossession; and the moral predisposition it forms utterly dis-positions and displaces me. Its inscription in the flesh breaches the very identity of this self, opening us forever to the other.

3. In a third configuration of meaning, "persecution" refers to my suffering with the other the other's persecution. I take Levinas to be saying that, through substitution, our pre-originary responsibility to and for the other causes the ego or self to participate in the sufferings of the other and to feel itself one with—and one of—the persecuted. In other words, the very structure of my identity is formed in a subjectivity that, before the awakening of egological consciousness, has already participated in the sufferings of the persecuted, because, even before the emergence of this consciousness, before the time of memory, and long before the awakening of moral consciousness, I have *already* been affected, wounded by the persecution suffered by others. Thus, I am not only (as in the first configuration) an agent of persecution, though my participation may be very indirect and remote; in my experience as a pre-originary self, already accused of persecution, already traumatized by this accusation, already guilty of persecution (as in the second configuration), I am also, in a sense that Levinas wants us to begin admitting into our consciousness, a victim of persecution, wounded in the very depths of my flesh—in a dimension of my being which radically opens and exposes me—by the persecution suffered by others. The other's suffering is my affliction, my own persecution.

In his intricate and subtle commentary on the question of persecution in Levinas, Robert Bernasconi writes: "Perhaps I am both persecuted and oppressor to the extent that the face which confronts me is both judge and accused."[7] This would seem to draw out the implications of a statement in *Otherwise Than Being* where Levinas says that the "enigma" of the face—the face of the other who faces me—is both "judge and accused" (*OB* 12, *AE* 14).

But in what sense, in what way, am I persecuted? And how could Levinas possibly be implying that I should be more concerned about myself than about everyone else? We might be tempted at first to suppose that it is merely a question of extending the normal concept, since everyone can appropriate the phenomenological "I" and because, since I am in no position to deny that others have suffered persecution, I must be willing to recognize that everyone may have an indisputable right to claim the suffering of persecution. But what he has to say cannot be reduced to this normal, still familiar conceptual terrain. A radically different configuration of meaning is in fact at stake. Moreover, as soon as I adopt the first-person position and conclude that this extension supports my own claim to be the victim of persecution, a voice in Levinas's ethics will intervene, serving as a reminder that this extension must in no way blind my eyes to the persecution suffered by others. The most unsettling point in Levinas's ethics is not, after all, that all of us are victims, but that all of us are guilty of persecution—and none can avoid the accusation.

But in what sense, then, am I persecuted? I want to suggest that, in the second and third configurations of meaning, Levinas is giving both the accusation of persecution and the suffering of persecution a deeper, radically new meaning—let us say a "pre-originary sense," not at all ordinary, not at all immediately recognizable, according to which the accusation of persecution and the suffering of persecution refer me to experiences relating to the other that are constitutive of the very deepest structure of my subjectivity: my substitution for the other, my pre-originary, pre-personal exposure to the other's suffering presence—and my ability to be responsive. Thus, for example, Levinas will refer us to a pre-originary exposure to the other, an "exposure [that] precedes the initiative a voluntary subject would take to expose itself" (*OB* 180, *AE* 227). It is in the substitution effected by this pre-originary exposure that I am first touched by the other's suffering and feel a responsibility for the other that accuses me of taking part—despite myself, despite my innocence—in the other's persecution.

A careful reading of the texts suggests, I believe, that there are ways in which realizing this pre-originary substitution could deepen and alter our understanding of the meaning of "persecution." Because this substitution shatters and alters our identity, contacting and realizing it could heighten our awareness of a shared experience of persecution and, at the same time, reinforce that sense of responsibility for the persecution suffered by the other which has already, in a time before time, claimed the flesh of our pre-originary self by opening and exposing it to the other. No one suffers persecution alone. When anyone suffers persecution, we all suffer, we all suffer persecution.

Whereas, in the first configuration of meaning, the extension of the experience of "persecution" to everyone involves a meaning that does not necessarily disturb the rule of egoism, the extensions in the second and third configurations involve interpretations of our experience that compel us to confront a radically new experience of persecution, an experience that requires interpretation in terms of a phenomenology of the flesh—a phenomenology, in particular, that registers the other's suffering of persecution and the other's pre-originary accusation of persecution in and as the formation of a pre-originary, bodily carried sense of responsibility for the other, not only in the most absolute passivity and in a time before consciousness, volition, and memory, but also in a certain identity-shattering and skin-traversing substitution.

Giving new meaning to a phrase from Habermas, we could perhaps call substitution "a deep layer of solidarity."[8] Because of the substitution, the exposure to alterity that takes hold of us at this deepest level of our experience, we must say that the ethnic and racial differences which are the shameful obsession of prejudice are only skin deep. Because, from the depths of the flesh, our skin is exposed to the other in the truth and justice of its nudity, and because all the seemingly incontestable boundaries of kinship, of race and ethnicity, socially constructed at the level we call "skin," are subjected to a trial coming both from within and from without that they can never completely ignore or suppress.

It should be clear by now why it is necessary to interpret Levinas's account, positing a pre-originary substitution and responsibility, in terms of a process of moral growth—and a corresponding palimpsest of the flesh.

4. But there is also, I suggest, a fourth configuration of meaning, one in which my responsibility for the suffering and welfare of the other constitutes not only an "accusation" but also a "persecution." For the responsibility borne of substitution—and the accusation of persecution that is registered in the other's face—is a burden and affliction which makes me suffer. Thus, in *Otherwise Than Being*, Levinas writes of

> the trauma of accusation [*le traumatisme de l'accusation*], suffered by a hostage to the point of persecution [*subie jusqu'à la persecution*], putting into question the very identity of the hostage [*me*], who substitutes himself for all the others: all this is the Self [*le Soi*], a defecting or defeat [*défection ou défaite*] of the Ego's [*du Moi*] identity. (*OB* 15, *AE* 18)

Levinas will also refer us, there, to "the irreparable wounding of the Self in the Me accused by the other to the point of persecution" (*l'incicatrisable blessure du Soi dans le Moi accusé par l'autre jusqu'à la persécution et responsable de son persécuteur; OB* 15, 126; *AE* 18, 162). This recurrent phrase, "to the point of persecution," each time perplexing, is at the very center of the fourth configuration of meaning within which Levinas situates the question of persecution, for his phenomenology shows us that the accusation of persecution which is inscribed prior to consciousness in the depths of the flesh always becomes, *at the level of consciousness*, an inevitable "persecution" of conscience, a burden that forever holds us hostage. We are *persecuted* by the accusation. We are relentlessly pursued by its exigency—by a responsibility and an accusation from which we can never be released. In a passivity more passive than the passivity that modern philosophical thought contrasts with activity, a passivity even more passive than the Husserlian "passive synthesis," I am overcome, "persecuted" (in what may be Levinas's most disturbing and provocative sense of this term) by this accusation, affected unto the very depths of my flesh, elected and destined to bear—as host and hostage—an undeclinable responsibility for the other (*CPP* 147, *HH* 94). Whether or not we realize it, our flesh forever bears the traces of its traumatic, secret election by the Good, an imperative moral assignment that is contrary to our natural egoism, but nevertheless inwardly incumbent.

But it is essential to recognize that this fourth configuration of meaning is registered differently in different phases or faces of individuation. Thus there is (a) a sense constituted by our egoism and (b) a radically different sense articulating itself through the self—and in fact, first of all, through the very flesh of the pre-originary self. Levinas never makes this differentiation clear, although it seems to me absolutely necessary, because how I respond to the accusation of persecution unquestionably differs, depending on whether I respond as an ego or as a morally developed self. In the ego, this accusation will be experienced as a totally hostile burden—as a "persecution" in the sense that it is an "election" which, as much as possible, the ego will try to deny and evade. Levinas's early work, *On Evasion,* diagnoses this experience with phenomenological insight into its motivation.[9] In a self that is more morally developed, however, this accusation would be experienced as a "persecution" in the *absolutely different* sense that it constitutes an "election" the self joyfully embraces to serve the Good of the other—a moral assignment which it must try to fulfill, knowing all the while that, no matter how hard it tries, it cannot possibly do enough to serve the other. Thus, the response of a morally developed self to its awakened consciousness of the accusation, its response to an awareness of the responsibility that summons it as a self, would be to take to heart the other's Good and dedicate itself ever more self-lessly to serving and caring for the other, even to the point of assuming responsibility for making the accusation of the other into an endlessly demanding "persecution," the relentless "persecution" of a moral conscience that constantly reproaches, constantly requires more self-sacrifice—even the sacrifice of its name, the possibility of public recognition for its service. In other words, a morally developed self would experience a consciousness of the persecution that has already taken hold of the pre-originary self, already overcome it, in a pre-originary time before consciousness, volition, and memory, and already bound it, flesh and spirit, in extreme subjection to the other. And to the extent that—thanks to the face of the other—I have become conscious of this assignment, its

responsibility to and for the other would assume the traits of an accusation, connecting me to the other's suffering and accusing me of persecution not only *despite* all good intentions but *even before* all good intentions.
This accusation could touch, wound, and expose me so deeply, pursuing
me all the days of my life, that it would become what Levinas wants to call,
radically altering the standard meaning of the term, a persecution. Thus,
a morally developed self would feel to some degree compelled by—and
indeed drawn to—the vocation of self-less service, to which, through its
very incarnation, through the very nature of its sensibility, it would feel itself to have been already called, already "elected." In the extreme of self-
sacrifice, this persecution by an extreme sense of responsibility could be
said, perhaps, to define for Levinas the figure of a saintly life.

Ego and Self: A Narrative
of Moral Growth

In order to understand Levinas's ethics, and in particular, what he is saying about responsibility, substitution, and persecution, it is necessary to
understand his phenomenological treatment of subjectivity, especially his
distinction between the ego (*le Moi*) and the self (*le Soi*). I will now show
that there is, in his analysis of subjectivity, an implicit narrative of moral
self-realization, and that this narrative requires, on a *diachronic* axis, the
recognition of four different phases or faces in moral self-development
and, on a *synchronic* axis, the recognition of four different structural dimensions—dimensions, in fact, of the flesh, the body that embodies these
phases or faces. In the course of development, the earlier stages of the
process are surpassed, but do not entirely disappear. Therefore, the moral
perspective of the earliest stage—our pre-originary sensibility—can always to some extent be recuperated for the guidance of present living; but
there is always also the possibility of occasional or more or less permanent
regression to the moral perspective and moral comportment of an earlier
stage. To facilitate discussion, let us call these four subjectivities (1) the
pre-originary self, (2) the narcissistic ego, (3) the enlightened ego, and
(4) the saintly self. As we shall see, the latter self embodies an ideal at-
tained only in the life of a saint or bodhisattva. Obviously, it is a phase, or
face we seldom see. (See figures 1 and 2.)

1. The figure of *the pre-originary self* characterizes the moral endowment of infancy: an endowment of "predispositions" that takes hold of the
utterly passive infant flesh. The pre-originary self receives this endowment, its election, in the form of an inscription bearing its assignment of

Figure 1
The Moral Journey

Saintly Self (by an effort to recuperate traces carried by the pre-originary self)	Transpersonal responsiveness, openness, compassionate exposure Selfless, joyous self-sacrificing: a saintly anonymity The one-for-the-other: a saintly heteronomy An asymmetrical relation: but this time in favor of the other Nonreversible, non-reciprocal responsibility (in favor of the other) Saintly volition (assumption of supererogatory responsibilities) A saint's experience of being persecuted: the saintly one sympathetically *shares* sufferings of others and feels pain at being unable ever to do enough
Enlightened Ego	Capable of an impersonal, universalizable moral standpoint (Kant's "mature" moral development) Autonomous (in the Kantian universalizable sense) Relations with others ruled by mutual recognition, symmetry, reversibility, reciprocity, equality Builds institutions of justice to achieve a pragmatic accommodation to an *enlightened* egoism Responsible (in critical, reflective, dialogical assumption of obligations) "Accused," "persecuted": in the sense that this ego sympathetically *understands* the sufferings of others and works for social change to achieve justice and equality
Narcissistic Ego	Unable or unwilling to adopt the impersonal, third-person standpoint of the other, of justice Self-centered, self-interested assumption of responsibility Oriented toward self-preservation (conatus essendi) Insists on a name (no anonymity in giving) Narcissistically asymmetrical (in ego's favor) Narcissistically heteronomous (immature moral development in the Kantian sense: actions more or less in prereflective or unreflective conformity; no reversibility of positions, only a pragmatic mutual recognition, a quid pro quo exchange, no principled reciprocity)

Figure 1
The Moral Journey (*continued*)

	Narcissistically persecuted (regards responsibility for others as an unwanted burden)
Pre-Originary Self	Pre-originary substitution for the other
	Pre-personal, pre-originally anonymous
	Pre-originally asymmetrical (in favor of the other); pre-originally heteronomous (in favor of the other)
	Involuntary subjection to the other: prior to consciousness, memory, volition
	"Accused" (called in accusative forms *se, me,* prior to any nominative)
	"Persecuted pre-originarily" (taken hold of in the flesh by responsibility)
	Traumatized
	In irreversible, nonreciprocal substitution for the other
	Taken hold of by an undeclinable pre-originary responsibility for the other (a-pre-originary)

responsibility for the other in the most radical passivity, heteronomy, and anonymity of its flesh. But, as Levinas emphasizes (*CPP* 137, *HH* 80), we must not think of these "predispositions" in terms of any "divine instinct," any "altruistic or generous nature," or any "natural goodness," because they do not fix moral development in any teleologically predetermined relation to the Good, and because it is also in the nature of the flesh to be endowed with libidinal drives that do not immediately recognize in generosity, altruism, and goodness their proper fulfillment. Thus, the flesh of the pre-originary self is riven by the marks of an extreme trauma, imposing and inscribing the secret of irreversible substitution, the asymmetry and heteronomy of the-one-for-the-other, on the palimpsest of the flesh, opposing and resisting the selfishness and aggressiveness of the natural drives, already accusing and persecuting the infant even before the time of the name. The self-lessness of the saintly self, its substitution for the other, would accordingly be a transformative *recuperation* of the "lower" anonymity and "lower" heteronomy of the pre-originary self. This would constitute a certain "higher" heteronomy, a responsibility for the other that would be higher than Kantian "autonomy" and that one might usefully compare with Kant's conception of "love" as the free reception of the will of another person into one's own maxims.

Figure 2
The Palimpsest of the Flesh

To the four configurations, the four faces of subjectivity, there correspond four phases or dimensions of our embodiment, our incarnation: the flesh as text and texture of the moral journey

Saintly Self (Transpersonal)	The flesh in its apotheosis, e.g., in tenderness and compassionate work, in service to the community, and especially to the needy; Proverbs 31: "She stretches out her hand to the poor; She reaches out her arms to the needy"
Enlightened Ego (Impersonal)	The flesh in its universality as the medium of mutual recognition, mutual respect, and peace
Narcissistic Ego (Narrowly personal)	The flesh in its social role as egological skin, site of sensuous pleasure, defining boundaries between ego and other, establishing and protecting the interiority and immanence of subjectivity, expressive and assertive, even to the point of aggressivity and certain habits of violence
Pre-Originary Self (Prepersonal)	The flesh prophetically inspired: the passive receiver and entrusted bearer of the message, bearer of the commanding inscription of the moral law, accusing, persecuting, taking possession of the flesh, binding it to an indeclinable responsibility for the other, preparing it for the responsiveness and communicativeness of a sensibility to the other, suffering for the other

2. The figure of *the narcissistic ego* characterizes that moral condition in which our intentions, motivations, and actions are determined to a great extent by self-preservation and self-interest.[10] In the social relations of the narcissistic ego, there is, as we would expect, not much—if any— reflectively mediated reciprocity. It lives by an asymmetry that favors itself. This ego emerges, of course, through socialization, and its rule involves the forgetting and concealing of the pre-originary self: "without [experiencing a deep sense of] persecution, the ego [*le Moi*] raises its head and covers over the self [*le Soi*]" (*OB* 112, *AE* 143). In effect, the narcissistic ego splits off from its earlier experience as a pre-originary self. In the moral comportment of this ego, then, there is a certain asymmetry and heteron-

omy—but in the Kantian sense, utterly different from the other two struc-tures of asymmetry and heteronomy, namely, those in the pre-originary self and the saintly self. However, despite the fact that the narcissistic ego is a socially constructed formation, its sovereignty is eventually contested by the moral exigencies of society. A society in which individual egos each selfishly pursue only their own self-interest, indifferent to the needs, in-terests, rights, and concerns of others, would be an anarchic society close to the fabled "state of nature." Consequently, socialization attempts to el-evate the individual to the moral perspective of an enlightened egoism, encouraging mutual recognition, equality, the exploration of common interests, and a commitment to principles of justice.

3. In contrast to the figure of the narcissistic ego, the figure of *the enlightened ego* characterizes the autonomous, reflectively mediated moral maturity of adulthood, a life of "enlightened egoism," voluntarily grounded, as Kant would have it, in critically appropriated moral prin-ciples, principles requiring the justice of symmetry, reversibility, and rec-iprocity. The enlightened ego will accordingly be recognizable in Levi-nas's texts as the form of subjectivity belonging to the liberal bourgeois State. In other words, the liberal State exists as a material accommodation to the freedom of a certain "enlightened egoism." Founded on the prin-ciples of a certain historical form of individualism, the State therefore at-tempts to establish a community of enlightened egos, whose different needs and interests, despite conflicts, would nevertheless be susceptible of negotiation, coordination, and harmony for the sake of the common good. The State established by bourgeois liberalism therefore does not negate egoism. On the contrary, the State affirms it; but at the same time, it attempts to elevate this egoism to the impersonal perspective of moral principles which the ego, in the "enlightened" exercise of its autonomy, should reflectively justify through uncoerced and respectful dialogue with others. As a formation of subjectivity, the enlightened ego is already a difficult achievement, requiring constant vigilance, the constant critical examination of motives and intentions, and a willingness to learn about ourselves from others and grow morally from our interactions with them. It is, of course, no more preordained than is the stage of the saintly self.

4. There is, finally, the possibility of *a saintly self*, a figure about which Levinas speaks only with hesitation—and only with the greatest precau-tions. Most adults would seem to live out their lives within the moral men-tality of egoism, or between this mentality and that of the enlightened ego. But Levinas speaks of "the recurrence of the ego to the Self," *du Moi à Soi* (*OB* 155–56, *AE* 121). I take this to indicate his hope that, through its encounters with others—through the "accusation" of persecution com-ing from the other's face, which *ramène le Moi à soi en deçà de mon identité*

(*OB* 92, *AE* 117), the ego might somehow be provoked to retrieve or recuperate the experience of substitution constitutive of its pre-originary self. In "Diachrony and Representation," Levinas says: "Approaching the neighbour [*le prochain*], the Ego [*Moi*] can no longer be an Ego."[11] In its relations with others, a self beneath the ego is summoned and a self higher than the ego is invoked, calling into question the ego's egoism, *l'impérialisme du Moi* (*OB* 128, *AE* 165; *TO* 108, *EN* 174). In the Hasidic tradition, the term "zaddik" names this "higher" self.

In the essay "No Identity," Levinas calls our attention to an existential possibility, one in which "the active ego [*Moi*] reverts to the passivity of a self [*soi*], to the accusative form of the oneself [*se*] which does not derive from any [prior] nominative, reverting thereby to an accusation that is prior to any fault" (*CPP* 147, *HH* 94). The saintly self is, of course, a never-ending, never-completed project of exposure to the other, "a divergency between the ego and the self" made possible by "an impossible recurrence, and an impossible identity" (*CPP* 149, *HH* 97). This return to the self consequently "becomes an interminable detour" (ibid.). In question, here, is the possibility of a truly higher, saintly life, a way of life that has made felt contact with, and to some extent recuperated, the suppressed, pre-originary moral endowment of infancy, so that this endowment of "predispositions," through which the "I" substitutes for the other, takes part in the other's suffering, and assumes responsibility for the other, could become the moral compass for a saintly life of self-sacrifice, a life, therefore, of selfless anonymity and heteronomy, devoted asymmetrically and without the expectation of reciprocity or recompense, to compassion and justice for the other. This stage, phase, or face involves the ultimate sacrifice of one's ego—the sacrifice of one's very name, and also the sacrifice of volition as it is ordinarily understood.[12] It also involves the assumption of a certain humility—will as humility, not as will to power—returning the ego to the pre-originary self beneath it, at the bottom of the ego, *au fond du Moi* (*CPP* 99, *HH* 52). Thus, everything depends on the ego's personal assumption of responsibility for the developing transformation of our pre-originary capacity to be responsively exposed to the other. The saintly life is motivated, is moved by the heteronomy of deepest compassion, by the accusation and persecution of a responsibility for the other that has come to obsess it. (It is worth noting here that the words "hostage" (*ôtage*) and "obsess" (*obséder*) derive from the same root, namely "sed-"). The saintly self, its egological identity deconstructed, lives by and for the responsibility of substitution, working for others with a passionate selflessness, working in the name of a higher anonymity, a higher namelessness, a higher heteronomy. Thus, as the two figures show, each of the four phases or faces corresponds to a dimension of our embodiment, our incarnation in a flesh that must be read hermeneutically—as if it were a palimpsest entrusted with words of sacred wisdom.

But the saintly self cannot emerge from the enlightened ego in any linear temporality, any straightforward and progressive continuum of development. Instead, it requires that the ego undertake—or rather, undergo—a passage of *récurrence,* a *retournement* (*OB* 92, 155–56; *AE* 117, 121). Under what Levinas will describe, in the next passage to be cited, as "the traumatic effect of persecution," the retrospective recognition of an inchoative, bodily felt sense of response-ability that is already in-the-making can enable us to effectuate that response-ability in the conduct of our moral life; but the pre-originary response-ability—a lower anonymity and heteronomy—nevertheless first comes to light in a sequence that "in reality" can be realized only afterward. Thus we would touch, and in turn be touched by, the summons to a moral responsibility for the other that would have taken hold of us in the time of a past that has never been present.

Leaving us to work through the multiple equivocations he has set in motion, Levinas tells us that "the more I [an ego] return to myself [the pre-originary self], the more I divest myself, *under the traumatic effect of persecution,* of my freedom as a constituted, willful, imperialist subject, [and] the more I discover myself to be responsible" (*OB* 112, *AE* 143). (Note the equivocations in the philosopher's uses of the words "I," "myself," and "persecution." Also note the ego's experience of "persecution" as it figures in the phrase printed in italics.)

This passage is of the greatest importance, because once we have disentangled the equivocations, it seems to be showing that Levinas's phenomenology implies and requires, as I have suggested, that we think of persecution in a radically new way—namely, in terms of what the "anatomy" proposed in this study has described as the second, third, and fourth configurations of meaning—and also that we must connect the question of persecution to a narrative of moral growth. The passage further seems to imply that the realization of a saintly life would depend upon an ego-breaking effort to retrieve, to whatever extent may be possible, at least a trace, however faint, of the body's sense of the substitution which has already affected it, already taken hold of it, already claimed, ordained, and dispossessed it—according to the most radical heteronomy and anonymity. In question is an effort that, even in the best of us, can be only partially successful in making contact with that sense of inordinate, undeclinable responsibility carried by the body in the very depths of its flesh, only partially successful in retrieving or recuperating, from the merest traces of traces that still remain, inscribed upon the deepest, oldest folds of the flesh, the felt sense of an imperative moral assignment, and only partially, imperfectly successful in making this assignment, which comes from a time before time, the creative, sustaining source of everyday life—the way one lives one's life.

It is essential to understand that the "return" in question here is not a narcissistic return to oneself—to a centeredness in one's ego, but rather a process provoked in *exposure* to the other and set in motion in *response* to the other's appeal. For the face of the other can reveal to me my violence, putting me in touch with an even deeper source of action—refractory traces of my pre-originary substitution for the other. Thus, the recurrence through which the ego would attempt to retrieve something of the pre-originary self's moral experience can be possible," according to Levinas, only

> under the traumatism where presence is deranged [*dérangé*] by the Other [*Autrui*]. Deranged or awakened. To experience [*éprouver*] the authenticity and value of this traumatism is to return again to this very traumatism, to this transcendence or this vigilance [*éveil*] where all these notions will signify for the first time for us.[13]

And once again, we note, responsibility for the other—for her suffering and welfare—is described as a "traumatism."

So the anatomy of persecution that I am suggesting in the present study is supported—I think implied—by what Levinas has to say. Likewise, many textual passages, including the last two, support, even imply and require, the narrative of moral growth outlined here. There is, Levinas tells us, "a prehistory of the ego" (*OB* 117, *AE* 150), a "subjectivity prior to the ego, prior to its freedom and its non-freedom"—a "pre-originary subject" (*CPP* 133, *HH* 74). He also says (*OB* 195n16, *AE* 142n16) that the ego (*le Moi*) is "constituted on the basis of the self" (*à partir de soi*), that "egoism is neither first nor last" (*OB* 128, *AE* 165), implying that I am both already a self and yet not yet a self (*OB* 118, 123; *AE* 151, 158). I take this to mean that there is a diachronic phase or face, synchronically a dimension—call it the pre-originary self—which *precedes* the formation of the ego, and that there is also the *possibility* of a diachronic phase or face, synchronically a dimension, *after* the formation of the ego. Call this latter the saintly self, that phase or face of subjectivity which would willingly assume, in its freedom—and as an election defining its life—a responsibility for the other that has already taken the evasive ego hostage, already obsessed it. Levinas says "it is in the course of the individuation of the ego in me [*le Moi en moi*] that is realized the elevation in which the ego is for the neighbor [*le prochain*], summoned to answer for him" (*OB* 126, *AE* 162).

Individuation is commonly thought to be a question of the ego's emergence and its assumption of an undisputed sovereignty—the final phase or face of moral individuation and self-realization. Levinas rejects this, arguing that we are capable of living our lives in relation to a greater moral height. But this greater moral height requires the humiliation of the ego, that the ego lower itself before the other. It requires that the ego renounce its sovereignty and return to the moral priorities it abandoned, in order to retrieve a pre-originary connection to the whole of humanity—a connection that already existed even "before the [actual] appearing of the other in sensibility" (*OB* 75, *AE* 95).

Let us therefore concentrate for now on passages that describe what we are calling the pre-originary self. There is, Levinas says, a self which is "older than the ego" (*OB* 117, *AE* 150): "the self does not begin in the auto-affection of a sovereign ego" (*OB* 123, *AE* 158). This self belongs to "an order which, beyond representation, affects me unbeknownst to myself, 'slipping into me like a thief'" (*OB* 150, *AE* 191). This, I suggest, is the experience of the pre-originary self—the self which, according to our reading of Levinas, is formed in and as "a substitution for the other [*l'autre*]" (*OB* 164, *AE* 208). This subjectivity is constituted by a responsibility for another that, he says, "requires subjectivity as an irreplaceable hostage. This subjectivity it denudes *under* the ego in a *passivity of persecution,* repression and expulsion outside of essence, into oneself" (*OB* 124, *AE* 159; emphases added). On my interpretation, this points to a moment of subjectivity—call it the pre-originary self—which, diachronically considered, precedes the formation of the narcissistic ego and which, synchronically considered, is preserved, at least as a somewhat retrievable "trace," "beneath" or "under" the "sovereign ego." My "obedience" to this pre-originary responsibility is, of course, radically passive—more passive than passive. So the self in question here is the pre-originary self, the "self in the ego" (*OB* 126, *AE* 162) that is hidden and suppressed by the narcissistic ego which emerges from the pre-originary self in the course of socialization. And from the very beginning, this pre-originary self is, as already noted, "accused by the other to the point of persecution, responsible for its persecutor" (*accusé par l'autre jusqu'à la persécution et responsable de son persécuteur*). But this accusation, which, consistent with the precedence of a radically passive pre-originary self, first comes to articulation not in the grammar of the ego's nominative, but instead in the grammar of the accusative case, and which Levinas also describes as "persecution," as a *blessure du Soi dans le Moi,* is constitutive of the very "being" of the pre-originary self. This self is nothing if it is not only a traumatic participation in the other's suffering—suffering, itself, to the very point of persecution, the other's experience of persecution—but also a traumatism *bearing responsibility* for the other's persecution: a suffering-for-the-other so intense, so obsessing, and so deeply disturbed by a sense of responsibility and guilt that it can make us want to describe it, despite the strangeness, by using the word "persecution." Since substitution constitutes the very existence of the pre-originary, it constitutes an "election" that has taken hold of subjectivity prior to the emergence of the narcissistic ego, prior to the "act-passivity alternative" (*OB* 117, *AE* 149).

The life of the pre-originary self is directed in accordance with its "involuntary election" by the Good (*OB* 15, *AE* 19). "Attachment to the Good," Levinas says, "precedes the choosing of this Good. How indeed choose the Good? The Good is good precisely because it chooses you and grips you before you have had time to raise your eyes to it" (*N* 135). It is the pre-originary self, of course, which is "elected" in this way by the Good—whereas it is in the life of an enlightened ego or in the life of a saintly self that the Good would instead be the concern of an "election." Thus, in two senses, "everything is from the start [*au préalable*] in the accusative": even before it knows its name, the self has always already been called to the Good; but this calling is a moral imperative that summons to a responsibility which the self will always have been too late to assume. Hence, the grammatical accusative of the summons to responsibility is also an "accusation" of dereliction, of failed responsibility. Hence also the deep, bodily carried, bodily metaphored sense of guilt that "persecutes" the pre-originary self, even before it takes action, as an ego, in relation to the Good. The pre-originary self, the first phase or face of one's life, is therefore a life radically heteronomous, asymmetrically exposed to the other—but without any realization of its originary alterity, its originary heteronomy in substitution for the other—and without any realization of the secret messianic promise buried in its ancient flesh.

The Victim's Responsibility

As Bernasconi realized some time ago, one of Levinas's most perplexing statements in this regard is undoubtedly this: "To bear responsibility for everything and everyone is to be responsible despite oneself. To be responsible despite oneself is to be persecuted. *Only the persecuted* must answer for everyone, even for his persecutor."[14] "Only the persecuted"? If there is a dimension of our existence wherein we are so deeply affected by the suffering of others that we not only bear their suffering with them, but have already taken their suffering into ourselves in substitution, are we not—all of us—victims of persecution? Was this not an implication that Bernasconi drew,[15] with apparent justification, from Levinas's assertion (see *OB* 12, *AE* 14, for example) that "the face which confronts me is both judge and accused"? So I too am one of the persecuted. But are we not—all of us—in any case responsible for persecution? What limitation is the word "only" introducing? Does Levinas not say that I am responsible for everyone, including those who persecute me? If the I is an agent of persecution, in what sense is such a person also one of the persecuted? Would Levinas want to deny that the Nazis should bear collective responsibility for the Shoah? Would he want to deny their collective guilt? If not, why the "only"?

As these inevitable questions show, the three sentences in this passage are not merely enigmatic; they are profoundly unsettling. And even now, I am not confident that my interpretation can give them moral lucidity without betraying them. In any case, I am proposing to interpret the philosopher as holding, by implication, (1) that despite ourselves, despite our intentions and beliefs, we are responsible—each of us, as an "I"—for everyone; and (2) that each one of us, made to feel responsible for the other despite ourselves, is accordingly "persecuted"—not only by the weight of this "undeclinable" responsibility, but also by the pre-originary substitution that has already determined our participation in the sufferings of the persecuted. But the third sentence remains perplexing.

Let us give thought to another passage where the phrase "only the persecuted" appears, bearing what seems to be a different message, but perhaps, after all, casting some light on that third, most enigmatic of sentences:

> The face of the neighbor in its persecuting hatred can by this very malice obsess as something pitiful. This equivocation or enigma *only the persecuted one* who does not evade it . . . is able to endure. This transfer [i.e., substitution] is subjectivity itself. . . . In the trauma of persecution it is to pass from the outrage undergone [undergone by the victim] to the responsibility for the persecutor, and, in this sense, from suffering to expiation for the other. (*OB* 111, *AE* 141–42; emphasis added)

Here, it seems, Levinas wants to solicit from within the victim's suffering not merely a *capacity* for forgiveness, but indeed the hold of a certain, almost unbearable, almost unendurable obligation—to forgive, to pardon, to expiate, and even to *feel* the intensely deep suffering of the agent of persecution, which has driven him to such consuming hatred and violence. For Levinas, such compassion for the agent of persecution, however difficult and exceptional, is nevertheless a moral comportment demanded first of all of the victim, because, as his phenomenology brings out, the victim is *already related* to the agent of persecution through a *pre-originary sub-*

stitution for the other which takes hold of the pre-originary self—takes hold of its sentient flesh; and also because, in the face-to-face relation, the victim of persecution is being summoned, despite her suffering, to make felt contact with that dimension of her experience and accordingly to respond to the other from out of that contact, that awareness.

In *The Drowned and the Saved* (*I sommersi i salvati*), Primo Levi, a survivor of Auschwitz, adverts to the survivor's experience of "a vast shame, a shame of the world" *(una vergogna più vasta, la vergogna del mondo)*. He observes that there are those who, before the guilt of others, or their own, turn their backs, so as not to see it and not to feel touched by it, while there are others—"the just among us"—who "experienced remorse, shame, suffering, for the misdeeds that others and not they had committed, and in which, nevertheless, they felt themselves involved, because they could see that what had happened around them, and in their presence, was irrevocable." If the Shoah proves, he says, "that man, the species man, we in short, are capable of constructing an infinite enormity of pain," the shame experienced by survivors is a shame that overcomes them at the realization that they were witnesses to this terrible truth—a truth that they could not, in spite of all efforts, deny.[16]

In "Franz Kafka," an essay written in commemoration of that writer's death, Walter Benjamin observes that "shame is not only shame in the presence of others, but can also be shame one feels for them."[17] Such an experience is made possible, I believe, when the other's comportment affects us so deeply that our feelings well up from the substitution for the other always already taking place in the very depths of the flesh.

Recalling, in *The Truce*, the faces of the Russian soldiers who were the first to enter the camp, Levi comments that what he saw was an expression beyond compassion, a certain "confused restraint" (*confuso ritegno*) that sealed their mouths. "It was," he writes,

> the same shame very familiar to us, the one that overwhelmed us after the selections, and every time that we were compelled to take part in or submit to an outrage: the shame that the Germans did not know, a shame that only the just experience before a wrong committed by another, consumed as they are by the fact that such a wrong could exist, that it could have been introduced so irrevocably into the world.[18]

In *The Drowned and the Saved*, where he returns to reflect on his earlier observation about the shame which he saw appear on the faces of the Russians, Levi says: "That many (and I myself) experienced "shame," and therefore a sense of guilt, not only during imprisonment but also after is a fact confirmed by the testimony of many survivors."[19]

Why, he asks, should people who were not responsible for committing atrocities nevertheless feel shame? Levi proposes more than one explanation. There is, for one thing, the shame over having lived like animals.[20] There is also a feeling of shame over having fallen short of solidarity, having turned away from someone in need, someone begging for help, even if only the kindness of a human word; and there is shame over having done nothing, or not enough, to destroy the system.[21] Finally, there is the deepest experience of shame, which is shame over surviving when others did not:

> Are you ashamed because you are alive in place of another? And in particular, in place of a man more generous, more sensitive, more useful, wiser, worthier of living than you? You cannot shut out such feelings: you examine yourself, you review your memories. . . . No, you find no obvious transgressions; you did not usurp anyone's place, you did not beat anyone (but would you have had the strength to do so?). You did not accept positions (but none were offered to you . . .), you did not steal anyone's bread; nevertheless, you cannot exclude it. It is no more than a supposition, indeed the shadow of a suspicion: that each man is his brother's Cain, that each one of us (but this time I say "us" in a much vaster, indeed universal sense) has usurped his neighbor's place and lived in his stead. It is a supposition, but it gnaws at us; it has nestled deeply like a woodworm; although unseen from the outside, it gnaws and rasps.[22]

For Levinas, such shame is not to be belittled as mere supposition: for him, the fact that one could experience shame over the misdeeds of another, or experience shame for surviving instead of another, is what confirms his phenomenology of substitution, the one-for-the-other.

So perhaps we should read Levinas's perplexing sentence in terms of this assignment of responsibility, summoning the victim to bear the unbearable—not only to rise above the egoism in revenge, returning hatred with hatred, and not only to suffer in substitution the suffering of the agent of persecution, but also to forgive and pardon, making expiation possible.

The Witness

As we know, Levinas repeatedly asserts not only that I am responsible for everyone—which means that I bear some responsibility for your persecution by the other—but also that my very identity is formed by substitution for the other. This is a position which would seem to imply that when others are persecuted, I also must suffer that persecution. And yet, at least in the first of the passages with the phrase "only the persecuted one," if not also in the second, Levinas seems to be limiting his recognition of persecution, suggesting that, in a certain sense, only the one who has been persecuted *in the standard sense of that word* is in the morally required position to bear witness to the persecution—to testify and bring it to justice, and that only the victim, the one who has been persecuted *in the standard sense of the word,* is in a position to forgive and pardon the agent of persecution. The point is that the pardon is ethically problematic when given by someone other than the actual victim or when given for anything other than what that victim actually suffered, because, outside the relation between agent of persecution and victim, it is always possible that the pardon could cause injury to others (*CPP* 30, *EN* 29). Thus, it is *only* the persecuted one—again, in the standard sense of the term—who can forgive, assuming responsibility for breaking through the repetition of suffering to the possibility of a redeeming repentence. For everyone, even his oppressor. Testimony, judgment, forgiveness, and pardon: this, I believe, is the calling, the "election" to undeclinable responsibility, absolutely singular, which the persecuted one—and only she—must assume. A statement from "La volonté du ciel et le pouvoir des hommes" ("The Will of Heaven and the Power of Men") supports this reading.[23] But restitution, returning the repentant individual to the embrace of humanity, is fully granted to the oppressor only when the one who has been persecuted first brings out the truth that judges and finds within his heart the miraculous power of forgiveness. Only the testimony, judgment, and forgiveness of the persecuted (in the standard sense of the term) can accomplish this restitution, helping the agent of persecution to return to humanity. Therefore, testimony, judgment, and forgiveness are the urgent responsibility of the one who has been persecuted—a responsibility that falls only on the shoulders of the persecuted (in the standard sense of the term).

But what do we want to say in response to Primo Levi, who asserts in *The Drowned and the Saved* that the survivors (*superstiti*) of the Shoah are not the true witnesses (*testimoni veri*), and that the only true witnesses entitled to testify to the horrors of the Nazi death camps are those who died? "We [survivors]," he says there, "didn't touch the bottom. Those who did, those who saw the Gorgon, did not return to tell about it, or returned mute; but it is they, the 'Musselmänner,' the drowned, who are the complete witnesses."[24]

Primo Levi's assertion also introduces another point of perplexity. This one concerns the "third": the third person, the third party, the third position or perspective. From etymology, we know that the word *tiers,* "third," comes from the Latin *testis,* the testimony of a witness. We also know that Levinas identifies the third, as witness, with the impartial, impersonal judgment of justice, the perspective of symmetry, equality and reciprocity that represents the whole of humanity.[25] But if only the victim, the persecuted one, can forgive the agent of persecution, does the logic of Levinas's position imply that only the victim can bear witness and judge? I think not. I think Levinas wants to say that, although only the victim (in the standard sense) can forgive and pardon, helping the agent of persecution to find humanity within himself and giving him, in effect, the gift of a prayer for his expiation, we others have a responsibility to bear witness and submit the agent of persecution to the judgment of justice, the justice of judgment.[26]

Messianic Time: The Temporality of the Pardon

In his discussion of the infinity of time, Levinas meditates on the paradoxical temporality of the pardon—the way it interrupts and breaches the linear continuum of time and history to inaugurate and participate in a different temporality, as if reversing the direction of time and allowing a certain retroactive transformation of the act being pardoned:

> The paradox of pardon lies in its retroaction; from the point of view of common time, it represents an inversion of the natural order of things, the reversibility of time. . . . Pardon refers to the instant elapsed; it permits the subject who had committed himself in a past instant to be as though that instant had not passed on, to be as though he had not committed himself. Active in a stronger sense than forgetting, . . . pardon acts upon the past, somehow repeats the event, purifying it. But in addition, forgetting nullifies relations with the past, whereas pardon conserves the past pardoned in the purified present. (*TI* 282–83, *TeI* 258–61)

Through the victim's pardon, then, "time adds something new to being, something absolutely new" (*TI* 284, *TeI* 260–61). This *novum,* breaking into the standard time-continuum, "liberates being" from fate (ibid.). The pardon of the persecuted can purify those responsible for their suffering—not by denying what happened, but only by touching them with the redemptive power of infinite time: "Infinite time is the putting back into question of the truth it promises. . . . Truth requires both an infinite time and a time it will be able to seal, a completed time" (*TI* 284–85, *TeI* 261).

Concluding this meditation, very reminiscent of Walter Benjamin's reflections on the paradoxes and intrigues of messianic time,[27] Levinas emphasizes that "the completion of time is not death, but messianic time, where the perpetual [the ever-the-same] is converted into the eternal. Messianic triumph is pure triumph; it is secured against the revenge of evil whose return the infinite time does prohibit" (*TI* 284–85, *TeI* 261). "Is this eternity," he wonders, "a new structure of time, or an extreme vigilance of the messianic consciousness?" Giving us no direct answer to this question, he leaves us to the provocations of this thought. Benjamin would speak here of the "image of redemption" which can suddenly flash up in the *Jetztzeit*, interrupting the endless repetition of the revenge of time and history, bringing time as we have known it to a standstill, and giving justice, if not love—a new beginning—a small chance.[28] Breaking the repetition of suffering, breaking the repetition of revenge—a terrible justice—the victim's pardon of forgiveness gives the unbelievable glory of humanity a certain chance to seal the end of persecution within its redemptive power. Perhaps forgiveness is ultimately the only gesture by virtue of which the agent of persecution, if wholeheartedly repentant, could be opened to the redemptive power of the Good.

Primo Levi, having survived the hell of Auschwitz, will not pardon any agents of persecution who are not wholeheartedly repentant, making restitution in words and deeds. Those remain agents of persecution, not deserving forgiveness. But, he says, not even the victim's pardon can erase or annul the guilt.

Of course, like Benjamin, Levinas will insist that the redemptive power of the pardon cannot be understood so long as messianic time continues to be represented in terms of a linear succession of now-points:

> Time must not be seen as "image" and approximation of an immobile eternity, as a deficient mode of ontological plenitude. It articulates [*articule*] a mode of existence in which everything is always revocable, in which nothing is definitive but everything is yet to come [*à venir*], in which even the present is not a simple coincidence with itself, but is always an imminence.[29]

In the Face of Persecution

Does the agent of persecution see humanity in the face of his victim? Why does the face not have the power to halt persecution? Why is the humanity of the face not visible—visible in an epiphany that would transform the evil intentions driving the persecution? If, as Levinas says, the face of the other manifests the commandment prohibiting murder, how is it nevertheless possible for murder to take place in the face-to-face relation? In *Time and the Other*, Levinas makes the messianic moment concrete, insisting that it is possible only in "the [ethical] relationship of the subject with the Other."[30] Later in this text, he says that "the situation of the face-to-face would be the very accomplishment of time. . . . The condition of time lies in relationships among humans, or in history" (*TO* 79, *TA* 68–69). Perhaps, then, messianic time would be the time when, even for the agent of persecution, the face of humanity would become visible, the time when humanity would become visible—visible in its invisibility—in the face of every other. Thus, in "Phenomenon and Enigma," Levinas tells us, making a point with his reference to our "weak sight" that recalls Benjamin's discussion, in his "Theses on the Philosophy of History," of a *schwache messianische Kraft*, a "weak messianic power," that

> the signifyingness [*signifiance*] of an enigma comes from an irreversible, irrecuperable past which has perhaps not left, since it has already been absent from the very terms in which it was signaled . . . The enigma is the way of the Absolute, foreign to cognition, not because it would not shine with a light disproportionately strong for the subject's weak sight, but because it is already too old for the game of cognition, because it does not lend itself to the contemporaneousness that constitutes the force of time tied to the present, because it imposes a completely different version of time. (*CPP* 71, *EN* 214)

In our time, the humanity of the other is still barely visible in the face-to-face relation—still barely visible as the forever invisible. Only a very weak messianic power connects the sight of our eyes to that dimension of our flesh where a pre-originary substitution has already taken hold of us. Only a very weak messianic power touches and moves our eyes. Hence the terrible reality—persecutions, pogroms, wars, murder.

What Resists Murder?

In "Is Ontology Fundamental?" Levinas connects the commandment that prohibits murder to the experience of the face. He argues that

> the Other [*Autrui*] is the sole being I can wish to kill. I can wish. And yet this power is quite the contrary of power. The triumph of this power is its

defeat as power. At the very moment when my power to kill realizes itself, the other [*autrui*] has escaped me. Certainly I can, killing, attain a goal; I can kill as I hunt or slaughter animals, or as I fell trees. But when [as in Heidegger's phenomenological account of *Mitsein*] I have grasped the other in the opening of being in general, as an element of the world where I stand, where I have him on the horizon, I have not looked him in the face, I have not encountered his face. . . . To be in a relation with the other face to face is to be unable to kill.[31]

But ordinary experience certainly seems to refute Levinas's phenomenology, unless we suppose that, in a certain, still enigmatic sense, the murderer does not really and truly *see* the face of the other, does not—not yet—really and truly see the *humanity* of the other even as he faces him and looks him in the face. Defying our skepticism, Levinas insists that, in the face of the other, "the infinite resistance of a being to our power affirms itself precisely against the murderous will that it defies" (*BPW* 10, *EN* 21–22). But what kind of power is this resistance to the power of murder? Whereas common experience would make this resistance an assertion of power on the part of the ego, a matter of self-preservation, survival, the resistance to which Levinas is trying to draw our attention does not come from the ego—and it is therefore not a recognizable form of power. "The human," he says, "only lends itself to a relation that is not power" (ibid.). But what is it that resists persecution, violence, and murder without being a power? In "Philosophy and the Idea of Infinity," Levinas asserts that "ethical resistance is the very presence of infinity." And he argues that

> if the resistance to murder, inscribed on a face, were not ethical, but real, we would have access to a reality that is very weak or very strong. It perhaps would block our will. The will would be judged unreasonable and arbitrary. But we would not have access to an exterior being, to what one absolutely can neither take in nor possess, where our freedom renounces its imperialism proper to the ego. (*CPP* 55, *ED* 173)

The other, as an infinite being, is "manifested," he says, "in the absolute resistance which, by its apparition, its epiphany, it opposes to all my powers" (ibid.). Continuing in a mode of discourse that paradoxically problematizes its apparent claim to register first-person phenomenological experience the longer we stay with it,[32] he adds that, to be sure,

> the other is exposed to all my powers, succumbs to all my ruses, all my crimes. Or he resists me with all his force and all the unpredictable resources of his freedom. . . . But he can also—and here is where he

> presents me his face—oppose himself to me beyond all measure, with the total uncoveredness and nakedness of his defenceless eyes, the straightforwardness, the absolute frankness of his gaze. . . . [Thus,] true exteriority is in this gaze [returned to me] which forbids me my conquest. (*CPP* 55, *ED* 173)

An enigmatic form of resistance! It is not that the powers of persecution are too weak, but rather that, facing the humanity of the other, facing "the resistance of what has no resistance," facing a certain "ethical resistance," the violence supposedly finds itself stripped of power, encountering in the other's face an opening which draws it into "the very dimension of infinity," where it is no longer able to have power (ibid.). Such is the powerless power of the other's face, the face in the exposure of its humanity, the face of the persecuted one, ever victorious—according to Levinas—in its reserve of humanity. And yet, murder happens. In brutal massacres, where victims and torturers encounter one another face-to-face. In wars between faceless enemies. In lynchings and crucifixions, murders of the innocent, victims because of the color of their skin or their sexual orientation. The face forbids murder—yet murder happens.

The Indestructible beyond Persecution

According to Bernasconi, persecution "is not directed at the universal: the Inhuman does not have humanity as its target. One is always persecuted as a Jew, an Arab, a heretic, or for one's color."[33] There is a certain truth in this observation. And yet the Nazis undertook a systematic effort to dehumanize the Jew—not only to exterminate Jews, but in the course of the master plan, to destroy the Jew's very humanity, reducing the Jew to bare organic life, a condition even lower than the animal.[34] Thus, I think we must recognize, in the inhumanity of the Nazi persecution of the Jews as Jews, the operation of what is perhaps an even more monstrous and evil intention: the intention to destroy, in them, through them, the very face of humanity—that universal humanity, living in mutual recognition, freedom, and equality, which it has been the historical mission of the modern Enlightenment to achieve.

In *The Infinite Conversation*, Maurice Blanchot undertakes a response to Robert Antelme, who, in *The Human Species*, his testimony regarding the Nazi extermination camps, asserted that "Man is the indestructible that can always be destroyed."[35] Blanchot writes:

Through reading such a book we begin to understand that man is indestructible and that he can nevertheless be destroyed. This happens in
affliction. In affliction, we approach the limit where, deprived of the
power to say "I," deprived of the world, we would be nothing other than
this Other that we are not. . . . This has the ring of truth, and yet we are
unable to know it through a knowledge that would already be true.

Blanchot is certainly right to recognize that the knowledge for which we
hope in order to ground Anthelme's thought escapes our grasp:

That man can be destroyed is certainly not reassuring; but that, because
of and despite this, and in this very movement, man should remain indestructible—this fact is what is truly overwhelming: for we no longer have
the least chance of seeing ourselves relieved of ourselves or of our
responsibility.

And yet there is, in this situation, a strange and enigmatic reality, which
demands that we make an effort to understand it: although the inmates
of the Nazi death camps are powerless, and nothing stands in the way of
their being murdered, the power of their persecutors is nevertheless
somehow limited:

And yet this force that is capable of everything has a limit; and he who
literally can no longer do anything still affirms himself at the limit where
possibility ceases: in the poverty, the simplicity of a presence that is the
infinite of human presence. The Powerful One is the master of the possible; but he is not master of this relation that does not derive from mastery and that power cannot measure: the relation without relation
wherein the "other" [*l'autre*] is revealed as "autrui."

Even when reduced to the condition of naked life, no longer a
sovereign subject, no longer an ego who can say "I," reduced to being
"someone who eats scraps," the death camp inmate, the victim, nevertheless bears within himself something that negates the power of the powerful, for the human is forever absolutely other, beyond the reach of the
agent of persecution. In the paradoxical presence of an indestructible
"humanity," the Nazi camp officials confronted the absolute limit to their
power: although not beyond the reach of a dehumanizing brutality, many
of the Nazi death camp inmates retained their humanity, a sense of the
Good that, even under deprivation and torture, could not be destroyed.
Nevertheless, what remained—their sense of humanity—must still

be called a remnant, or, since we must be careful to avoid reducing it to ontology or essence, the merest trace of a trace. Perhaps that is the only way we can say, within the discourse of our time, what our humanity "is." Nothing objective—but of the utmost importance.

The Remnant of Our Humanity

But what do we mean when we say, for example, that under extreme torture someone died with sublime dignity, with his humanity intact? Levinas's allegorical figure of the trace is of course prefigured by the notion of the remnant in the Old Testament (Isa. 10:20–22) and presupposes Franz Rosenzweig's interpretation of this remnant, which is introduced in part 3, book 3 of his *Star of Redemption*.[36] According to Rosenzweig, "man is always somehow a remnant. He is always somehow a survivor" (*SR* 404). The remnant—our innermost humanity—preserves the connection between the kingdom of heaven and the sanctified life here on earth, so that "if the Messiah should come 'today,' the remnant will be ready to receive him" (ibid.). The remnant is that universal humanity within us which remains "waiting" for redemption, waiting in the time that remains between the "already" of a revelation beyond memory and the "not yet" of a redemption beyond rational hope (*SR* 417). "Just for this," he says, "we remain within the boundaries of mortality. Just for this we—remain" (*SR* 416).

In the Time Remaining

In the time remaining—that is to say, not in the "normal" order of time, but in the time announced by the prophets, the messianic time between revelation and redemption—we remain separated from the glorious epiphany of our humanity, separated from a revelation making visible at last that which must remain invisible: that dimension of each person through which the lives and destinies of all human beings are, and have always been, inextricably interconnected. In these dark times, what can seeing the humanity of the other possibly be, if not the paradoxical seeing of an invisible remnant, almost nothing, a ghostly reminder of the indestructible bond that makes each one of us for-the-other?

In "The Ego and Totality," Levinas tells us that "when face to face, I can no longer negate the other; the noumenal glory of the other [*d'autrui*] alone makes the face to face situation possible" (*CPP* 43, *EN* 45). But the noumenal glory of the face, in which the humanity of the other would reveal itself, will be seen as such only in a world where social relations are grounded in substitution, the one-for-the-other, the deepest dimension of subjectivity—there where, in words taken from Merleau-Ponty, "I live in the facial expressions of the other, as I feel him living in mine."[37]

In the time remaining, however, when there is at work only what Benjamin calls a "weak messianic power," the "noumenal glory" of the face is not often to be glimpsed and imparted in the concreteness of one's relation to the other person.[38] It remains withdrawn from knowledge, without intelligible speech, made invisible by the violence of our world. In the time remaining, therefore, we are called upon to work for justice in the name of a humanity that does not yet exist—a humanity visible in the other's face only as an indestructible remnant, as that enigmatic something, not a universal, not a genus, nothing that our present ontology can possibly conceive, which remains, utterly invisible and incomprehensible, to haunt our consciences, in a world where the other person, my neighbor, is still all too frequently the victim of hate, persecution, and murderous violence.

Questions

I would like to conclude with two questions. How could the compassion borne in the heart of substitution be touched, reached in a way that would break the returning cycles of hate, persecution, and violence? How can we hope to teach the possibilities for moral growth when what we are teaching in the name of "morality"—and the way we are teaching it—in so many ways unnecessarily perpetuates cruelty, hatred, and violence?

Notes

The first epigraph is from Ralph Waldo Emerson, *The Early Lectures of Ralph Waldo Emerson*, eds. Stephen E. Whicher, Robert E. Spiller, and Wallace E. Williams (Cambridge: Harvard University Press, 1961), 3:251.

The second epigraph is from George Santayana, *Platonism and the Spiritual Life* (New York: Harper and Row, 1957), 260.

1. Levinas, "Sans identité," in L'Humanisme de l'autre homme (Montpellier: Fata Morgana, 1972), p. 99; "No Identity," in *Collected Philosophical Papers* (Pittsburgh: Duquesne University Press, 1998), p. 150. Hereafter cited as *HH* and *CPP*.

DAVID MICHAEL KLEINBERG-LEVIN

2. See Emmanuel Levinas, *Otherwise Than Being, or Beyond Essence,* trans. Alphonso Lingis (The Hague: Martinus Nijhoff, 1981), 117; *Autrement qu'être, ou au-delà de l'essence* (The Hague: Martinus Nijhoff, 1974), 149, where, for example, the philosopher explicitly describes the assignment of obligation as an "inscription"; but he never sufficiently articulates this moral appropriation, this "election" of the flesh—although I recognize in the traumatism of circumcision, inscribing the covenant between Israel and God into the flesh of the male, the archetype for this feature of Levinas's phenomenology of responsibility. Hereafter cited in the text as *OB* and *AE,* respectively.

3. According to Levinas, the first and most fundamental experience I undergo in encountering the face of the other is the commandment that prohibits murder. But if, as Levinas maintains, I am bound to responsibility for the other through the assignment of a pre-originary "election," I must not be wholly evil, wholly disposed to murder. It is thus difficult to understand why Levinas insists that the first and most fundamental experience of the other's face is an experience in which the commandment prohibiting murder speaks to us. Is this phenomenology—or is it perhaps another way of telling the mythic Hobbesian narrative?

4. Regarding the question of traces, see my discussion in "Tracework: Myself and Others in the Moral Phenomenology of Merleau-Ponty and Levinas," *International Journal of Philosophical Studies* 6, no. 3 (1998): 345–92.

5. See Primo Levi, *I sommersi e i salvati* (Turin: Giulio Einaudi, 1986), 34–35. Levi asks whether we are all oppressors, all guilty of persecution, and writes: "I don't know, and it interests me little in knowing, if in my depths there lurks [*si annidi*] an assassin, but I know that I was an innocent victim—and an assassin, no, . . . and that to confound [murderers] with their victims is a moral affliction [*malattia morale*] or a sinister symptom of complicity" (my translation). For the English, see Primo Levi, *The Drowned and the Saved* (New York: Vintage Books, 1989), 48.

6. Sigmund Freud, *The Ego and the Id* (New York: W. W. Norton, 1962), chap. 5, p. 42.

7. Robert Bernasconi, "'Only the Persecuted . . .': Language of the Oppressor, Language of the Oppressed," in *Ethics as First Philosophy,* ed. Adriaan T. Peperzak (London and New York: Routledge, 1995), 78.

8. Jürgen Habermas, "Historical Consciousness and Postraditional Identity," in *The New Conservativism: Cultural Criticism and the Historians' Debate* (Cambridge: MIT Press, 1989), 249–67.

9. See Emmanuel Levinas, *De l'évasion* (Montpellier: Fata Morgana, 1982).

10. Emmanuel Levinas, "Philosophy and the Idea of Infinity," in *Collected Philosophical Papers,* 47–59; "La philosophie et l'idée de l'infini," in Emmanuel Levinas, *En découvrant l'existence avec Husserl et Heidegger* (Paris: Vrin, 1967), 165–78. *En découvrant* hereafter cited in the text as *ED.*

11. Emmanuel Levinas, "Diachrony and Representation," in *Time and the Other,* trans. Richard Cohen (Pittsburgh: Duquesne University Press, 1987), 108; "La diachronie et la représéntation," in *Entre nous: Essais sur le penser-à-l'autre* (Paris: Éditions Grasset et Fasquelle, 1991), 174. Hereafter cited in the text as *TO* and *EN,* respectively.

12. Levi, *I sommersi e i salvati*, 42. Levi holds that it is perhaps necessary that there is no proportionality between the sympathy we experience and the magnitude of the suffering which solicited that sympathy: necessary because "if we could and had to suffer the suffering of all, we couldn't live. Only to saints is it granted the terrible gift of compassion for the many." The rest of us are limited to the flesh and blood human beings in our proximity. My translation.

13. Emmanuel Levinas, "La volonté du ciel et le pouvoir des hommes," in *Nouvelles Lectures Talmudiques* (Paris: Éditions de Minuit, 1996), 34. Hereafter cited in the text as *N*.

14. Levinas, *Nouvelles lectures talmudiques*, 114–15; Emmanuel Levinas, *Du sacré au saint: Cinq nouvelles lectures talmudiques* (Paris: Éditions de Minuit, 1977), 46, emphases added. *Du sacré au saint* hereafter cited in the text as *S*.

15. Bernasconi, "Only the Persecuted," 78.

16. Levi, *I sommersi e i salvati*, 66–67 (my translation); *The Drowned and the Saved*, 85–86.

17. Walter Benjamin, "Franz Kafka," in *Illuminations*, ed. Hannah Arendt (New York: Schocken Books, 1969), 129–30.

18. Primo Levi, *La tregua* (Turin: Giulio Einaudi, 1991), 158, my translation.

19. Levi, *I sommersi e i salvati*, 55, my translation.

20. Ibid., 57:

> We had tolerated filth, promiscuity and destitution, suffering
> from them less than we would have in normal life, because our
> moral measure [*il nostro metro morale*] had changed. Besides,
> everyone had stolen: from the kitchen, the factory, the camp, in
> short, "from the others". . . and some (a few) had fallen low
> enough to steal bread from their closest companion. We had for-
> gotten not only our country and our culture, but also our fami-
> lies, the past and the future, because, like animals, we had been
> reduced to the present moment. (My translation)

For the English, see *The Drowned and the Saved*, 75.

21. Levi, *I sommersi e i salvati*, 58–60; *The Drowned and the Saved*, 78.

22. Levi, *I sommersi e i salvati*, 61–63; *The Drowned and the Saved*, 81.

23. Levinas, "La volonté du ciel," 20.

24. Levi, *I sommersi e i salvati*, 64, my translation; *The Drowned and the Saved*, 83–84. Also see *La tregua*, 354, where Levi says that, in his book *Se questo è un uomo*, "it seemed to me that the theme of indignation should prevail: it was a testimony almost juridical in nature, and in my intention it was to be an act of accusation—not in order to provoke retaliation, a vendetta, a punishment—but simply to render testimony" (my translation).

25. Emmanuel Levinas, *Totality and Infinity*, trans. Alphonso Lingis (Pittsburgh: Duquesne University Press, 1969), 213; *Totalité et infini* (The Hague: Martinus Nijhoff, 1961), 188. Hereafter cited in the text as *TI* and *TeI*, respectively.

26. See Levi, chapter 6 in *I sommersi e i salvati*, 100, and the appendix to *La tregua*, 330–31. Levi insists that pardon cannot retroactively undo what has happened nor cancel guilt for evil deeds; nor is he willing to pardon those who *remain*

enemies. He will not pardon any of the guilty—unless, he says, they have demonstrated, not with fine words but with significant deeds—and not too belatedly—that they accept responsibility for the horrors of fascism and are determined to fight against racism, ethnic hatred, nationalism, and all forms of state terrorism. This, he says, may be pardoning one's enemy—but such an enemy has ceased to be an enemy!

27. See Walter Benjamin, "Theses on the Philosophy of History," in *Illuminations,* 253–64; and his notes called Konvolut N in "Re: The Theory of Knowledge, Theory of Progress," in *Benjamin: Philosophy, Aesthetics, History,* ed. Gary Smith (Chicago: University of Chicago Press, 1989), 43–83.

28. Benjamin, "Theses on the Philosophy of History," 253–64.

29. Emmanuel Levinas, *Difficult Freedom,* trans. Seán Hand (Baltimore: Johns Hopkins University Press, 1990), 292; *Difficile liberté,* 2nd ed. (Paris: Albin Michel, 1976), 407.

30. Levinas, *Time and the Other,* 39; *Le temps et l'autre* (Paris: Presses Universitaires de France, 1983), 17. *Le temps et l'autre* hereafter cited as *TA.*

31. Emmanuel Levinas, "Is Ontology Fundamental?" in *Emmanuel Levinas: Basic Philosophical Writings,* ed. Adriaan Peperzak, Simon Critchley, and Robert Bernasconi (Bloomington: Indiana University Press, 1996), 9; "L'ontologie est-elle fondamentale?" in *Entre nous,* 21.

32. See my discussion of Levinas's use of language in "The Invisible Face of Humanity: Levinas on the Justice of the Gaze," in my book *The Philosopher's Gaze: Modernity in the Shadows of Enlightenment* (Los Angeles: University of California Press, 1999), 234–334.

33. Bernasconi, "Only the Persecuted," 82.

34. See Jean-Luc Nancy, *The Experience of Freedom* (Stanford: Stanford University Press, 1988), 128: "Wickedness does not hate this or that singularity: it hates singularity as such and the singular relation of singularities." And see Primo Levi's chapter on "la violenza inutile" in *I sommersi e i salvati,* 83–101, which supports my argument here. There can be no doubt, according to Levi, that the Nazis resolved first to "annihilate us [Jews] as human beings in order to murder us later slowly" (*Se questo è un uomo,* 45). In *La tregua* (332), Levi observes that, in these conditions, it becomes possible, even if not always easy, to torture and murder, violating human nature through and through. Earlier, in *Se questo è un uomo* (133), he had written that "to destroy man is difficult, almost as difficult as creating him." And addressing himself directly to the agents of persecution, he says: "It hasn't been easy, hasn't happened quickly, but you Germans finally succeeded in doing just that. Here we are, docile beneath your watch; from us [prisoners], now, you have nothing more to fear: not acts of revolt, not a word of resistance, not even a judgmental look [*neppure uno sguardo giudice*]" (*Se questo,* 23; my translation). For the Nazis took everything human away from their victims: everything, even including their names. The inmates of the camps had been reduced to the condition of phantoms: "non-humans that march and labour in silence, the divine spark extinguished in them, already too empty even to suffer" (ibid., 82). "One even hesitates," he adds, "to call them living: one hesitates to call death their death, before

which they are no longer afraid, since they are too exhausted to comprehend it" (ibid., my translation).

35. Maurice Blanchot, *L'entretien infini* (Paris: Gallimard, 1969), 192; *The Infinite Conversation* (Minneapolis: University of Minnesota Press, 1993), chap. 5, §2, p. 130. And see Robert Antelme, *L'espèce humaine* (Paris: Gallimard, 1978).

36. See Franz Rosenzweig, *The Star of Redemption* (Notre Dame: Notre Dame University Press, 1985). Hereafter cited in the text as *SR*. See also Emmanuel Levinas, "Franz Rosenzweig: A Modern Jewish Thinker," in *Outside the Subject*, trans. Michael Smith (Stanford: Stanford University Press, 1993), 49–66; "Franz Rosenzweig: Une pensée juive moderne," in *Hors sujet* (Montpellier: Fata Morgana, 1987), 73–96.

37. Maurice Merleau-Ponty, *Les relations avec autrui chez l'enfant* (Paris: Centre du Documentation Universitaire, 1975), 69; "The Child's Relations with Others," in *The Primacy of Perception* (Evanston: Northwestern University Press, 1964), 146.

38. See my chapter on "The Invisible Face of Humanity," in *The Philosopher's Gaze*, 234–334.

Returning Violence

Antje Kapust

In his monumental historical oeuvre, Herodotus made a recommendation to posterity that seems seductive in its simplicity but that, nevertheless, represents one of the most crucial problems of humanity: he claimed that a human being would be unwise to prefer war to peace.[1] What appears to be a simple and reasonable statement in Herodotus turns out to be more complex in the optics of Levinas. Raising the difficult problem of humanity from a new angle, he explores what would contribute to the interruption of recurrent violence. Against traditional concepts of meaning, which according to Levinas include even Merleau-Ponty's project of a lateral meaning, he questions the specific orientation which directs a French person to learn Chinese instead of considering the Chinese-speaker as something barbaric excluded from language, an orientation which directs the French-speaker to prefer speech to war.[2]

This question is all the more relevant when contrasted with a remark that suggests resignation in the face of the eternal return of violence and that seems to anticipate and confirm a specific irreducibility of Hobbes's *bellum omnium contra omnes*. In one of his late dialogues, *The Laws*, after having argued for the superior force of the Idea of the Good over the power of *polemos*, Plato concludes with a pessimistic resignation: "What most people name peace is nothing more than a name, in reality we always have to deal with a natural, non-declared war of all states against all states."[3] For Plato, no remedy against the inextinguishable return of violence seems to exist. Peace, this precious matter, given preference in the thinking of Herodotus, is degraded by Plato from the status of a real "thing" to a mere word; to a "bare wish without reality," as Kant put it; to a pure change without fundamental substance, as Husserl claimed in the famous *Crisis;* and to a "blind touching," as Levinas suggests, a lip service

without work, an economics of empty meanings without liturgical substitution.[4]

At this point it would be easy to take an apparently "short way," en-
listing the hyperbolic chain of arguments presented by Levinas as a way
out of this question, a chain of arguments that concludes in the recommendation that the final word of philosophy would end in God, as described by Levinas in "Meaning and Sense."[5] But instead of this comfort-
ably short and direct way, Plato recommended—indeed already in his
dialogue *The Statesman*—a long way full of detours and apparent absurdities, an *oratio obliqua*, which is also taken up with delight by Foucault in
order to find an example of the turning around of the fixed *mathesis* of
Western rationality.[6] In *The Statesman*, Plato attempted to come to terms
with a political pragmatism that had been perverted from its original ideal
to one of the worst forms of the betrayal of peace—a fall exemplified and
incarnated in the politician Alcibiades. Political pragmatism is degraded
to a political opportunism that does not take into account the harm it
causes to all the innocent lives devastated by this betrayal. It is therefore
not surprising that Plato tries again and again to save the realization of
peace as a non-betrayed task of the political, like the waves of the sea
running against the shore, like contesting the adversity of things, which
Sartre, Freud, and Merleau-Ponty named the reverse side of the coin.[7]
Again and again he tries to make sure that the speech of peace does not
fall prey to an irreducible violence or get deformed into the simulacrum
of a blind dramatic device which consists of an *illusion of peace without
reality*.[8]

It seems that Levinas tries to intervene exactly at this blind spot between the ethical and the violent. I therefore want to work through the
sides of the ambiguity of returning violence—an ambiguity that Merleau-
Ponty analyzes in his thinking on war and peace in his essay "The Adversity of Things."[9] It is for this reason that I want to subject Levinas to a sort
of cross-examination by placing his quest for an ethical orientation under
pressure and by constantly confronting it with its refutation of ontological
violence. In a fictional dialogue with Levinas, I will proceed in five steps:
(1) I will look at the close relationship between speech and violence; (2) I
want to briefly retrace some aspects of the degradation of political speech
by the warlike element and then (3) return to the question of the so-
called bad effects of rationality itself; (4) I turn to the relevance of speech
in the deconstruction of violence; and (5) I want to try to defend the ethical claim against the repetition and return of *polemos*.[10]

The Ethical Challenge in Face
of the Extreme

My main concern can be articulated in this thesis: the two aspects of violence and speech are not independent from each other but are related in a figure that I will call "the asymmetry of mutual exclusion and overlapping." I argue that this interrelation constitutes one "law of violence" which is performed according to a pendulum movement: the ascension of force coincides with a decrease of ethical speech to a minimal level. But besides this pendulum movement, violent force also borrows the mask of a specific language and speech in order to abolish ethical speaking.[11] In *Totality and Infinity,* Levinas had demonstrated how the ontology of violence is focused in the phenomenon of mobilization, which itself dissolves ethical speech. It may be that Levinas did not suspect how proper it would be to deconstruct the crucial point of force that is given with this mobilization. The benefit of this gesture becomes evident when we put this ethical optics into a coherent deformation by contrasting it with the philosophy of war presented by Ernst Jünger. This parallelism is all the more relevant since Jünger himself considers mobilization as the central nerve of force in his work *The Genius of War and the Warrior.* To trace the divergence of both thinkers is urgent, since Jünger derives the abolition of all speech from this phenomenon and thereby destroys the ethical orientation called for by Levinas. In contrast to Levinas, he draws a contrary conclusion—one which even includes a specific "praise" of war, as was very common at the beginning of the twentieth century, also expressed, for example, in Scheler's *Genius of War.*[12]

The potency of mobilization consists in the abyssal power to dissolve every potential surplus of an ethical beyond, dissolving it to the degree that no resistance is possible. Jünger describes this pendulum movement by taking up the metaphor of the electric circuit: violence is presented as a form of energy that sets free a demonic genius capable of invading the most intimate contours of a pacifist or eschatological position. The demonic nature takes hold of each being in an uncanny manner. It is so effective in its encompassing mechanism that even speaking itself is finally abolished, because there are no means or necessity to speak. Speaking regresses to a politics of force, which Jünger tragically justifies by referring to a specific idea of the infinite. This idea of the infinite comes into play when the genius of war performs the transition from the territorial order to the order of a higher eternal reality.[13]

The modulation of the same element, the factor of mobilization, allows Jünger to draw different consequences than Levinas. Civilization does not find its genesis in the claim of the other but in the spirit of war. War itself is given a sacred mask insofar as it cannot be reduced to an analytic of mass death and mass murder, but instead has to be considered as the symbol of a higher work. All theories of war worked out in that historical context draw on the same power of genius; a genius derived from Kant who, however, provided it with a different mask. To consider war in terms of death and destruction is to end up in a naturalistic point of view that ignores the creative power of nations enacted by the spirit, i.e., the so-called genius of war. The higher work claimed of this genius performs a transition from the sensible order to the central realm of the guiding idea: "By giving their life in battle, the fallen soldiers went from an imperfect order to a perfect reality, from a Germany in its temporal appearance to an eternal Germany."[14] Under the sign of this transition, every recommendation for peace, such as that made by Herodotus, is degraded into mere sounds. The destruction of Levinas's preference to talk with the so-called barbarian and stranger could not be more dramatic. In contrast to Levinas, the final point of human existence does not lie in God but in the fallen soldier: "The unknown soldier finds rest in the heart of Paris beneath the Arc de Triomphe. Western consciousness memorizes him in the symbol of the Paladin of civilization."[15] For Jünger, the reason for the defeat of German civilization lies precisely in falling prey to the "barbarian." This falling-prey occurs when a spirit turns toward the other by learning his or her language, the speech of the "barbarian," instead of insisting on its own *conatus* of force: "The secret chronometer of civilization is guarded in Paris, and whoever acknowledges this will be measured instead of giving himself the measure. Germany has become accustomed to speaking a foreign language— is it astonishing that the stranger comes into domination and reign?"[16]

In order to keep the question of an ethical orientation alive, Levinas would have to raise the question of how we could remain aware of the consequences of this hidden transformation. He would have to reread a long and troublesome genealogical trace. This trace makes visible the law of mutual and asymmetrical exclusion in a "pendulum movement," and it displays the tragic fate of a prophetic speech always overlapped by the speech of violence.

The Degradation of Political Speech by Infiltration of the Warlike Element

This law of the pendulum movement erects itself on a long and successful prehistory in which the ontology of war corresponds to a politics of force. Contrary to the *opinio communis* that reason and force, the politics of logos and the logos of the warlike element, are separate, Plato's insight seems to indicate a different logic: political reason is shaped by a silent and masked infiltration of warlike elements. This infiltration is the reason why Foucault questions the origins of modern rationality in terms of a *perversion of language:* "How, since when and why, did we become aware of the fact that it is war that works below and within political relations?"[17] It is revealing that Foucault does not develop this argument in the shape of a *polemological shadow* of rationality itself. Let us remember that Levinas himself does not locate the main element of war in a *polemological structure,* which is only *one* manifestation of war.

Levinas briefly analyzes different definitions of war: polemology, annihilation, logic of destruction, negation, and combat.[18] But his criticism of these definitions refers to the fact that all these types ignore the a priori of the face as the vulnerability of the other. This is the reason why, according to Levinas, the main aspect of war has to be recognized in *vulnerability.* We might discover the impact and the value of this definition by contrasting it with the position taken up by Foucault, who places an emphasis on the infiltration of political language by the spirit of military language. This perversion of language is mirrored in the fact that the language of power relations between nations reflects the vocabulary of war and its techniques of annihilation. Foucault denounces the political insofar as it is shaped and dominated by central terms of strategic thinking and the tactics of war. It is precisely this infiltration of civil speech by the warlike element that leads him to advance the thesis that military thinking marks the center of not only political institutions but also the civilian order, in which is hidden the mechanics of the order of battle.[19]

We may wonder if this perspective ever reaches the point Levinas is aiming at—to remember those human beings who are exposed to violence in their passivity, those whose cries are smothered by the language of violence, and who have never even been granted a memory in the course of history, a history that is written in the voice of the victors, a history that has always been written under the seal of the emperor. Recent activities—such as the exhibitions on the war of annihilation led by the Wehrmacht, the black book on communism, or discussions in international law about crimes of war and crimes against humanity—uncover one of the darkest aspects of humankind in their oblivion of the elemental: the legitimate voice of a victim to be remembered not only against the political gestation of powers but also against their thanatological effects of repetition in history.[20]

Without being explicitly aware of these concepts, Ricœur has already attempted to question the shadowy sides of history by formulating a paradox: the origin of the political goes back to a *tragic* dimension that he locates in a fatal connection of the rational and its own *malum*. A specific rationality produces bad effects.[21] However, he derives a fatal conclusion from this: "The political shows its sense only if its intent and its telos is connected with the fundamental intention of philosophy itself: with the good." Does this perspective imply the repetition of the dangers of history itself, the eternal return of violence? The emergence of new strategic principles as the authentic speech of the military caused an important modification. This factor increases with the impact of the nuclear *Gestell:* civil forms deliver their contribution to war, as Virilio shows in his book *The Negative Horizon*.[22] Human inventions, such as the railroad, turn from harmless service into an organized structure of mass death, into the calculation of the subject under the sign of death, as Edith Wyschogrod shows in her book on mass death, *Spirit in Ashes*.[23] Basic economic structures, geopolitics, strategies of administration, communications systems, etc., become the decisive turning points in a logic where the finitude of human being overturns into the infinite of annihilation. It produces a form of rationality that takes up the form of the *commercium,* denounced by Levinas, in which human beings remain under the force of mobilization. The wars of the twentieth century turned out to be total wars, i.e., wars of the total mobilization of masses and material. Given this real power of the shadowy side, all recommendations for peace seem to be nothing more than wishful thinking.

The Evil of Rationality: Failing to Hear the Speech in the Pendulum Movement

It is surprising that the theories developed as remedies ignore the relevance of speech. The tradition is known for having put all solutions on a one-sided card, presented in the figure of unity, against the warlike forces of dispersion. Against the evil of violence, classical *topoi* concentrate on the figure of unity or the unification of the heterogeneous, for example, in the politics of the friendship, in the model of the polis and Augustine's *City of God*. The corresponding concepts that reflect this unity are cultivated like a red guiding thread through the history of thinking: the politics of *homonoia*, the politics of *harmony* against politics of difference, and the ethics of *concordia*. It is well known that Levinas attacked the ethical implications of these models in his criticism of the neutrality of the one as it is expressed in the philosophy of Plotinus. The necessity of a deconstruction of the one imposes itself in view of the incredible impact of this figure, which continued to resonate in the philosophies of the twentieth century. This impact can even be found in Husserl. Having survived World War I, in which his son perished, he wonders about a remedy against violence. But it is dramatic to see that he falls back into the same structure that had contributed to the generation of violence—a guiding form of unity, which ignores the traumatic traces of violence and the phenomenon of the destruction of speech. Husserl only briefly mentions the traumatic traces of modern wars in his reflection entitled "Kaizo" and, even then, reduces them to a mere annotation before quickly turning his philosophical focus to a uniform ideal of a *renewal of humankind* that would leave the destructive and dysfunctional forces of violence behind.[24] It is no coincidence that this solution is constructed on the basis of a paradigm that is oriented by analogy toward the *mathematical* structure, thereby carrying forward the inherent potential of the homogeneity and leveling of the same.

In his book *Truth and History,* Ricœur analyzes a similar gesture, one caught in the underlying structure of violence. He also claims to break with totality, but falls back into the idea of a humanity grounded in a structure of reason oriented toward the mathematical ideal. This ideal is defended in the form in which it was inaugurated in antiquity and as it is still conceptualized in Husserl's demonstration of the inner historicity of geometry: "One cannot forget that science, that was Greek in its origin and became European with Newton, Galileo, and Descartes, has not been initiated as Greek or European but as human."[25]

Although Ricœur emphasizes the human effect of those movements, not the classification as European or Greek, this prospect of humanity is grounded upon a form of unity that leads to the project of the colonization of other cultures.[26] It is strange that Ricœur is able to articulate this unity but does not acknowledge fully enough the possibilities of its abuse. Should we consider this as the impact of the returning pattern of violence, leaving no place for the beyond? Ricœur first remarks: "The Greek-European rationality produces a type of unity *de jure,* that presses its stamp on all other cultures of this civilization."[27] The forming power of this homogeneity, which tragically does not only evoke the forming power of Plato's *chora* but the generating and constructing power of the genius of war, is already illustrated in a metaphor that Pascal puts into play: "The entire humanity can be considered as one single man that learns continually and forgets nothing."[28] Ricœur's interpretation of this metaphor (which is the type of metaphor that Levinas denounces) illustrates the degree to which a certain type of philosophical speech itself leads to a ground that can be so catastrophically abused against its own "good will": "Pascal means nothing else with this sentence than that each human being, confronted with a geometrical task, is to come to the same conclusion—presupposing, of course, he/she possesses the necessary knowledge. It is an abstract unity *de jure* of humankind and all other manifestations are conditioned by this unity."[29] The language of the one Levinas attacks could not be more perpetual.

What is the power or the orientation that prevented the "recognition" that the human cannot be reduced to the language of neutrality or to the exchangeable formulas of an algorithm?

The "Law" of the Pendulum Movement: Mutism of the Victim and Absence of Speech

Let us therefore go back to the previously mentioned pendulum movement and its consequences for the absence of ethical speech. The law of the pendulum movement stated that violence takes place in the destruction of ethical speaking. Killing requires no more language; it proceeds without words, eventually only accompanied by the threat expelled by the same. The only tolerated forms of language used by violence are reduced to the patterns of *command* of the same: "Go away," as in forms of ethnic violence when the victim is not immediately killed; "tell us what you know," as in instrumentalization of torture; "shoot and kill," as in the order to kill the enemy that war enacts; and "betray," as in espionage operated in all forms of violent aggression against others.[30] All such commands leave their language of violence as a trace in the soul of the violated: moral devastation in the face of destruction, lifelong patterns of escape and evasion of the unsaved soul, and the devastation and undoing of character in killing, as it is already depicted in the case of Homer's warrior Achilles.[31]

Even in the one-sided dictation of peace, it is the merciless fist of the winner that dictates all language after a capitulation.[32] It is just in this vacuum, in this discontinuity of two different logics, that the absence and withdrawal of ethical speech takes place. From antiquity to modern times, it was always the other as barbarian, as horrid animal, and as uncivilized being, who was all too often decreed to be a legitimated target for extinction. This "labeling" coincided with an ambivalent refusal of situating him or her in the reign of ethical speech.[33] Passing from the late concept of *polemos* to the holy doctrine of sacred war, from conquest of civilizations to ideological legitimations of persecutions of others, rationality developed many ways of interrupting the orientation that Levinas advances—that of preferring to talk to the so-called barbarian instead of killing him.[34] Even the calling into memory of this orientation does not take place; violence is enacted in the sphere of mute acts of brutality such as took place in the mass execution of Jews, a mass murder which was set forth in the final solution of National Socialism: "We have drunk a lot of alcohol during this time in order to stimulate our verve and exhilaration for work."[35] Victims are deprived of any possibility of speech, since any request for deliverance, rescue, or survival has to be immediately denied and repressed: "The Jews who were still living after mass execution as well as those who were only shot and still wounded in the lower layers were suffocated by the upper layers or were drowned by the blood of the upper layers."[36] The force of violence replaces the creative function that Hannah Arendt attributed to the political word. An agonistic productivity of political speech shifts all too quickly to a dysfunctional and destructive force. Ricœur describes the logic of this collision in a metaphor which dismisses Levinas's ethical point, since violence is described as the mechanical action and reaction of two forces—an image that is applied to illustrate the phenomena of battle and combat from modern philosophy to the military discourses of the nineteenth and twentieth centuries.[37] But it is important that he links this collision of forces with a degradation of language. Ricœur describes precisely the ontological dilemma of this violence: it consists in the dominance of the blind spot in which "two powers of command confront each other at the same point of pretension where they cannot sustain both at the same time."[38] In this blind spot of collision, speech gets destroyed and is replaced by a *myth* that imposes a stigma upon the target of extinction, as Levinas, Merleau-Ponty, and Ricœur describe in similar ways.

In "The War Has Taken Place," Merleau-Ponty describes how, if the victim were not enclosed within the myth of "the Jew," the anti-Semite could not torture and extinguish the Jew, if the anti-Semite would only open to the face of the other: a face, where the gaze is silent speech.[39] Ricœur discovers a similar pattern displaying the active factor of violence done to another by abusing his or her exposure, passivity, and vulnerability. In this confrontation, which reveals an asymmetrical relation of power, a process of stigmatization is set forth, transforming the political into a violence of annihilation: "The angel of all violence is therefore always the deliberate and real murder: In the moment where violence takes place the other is labeled with the stigmatized sign: to be extinguished."[40] This extinction proceeds without an orientation to speak with the other.

As Simone Weil shows in her impressive interpretation of Homer's *Iliad,* the annihilation of the warriors takes place without words. All fighters are enclosed in their own universe, cut off from the other, only related to the body to be killed.[41] Language is once again reduced to the mathematical form of an economic conclusion, measuring the force required for efficient destruction. It is for this reason that Bertrand Russell tries to destroy the mask of command and dissimulation of violent force, in an attempt to make visible their real impact. He accomplishes this by replacing the habitual formula "I am ready to die for my fatherland" by the enunciation "I am ready to kill for my fatherland." Elaine Scarry, taking up this example in her reflections on war, goes even farther and suggests this explicit formulation: "The defense of a just matter means to kill for a just matter and to accept the danger of an unfair and unjust death."[42] It is therefore astonishing that even Scarry, in her analysis, does not accent the decomposition, the cancellation and the enforced impossibility of ethical language; instead, she concentrates on the structural logic that generates those patterns, which she describes as an invasion into human flesh.

But this loss of language and speech is extremely relevant, as becomes visible when we turn to the side of the victim. To employ Husserl's description of intentionality in this context, we could describe the phenomenon in the following way: speaking marks a space or vacuum that is not filled by being heard. Severely hurt victims or traumatized persons lose their language and become mute. The ideal that Hannah Arendt articulated as the telos of the political is driven to the most extreme limit of impossibility: shaping and gestating a common world through speaking and shared perspectives breaks down into a state where no speech will ever take place.

This loss of speech can even be discovered in one of the most famous case studies in philosophy, the patient "Schneider" discussed by Goldstein and Merleau-Ponty, a "case" that could have drawn attention to the relevance of language. We may wonder if the phenomenologists failed to capture the pendulum law, since they are missing one crucial element. The anatomy and the physiology of violence have to be completed by a traumatology, and it is this which Levinas is thematizing. Merleau-Ponty was unaware of the phenomenon of trauma, since the concept had not yet emerged at that time. So the traces of violence that he analyzes are not described as the signs of a suffering of the loss of language, but only as the shrinking of the world to a world of a few silent gestures.[43]

What, then, is acted out in history in the case of the eternal return of violence? In response to this question, we might place the issue of the Goldstein case into the language of an analogy in order to demonstrate what philosophy itself could learn, if it would *lend an ear* to the speech of the sensible, if it would open the senses to the flesh of being, as Merleau-Ponty says, and if it would not enclose itself in a space of concepts which muffles the cries of violence.[44] The famous "principle of sufficient reason" has "existed" as a problem in the horizon of philosophical perception, but it took—as Heidegger shows us in his wonderful analysis—an incubation of two thousand years before finally getting articulated.[45] Silently a problem was indicated that could have been put into words already, if only the silent speech of the victims of history had been acknowledged. This is what Levinas is claiming: hearing, following the orientation of talking with the barbarian.[46]

But in spite of this invisible horizon, the National Socialist butcher does not care about the speech of suffering. It is already exceptional if he mentions it as a vacuum and extreme limit in his daily notes: "Every night the crying of the desperate children and the miserable screams of those who have lost their mind/reason are audible from the other end of the camp."[47] It is worthwhile to have a closer look at this example. First, the difference between "audible" and "listen to" or "lending an ear" is of extreme importance. But the topological rupture is also significant. The cries are coming from the other end; they overcome the separating distance; but they do not reach the traitor so as to touch him with the claim of those others who are persecuted.[48]

Anamnesis of a Problem

Returning violence is accompanied by an irreducible question, one which Plato already predicted and had raised as a question, the problem of deafness in the face of the cry of the suffering. This "deafness" seems to imply an ontological refutation of the orientation asked for by Levinas. Let us make another detour: Ricœur had analyzed the mechanism of violence by questioning its anatomy and its physiology. It seems that a central aspect was forgotten in this context—the relevance of traumatology. This point implies more than a bare account of mental, emotional, or psychic mutilations. If Ricœur says that a specific rationality produces bad effects, we have to confront the ambiguity of rationality itself and question the way in which the rationalization, organization, and instrumentalization of violence and mass death have played a part in excluding and mutilating speech; for example, the speech of pain, the claims of rights, and the cries of suffering.

The above-mentioned rationality of the one results in one of the worst paradigms of blindness to these phenomena. Levinas could deconstruct this ignorance by deconstructing the philosophy of Plotinus. Plotinus solved the problem of how to insert factical violence into the harmony of the one by presenting a model in which the parts are arranged according to a perfect harmony, by means of a dramatic configuration—a trick that we could denounce as a verbal dissimulation of violence. This dramatic configuration allows Plotinus a fatal misinterpretation of violence, one which became constitutive throughout history: "All combat led by mortal human beings, arranged in a beautiful order and joyful dances of weapons, tells us that human life is nothing else than a game and that death is no horror."[49] Traumatic consequences of violence vanish away in a philosophy that relies on the primacy of the concept, which disguises the speech of pain as a blind shadow without real substance: "Since in this case the same is true as for all casualties of life. As on stage, it is not the inner human being, the soul, who laments and cries, but only its shadow, the external human being who transforms the world into a stage whereas the inner soul is indestructible."

It seems as if mythical thinking gave evidence of a more subtle wisdom than the naive oblivion of philosophy. This becomes visible in the silent intuition that mythical thinking displays in the power of the rhapsodic word: Athena, the goddess of logos and the source of Western rationality, is the reverse side of bare irrational force. She not only accompanies Ares, the god of war; she complements brute force with the instrumental force of strategic thinking and rational tactics.[50] In addition, she rules over another violent power: while she is the goddess of logos, thinking, and speech, she is also responsible for cutting speech and transforming normal persons into mute victims. She does so by the assistance of the Gorgons, those feared goddesses of terror, panic, and cruelty, which appear as her attributes in her early stage. Panic, terror, and fear are the forces that mutilate persons into silent suffering. This is due to petrification by paralysis, which has to be considered as one origin of the loss of speech. Petrification takes place as the degradation of the human being into an objectified mass of matter, what Simone Weil described as a zombie. The victim is neither dead nor alive—in a tragic manner of eternal repetition, the zombie turns out to be a cipher for cultural and human-made traumatic violence, insofar as this figure of mythical thinking resembles those living dead persons at the edge of the silent world of the concentration camps of the twentieth century.[51] It is only in the philosophical era that repressive philosophical discourse sublimates Athena into the fully enlightened goddess of rationality. For this reason, Ricœur is right when he reminds us not to forget the bad effects that cannot be separated from rationality itself: Athena is sublimated; however, invisibly and disguised, she still carries her bad effects with her, insofar as the Gorgons are still inscribed in her in a displaced way, appearing on her shield of war. Perhaps it is precisely in this mechanism of philosophical sublimation that we could discover the point where Levinas could interrupt the violence of speech. The described sublimation of Athena could be read as a trope of philosophical thinking—elevating the sensible myth to the primacy of concept.

Levinas could aim at a deconstruction of this eternal repetition of violence, hidden in rationality itself, by making a twofold detour: the deconstruction of this primacy of representation (for example, as it occurs in the trace of the other) converges with an ethical phenomenology of the sensible, which is described as the pain of trauma.[52] And it is precisely at this point that another advantage can be drawn from Levinas's conception of violence. Let us remember that he grounded diverse theories of the polemological, the work of annihilation, conquest, and combat, in the hidden presupposition of abusing the vulnerability of the other. If it is just this sensible vulnerability that is ignored in the primacy of representation, the deconstruction of representation would unmask that which violence always dissimulates in order to be effective.[53] One might object that this ethical dissimulation would only account for specific types of violence (those linked to the factor of nearness) but does not account for all kinds of violence, such as the mediated violence linked to the paradigm of hyper-technology, which Virilio and Baudrillard make visible. The classical trope in this context would be the atom bomb.[54] The pilot, who puts this logic of destruction into effect by destroying from total distance without any nearness, cannot be deconstructed in an ethical paradigm which centers around sensible affection.[55] But does this shift or absence mean that we again fall back into an undecided situation, where the logic of violence keeps the "last word" by subverting the speech of ethical resistance? Are we again confronted with the irreducible remainder of *polemos* that Plato lamented? Is war, then, the father of all things? Is the unknown soldier the law of civilization, or is the attribution of pain the invention of culture?

Let us try another turn in order to subvert these ontological ghosts. The speech of ethical resistance means tearing away the masks of a context, and this also concerns the legitimations that war has generated in order to dissimulate itself as the extreme consequence. If the *polemos* seems to establish itself as the final accord of all spoken words, Levinas could show that there is still a beyond. War tries to get hold of persons without being recognized as war. War manifests itself by the command of mobilization and becomes visible only afterward in its real effect—mostly when it is too late to withdraw, too late for other solutions, or too late not to suffer from the destruction and crimes of war. But this strategy of dissimulation is parallel to an invisible strategy of legitimization that subverts the doctrine of the official legitimization of war and violence. It appears "on silent feet," as Merleau-Ponty says, using the words of Nietzsche.

This can be shown in a fragment from Heraclitus: "Also the *Kykeon* disintegrates itself [*distatai*] if one does not stir it [*me kinoumos*]."[56] This dark and mysterious fragment seems harmless, but it dissimulates one of the most dangerous strategies. The *Kykeon* is the mixed drink of the Eleusian mysteries. It consists of barley flour, water, and peppermint, which are three heterogeneous elements. And it disintegrates if one does not stir it. This object is only the mask for an invisible but eminent political problem. The mixture symbolizes the coexistence of heterogeneous forces. The meaning of the fragment could be *translated* in the following way. So that the beverage does not disintegrate itself, one must stir; so that a political community does not fall apart, one must practice a politics of movement which also implies violent movement against the danger of inertia. The hidden paradox of this position consists in its connection of the ideal of unity with ongoing violent motion. Plutarch is exactly on the point, as demonstrated by his telling of the following story about Heraclitus. Asked by the Ephesian for advice about how harmony (*homonoia*) could be maintained in the community, Heraclitus does not let one single word cross his lips—and this in a meeting where talking and discussion are on the agenda. Instead of using language, he takes a glass of water, adds barley flour and mint, preparing a mixture of these ingredients, stirs it a while, drinks it and retreats silently. The point of this ironic anecdote is to be found in the title under which Plutarch tells it: " Of Garrulity."[57]

Here the ethics of substitution, as well as a politics of balance and a politics of difference, are pushed to the limit. The infiltration of the political through warlike elements not only profits from a movement of totalization by mobilization but also through the affiliated ideological speech. The decline and disintegration of a community, which was all too often attributed to an inert and therefore disintegrating peace, could only be avoided by a stimulating force. A whole spectrum of forces, from the nineteenth century until recent times, speaks this language of the blindness of an ideological logos of argumentation that has been grasped by the *kratos*—just as Jünger had predicted. Have we again arrived at a stalemate? Was Plato's pessimistic resignation right after all? Is there no escape from the trauma of repetition?

Let us try a last detour: the necessity associated with the "one must stir" seems to hide another presupposition. This presupposition can be made visible by transforming it into an explicit formulation, and thereby stripping the mask of its context. The claimed movement cannot be performed without participation, e.g., the silent complicity or active engagement that Merleau-Ponty tries to deconstruct in his "La guerre a eu lieu."[58] Even movement has to enact power in language, for example, in the language of the command of mobilization, if it is to subvert the language of ethical resistance. But, in contrast to those who propagated this movement of violence, Heraclitus refrains from making explicit normative claims. He did not say, "You must create violent movement so that inert peace does not disintegrate your community." By the same token, neither

Levinas nor Heidegger speak in a normative way. What at first glance looks like nothing more than a mere reversibility or correspondence could bear an invisible surplus or beyond. There is war, and Plato is unfortunately right about this. Nevertheless, it might be possible that the claimed necessity could be subverted by the ethical impact. Ethics is my business, as Levinas says. It is mine by my *performing* it, even in the act of talking with, rather than killing, the barbarian. But it is precisely in this self-perception of oneself as an ethical performance that a plurality of singularities could create a non-inert peace beyond violence.

Notes

1. Herodotus, *Historien* (Stuttgart: Alfred Kröner, 1971). Concerning the reception and transformation of Herodotus, see also Hans Joachim Diesner, ed., *Stimmen zu Krieg und Frieden im Rennaissance-Humanismus* (Göttingen: Vandenhoeck und Ruprecht, 1990); and Franz Josef Worstbrock, *Krieg und Frieden im Horizont des Rennaissance-Humanismus* (Weinheim: Acta Humaniora, 1986).

2. Emmanuel Levinas, *Humanisme de l'autre homme* (Montpellier: Fata Morgana, 1972), 39.

3. Plato, *The Laws*, 626a.

4. Phenomenologists will immediately recognize that the important difference between economic and ethical meaning, or that between exchange and gift, is at stake. For more discussion, see my book *Berührung ohne Berührung: Ethik und Ontologie bei Merleau-Ponty and Levinas* (Munich: Wilhelm Fink, 1999), 54ff. and 80ff. A translation is in process.

5. "Mais le 'terme' d'un tel mouvement à la fois critique et spontané—et qui n'est pas, à proprement parler, un terme, car il n'est pas une fin, mais le principe sollicitant une oeuvre sans récompense, une liturgie—ne s'appelle plus être. Et c'est là, peut-être, que l'on peut s'apercevoir de la nécessité où une médiation philosophique se trouve de recourir à des notions comme Infini ou comme Dieu" (Levinas, *Humanisme*, 57).

6. Michel Foucault, "Omnes et singulatim: Zu einer Kritik der politischen Vernunft," 65–92, in *Gemeinschaften: Positionen zu einer Philosophie des Politischen*, ed. Joseph Vogl (Frankfurt am Main: Suhrkamp, 1994), 72ff.

7. See Maurice Merleau-Ponty, "L'homme et l'adversité," in *Signes* (Paris: Gallimard, 1960), 284–308. This text is published in English translation as "Man and Adversity" in *Signs,* tran. R. C. McCleary (Northwestern University Press, 1968), 224–243.

8. Interestingly, Levinas opens up the discussion of this problem explicitly in his final reflections on peace at the end of *Totality and Infinity,* trans. Alphonso Lingis (Pittsburgh: Duquesne University Press, 1969), 281–84.

9. See op. cit. "Man and Adversity," 224–243. See also "La guerre a eu lieu," in

Maurice Merleau-Ponty, *Sens et Non-Sens* (Paris: Gallimard, 1966), 252ff. It is available in English translation as "The War Has Taken Place" in *Sense and Non-Sense*, trans. Hubert L. Dreyfus and Patricia A. Dreyfus (Northwestern University Press, 1964). The "solution" cannot be found in shifting the legacy of the opposition between the transcendental and the empirical toward the polarity of normativity and facticity, where moral knowledge directs "how persons have to behave," and where deviation can be neglected as empirical failure. See Jürgen Habermas, "Richtigkeit versus Wahrheit—Zum Sinn der Sollgeltung moralischer Urteile und Normen," 35–54, in *Moral im sozialen Kontext*, ed. Wolfgang Edelstein and Gertrud Nunner-Winkler (Frankfurt am Main: Suhrkamp, 2000), 36. The orientation toward a consensus achieved by discursive rationality is not the result of a "matter of fact," but establishes a norm which expects acknowledgment by all partners of communication who take their point of departure in the premise that they can establish this consensus under ideal conditions of rational discourse. Habermas degrades the problem that I call the "repetition of the agonistic" to the status of an empirical failure on the part of those who refuse to participate in consensus that does not need to be considered more deeply, which allows him to return immediately to his premise (46–47).

10. Under the heading of returning forces and by taking Levinas's question of orientation as a guideline, I present an extended analysis of the relation between the power of war and the mutilation of speech in my book *Der Krieg und der Ausfall der Sprache* (München: Wilhelm Fink Verlag, 2004).

11. Compare Elaine Scarry, *The Body in Pain: The Making and Unmaking of the World* (New York: Oxford University Press, 1985). The question of the transformation and mutilation of speech is normally eclipsed in reflections on violence. It is therefore extraordinary that some rare reflections can be found. For example, concerning the instrumentalization of speech in the operation in the crime of violence, see Yves Ternon, *Der verbrecherische Staat: Völkermord im 20. Jahrhundert* (Hamburg: Hamburger Edition, 1996), 78ff. For Todorov's reflections on the connection between speaking, judging, and understanding as the attempt of victims of the Holocaust to face evil, see Tzvetan Todorov, *Angesichts des Äußersten* (Munich: Wilhelm Fink, 1993), 232ff.

12. See Max Scheler, *Der Genius des Krieges und der Deutsche Krieg*, in *Gesammelte Werke*, vol. 4, ed. Manfred Frings (Bern and Munich: Francke, 1982). This influential book, mostly avoided by phenomenologists, is discussed in all its horrendous effects by Kurt Flasch in *Die geistige Mobilmachung: Die deutschen Intellektuellen und der Erste Weltkrieg* (Berlin: Alexander Fest, 2000). In contrast to Flasch's interpretation that texts such as those presented by Scheler (but also by other phenomenologists such as Theodor Lipps, etc.) functioned as retrograde legitimations of the event of war, I am inclined to consider them as opening up categorical frames that, like a *chora*, shape an event like war. It seems that it is precisely in this gesture that their dangerous potential of a warlike orientation is hidden.

13. Ernst Jünger, "Die totale Mobilmachung," in *Krieg und Krieger*, ed. Ernst Jünger (Berlin, 1930), 9–30. In a fatal way, the extreme perversion of philosophical motives is made visible by Jünger's adaption, which can be taken as emblematic of a specific "spirit of time."

14. Jünger, "Mobilmachung," 29.

15. Ibid., 27.

16. Ibid., 26.

17. Michel Foucault, *Vom Licht des Krieges zur Geburt der Geschichte* (Berlin: Merve, 1986), 7. The text is a lecture given at the Collège de France on January 21 and 28, 1996. It should be mentioned that the publication is still not authorized.

18. In *Levinas: Darstellung seines Denkens* (Freiburg, 2005), I discuss different modes of war briefly announced and only indicated by Levinas.

19. Foucault, *Licht des Krieges*, 7. For the broader and interdisciplinary horizon, see also Jeremy Black, *European Warfare 1660–1815* (New Haven and London: Yale University Press, 1994); Theodor Fuchs, *Geschichte des europäischen Kriegswesens* (Munich: Bernard und Graefe, 1977); Azar Gat, *The Origins of Military: Thought from the Enlightenment to Clausewitz* (Oxford: Clarendon, 1989); and Maurice Pearton, *The Knowledgeable State: Diplomacy, War and Technology Since 1830* (London, 1982).

20. See Roy Gutman and David Rieff, eds., *Crimes of War: What the Public Should Know* (New York and London: W. W. Norton, 1999); Aryeh Neier, *War Crimes: Brutality, Genocide, Terror, and the Struggle for Justice* (New York and Toronto: Random House, 1998); and Hannes Herr and Klaus Naumann, eds., *Vernichtungskrieg: Verbrechen der Wehrmacht 1941–1944* (Hamburg: Hamburger Edition, 1995).

21. Paul Ricœur, *Geschichte und Wahrheit* (Munich: Paul List, 1974), 249. Ricœur reflects on this *malum politicum* as the dominant political paradox.

22. Paul Virilio, *L'horizon négatif* (Paris: Galilée, 1984). See also Dierk Spreen, *Tausch, Technik, Krieg: Die Geburt der Gesellschaft im technisch medialen Apriori* (Berlin and Hamburg: Argument, 1998); and Stefan Kaufmann, *Kommunikationstechnik und Kriegführung 1815–1945. Stufen telemedialer Rüdstung* (Munich: Wilhelm Fink, 1996).

23. Edith Wyschogrod, *Spirit in Ashes: Hegel, Heidegger, and Man-Made Mass Death* (New Haven and London: Yale University Press, 1985).

24. Edmund Husserl, *Aufsätze und Vorträge,* ed. Thomas Nenon and Hans-Rainer Sepp (Dordrecht: Martinus Nijhoff, 1989), 3.

25. Ricœur, *Geschichte und Wahrheit,* 277. Ricœur discusses the problem of power, especially in the totalitarian system of socialism.

26. See Levinas, *Humanisme,* 31, 54, 56, 41); Merleau-Ponty, *Signes,* 47, 174–75; Edmund Husserl, *Die Krisis der europäischen Wissenschaften und die transzendentale Phänomenologie* (The Hague: Martinus Nijhoff, 1962), 325; Robert Bernasconi, "One-Way Traffic: The Ontology of Decolonization and Its Ethics" 67–80, in *Ontology and Alterity in Merleau-Ponty,* ed. Galen Johnson and Michael B. Smith (Evanston: Northwestern University Press, 1990), 78, 71, 76. Also see my discussion in *Berührung ohne Berührung,* 262–77.

27. Ricœur, *Geschichte und Wahrheit,* 277.

28. Ibid.

29. Ibid.

30. This phenomenology of the deformation of speech makes visible the

transformation via rhetoric of an original "logos" to the final expiation of speech in "language as command" as it is conceptualized in Hobbes. The shift between warlike command and ethical command cannot be more disastrous.

31. See the interpretation of the transformation of Achilles as an indication for what has been considered to be a post-traumatic stress syndrome of Vietnam veterans (and others) in Jonathan Shay, *Achilles in Vietnam: Combat Trauma and the Undoing of Character* (New York: Simon and Schuster, 1994); and Dave Grossman, *On Killing: The Psychological Cost of Learning to Kill in War and Society* (Boston: Back Bay Books, 1995). Martha Nussbaum has already described the mutilation of characters by violence:

> Hecuba had argued that nomos, though human and contingent, is stable, and that through nomos humans can make themselves stable. The events of this play show us that the annihilation of conventions by another's act can destroy the stable character who receives it. It can, quite simply, produce bestiality, the utter loss of human relatedness and human language. Bestiality, in the final scene, is shown us most clearly in the person of Polymestor, who, after the blinding, enters half-naked, on all fours, a "mountain beast" (1058), wild for the blood of his injurers. (Martha Nussbaum, *The Fragility of Goodness: Luck and Ethics in Greek Tragedy and Philosophy* [Cambridge: Cambridge University Press, 1986], 417)

32. See, for example, Tacitus, *Historien*, 1.50; Caesar, *Bellum Gallicum*, 8.2.4–5.1. See also Gerhard Binder, "Saeva Pax: Kriegs- und Friedenstexte," in *Krieg und Frieden im Altertum*, ed. Gerhard Binder and Bernd Effe (Trier: Wissenschaftlicher Verlag, 1989), 219–45.

33. See my text "Zivilisierte Grausamkeit: Feindschaft und Vernichtung," in Mihran Dabag, Antje Kapust, and Bernhard Waldenfels (eds), Gewalt: Strukturen, Formen, Repräsentationen (Munich: Wilhelm Fink, 2000), pages 199–220.

34. This is not to be understood as the possibility of choice or decision, but as the ethical paradox of "doing before hearing," as Edith Wyschogrod points out in her text "Doing before Hearing: On the Primacy of Touch," in *Textes pour E. Levinas,* ed. François Laruelle (Paris: Éditions Jean-Michel Place, 1980), 179–203.

35. Gerhard Schoenberner, *Der gelbe Stern: Die Judenverfolgung in Europa 1933–1945* (Frankfurt am Main: Fischer, 1991), 122.

36. Schoenberner, *Der gelbe Stern*, 122.

37. This structure of combat, which is central in Clausewitz's classic book on war, which shaped the European spirit of the nineteenth and twentieth centuries, and which finds a philosophical equivalent in Hegel's famous combat of master and slave, is so persistent that even Heidegger fell prey to it in his thinking on aesthetics and did not overcome these dark sides.

38. Ricœur, *Geschichte und Wahrheit*, 224. Ricœur discusses this structure under the heading of the growing conscience of violence.

39. See Merleau-Ponty's discussion in "La guerre a eu lieu," in *Sens et Non-Sens,* 252. I questioned the relevance of this motif at the meeting of the Society for Phenomenology and Existential Philosophy in Lexington, Kentucky in September

1997 under the title "The Ethical Eminence of the Flesh: Toward Being with a Plurality of Faces"; my discussion there will be inserted in a project entitled "Tropes of Violence." An "empirical" example of the power of ethical resistance can be found in Pressac, who describes how an SS officer, expected to supervise the crematorium of Auschwitz, was unable to "continue his job" after having encountered some playing children. See Jean-Claude Pressac, *Die Krematorien von Auschwitz: Die Technik des Massenmordes* (Frankfurt am Main: Piper, 1995), 132.

40. Ricœur, *Geschichte und Wahrheit,* 225. Ricœur describes this structure in his reflections on becoming aware of violence.

41. Simone Weil, "L'Iliade ou le poème de la force," *Cahier du Sud* 230/231 (1940–41); also in Simone Weil, *La source grecque* (Paris, 1953).

42. Elaine Scarry, *Der Körper im Schmerz: Die Chiffren der Verletzlichkeit und die Erfindung der Kultur* (Frankfurt am Main, 1992), 120; Bertrand Russell, *Hat der Mensch noch eine Zukunft?* (Munich: Deutscher Taschenbuch, 1963), 90.

43. Maurice Merleau-Ponty, *Phénomenologie de la perception* (Paris: Gallimard, 1945), 127.

44. It is for this reason that the chapter on the flesh in *Berührung ohne Berührung,* 279–314, deals with the question of how Merleau-Ponty's notion of flesh can be worked out in a way that the hearing of the other is practiced against the occlusion of the other.

45. Martin Heidegger, *Der Satz vom Grund* (Pfullingen, 1992). Many similarly constructed phenomena can be found; for example, the rise of concepts of conscience, human rights or respect.

46. Xenophon describes how, instead of being talked to, the other is "hunted like a dog"; see *Anabasis,* 3.2.35. See also the excellent book by Y. A. Dauge, *Le barbare: Recherches sur la conception romaine de la barbarie et de la civilisation* (Brussels, 1981); and the interesting and excellent book by Jean-François Mattéi, *La barbarie intérieure: Essai sur l'immonde moderne* (Paris: Presses Universitaires de France, 1999).

47. See the witness of Georg Wellers in Schoenberner, *Der gelbe Stern,* 156.

48. "Touching" seems to be an eminent way against diastasis and splitting and also "guarantees" two other advantages—to keep open the necessary separation claimed by Levinas and to "constitute" a re-ligio toward the other by sensible means beyond the pitfalls of representation. Compare the "untouchable" in Jacques Derrida, *Le toucher, Jean-Luc Nancy* (Paris: Galilée, 2000), 81ff., and, from a different point of view that includes the question of gender, Cathryn Vasseleu, *Textures of Light: Vision and Touch in Irigaray, Levinas and Merleau-Ponty* (London and New York: Routledge, 1998).

49. Plotinus, *Enneaden* (Jena and Leipzig: Eugen Diederichs, 1905), 1:254.

50. In his famous eighth letter on aesthetic education, Friedrich Schiller denounces the ambivalence concerning the goddess of wisdom as an elemental part in the pattern of war as it is visible in mythical thinking; and asserts that philosophy, instead of working through that ambivalence, covers up. This gesture could be considered to be one more source of returning violence. See Friedrich Schiller, *Über die ästhetische Erziehung des Menschen, in einer Reihe von Briefen* (1795; Stuttgart: Reclam, 1965), 30.

51. See the subtle study of Jean-Pierre Vernant, *Tod in den Augen: Figuren des Anderen im griechischen Altertum: Artemis und Gorgo* (Frankfurt am Main: Fischer, 1988). Wolfgang Sofsky presents a phenomenological analysis and shocking portrait of the "Muslim" in a section dedicated to this phenomenon in his book *Die Ordnung des Terrors: Das Konzentrationslager* (Frankfurt am Main: Fischer, 1997).

52. This is one reason for the breakdown of the primacy of conception. Traumatized persons describe the catastrophe of violence by referring to the semantics of the sensible (the sound of tanks, the coldness of the snow of Stalingrad, the smell of cadavers, etc.), a phenomenon that can also be found in classic texts. One of the best examples is the description of the wound of Philoctetus as it is described in Sophocles and Homer. It has established the pattern of a located and sensible memory in the French discussion (Pierre Nora), which is taken up by Aleida Assmann in her research on memory, especially on the memory of the Holocaust. See her article "Funktionsgedächtnis und Speichergedächtnis—Zwei Modi der Erinnerung," in *Generation und Gedächtnis: Erinnerungen und kollektive Identitäten*, ed. Kristin Platt and Mihran Dabag (Opladen: Leske und Buderich, 1995), 169–86. The problem of trauma is discussed in her excellent book *Erinnerungsräume. Formen und Wandlungen des kulturellen Gedächtnisses* (Munich: Beck, 1999). Rudolf Bernet presents a different approach to the question of trauma in his excellent text "The Traumatized Subject," presented at a colloquium in honor of Bernhard Waldenfels in November 1999 in Bochum, and which can be considered as an answer to Waldenfels's philosophy of responsivity. In his discussion of Levinas, Freud, and Lacan, Bernet shows how the subject is only as long and insofar as he or she resists the traumatic event—a clear deviation from the Cartesian definition. The impact of this "annihilation of subjective identity by a traumatic event that cannot be appropriated" leads to a repeated structure of double impossibilities that also shapes his "responsivity." Being a passive subject in the exposition to that event, it cannot answer to the trauma (being "turned around," it is impossible to be in the state to answer), even though it is also impossible not to answer (for it only survives by resisting against the traumatic event).

53. It becomes evident why Levinas dedicates so much care and effort to the breakdown of the primacy of representation, including the different notions of representation which are at work in Husserl's famous Fifth Logical Investigation.

54. Hannah Arendt takes up the example of the atomic bomb in order to illustrate a fatal paradigmatic turn—the annihilation of politics by the destruction of the world, which is not mere physical or material destruction but abolition of the political logos and the loss of the memory of cultures. The enframing (*Gestell*) of nuclear power destroys the human legacy of different perspectives. See Hannah Arendt, *Was ist Politik? Fragmente aus dem Nachlaß*, ed. Ursula Ludz (Munich and Zurich: Piper, 1993), 81ff. In addition to possible Levinasian arguments against this approach, it is symptomatic that the traumatic background of this evolution is unfortunately also missing.

55. See, for example, Jürgen Seifert et al., eds., *Logik der Destruktion: Der zweite Golfkrieg aks erster elektronischer Krieg und die Möglichkeiten seiner Verarbeitung im Bewußtsein* (Frankfurt am Main: Materialis, 1992).

56. Heraclitus, *Fragmente, Griechisch und Deutsch,* ed. Bruno Snell (Darmstadt: Wissenschaftliche Buchgesellschaft, 1995), frag. B 125, p. 37; Hans Diels and Werner Kranz, *Fragmente der Vorsokratiker* (Zurich and Berlin: Artemis, 1964), 1:144.

57. Plutarque, "Du bavadarge," in *Oeuvres morales,* ed. by Jean Dumortier and Jean Defradas (Paris: Les Belles Lettres, 1975), vol. 7, pt. 1, "Traités de Morale" 27–36; 511B, pp. 219–57, here p. 247ff.:

> Comme ses concitoyens lui avaient demandé de leur donner son opinion sur la concorde, Héraclite monta à la tribune, prit une coupe d'eau froide, la saupoudra de farine qu'il remua avec un brin de menthe, vida la coupe et se retira, leur montrant ainsi qu'à se contenter de ce qu'on a pour rechercher les choses coûteuses, on maintient les cités dans la paix et la concorde.

A specific mixture and a balanced kinesis, both of which also represent extreme problems in Plato, and which must be reflected in the *Parmenides* so that an ontology of the good is not "grounded" on the unphilosophical gesture of avoidance, constitute the central elements in Heraclitus's ontology of war. A further personification of war, the force of strife (*Eris*), combines these two aspects, constituting a long-hidden "stream of historicality," which is also again and again enacted as the power of war by different discursive backgrounds (i.e., Kant's reflections on the role of antagonism). It seems that these hidden backgrounds should be uncovered. I tried to indicate one pattern of this in my article "Figures of Conflict and the Violent Logic of Exclusion," in *War and Its Uses: Conflict and Creativity,* ed. Bruce Butterfield and Jürgen Kleist (New York: Peter Lang, 1999), 277–86.

58. See Merleau-Ponty, "La guerre a eu lieu," 250ff.

Levinasian Responsibility and Freudian Analysis: Is the Unthinkable an Un-Conscious?

Bettina Bergo

Faust: Doch im Erstarren such ich nicht mein Heil
Das Schaudern ist der Menschheit bester Teil.
— Goethe, *Faust,* cited by Levinas, *Otherwise Than Being,
or Beyond Essence*

What bound me to Jewry was (I am ashamed to admit) neither
faith nor national pride, for I have always been an unbeliever . . .
[Yet] beyond this there was a perception that it was to my Jewish
nature alone that I owed two characteristics that had become
indispensable to me . . . Because I was a Jew I found myself free
from many prejudices which restricted others in the use of their
intellect; and . . . I was prepared . . . to do without agreement
with the "compact majority."
— Freud, "Address to the Society of B'nai B'rith," May 6, 1926

Energies and Traumas: Confluences in the Thought of Freud and Levinas

The analysis that follows is part of a work in progress. I propose to begin
by drawing a schema whose cardinal points consist of two sets of citations:
one from Freud's "Beyond the Pleasure Principle" (1920), the other from
Levinas's *Otherwise Than Being, or Beyond Essence* (1974). These citations
suggest that confluences between psychoanalysis and Levinas's "first philosophy" argue for the notions of an unconscious and a preconscious—
if only as a heuristic measure. The question, of course, concerns their na-

ture. That is, what are the preconscious and the unconscious; what do we gain from their hypothesis and from speculation about their structure? Levinas dismisses the Freudian unconscious as modeled upon a classical understanding of consciousness. Yet his notions of responsibility and sub-stitution are pre-reflective, pre-intentional, and his responsibility gets likened to a psychosis—indeed, one that "speaks." A painstaking reading of the works of Freud alongside those of Levinas could show us how the resemblances between their thought point beyond themselves. I hope that this is the beginning of such a reading. Still, the resemblances will never be systematic. The depiction of immanence as fissured, that of the impersonal forces of alterity-in-immanence, and of their "movement" are all shared by Freud and Levinas. They are the property of both phenom-enological reconstruction and transcendental speculation, whether psy-choanalytic or fundamental ontological and ethical. I will return to the re-lationship between ontology and ethics when I turn to Levinas.

Two things are striking: first, the similarity in the nature of the "material" that Freud and Levinas uncover, particularly in light of pre-conscious forces and anxiety; and second, that Levinas's dismissal of psy-choanalysis is founded upon a terse argument that psychoanalysis's un-conscious is modeled upon consciousness.[1] Therefore, the notion of the unconscious entails a projective transformation of conscious faculties, such as memory, motility, and conceptuality. Simon Critchley has argued that Levinas's critique of Freud is not quite fair.[2] Yet Michel Henry has demonstrated that the unfolding of the Freudian unconscious gives rise to debilitating contradictions. As a hybrid aggregate of neurophysical forces, *and* their very production, *and* the "site" thereof, the unconscious is not *one entity* but a plurality. Moreover, its pathological states depend upon notions like "unconscious" thoughts, concepts, and affects, which clearly suggests the strange parallelism between the conscious and the un-conscious mind that Levinas decried. These notions function to explain what gets stored in the "there" of the unconscious, how the drives origi-nate, what they attach themselves to, and how they contribute to psychic pathologies. Because nonreflective, affective "life" (e.g., self-affection, and the imagination that is active in dreams) is described in concepts that reproduce the representational activities characteristic of consciousness, and because this "life" is made visible by being brought, or reduced to, consciousness, Levinas's objection appears to reach its target.[3] Thus, the thinkers who have discussed Levinas's relationship to psychoanalysis di-vide into two groups: those who feel that Levinas misunderstood signifi-cant aspects of psychoanalysis (which in turn illuminate Levinas's own notions of immanence and responsibility), and those who argue that psychoanalysis largely overinterprets immanence. Among the first group are Simon Critchley[4] and Paul-Laurent Assoun.[5] Among the second group we find Michel Henry. I will limit my remarks here to Assoun and Henry, because the first is the historian of psychoanalysis who came later to Levinas via Rosenzweig. The second, Henry, is the philosopher who criticizes psychoanalysis from a philosophical perspective that engages a hermeneutic phenomenology (he calls it "material phenomenology") sometimes close to both Heidegger's and Levinas's work.

It is Paul-Laurent Assoun who has shown the extent of the resemblances between technical terms and concepts in Lacan and Levinas. He also demonstrates that these resemblances are never decisive; they arise at different points in the unfolding of each man's work, and they serve different purposes. The oft-noted Kojève connection (both Levinas and Lacan attended Alexandre Kojève's seminars on Hegel's *Phenomenology of Spirit*)[6] is not deep, because Levinas is a reader of Rosenzweig, the opponent of synthesizing dialectics, before Levinas is a partner in dialogue with Kojève and his particular logic of desire. It is otherwise for Lacan. Nevertheless, writes Assoun, we should avoid speculating about Lacan's and Levinas's silence about one another. It is less a symptom of the will to ignore an unavoidable presence, than the situation of two men speaking a language whose root is outwardly common but whose dialects are mutually unintelligible. What is the common root? It is the project of unfolding a discourse about interiority and otherness that is not regulated by spatiotemporal binaries (e.g., inside *versus* outside a self; prior to intentional activity *versus* as a mode of intentionality). I mean "otherness" here in two senses: "other" as the margin of philosophical systems, and otherness as the impact of what is not-I upon an I. So far I am not saying much that Assoun does not discuss. But in arguing for their differences, Assoun fails to note one connection between Levinas and Lacan: both men were familiar with Merleau-Ponty. This pivotal point from Merleau-Ponty is suggested to us by Henry. It is the concept of "affectivity" I will return to shortly. First, the citations from Freud in 1920:

> As a new factor we have taken into consideration Breuer's hypothesis that charges of energy occur in two forms; so that we have to distinguish between two kinds of cathexis of the psychical systems or their elements—a freely flowing cathexis that *presses on* toward discharge and a *quiescent* cathexis.

Over the course of Freud's career, these two types of force will take different names. They are already present in a shadowy form in the 1895 "Outline for a Scientific Psychology"[7] and will be discussed in a different way in the "New Introductory Lectures" of 1933.[8] Concepts denoting aggressive or destructive forces include the "pleasure principle," the "Nirvana principle," and the "death drive." In Freud's thinking by 1920, pleasure accompanies the discharge of energy and the destructive instinct is released when the normal, muscular discharge of energies is blocked. The counter-forces include the notion of eros, in which pleasure accrues to the accumulation of energy or drives. Despite considerable internal inconsistencies in their operation and relationship to pleasure, the principles are two and generally intertwined with each other, although the destructive drive is ordinarily "invisible." In many significant works from the 1920s, the "quiescent cathexis"—necessitated by the central nervous system's requirement of homeostasis—is interpreted as the organism's fundamental drive to return to a conservative, *preorganic* state (death).[9] Thus, when the two drives "defuse" in neuroses, the quiescent cathexis does not just dampen the organism's life force, it holds sway over it—theoretically, to moderate the vagaries of a quantitative internal accumulation of energy whose excesses could produce trauma. But the difficult "reign" of the death drive is rooted here in the mechanistic principle of the ego discharging energies through motility. When discharge is not possible, e.g., in cases where excesses arise from "invisible" internal or physiological "events," then the system of energy balance is effectively threatened. Let us return, for now, to the 1920 essay "Beyond the Pleasure Principle." It will presage the utter tangle that the conceptualization of these drives entails.

> We may . . . venture to regard the common traumatic neurosis as a consequence of an extensive breach being made in the *protective shield* against stimuli. [What] *we* seek to understand are the effects produced on the *organ of the mind* by the breach in the shield . . . and by the problems that follow in its train. . . . It is caused by lack of any preparedness for anxiety . . . In the case of quite a number of traumas, the difference between systems that are unprepared and systems that are well prepared through being hypercathected may be a decisive factor in determining the outcome; though where the strength of a trauma exceeds a certain limit this factor will . . . cease to carry weight.[10]

There follows a comparison between the dreams that are wish fulfillments and the dreams of "patients suffering from traumatic neurosis." The interpretation of dreams has provided Freud's critics with extensive material. If the dream has meaning insofar as it is produced by unconscious drives and desires, then is this production of a dream-sign, or its "representative content" by the unconscious, not disturbingly analogous to the production of a meaningful statement by an intentional consciousness? If so, is not the unconscious functioning here in the way that conscious activity does when it produces ideal meaning? Because of, or despite, this evident objection to the oneiric "meaning creation," Freud ventures another distinction. There are two sorts of dreaming: that of neurotic patients and that of "normal" dreamers. Unlike ordinary dreams, neurotics' dreams do *not* operate under the pleasure principle. They attempt to master a traumatic stimulus by "developing the anxiety" that should keep the "breach in the shield" from resulting in trauma. There would thus be two principles for dreams, determined by the depth and persistence of trauma.

For all that, Freud's conclusion is *not* primarily about neuroses and the divergence between normal dreams and the dreams of the traumatized.[11] It concerns the dynamism of forces that led him to revise his topography of the mind. These forces are the quiescent and free-flowing cathexes noted earlier. And by 1920, the primacy of the destructive drive in neurotic patients (especially visible in phobias and "obsessional neurotics") led Freud to assert that consciousness not only is "*not* the most universal attribute of mental processes, [it is] a function of them" ("BPP" 606). Nevertheless, it is the explanation of the possibility of consciousness that eludes Freud. In neuroses, consciousness *shows* that it is structured traumatically by the operation of the invisible death drive, which has *separated* from the erotic drive. But we must not take consciousness topographically as the "site" of the interaction of drives. It is a convenient metaphor to conceive of drives placed in a site; this is why the "es" or "id" refers ambiguously to drives and is also their site, though it has an indefinite locus. Moreover, consciousness itself is not strictly speaking interiority, whether representational or passional. Freud insists that, as bodily ego, it "must lie on the borderline between outside and inside" (ibid.). Thus, "all excitatory processes that occur in the *other* systems leave *permanent traces* behind in them which form the foundation of memory" (ibid.). They are both pre-memorial like an a priori condition of possibility, and *never* conscious. Consciousness is the palimpsest that Freud's wax slate figures. It is irremediably and chaotically marked by internal and external events, like his mystic writing pad.[12] The analogy stops there, however, for consciousness was, itself, never like a surface that was wholly unmarked *and also conscious.*

I propose to hold off discussing the ambiguous status of consciousness. What has been said is enough to concede a point to those who doubt that Levinas's criticism of Freud is unequivocally true.[13] Instead, I emphasize three points. First, the metaphors of "protective shield" and "organ of the mind" denote Freud's search for some principle of continuity between the various mental events and systems. Of course, the expression of this principle is redolent of the scientism often found in Freud, for which he has been duly criticized. Whatever the extent of this continuity, it appears *clinically* in obsessional neuroses and, more tenuously, in the phenomena of negation, isolation, and undoing. It would be fatal to a cure or to the explanation of these phenomena to abandon it. And it would be philosophically regressive to repudiate all continuity.

Second, note *here* the causal priority of trauma over anxiety. Unable to maintain trauma as a cause, Freud will revisit this order after 1924. At that point we see him making a move that recalls one of Levinas's innovations in *Otherwise Than Being*. For now, noteworthy is the sheer breadth of *trauma* per se, which can be caused physiologically by important modifications in the organism (e.g., birth) or by relational conflicts arising as the ego develops. Also note the extent of anxiety: it arises in response to external threats and it is triggered by various internal conflicts of forces. Indeed, anxiety functions dually as sign of, and protection against, anxiety.

By his 1932 lecture "Anxiety and Instinctual Life," Freud will abandon the distinctions he traced in 1920 between neurotic anxiety, realistic anxiety, and moral anxiety. In the late work all our anxieties are in some sense "realistic," since all anxiety concerns a loss—castration, loss of love, or loss of self. Like the life of the imaginary in Lacan, these concepts describe preconscious events in which the metaphoric and metonymic are not less valid or "real" than what is external and experiential. Thus conscious life loses its strict connection with "reality," understood as perceptual givens and their system of reception; it now touches the processes whose energies it receives but cannot perceive. The innovation of 1932, however, concerns the *fact* of anxiety: it is there *prior to* trauma and repression. Anxiety is no longer their product. Instead, anxiety gets tied speculatively to Rank's trauma of birth, but especially to a law established by the alterity called the "father." This so-called law will soon bring us to a point of comparison between Levinas and Freud.

Third, the description of consciousness as a "borderline between outside and inside" is designed to explain why *any* excitation leaves its "trace" in consciousness. It leaves a trace to the degree that "consciousness" is neither the synthetic activity of idealism nor the intentionality Husserlian phenomenology. Freud's consciousness as "borderline" wants to undercut the metaphysics of adequacy or fit between intellection and objects. A comparable undercutting is of importance to Heidegger, and to Levinas (as Heidegger's student and as his adversary) from the 1940s through the 1970s.[14] Levinas's later work explores affectivity as the vulnerability of the skin, which becomes the folded borderline or (null-)site between outside and inside.[15] Like Freud's, Levinas's borderline has no static topography. Though it can be considered from inside or from outside itself, a traumatic event has the metaphoric effect of thrusting the outside inward, or peeling the inside back and folding it inside-out.

This sort of play space in Levinas has an ethical quality. This is why the descriptive symptomatology of trauma in Levinas's work flows out of an *anthropology* of transcendence to-the-other or, again, out of a transcendental "aesthetic" rooted in the other who constitutes "me" as a self-in-suffering. In *Otherwise Than Being,* ethics *means* being inhabited by an other, but one whose force of impact has nothing to do with his de facto appearing in the world. This momentary inhabitation produces, *unchosen and unconsciously,* exceptional speaking and action. That is the end that the concept of "borderline" serves in Levinas's philosophy. In Freud, the struggle to delimit and clarify consciousness as more, or other, than a *convenio* of thoughts and things vitiates the economy that separates unconsciousness and consciousness, even as it highlights the irreducibility of conscious embodied *life.*[16] In light of the alterities that are "other man" and the unconscious forces, and given the constitutive difficulties they pose to Levinas and Freud respectively, I will cite a collection of short statements from *Otherwise Than Being* in which the attempt to undercut binary "solid logics" is clear. This move is essential to the possibility of Levinasian "substitution," which is affective and paradoxical. Substitution is *constitutive* of a self (*moi*) and *disclosive* of a way of better-than-being, but it has no conscious content other than suffering and anxiety. Levinas characterizes substitution broadly as follows:

> Man is not to be conceived in function of being and not-being, taken as ultimate references. Humanity, subjectivity—the excluded middle, excluded from everywhere, *null-site*—signify the breakup of this alternative, the one-in-the-place-of-another, substitution, signification in its signifyingness qua sign, prior to essence, before identity. (*OB* 14)

Levinas is not the first to undercut binaries. The notions of inside *versus* outside, even when their opposition is dynamic or dialectical, are already displaced in Husserl's and Heidegger's phenomenologies. This is, arguably, a response to German idealism. The outcome of this displacement was to make immanence more interesting: think of Husserl's demand that Descartes' cogito be enlarged to encompass all its acts. Think, too, of Heidegger, for whom *Dasein* is always world-bound, a site within a site: "Dasein's Being . . . must be understood *a priori* as grounded upon that state of Being which we have called 'Being-in-the-world.'"[17] For his part, Freud eschews the inside-outside distinction in various ways. Notably, he insists that the ego is neither just conscious, nor just preconscious. Above all, it is a bodily ego. Body is at once the site of sensation and perception, the sign and agent of "inhibitions" and "symptoms," and, as a living body, it *is* those internal drives which create tensions in it.

When Levinas wrote *Existence and Existents* between 1940 and 1945, he was already reworking Heidegger's logic of inside-outside; Being and the beings for which Being can be their own; consciousness/unconsciousness.[18] There was, for Levinas, a problematical yet irreducible *continuity* joining consciousness with its birth in waking up and its self-dissolution in sleep. Consciousness is, even before it is "in-the-world." Thus a human being can be *interested* in the being of entities only because he takes a position or has an attitude toward *his* existence. But if Heidegger characterized such an attitude as "concern," Levinas examined other modes of being; namely, those of fatigue and indolence, whereby the conscious being is slow to emerge *from* himself "into the world" (*EE* 24–25). These modes *precede* Heidegger's concern, he argued, and differentiate immanence into interpenetrating layers (with varying degrees of consciousness) to which Heidegger failed to attend.

Moreover, indolence and fatigue are not "contents of the mind." Levinas argues, "To take them as contents of the mind is to start by situating them in the flux of consciousness as 'psychic realities,' and then to ascribe to them, as a secondary property . . . an intention of refusal, a refusing thought" (*EE* 24). Instead, indolence, fatigue, the inner straining to get out or away (which occurs at a level *prior* to the desire to escape from one's de facto situation), are modes that are only possible in a being that does *not* begin in the world, alongside of things. Heidegger's notion of concern "is not . . . the very act of being on the brink of nothingness; it is rather imposed by the solidity of a being *that begins with and is already encumbered with the excess of itself*" (*EE* 27, emphasis added). This beginning does *not* presuppose an "in" that is worldly or a consciousness that is temporally ecstatic or ahead of itself. It is prior to a consciousness that is out ahead of itself. It describes a highly articulated immanence.

Waking up, "prior to interpretation" (*EE* 35), like fatigue, creates "the interval in which the event of the present can occur" as the "upsurge of an *existent*" which takes up its existence prior to distinctions between what is *its own* or not, whether it holds its existence as a question or not. If Levinas's archaeology of the self in the instant of the present suggests a discontinuity between being and nonbeing at the level of waking states and sleep (nonbeing), that distinction will not be his ultimate intent. In the same work, he introduces the concept of *veille*, or "wakefulness." This reverses the Heideggerian negativity of anxiety *and* establishes a certain *continuity* between the "states" of a self. Although a self, or an "I," comes out of itself in waking, this does not reintroduce a binary of sleep versus being-awake. The concept of wakefulness is a preconscious state that surrounds our intentional consciousness. As hypnotic or trancelike, wakefulness is without objects. It is characterized by the mood of anxiety, in which beings do *not* slip away or fail to interest the self, they rather oppress the self in their positive indeterminacy and "absolutely unavoidable presence . . . like a field of forces" (*EE* 58). And again,

> The distinction between the attention that is directed upon objects—
> *whether they be internal or external*—and the vigilance that is absorbed in
> the rustling of inevitable being goes farther than this. The I [*le moi*] is
> carried away by the fatality of being. There is *no longer any outside, or any
> inside*. Wakefulness [*la vigilance*] is absolutely void of objects; which does
> *not* amount to saying that it is an experience of nothingness. (*EE* 65,
> translation modified, emphases added) [19]

Digging beneath the binaries of inside versus outside alters the relationships between Being and nothingness, *Dasein* and world, ecstasy and the *nunc stans*. It also suggests a passage, a movement, between unconsciousness and consciousness.

By the time he writes *Otherwise Than Being* (1974), the pre-intentional, pre-self-affective mood of anxiety is what characterizes the specifically "borderline" nature of *sensibility*. Although Levinas wrests sensibility from the philosophies of finitude in which it was dominated by suffering, and although he gives it a mechanistic quality—i.e., to be governed by enjoyment (*jouissance*) [20] or a pleasure principle—in its *ethical* dimension sensibility cannot be divorced from anxiety. [21] Indeed, in a reversal of Heidegger's notion of transcendence as futural ecstasis, enjoyment is a mode of transcendence *in the present*. In *Otherwise Than Being*, enjoyment and pleasure are thus deformalized and de-objectivated using the example of the caress which, unlike the collaborations of the hand and the eye, identifies nothing and has no telos outside the gratuity of enjoyment. At the ethical level, however, sensibility takes the privileged form of *trauma*. Indeed, for Levinas, ethics is first philosophy because it is the logic of *human* being, and sensibility is ethical only because the self is structured traumatically, with an unexpungeable alien force at its core that keeps it from congealing. Though he articulates this structure with his concepts like "recurrence," "obsession," and "persecution," trauma and anxiety are here coeval (as they will ultimately be in Freud as well), and anxiety remains the affective tonality of generous intersubjectivity. [22] Thus Levinas:

> Vulnerability, exposure to outrage, to wounding, passivity more passive
> than all patience, passivity of the accusative form [*me*], the trauma of

accusation suffered by a hostage to the point of persecution, implicating the identity of the hostage who substitutes himself for the others: all this is the self, a defecting or defeat of the ego's identity. And this, pushed to the limit, is sensibility, sensibility as the subjectivity of the subject. (*OB* 15)

Three points are worth examining. First, note the effort that characterizes *Otherwise Than Being*. It is to explore subjectivity *beneath* the thrust of metaphysical constructions of subjectivity, including Husserlian intentionality. At its core, subjectivity has become the *contradiction* of a site that is a null-site, an excluded middle, or a "borderline," like Freud's ego, and not unlike the "contradiction" that Levinas perceived in the unconscious itself. This reconstructive phenomenology, searching beneath dialectics of outside-inside, *noesis-noema*, represents Levinas's protracted strategy against those philosophies, including psychoanalysis, phenomenology, and ontology, for which the subject is likewise a different kind of "site."[23]

Second point: Sensibility and affect have an enigmatic intelligibility which precedes and "attunes" reflective acts and identity. This claim is not unique to Levinas or Freud. In idealism, sensibility also has an uncoercible quality to it. It is something that resists intuition and understanding because it precedes them. To be sure, this theme has a marked and different importance to psychoanalysis and Levinasian phenomenology. Yet despite its positivism, Freud's speculative reconstruction of consciousness offers the explicit novelty of a bodily ego in which the body is neither strictly a subject nor an object.[24] Now, when Henry takes up this question of sensibility and affect, he will argue, in a way that evokes the later Levinas, that Freud's unconscious would be better understood above all as living, irreducible "affect." I cite Henry:

> In summary, the unconscious does not exist—if one puts aside the fact [upon which Freud insisted in its regard], in this case the a priori law of all ecstatic phenomenality, that almost everything represented is excluded from representation. Outside representation, what is represented does not, for all that, subsist in the form of "unconscious representations," those entities for which Freudianism imagined such fantastic destinies.
>
> As for the unconscious that designates *life*, it cannot be reduced to the empty negation of the formal concept of phenomenality if life is the initial *coming into itself of being in the form of affect*.[25]

Whatever we make of Henry's elaborate criticism of unconscious concepts and affect, he too must deformalize causal and binary logics. Thanks to him, we can trace a red thread between Freud and Levinas in two directions. In one direction, we find it between their deformalizations of the "borderline" that is "ego," or consciousness/preconsciousness, *or* vulnerability (for Levinas). In the other direction, we find it between Levinas's interpretation of sensibility, which, in its work of deformalization, undermines classical phenomenology's (pre)consciousness as passive synthesis in favor of non-unifiable split self *and* what I consider, against Henry, to be Freud's *struggle* to restore the specificity of the bodily ego, as a one-and-a-many, through his analogy with the ludic palimpsest, or *Wunderblock*. Note, too, that Levinas works *against* Husserl's principle of continuity (as passive synthesis), even as he takes vulnerability as providing a continuity between self, world, and other. Freud too never ceases examining the value of *his* principle of continuity, even though he recognizes the necessity of irreducible forces and loci. Indeed, Freud eventually gives up a simple, genetic account of anxiety and trauma, and with this, also his earlier distinctions between types of anxiety.

Third point: Levinas's "trauma of accusation" evokes Freud's problematical notion of "unconscious activity,"[26] or the "unconscious concept,"[27] or "unconscious representation."[28] Here we see clearly why Levinas accused Freud of modeling his unconscious upon the activities of consciousness. But things prove more complex than that. As Levinas himself argued in *Existence and Existents,* "consciousness" is more and other than intentionality as perception and representation. The very notion, borrowed from Heidegger, that it is modal, or tuned through moods, extends it into metaphoric regions that do not admit of exhaustive determinations. We cannot say *why* we are indolent, or vigilant in insomnia. We cannot say *when* we will "be" in these moods. Although, as Levinas suggests, the "effort" made when we are in a state of fatigue and despair is a "creation ex nihilo" (*EE* 31), it certainly is not ex nihilo at the bodily level! There is a tension in Levinas that arises in his treatment of the body. Inasmuch as he describes certain of its affective and sensuous states, he is not directly interested in the physiology of that body. Of course, this spares him discussions of mechanistic causality, but it also pulls the Levinasian body in the direction of the purely spiritual.[29] But the duality-in-unity of the body implies that it is not just the Freudian ego that is dynamically spread through the conscious, the preconscious, and the unconscious. The Freudian drives also have two sides to them, even if both sides do not reach conscious recognition. Like sensation understood by idealism, like Levinas's pre-reflective "passivity in the accusative form," Freud's drives exert a part of their force in somatic and affective expression. If Freud, dealing with pathology in a way that Levinas does not, pursues the causes of these "expressions," then at that level he uses terms that *resemble* but do not reproduce the products of a thematizing consciousness. For Freud, these expressions escape the *laws* governing conscious thematization. That is, drives may or may not become attached to an idea and then be *represented* consciously; however, the possibility of this attachment has an enigmatic dimension to it. That is, the possibilities and occasions of *translations* (in the etymological sense) of drives are unclear. As Levinas puts it, and as Freud knew well, "consciousness, in its opposition to the unconscious, is not constituted by the *opposition*, but by this *proximity*, this communication with its contrary" (*EE* 67). In Levinas, this proximity is as constitutive of the self in the 1940s as it is in the 1970s. But maintaining the possibility of such an indirect communication necessitates economic choices by both Levinas and Freud. The latter will underscore mental *dynamism* in view of such a communication. Levinas's choice will be effected in 1945 through modes of (pre)consciousness like insomnia and indolence, and in 1972, viewed from the side of consciousness, through the concept of the third party.[30] For different reasons, neither man's choice will be fully satisfactory. But both choices will have ties to the voice of the other or to immanent audition (Freud's preconscious is principally auditory), and to the possibility of expression ("Saying" in Levinas) or tying a word or cry to an event that would otherwise be lost (Freud).[31]

In Levinas, too, the "trauma of accusation" also escapes the laws of conscious thematization. It escapes the successive syntheses of time-consciousness. It escapes the logic of inside/outside, I/not-I. And so, not governed by principles of identity and sufficient reason, trauma may also escape, in its effects, the principle of non-contradiction. How then does Levinas describe it? He faces difficulties comparable to those Freud faced. These include the surreptitious realism and linearity of our everyday syntax and predication, *and* the usual economy of metaphors and similes. Thus, *Otherwise Than Being* is self-consciously a text whose many tropes do not simply stand, like ordinary tropes, in the place of some other idea recognizable through them; instead, they are emphatic and point to nothing necessarily in the world. This is close to what I have been arguing about psychoanalysis' use of paradoxical terms like "unconscious concepts": these are *not* just concepts preserved in the unconscious like an object in a block of ice.

For all that, Levinas's text is the more subversive one. Reduced to a single voice that must use a language that immediately universalizes it, the text *enacts* its own traumatization. It is frequently a discourse of trauma; or "a psychotic discourse" (*OB* 142), "obsession" (*OB* 158), a "pre-originary saying" (*OB* 45). Levinas adopts the very term "psychotic" at certain points. Elsewhere, he will call his discourse "the prophetic said," and "the poetic said" (*OB* 170), or a "dialogue delayed by silences, failure, or delirium" (ibid.). And like a patient recounting his pathology, he underscores himself the performative dimension of his speech. He remarks, "That is true of the discussion I am elaborating at this very moment" (ibid.). For these reasons, the Belgian philosopher Marc Richir argued that Levinas describes a "phenomenological unconscious."[32] But is Levinas's trauma unconscious? Certainly, if as Freud remarked earlier, trauma to *any* "system" *leaves a trace;* yes again, if what escapes conscious notice, or intuitive synthesis and retention, has any sense at all and *can* get tied to an idea and be represented later on. For Levinas, this X, or trace, will get tied *not* to an idea, but indeed to an entire poetics: a poetics of responsibility that expresses itself only to undo its own expression. This is why his ethics as first philosophy has no object and no structure, only constitutive trauma.

Why a Logic of an Unconscious?

I have juxtaposed quotations from Freud and Levinas, and highlighted three aspects of each of them. Rather than contesting Assoun's argument that Lacan and Levinas come together in only the most accidental, even insignificant ways, I am making two claims. The first is inspired by Richir's audacity, namely, that Levinas's work recovers a logic and spirit found in psychoanalysis at its least positivistic moments. This is the logic and spirit that focus upon traces of a psychic "life" which can never be brought to light, and which cannot stand above the conceptual suspicion that anything that disobeys the law of non-contradiction "is" not, has no existence. Second, I am saying that the strategy of reconstructing a "logic" of the not-conscious is unavoidable given Levinas's three "methodological" objectives. His objectives are as follows.

First, as we know, Levinas's phenomenology, initiated "in the spirit of Husserlian philosophy" (*OB* 183), nevertheless "ventures beyond phenomenology" (ibid.). It does so by venturing an ultimate reduction, not attempted by Husserl: that of human signification. This ultimate reduction is *not* phenomenological. It is hermeneutical, speculative, and is designed to take us "behind" Husserl's passive synthesis of consciousness. What lurks behind passive synthesis is a fissured subject in the accusative, a "me" without an owner. Such a presubjectivity argues for a specific kind of time, which Levinas calls "diachrony." This "time" does not belong to Husserl's flowing now-moments which are always brought into the flow of consciousness and through which sensation is always on the verge of becoming a thought. It also does not have the character of Heidegger's ecstasies. Against these, Levinas is looking for the unique ethical significance of sensibility. This significance is disturbingly untranslatable outside of Levinas's own speech, which is tensed by the slippage of description into enactment, by parataxis, indeterminate metaphors, and by the use of metonymy at a level of nonconsciousness where it cannot apply because there are no longer parts versus wholes. To reach this ethical preconsciousness, Levinas uses a language that is overdetermined. It condenses, displaces, and associates in ways that recall Freud's speculations on dream grammar.

Second, Levinas opposes the primacy of all thinking of being. His explicit opposition begins in 1935 with his first original work, *On Evasion,* and is fully elaborated in 1974 with *Otherwise Than Being.* The opposition continues, moreover, beyond that point. This project of opposing the thinking of being has many sides to it. Levinas's insistence that some dimension of subjectivity *not* be situated "in the world" remains, as does his argument against Heidegger's transcendence. The Levinasian "self" does *not* have a futural time structure. Instead, as we have seen, the self that Levinas describes comes from and returns to itself, except insofar as it is repeatedly "obsessed" by the (non-phenomenal) other. Thus it will be traumatized by beings, *not* summoned by Being. This dimension unfolds as sensibility and affect, in a number of modes already alluded to.

Finally, and most important, the constitutive Other of this dimension of subjectivity will be human, *not* ontological. Nevertheless, for all his divergences with Heidegger, Levinas will borrow from the latter a crucial logical distinction: the difference between entities that appear and *that they appear,* i.e., *appearing's pure condition in its pure activity.* This is Heidegger's distinction between beings and Be-*ing,* where Being is understood verbally. By maintaining his version of Heidegger's ontological difference, and using it to set up a level of everyday existence *opposed to* a level where that existence is suspended, or temporarily transcended, Levinas avoids Freud's structural hypothesis of the unconscious, the preconscious, and the conscious. In other words, it is perhaps less that Levinas deliberately *avoids* a Freudian economy of the psyche based on three dynamic regions or instances, than that he argues for the primacy of a *qualitative* (also Heideggerian in structure) distinction between the level of being and that of ethics, thereby rejecting *quantitative* notions of energy or drive. But Freud also abandons his positivistic analyses of energy, because quantities of neuronal energy could never explain the quality of consciousness.

Levinas's third methodological objective concerns positivism, dialectics, and systems. Using Franz Rosenzweig's *Star of Redemption,* Levinas examines the human "relation" to the world, to immanence, and to the transcendent Other in a way that does not permit these levels to intersect durably or to be taken up in a dialectic that reduces each of them to moments in movement toward a final realization of substance as subject—

Hegel's apotheosis of spirit and world. His resistance to Hegelian dialectic refuses the reflective, or observer, position that remains outside the confrontation of self and other, and speaks to *us* who hear him as we would a teacher. At the ethical level, self and other are never symmetrical positions. And *we* readers are not Levinas's *semblables*. Unlike Hegel's phenomenology, the same or the subject neither recognizes nor reduces the desire of the Other to the subject's own desire. Any struggle for reciprocal recognition, in Levinas, would be a secondary moment, inaugurated by the force of the third party. More important, such a struggle would be a regressive, "interested" intersubjectivity: one in which ethical force is not discernable. In other words, struggle and reciprocity cannot constitute by themselves the particularity of the human as ethical, and they are not themselves constituted by the human. On the contrary, the human encounter with the other is an encounter with an elevation, that is, with something that had a claim upon a "me" before I was aware of it. This encounter belongs to what is *lived*, not thematized from a theoretical posture. But this suggests that there are *two sorts of living* in Levinas: a generic animal living that belongs to the will or the drives, indeed, to ontology; and another that constitutes the specifically human form of singularity through repeated, traumatic interruptions of the animal consciousness.

Having pushed Husserl's phenomenological method past its breaking point, having refused the original meaning of Heidegger's ontological difference, and having dispensed with almost all dialectics—save perhaps that of Jean Wahl's unhappy consciousness—it remains for Levinas to work in a way not unlike Freud had done.[33] This is too easily said. Obviously, Levinas is not concerned with science and clinic. But his thought is otherwise reductive (e.g., of being), and invariably less influenced by speculative positivism and concern with topographical structures. For all that, three objects are shared by Levinas and Freud, and later, too, by Lacan and Henry. These are: (1) sensibility and affect, in themselves and as signs or traces of something invisible; (2) alterity as a non-phenomenal, foreign *force* that is simultaneously within us and without us; and (3) speaking in its genesis as an upsurge of meaning and gift. Despite his innovative "humanism of the other man," Levinas, like Freud, belongs to a powerful current in Western modernity. Curiously, it is *not* the same current that Levinas identifies as exemplifying the spirit of his project. He credits Platonism, Neoplatonism, and Cartesianism as giving privilege of place to the Good-beyond-being. I am arguing, on the other hand, that in addition to this, his emphasis on sensibility and affect—especially on suffering, on an absent other, the urge to escape from Being, and the qualitative leap out of being—places him in proximity to Schopenhauer, Kierkegaard, and Nietzsche. A similar argument is made by Henry about Freud.[34]

Remarkably enough, Levinas will do more than oppose *this* latter current, especially its Nietzschean avatar; he will appropriate its claims, limiting them to ontology. That is, he will use the current to return to life, body, and affectivity. Consequently, for Levinas, immanence is a closed circle at the ontological level. No alterity really penetrates it, whether the alterity is human or the fact of death, whether it is sensed or dreamed. The law of existence, Spinoza's *will to persist in existence,* and the dyad of Being and its site, or *Dasein,* hold good in Levinas. But this structure gets interrupted by difference, whose coming on the scene is pathology, a glorious pathology. Certain affects are traces of this interruption: the anxiety of insomnia, the *fear* over the Other's death, the subject's dissolving into sheer sobbing, and the obsession and recurrence into self in the approach of the other whose force is its expression.

These interruptions are lacunae in everyday time and consciousness. This is why Levinas's interruption is *not* equivalent to a permeable immanence. In Freud we find lacunae in consciousness as well; and indeed in Lacan, lacunae in the imaginary. If they are discerned at all, interruptions are found as traces of events *out of time,* shocking, deniable, but above all meaningless to consciousness per se. It is important to note that by 1932, the mature Freud—suffering from the recurrence of his cancer and revising his 1916 *Introductory Lectures on Psycho-Analysis*—turned his earlier theory of anxiety on its head. He now argued that anxiety, as an affective state, is not libido that has become unusable, nor is it the result of unconscious repression. Rather, it is a fundamental mode of being. Or, as he put it, "anxiety was there earlier; it was the anxiety that made the repression. But what sort of anxiety can it have been? Only anxiety in the face of a threatening external danger."[35] However, at this level, "external danger" is not really separate from "internal instinctual danger." And so distinctions fade between realistic, phantasmatic, and moral anxiety.

> A particular determinant of anxiety (that is, a situation of danger) is allotted to every age of development as being appropriate to it. The danger of psychical helplessness fits the stage of the ego's early immaturity; the danger of loss of an object (or loss of love) fits the lack of self-sufficiency in . . . childhood; the danger of being castrated fits the phallic phase; and finally fear of the super-ego . . . fits the period of latency.[36]

The heart of the danger is fundamentally *disablement,* or the loss of modes of being potent or whole, and a similar danger founds ethics in Levinas. Now, Lacan interprets Freudian castration as a *split* in the subject. In other words, the law of existence and the legal "life" of the ego entail an early interruption that gets repeated at ever higher levels of being. Since, for

Freud, this is what makes way for memory, no inaugural interruption could be recollected. To put it differently, the will to persist in being (understandable as a partly conscious drive) has lacunae which we discern through their traces. The traces do not *make* sense, because they cannot be brought under conceptuality without assimilation to conscious events. They do not fit into a thinking that reconstructs existence at a distance from affect, body, and trauma. The same can certainly be said of Levinas's concepts of recurrence and obsession.

When Marc Richir, who coined the term "phenomenology's unconscious" for his own purposes, speaks of these lacunae, he calls them "hiatuses" ("PI" 229–31, "PaI" 158–60). If intentional consciousness is the construction and pairing of subjects and objects, and if Husserl's phenomenology shows the doubling up of intentional acts and the intentional objects as a *tautology*, then the dimension of affectivity gets reduced to an intention about-to-be-born. But this reduction is untenable without interruptions. Richir writes: "From phenomenality to the tautology [of act and object] . . . there would be an irreducible *hiatus* and the unresorbable passivity of the subject would not only be that of a subject assigned to the other and for the other in the ethical dimension"—in other words, the dimension Levinas elaborates—"but also the passivity of what we are calling the *phenomenological unconscious,* where it is true that phenomenality overflows or is held on the in-side of all intentionality and of every teleology" ("PI" 231, "PaI" 160).

That such overflows occur explains why sensation is more, or finer grained, than intuition and representation. Further, just as Freud tentatively advanced his exploration of the parallels between drives in the unconscious and their "translations" and effects in culture, Richir will add that the hiatus in subjective life and the overflow of phenomenality together clarify "that savage and unstable mobility that keeps humanity from becoming fixed in systems" ("PI" 232, "PaI" 160). In short, as Levinas saw in 1961 in *Totality and Infinity,* history itself is not just Hegelian reason on the move; it evinces moments of ethical unpredictability and generosity, which have nothing to do with the ill-discerned operation of Reason.

Clearly, one should not move overconfidently in placing Levinas face-to-face with Freud. There are three additional reasons why Levinas rejects psychoanalysis. These can be expressed as (1) the ambiguity of "life" and the hypothesis of the unconscious; (2) the claim made by phenomenology in regard to other "transcendental" logics; and (3) the amorality of psychoanalysis.

I borrow the concept of the "ambiguity of life" from Michel Henry. His *Genealogy of Psychoanalysis* argues, in a Levinasian vein, that the hypothesis of a mechanistic unconscious is rendered unnecessary by an exhaustive exploration of the distinction, or "hiatus," between representation and life. Understood as a contained dispersion of forces, life requires representation only in order to be made the object of consciousness.[37] Without our intentional consciousness of it, "life" is already at work; it holds sway. This is Nietzsche's word, Henry reminds us. Now, if Freud maintained that affect is "the qualitative expression of a quantity of instinctual energy and of its fluctuations" (*GP* xvii), then those quanta of energy that interested the early Freud, and which he later on called "drives," come to consciousness through their qualitative traces, as affects (*GP* xvi). Without reopening the perplexities of energetics, let us just say that it is not a matter here of chickens and eggs. Quantities of drive condition qualities, understood as affective tones; such quantities are not accessible to consciousness, but qualities of affects *are* accessible. Moreover, if affect, or those quanta of which affect is a transformation, is *not* conscious, then why should the quanta be subject to the laws of identity? Why should they have to be integrated into the temporality of a synthesizing consciousness? These questions seem congenial to Levinas's thinking on trauma. But a significant distinction remains. Whether we follow Henry or Freud here, the character of drives and affect is for them interwoven with a will to power. For Henry, "the essence of affectivity is self-affirmation," "potentiality," or "Life's hyperpower" (*GP* xxvi, 325). Not entirely so for Freud, or for Levinas. The goal of Levinas's project is to affirm the impossibility of an affectivity that is simply self-affirmation and has no traces of other coeval forces. For Levinas, affect must have layers; certainly, the lion's share of the forces translated by affect is engaged in the will to persist in being. But another level shows that self-affirmation is interrupted, not by itself, but by something *other* than it, something both within and without it. "Other" here means not-assimilable: qualitatively different. Despite the qualitative distinction, these interruptions are indissociable from intersubjectivity in Levinas, and they give rise to ideas like the Good-beyond-being, or indeed, "God." Yet even when he speaks of Levinas's phenomenological unconscious, Richir devotes little attention to the former's emphasis of the singularity of the Good or the co-genesis of religion and morality in it. Like Henry, Richir wants his hiatus to extend back *into* life as perseverance, not as ethics or religion, but as a trial of the sublime. "To bear the weight of the other and of the world is . . . 'divine discomfort' only insofar as it is *also*, for us, the very discomfort of the *sublime*, of that which . . . summons me beyond limits which nevertheless cannot be located in the world" ("PI" 250, "PaI" 178). Yet the uniqueness of the Levinasian project is precisely his emphasis upon the Good, which arises in the midst of suffering and trauma as "for-the-other," and thereby alters, and spiritualizes, the fact of suffering by lifting it from its bodily ground. This alone, Levinas argues, takes from death the sting of *its* otherness. The spiritualization of suffering notwithstanding, death *and* the human other (or death and "love," death and *eros?*) remain the *two deformalized forms* of alterity for Levinas; and all trauma has something of dying.[38] No comparable "Good beyond being" is found in the theory of drives in Freud's unconscious. But this does not mean that Freud's drives are static, or that the unconscious is fixed like a world behind the world. The indeterminate movement back and forth of opening and closing in the self, described by Freud as tension and release, or as free-flowing versus quiescent cathexes, figures as the "systole and diastole of the heart" in Levinas (*OB* 109). For both Levinas and Freud, a twofold dynamism is required by the enigma that sensibility holds for conscious life.

Levinas's rejection of psychoanalysis is just and unjust. It is correct yet reductive when it is argued that the unconscious mimes the functions of the conscious and that it is demonstrable only on the basis of what *shows itself in pathology*. I have already addressed why this must be so. On the other hand, Freud faces the terminological difficulties of one who seeks to develop a new science. He is not attempting to *assimilate* the unconscious to the conscious, especially to its mechanistic aspects; he is attempting to thematize the unconscious in a nonpoetic, nonreligious way. There is, admittedly, something disturbing about the Freudian drives. They are themselves mechanistic, speculative, and they appear positively Manichean (in the sense of the equipollence of obscure, good and evil forces opposed to each other) when a trauma causes them to come apart. And, of course, they have a problematical relationship to pleasure and pain. That is, confronting the source of pleasure in a drive, Freud oscillated between pleasures arising from the *release* of tension (tied to the Nirvana principle or the death drive) and pleasures arising from the *accumulation* of tension (tied to the eros, or the life, principle).[39] As we have seen in "Beyond the Pleasure Principle," Freud will argue for two irreducible drives intertwined with unpleasure and pleasure: one that increases endogenous excitation; and the other, quiescent, that functions to reduce nervous system excitations and is accompanied by pleasure. If the quiescent drive holds primacy, then that is because it is more archaic and conservative. What makes it more archaic? Freud argues that the answer is found at the physiological and phylogenetic levels of the human.

Is this drive necessarily more archaic and conservative at the levels, preconscious and conscious, of sensibility and affect? Apparently so, for the quiescent drive is only visible when, defusing itself from its connection with eros, it shows itself in patients' repeated strategies of *trauma-creation*. The repetition compulsion represents Freud's avowal of a firm limit to the therapeutic possibilities of psychoanalysis. It leads him to speculate that the repetition of trauma within the therapeutic relationship—which is, after all, an intersubjective relationship before it is a scientific investigation—permits a necessary, but rather tragic, release of accumulating tensions. The tensions are immanent; they were partly "there" already, passively, but they *increase* within the context of the transference. They are released by way of the faculty that controls motility: the ego—but their release is also affective. The underlying supposition is that significant trauma, no matter what its initial source, leaves an unreadable trace of itself, and that trace is at times "passive," and at others, "active" over the history of the individual. If we bracket Freud's express etiological speculations about the death drive and its functions, here, then Freud's words become redolent of Levinas's:[40]

> On an unprejudiced view one gets an impression that the child turned his experience into a game from another motive. At the outset he was in a *passive* situation—he was overpowered by the [traumatic] experience; but, by repeating it, *unpleasurable though it was,* as a game, he took an active part. ("BPP" 600, final emphasis added)

And in regard to adults, the situation is similar:

> Twenty-five years of intense work have had as their result that the immediate aims of psycho-analytic technique are quite other to-day than they were . . . But it became *ever clearer* that the aim which had been set up— the aim that *what was unconscious should become conscious*—is not completely attainable by [the interpretive] method. The patient cannot remember the whole of what is repressed in him. . . . He is obliged to *repeat* the repressed material as a contemporary experience instead of . . . *remembering* it as something belonging to the past. ("BPP" 602)

Repetition is unavoidable because trauma, albeit relational, occurs beyond, on the "hither side of" (as Levinas puts it) the signifying capacity of words: trauma surpasses the nominalization and undermines the predicative operation of language. As Levinas noted in the 1940s, no subject-verb structure can be found in trauma. With repression and repetition, a dynamic and ongoing "lack" takes the place of Freud's oft-criticized topographical unconscious: in the place of a site, we now have an activity. Nietzsche's notion of the creation of an animal that remembers by way of traumas to its body, echoes in "Beyond the Pleasure Principle." So, too, does the Levinasian description of bodily vulnerability, "originary susceptibility," and "obsession" by the other.

The implication is that trauma divides, it splits something in the subject: a profoundly Levinasian notion. In Freud, it divides the drives, separating them from one another. If this were not so, and if we did not see some compulsion to repeat a trauma by harming or destroying one's self or one's relation to the therapist, then the claim that the drives were governed by the pleasure principle alone, could be maintained. But the compulsion to repeat is found in actual relationships *and* in dreams. Freud writes, "Patients repeat all of these unwanted situations and painful emotions in the transference and revive them with the greatest ingenuity. . . . They contrive once more to feel themselves scorned, to oblige the physician to speak severely to them and to treat them coldly" ("BPP" 604). Henceforth, it seems impossible to claim that psychic energy is homogeneous. Just as impossible as it is to "cure" certain traumas. Although this dualism of immanent forces is Manichean, and has earned the charge of mechanism, Levinas, for his part, would be the last to deny the persistence of trauma, given his own concept of "recurrence," in which he appropriates significant Freudian themes. Moreover, Levinas would not deny that trauma comes to pass at the intersection of incarnate sensibility and an archaic level of the psyche that he calls the "self." In Levinas, as we have seen, Freud's dualism of forces becomes the opening and closing of the split self under accusation by the other, like the systole and diastole of the heart.

In a move that brings him still closer to Levinas, Freud argues that the compulsion to repeat is *not limited* to neurotics. Moreover, the essence of trauma is found not in its shaping our character, but in the way in which it operates in a *passive* subject. This leads Freud to a logical conundrum: what really is passive, and what is active when we are dealing with immanence? He writes:

> What psycho-analysis reveals in the transference phenomena of neurotics can also be observed in the lives of some normal people. The impression they give is of being pursued by a malignant fate or possessed by some "daemonic" power. . . . This "perpetual recurrence of the same thing" causes us no astonishment when it relates to *active* behavior on the part of the person concerned and when we can discern in him an essential character-trait which always remains the same and which is compelled to find expression in a repetition in the same experiences. We are much more impressed by cases where the subject appears to have a *passive* experience, over which he has no influence, but in which he meets with a repetition of the same fatality. ("BPP" 604)

Given Freud's grappling with passivity, it is hard not to think of Levinas's description of "recurrence." He argues for its pre-reflective status, using a bodily metaphor that is more than a metaphor. "The reflection on one-self proper to consciousness, the ego perceiving the self, is not like the *antecedent recurrence of the oneself,* [which is] from the first backed up against itself . . . or *twisted over itself in its skin,* too tight in its skin, in itself *already outside of itself*" (*OB* 104). I am not saying that the concept of "recurrence" has the precise sense of Freud's compulsion to repeat. But it borrows from Freud the impressive blurring of inside-outside, same-other distinctions, which characterize traumatic affect. As a state of being, recurrence has no "status." Its description gives us a phenomenology of Freud's *Todestrieb:* it is a tensing or a throbbing like a *nonerotic* (Levinas insists) Freudian buildup of tension.[41] This is all the more apt that eros, in Freud, is the counter-drive; and, in cases of trauma, these drives come undone. Levinas's sense of recurrence both borrows from Freud and does not cancel his definition of the compulsion to repeat. Moreover, the famous Levinasian "obsession" by the other—by which he means responsibility as "being *under siege* by the other"—does repeat itself. It is, he writes, "a writhing in the tight dimensions of pain" (*OB* 75); "witness or martyr-dom" (*OB* 77); a persecution like "the content of a consciousness gone mad" (*OB* 101), but *better* than this: it is "the outdated notion of the soul" (*OB* 103).

I will not attempt to compare the religious sensibility as a theme in Levinas and Freud. That would take us too far off course. Yet it is clear that the significance of the religious concerns Levinas more than that of the psychoanalytical. And "religious" should here be understood in a way close to that of Kierkegaard in his discussion of "spirit" and "the leap," or the transcendence that eludes the understanding, in his *Concept of Anxiety.*[42] By 1974, Levinas had definitively taken what could be called a religious path toward trauma and the alterity for which a self is responsible. He chose a religious language of illustration rather than a positivist discourse grounded upon causal sequences or objective visibility. He further qualifies his choice by ruling out those religious discourses (i.e., the majority) that belong to the ontological domain; that is, all those discourses for which the Other is a *being,* albeit a supreme being.[43] Freud's path and that of Levinas are distinct and irreconcilable. But there is something symptomatic of a refusal in Levinas when he tersely rejects psychoanalysis and *its* unconscious. Common to both of them is, fundamentally, the attempt "to preserve psychical specificity against all physico-biological reduction," as Henry said of Freud alone (*GP* 299). I would add that both sought to preserve psychical specificity *not* just from physiological reductionism—into which both also fell: Freud with the source of drives, Levinas with being as *conatus essendi*—but also from spiritualizing reductions; and skeptical reductions in which the psyche loses access to body and other. A fecund inquiry would read Levinas's ethics of trauma next to Freud's repetition compulsion, especially in light of their different interpretations of alterity-in-sensibility, or the other-in-the-same. Indeed, Simon Critchley has begun such an examination with reference to Lacan as well.[44]

For now, I am only examining Levinas's refusal of two concepts in psychoanalysis: the unconscious and *life* as drives. My intention is to emphasize how close Levinas and Freud come to each other in their thematization of repetition and recurrence.[45] If the logic of being and better-than-being cannot be assimilated to that of bodily consciousness and the unconscious, then both Levinas and Freud will contend differently with a "two-world" logic and with the challenge of articulating the worlds. For Levinas, the two are conjoined as the chiasmus of a particular temporality: diachrony. They are not dialectized—except for a time in 1961, when "paternity" and "filiality" serve as natural and symbolic mediations between self and other. For Freud, the mediation of the preconscious posed the difficulty of determining what, in the unconscious, could effectively become conscious, and in what form. For Levinas, we find a circle: the two-world logic can be said to make his thought religious—over and above his use of "religion" as ethical sociality. And again, it is his opting for a religious, ultimately Talmudic, reading of the encounter with alterity that impels him to posit, not an ontological difference, but an "ethical" one between Being and the Good-beyond-Being.

Things are otherwise complex with Freud. The two "worlds," consciousness and unconsciousness, recall appearance-reality and mind-brain dichotomies. Although the adumbration of an unconscious affords explanatory paths for certain pathologies, because they can be restored to consciousness, the ultimate relation of the unconscious to the conscious never ceases posing a problem: in what ways does the unconscious mirror the conscious? What is the nature of conscious or perceptual elements when they become unconscious? Do they still have a "nature"? Since it is almost impossible to think without the principles of non-contradiction and sufficient reason, we could say that two worlds arise when the meaning of what is without intentionality (the unconscious) is sought. At that moment the formalism of non-contradiction and sufficient reason insinuates itself into a domain, the unconscious, in which their value is open to doubt.

Focusing on Freud's most positivistic arguments, Henry vehemently opposes the notion of an "unconscious psyche":

> [The] being of Psyche itself is merely the representative of something
> else, something not psychical but a system of physical energy. Thus the

psychical stands for a reality other than itself; . . . it has only a pseudo-autonomy, pseudospecificity, and pseudoreality. The affirmation of the existence of a psychical unconscious is acceptable only with that one essential restriction, namely that the unconscious . . . is merely a stand-in, an equivalent, a substitute [for somatic processes]. Insofar, however, as the psychical being of drives, of the unconscious . . . is understood as "representative," modeled on representation, it is secretly at one with . . . representational consciousness. (*GP* 299–300)

Henry's objection is that Freud's unconscious plays two roles badly: if it is the site, or sum, of somatic drives, then it redoubles these drives. If it "contains" anything symbolical or with links to images and words, then it becomes a ghostly stand-in for representative consciousness. The difficulty lies in positing a duality that is also just one thing. And it lies in the logic of containment; i.e., what site, or forces, contains or surrounds consciousness; in what way does the somatic give rise to idealization? Henry's objection is that the logic of containment slides into logics of assimilation or subsumption: do the body's drives generate the unconscious as an *epiphenomenon*, like Freud's preconscious *Hörkappe* (cap of hearing), which has both developmental and anatomical grounds?[46] Moreover, do the phenomena of perception and communication "go" anywhere when they are retained, then forgotten, then recollected? Henry does not allow Freud to defend his "unconscious psyche" by bracketing the objective, worldly sense of concepts like "sequence," "causality," and "site." Perhaps Henry is right in refusing such ambiguity. Perhaps, however, the deformalization of these categories would be so complex that a different vocabulary would have to take their place to avoid the traps of logic (identity, sufficient reason, containment, and subsumption). For all his conceptual innovations, Freud does not take this "philosophical" step in a way that satisfies Henry. Indeed, Henry would be equally dissatisfied with Levinas's two worlds. We must thus work with notions fraught with metaphysical weight, like that of the "psyche." For the purposes of this essay, let us pause at this notion and observe that it is preserved by both Freud *and* Levinas. Their recourse to it implies, above all, their own struggle against the two worlds, or the dichotomous logics, which arise for the conscious/unconscious, and for Being/Good-beyond-Being.[47]

There are two additional reasons why Levinas rejects psychoanalysis. Let us look at the claim of phenomenology first. Despite Husserl's turn to a transcendental phenomenology with the *Ideas*, first published in 1913, his philosophy was never "transcendental" the way Kant's was.[48] As we know, in the place of Kant's a priori/a posteriori dualism, and setting aside Kant's construct of the noumenon,[49] Husserl developed the phenomenological reductions.[50] His argument in favor of phenomenology held consistently that the contents of consciousness were brought to light without a transcendental deduction. They could be *shown* provided one bracketed the presuppositions of everyday life and of subject-object epistemologies in one's reconstruction. No transcendental deduction of categories was required to explain the possibility of knowledge for "consciousness in general," which was grounded upon judgments of experience. Even the conditions of the possibility of intellectual intuition were available to a phenomenologically reduced consciousness. No noumenal ghost world surrounds the appearances "produced" by a schematism of intuitions and categories, because the schematism is replaced by passive syntheses.

Following Husserl's inspiration, Levinas employs several phenomenological reductions. I mentioned his most radical elaboration of these earlier. The hypothesis of the *manifest* quality of the contents of consciousness represents, for Levinas as for Husserl, a step beyond Kantianism. But for Levinas, this step must also take us beyond Husserl and Freud. It must move beyond the deductive hypotheses of the unconscious and the preconscious; but it must also show that what is manifest relies upon what is not manifest (e.g., the face). Although Levinas requires a concept of self that is rooted in relational affectivity, the Freudian constructs represent a step backward, prior to Husserl's and Heidegger's phenomenological insights. Levinas does not say this explicitly, but clearly, for him, Freud's scientific a priorism remains formalistic and modernist. Like its predecessor, this reason for rejecting psychoanalysis is fraught with difficulties. Freud's argument for *traces* of drives in affect, not to mention both Freud's and Lacan's insistence that a drive is "not an instinct" in a deterministic biological sense, illustrate some of the difficulties in conceiving a formalist Freud.[51] Indeed, notions of the trace, and immanent forces accompanied by affectivity, are indispensable to Levinas's own philosophical de-formalizations.

Finally, consider the objection of the anethicality of psychoanalysis. As a therapeutic practice, there is an undeniable ethic in psychoanalysis. This is true even if the "cure" is incompletable and its meaning ambiguous for both the analyst and analysand. One difficulty, in this question of ethics, concerns the meaning of desire and sexuality for Freud and for Levinas. It is not possible to discuss Levinas's ambivalence about desire and sexuality at length here; much less their place in an ethic of being-for-the-other. Let us only say that, in his 1961 work, Levinasian eros is naturalistic (serving procreation) and ontic (compare the vulgarity but irresistibility of the seductive, feminine face). In his 1974 work, Levinas makes the caress an instance of pre-intentional proximity and vulnerability. Despite this innovation, eros, as desire and love, is *never* ethical, never better-than-

Being, the way responsibility and obsession are. But are the Freudian accounts of desire and sexual development anethical or amoral?

Let us return to the objection as it was aimed at Freud. In his remarkable work *At the Boundaries of the Analytic Act,* the French analyst Louis Beirnaert argued what is by now clear to most readers of Freud:

> Freud proposes no morality because he is concerned with that which precedes and founds all cultural forms, including moralities. It follows from this that, to enter into Freud's contribution, it is indispensable to avoid translating the terms and concepts that he uses in his psychoanalytic theory into a culturally specific morality.[52]

In Freud, the archaeological inquiry into morality is doubled by a genealogical one. And there is a genealogical strategy in Levinas as well. However, Freud and Levinas differ radically in their respective genealogies. Turning to Freud, it was only late in life that he devoted a long study to the genealogy of morality and religion. His midcareer work, *Totem and Taboo* (1913), moved between archaeology and genealogy. It sought to escape the binary of moral guilt and the transgression of a moral law by going behind them to the primary taboo on incest. The interest of this taboo lay in its translation of the peculiar Oedipal "identification" of the male child with the father. And already, in this work, the *source* of the taboo is the other as dead father; that is, the *imaginary father.* Later on, in *Civilization and Its Discontents* (1930), Freud addresses the (deformalized) incipience of moral conscience in the emotion of "remorse." Similar to the taboo and its source, remorse has an unconscious ground. But here the ground is an affect that is both unconscious and conscious. It gets tied to the emergence of the superego at the resolution of the Oedipal drama.

Despite obvious parallelisms between the conscious and unconscious tensions, parallelisms that might give Levinas and Henry another reason to accuse Freud of reductionism, let us note two things. First, there is an *ethical quality* to the way in which the Oedipal conflicts are resolved in favor of familial harmony, even when their resolution comes at the expense of the *health of the subject.* Think of the suffering little Hans and his horse phobia, which allowed him to love his father without ambivalence.[53] Second, the ground of remorse lies in a *law* that remains unconscious, because it is "outside the series of all cultural formations" (*AFAA* 109). What is this law? It is a law of *relationality* with an assimilated other (the mother) and a commanding, speaking Other (the father and voice of the father). And it is a law of eros (with the mother) and the interruption of eros's indeterminate temporality of enjoyment (by the intrusions of the "external" other), which arises *as simultaneous with* the genesis-in-fission of the ego it-

self. This amounts to a modified Levinasian structure. Returning to Beirnaert's remark about ethics: of course Levinas would reject any theory of
the anethical formation of moral and religious forms, even if their source
were traceable to a conflict that gave rise to a legislating other-within-the-
self (whether as the superego, the dead father, or the other who obsesses
me without appearing). But, as I have shown, the question of ethics in psychoanalysis is more complex than that. It confronts a desire too ontic to
qualify as Levinas's 1961 concept of "metaphysical desire." And therapeutic practice engages a complex responsibility that is superficially different
from Levinas's concept of responsibility. The psychoanalytic invites the
analysand to be responsible for his or her own desire; i.e., not to give way
to internal or external demands that this desire be abandoned. If we conceive this as normative, or as discouraging responsibility for the other,
then we will have misunderstood the meaning of desire in psychoanalysis.
Beyond objections to the anethicality of psychoanalysis, the structural
resonances between *Civilization and Its Discontents* and Levinas's *Totality
and Infinity* are remarkable. As Levinas writes there:

> There exists a tyranny of the universal and of the impersonal, an order
> that is inhuman though distinct from the brutish. Against it man affirms
> himself as an irreducible singularity, exterior to the totality . . . and
> aspiring to the religious order where the recognition of the individual
> concerns him in his singularity, an order of joy which is neither cessation
> nor antithesis of pain, nor flight before it. (*TI* 242)

Levinas's "irreducible singularity" is also a being-under-Law, threatened
by and expiating for the absent other, whatever the phenomenological difficulties of framing that absence.

Totality and Infinity defines the "religious order" as one of joy and
pain. It is an order required by beings that are human. This order comes
to be because an other interrupts the tyranny of the universal, that is, history and being. Access to the origin of this interruption is foreclosed by
Levinas. He shares Husserl's opposition to psychological speculation. But
access to the law in Freud is only possible as a heuristic. This law refers to
an immanent "force." Therefore the speculative understanding does and
does *not* capture its meaning; understanding neither establishes nor un-
does this law insofar as it is constitutive of an ego that emerges between
perception and drives. If we return to Levinas and his particular understanding of the religious, we note that within the anonymous judgment of
history, where force reigns, there is found occasionally a "religious" judgment. In a provocative tone reminiscent of Kant's practical reason, Levinas calls this the judgment of "God":

> The idea of a judgment of God represents the *limit idea* of a judgment
> that . . . takes into account the invisible and essential offense to a singu-
> larity that results from judgment (even from a judgment that is rational
> and inspired by universal principles) and . . . [which] does not silence by
> its majesty the voice and the revolt of apology. (*TI* 244)

Dare we add to this revolt, the return of *remorse?* Be that as it may, singularity has privilege of place at the level of *practical truth* rather than as an
epistemic notion. This is thanks to the idea of the "judgment of God." This
judgment lies in the sense, or the conviction, that something or someone
greater than oneself and surpassing both history and biography "sees" the
invisible harm to the other. Here begins Levinas's constitution of an ethics
under the eyes of the Other/Father (who is *not* a supreme being). It is less important, to Levinas's ethics, to determine whether this event is imagina-
tive, or experienced, or both. What counts is that the idea and sentiment
simply arise and that the idea is both incomplete and indissociable from
a sentiment.

In regard to the ethics of psychoanalysis, a different question arises
when we ask what is the relationship between Levinas's idea that I, and
others, are observed by one whom we will never perceive, and the imaginary expectation directed toward the silent analyst. This question is taken
up by Lacan in his discussion of the desire of the analyst. But it also sheds
light on Freud's perplexity over the repetition compulsion within analysis.
For, if the analyst's silent gaze *constitutes* that which "takes into account the
invisible and essential offense," then the repetition compulsion argues for
a desire *either* to dramatize this offense in its excess through continuous
reenactments, *or* to deny the possibility of any "other" who can take the invisible into account, can constitute singularity, and can interrupt the
tyranny of the impersonal. Caught in the repetition compulsion, the
analysand wavers *between* two orders: first, Levinas's religious order and
the access to the judgments of the ego-ideal, which is part of a psychoanalytic "cure"; and second, the atheism of an impersonal, anethical order
in which the other is absent.

Levinas writes that "God sees the invisible" (*TI* 244), and the "invisible is the offense" (*TI* 242) *done to the single person.* But who "sees" that
God sees? The relationship expressed by revolt must be the "seeing" in
question. Is it the victim *and* the aggressor, or just the victim who thus
sees? Important above all is that it constitutes a "me" in the moment that
I find myself under an unanticipated law that is "imaginary" insofar as it
runs against being and history. Under the judgment of "God" means
simultaneously the end of innocence—i.e., willed or unwilled ignorance—and the halting of violence. It implies both guilt, as my guilt be-

fore the other person, and the possibility that the violence implicit in the historical forces that destroy particular persons is not the last word on the human condition.

For Freud, too, the origin of morality and religion lies in a primordial guilt. This is the other "hiatus," as Richir puts it, which arises through a desire that precedes the formation of the ego. This desire is to remain unindividuated and fused with the mother (i.e., to remain one yet non-singularized), under some principle of pleasure. In another Freudian economy, it is the desire for release, for a return to a pre-live state: death. So the proto-subject enacts, or fantasizes, the violation of the law that separates and constitutes. It destroys the other as the imaginary "father" (God) and the principle of individuation (the Other, the interruption). But it does not escape obsession by the other. Here we see that whatever the historical and explanatory value of Freud's account of the forces that constitute religion and the subject, the parallels that these evince—between Levinas's and Freud's economies of desire—are arresting. Only consider the placeholders of father-introject and God-the judge in Freud and Levinas. It may even be argued that these parallels remain, despite evident differences in the deduction and purpose of these economies.

Is it the amoralism of psychoanalysis, then, that led Levinas to avoid it, or is it the question of desire and the difficult parallel between Levinas's judgment of God and Freud's law of the father that explains his avoidance? If this is the case, then is not the supposed amoralism of psychoanalysis plausible only because the destruction of the Other/father leaves the latter as a *given* or an introject, and as indissolubly a part of our cultural productions, such that we do *not need* to append another, more factical explication of ethics and religion? How could Levinas respond to this question if he does not venture to explore the *ontological* status of "being under God's judgment?" How can this "being-under," this peculiar seeing or sentiment, be rooted in anything but the imaginary if it is better-than-being?[54] It is enough for now to emphasize that the dual logics I attributed earlier to both Levinas and Freud are not vicious if we suspend the category of identity and the principle of non-contradiction. That is, the desire for pleasure—say, as the desire for the imaginary mother, who is all and no thing—and the law of the father that forecloses access to pleasure in the name of the distant other, or the excluded third party, together inaugurate two dimensions of existence: that of unconscious guilt and the primordial anxiety, *and,* at the level of consciousness, that in which morality and religion are possible. For Levinas, to be under the judgment of God describes that moment where I am caught in an invisible gaze *and* I realize this consciously. This double moment, wherein A and not-A seem to coexist, holds joy and suffering in tension. It is intermediary between affect and reflection. As "the order of joy" and religion, it is always also the order of guilt and remorse, wherein an "I" suddenly "sees" violence, because the force of the other, who is not "there" as "I's" ob-ject, has individuated that "I" in its desire—and its desire is "to see" the invisible; to expiate, or to pronounce the word "God" as the paradoxical interruption of force, or life, or conflict itself.

Concluding Remarks

In sensibility and affect, Levinas and psychoanalysis find a common terrain. I cannot present further Henry's arguments why Freud approaches and dismisses affect as the truth of his unconscious. Henry admits that Freud himself struggled with the meaning of affect (*GP* 315–16).[55] And I have suggested three reasons why Levinas would reject psychoanalysis. Beneath them, however, I found other parallels which, despite their imperfections, suggest that Levinas had deeper reasons for looking away from psychoanalysis. The relational logic that gave rise to both philosophies, as it were, comes from similar tasks and comparable evasions: among these, the indeterminacy of being and the forces of desire or will. Freud is not to be faulted for attempting to go beyond Schopenhauer's and Nietzsche's concepts of affect, suffering, will, and impersonal force. Freud is explicit about this in 1923 when, following Georg Groddeck, he argues that we are "'lived' by unknown and uncontrollable forces," and adopts the originally Nietzschean term of *es* for these forces.[56] In Levinas, two uncontrollable forces inhabit the reduced self as well: that tensing of obsession which he calls "being too tight in one's skin," and the horror engendered by our dissolving into the purely elemental (i.e., the *there is*). Contradictory reasons can be adduced to explain Freud's suspicion of philosophy.[57] For instance, to avoid transcendental construction, his theories ground their legitimacy in decades of clinical observation, but this leads him to deduce explanatory conditions that are both transcendental and unstable. Anxiety and trauma are a case in point: their relationship and causal sequencing is reversed between the dream interpretations of 1901 and the "New Introductory Lectures" of 1933. Moreover, neither Freud nor Levinas embraced the idealistic conception of reason and history.[58] But their discourses, more than most others, resolutely address alterity as a force, cast suspicion on humanism and everyday morality, and reframe the concepts of desire and ethics. Heidegger should not be ignored, but his alterity lies essentially in the question of Being. Posthumous works of Merleau-Ponty like *The Visible and the Invisible* also deserve an eminent place in this discussion. Perhaps more than any other contemporary philosopher, Merleau-Ponty reconceives the meaning of sensibility outside of binary logics.[59] However, establishing his contribution exceeds the comparisons attempted in this essay.

Notes

1. See Emmanuel Levinas, *De l'existence à l'existant* (Paris: Vrin, 1986), 57; *Existence and Existents,* trans. Alphonso Lingis (The Hague: Martinus Nijhoff, 1978), 38. *Existence and Existents* herefter cited in the text as *EE.* Levinas writes there, in a work whose redaction dates from the 1940s:

> Since the *discovery of the unconscious*—and this contradiction in terms is evidence of a considerable intellectual upheaval—philosophy has been conceiving of the unconscious as another consciousness, failing to recognize the ontological function of the unconscious and its specific relationship with conscious clarity . . . The unconscious is interpreted in terms of consciousness, or the reverse. The unconscious appears as a possible, a germ, or as something repressed.

The omission of the term "psychoanalysis" is striking enough here. But Levinas wants to refer to more than Freudian psychology and analysis. The ontological relation he refers to, between consciousness and unconsciousness, involves a Cartesian contrast between the clear and distinct and the "obscure" and "ambiguous" (38). This contrast will allow him to discuss stages between sleep and complete wakefulness. These stages—or anything we can *perceive and describe*—are what is thematizable for philosophy *without speculation.* They are amenable to an interpretive phenomenology that resembles Heidegger's own, while opposing Heidegger's purposes.

Levinas makes a similar statement—this time, however, in the form of a denial or negation—in 1980 at a conference entitled "La psychanalyse est-elle une histoire juive?" He says, "My discomfiture comes . . . from the fact that I am entirely outside of psychoanalytic investigations, whatever the forms under which they are pursued, and I am neutral before the battles they wage." But Levinas's disinterest here is precisely *not* a Freudian *Verneinung.* There is a profound kinship, and a competition, between the analytic interpretation of dreams (and so of desire and the unconscious) and Talmudic dream interpretation, which loosely shares with analysis certain techniques of idea association. See Emmanuel Levinas, "Quelques vus talmudiques sur le rêve," in *La psychanalyse est-elle une histoire juive? Colloque de Montpellier,* ed. Adélie Rassial and Jean-Jacques Rassial (Paris: Seuil, 1981). Cited in part by Simon Critchley, "The Original Traumatism," reprinted in his *Ethics, Politics, Subjectivity* (London: Verso, 1999), 185.

2. See Critchley, "The Original Traumatism," 186–88.

3. For a fuller development of these criticisms, see Michel Henry, "Man's Mon-

key: The Unconscious?" in *The Genealogy of Psychoanalysis,* trans. Douglas Brick (Stanford: Stanford University Press, 1993), 281–327.

4. See Critchley, "The Original Traumatism," 183–97.

5. Paul-Laurent Assoun, "Le sujet et l'Autre chez Levinas et Lacan," in *Rue Descartes,* vol. 7, June 1993, 123–45; English translation by Sarah Harasym in *Levinas and Lacan: The Missed Encounter* (Albany: State University of New York Press, 1998).

6. See Marie-Anne Lescourret, *Emmanuel Levinas* (Paris: Flammarion, 1994), 108 and 223.

7. Sigmund Freud, "Project for a Scientific Psychology" in *The Standard Edition of the Complete Psychological Works of Sigmund Freud,* trans. and ed. James Strachey and Anna Freud (London: Hogarth, 1964), 1:283–397. In this text, what will later be called drives are separated into exogenous and endogenous "excitations." The operation of the endogenous excitations is defensive and conservative, following the initial motivation of the work, which was to examine the neurological meaning of defenses. There is no real discussion of instincts, here; this is, rather, the Freud of a nineteenth-century energetics, a discipline that Freud himself will promptly disown. Common themes with later works include the function of memory, perception, and the maintenance of a quantitative homeostasis of forces in the individual.

8. Sigmund Freud, "New Introductory Lectures on Psycho-Analysis," in *The Standard Edition,* vol. 22.

9. See also Sigmund Freud, "The Ego and the Id," in *The Standard Edition,* 19:40–41. "The emergence of life would thus be the cause of the continuance of life and also at the same time of the striving toward death; and life would be a conflict and compromise between these two trends."

10. Sigmund Freud, "Beyond the Pleasure Principle," in *The Freud Reader,* ed. Peter Gay (New York: W. W. Norton, 1989), 608–9. Hereafter cited in the text as "BPP."

11. See Simon Critchley, "The Original Traumatism," 192ff., for a discussion of dreams of traumatic neuroses and the phylogenetic account of the death drive and its consequent repetition compulsion.

12. And at *that* level, it is not easily "read." The survival of traces depends upon their fragmentary quality, which means that for the perceiving "consciousness," it is as though they had never "been" otherwise. See Sigmund Freud, "A Note on the 'Mystic Writing-Pad'" (*Wunderblock*), in *The Standard Edition,* 19:227–32.

13. Indeed, it is not that Freud just takes consciousness over from philosophy whole cloth, as Henry suggests. In itself, consciousness remains a mystery to him. But consciousness is, obviously, the only "state" from which we can thematize. It is, for Freud, "in the last resort our one beacon light in the darkness of depth psychology" (see "Ego and Id," 19:18). And it is the "fact without parallel, which defies all explanation *or description*" (see "An Outline of Psycho-Analysis," in *The Standard Edition,* 23:157). For this reason above all, Freud gave up his speculations on neurons in the "Project": there was no way to map neuronal function onto consciousness; there was no passage between the physiological and the symbolical.

This is why the unconscious must sometimes "look like" conscious processes do. There is no other "beacon light" to guide us but conscious processes. Henry knows this and finds it an unsatisfying response. But we should emphasize that we are dealing with dynamics, with functions, *not* identities, and we should grant Freud that metaphors for conscious functions *are as ambiguous* as those for unconscious ones, no matter how familiar the former are to us. Indeed, if there is no point of communication between neurobiology and symbolic activity, between drives and conscious processes, then we are forced back onto a dualism as radical as that of Descartes. Such a dualism would be tasteless to us, but logically unavoidable unless we begin from the visible and use language that suggests possible structures of unconscious activities, without carving them in stone.

14. Martin Heidegger, *Being and Time* (New York: Harper and Row, 1962), pt. 1, chap. 5, p. 176.

15. Emmanuel Levinas, *Otherwise Than Being, or Beyond Essence,* trans. Alphonso Lingis (Dordrecht and Boston: Kluwer Academic Publishers, 1991), 107. Hereafter cited in the text as *OB*.

16. See Henry, *Genealogy of Psychoanalysis,* 285ff.

17. Heidegger, *Being and Time,* pt. 1, chap. 2, para. 12, p. 78.

18. See Levinas, *Existence and Existents,* chap. 1, "Introduction: The Existent and the Relationship with Existence," for a re-situating of the meaning of the "instant" and the present, such that consciousness emerges a priori from itself, before finding itself in-the-world. This is Levinas's notion of the hypostasis. Levinas writes:

> The renewal of ontology in contemporary philosophy has noth-
> ing in common with realism. Its inquiry does not presuppose an
> affirmation of the existence of the external world and of its pri-
> macy over consciousness. It affirms that what is essential in
> human spirituality does not lie in our relationship with the things
> which make up the world, but is determined by a relationship . . .
> with the pure fact that there is Being. . . . If at the beginning our
> reflections are *in large measure inspired by the philosophy of Martin
> Heidegger,* . . . they are also governed by a profound need to leave
> the climate of that philosophy. (19)

19. These analyses suggest a phenomenological corollary to Freud's discovery of those pathologies that caused him to infer that being is as if driven by a conservative urge, *back,* as it were, toward a pre-living, pre-animal state, which would be the non-livingness of minerality. Now, although the pathologies exhibited by patients who would not get better, or who would not let go of compulsions to repeat traumatic moments, or who seemed to hold fast to the symptoms that bound up the traumas and held them in invisibility, are extremes, they too are always accompanied by certain irregular rhythms of the present. That is, they entail weariness, indolence—attitudes or positions vis-à-vis the presence of the upsurge of the self—and the very Levinasian anxiety that is a sign of being as if crushed by the present. One might argue that Freud's patients were not crushed by the present but oppressed by the past, through unconscious memories. But this does not ad-

dress the fact that, whatever the status of their memories (their past), the phenomena of symptoms, inhibitions, etc., impede other taking-positions *in the present;* these phenomena have tonalities similar to those described by Levinas. Freud, uninterested in phenomenological description and interpretation, describes these states within his general strategy of searching for their causes. Therein lies a fundamental, and problematic, difference between psychoanalysis and phenomenology. In addition, the replacement of Heidegger's "call of Being" with Being's "fatality" precludes its appropriation as a question. Being becomes a trauma that is both ontic and ontological. It is ontic as the im-press of indeterminate beings; it is ontological as the condition that ties our passivity up with a pre- or a para-consciousness. This "experience" of trauma has an obsessive quality, it repeats itself, but it fades when we fall asleep or get up. Compare this with Freud's discovery about traumas from conflicts, which lead to phobias.

20. As Levinas writes in *Totality and Infinity,* "will to power" and indeed "any philosophy of power . . . which does not call into question the same [is] a philosophy of injustice." He will reverse philosophies of will, life, and power—with which he groups Heidegger's—and set in the "site" of living, not power, but pleasure; if one will, a deformalized *pleasure principle.* See Emmanuel Levinas, *Totality and Infinity,* trans. Alphonso Lingis (Pittsburgh: Duquesne University Press, 1969), 46ff. Hereafter cited in the text as *TI.*

21. In *Totality and Infinity* (published in French in 1961), pleasure was already definitive of lived and pre-reflective life and it characterized human transcendence at both the ontic level of experience of things—eating, enjoying the sunlight—*and* the ontological level as the enacted possibility of the "love of life."

22. In its ontological meaning, anxiety appears to be more frequent an "occurrence" than it is in Heidegger. Perhaps because, for Heidegger, anxiety is prima facie non-relational. It is non-relational because it reveals one's own most possibility of being, that of getting *Dasein* in view as a whole; facing it in its constitutive finitude. See *Being and Time,* paragraph 51. Note Heidegger's remark in paragraph 40, "The Basic State-of-Mind of Anxiety as a Distinctive Way in which Dasein is Disclosed": "And only because anxiety is always latent in Being-in-the-world, can such Being-in-the-world, as Being which is alongside the 'world'. . . ever be afraid. Fear is anxiety, fallen in the 'world,' inauthentic, and . . . hidden from itself. . . . Moreover, under the ascendancy of falling and publicness, '*real*' *anxiety is rare*" (234).

23. Of course, for Heidegger the "subject" is a Being-*there;* such it finds itself alongside of beings and is called by Being, rather than driven into itself by an other.

24. We see a development of this productive ambiguity of the bodily ego in Merleau-Ponty's studies of affect in perception.

25. Henry, *Genealogy of Psychoanalysis,* 315, emphasis added. Hereafter cited in the text as *GP.*

26. See François Roustang's remarks on Freud in his introductory essay to Michel Henry, "A Philosophy for Psychoanalysis?" in Henry, *Genealogy of Psychoanalysis,* xvi. See also, for example, Freud's (1933) "New Introductory Lectures on Psycho-Analysis" in *The Standard Edition,* 22:71:

Under the new and powerful impression of there being an extensive and important field of mental life which is normally withdrawn
from the ego's knowledge so that the processes occurring in it have
to be regarded as unconscious in the truly dynamic sense, we have
come to understand the term "unconscious" in a topographical or
systematic sense as well . . . The discovery, actually an inconvenient
one, that portions of the ego and super-ego as well are unconscious
in the dynamic sense, operates at this point as a relief . . . "The
"inconvenient discovery" vastly complicates the sense of "unconscious concept" or "unconscious activity." This is because the limit
that "latency," that "time," if one will, during which a thought or
perception is not "in mind," is not a simple declaration that it is
stored away in a black box, or waiting to return to consciousness
unaltered, or even that it has a representational status in the mind
at all. [Freud writes,] if it were at all certain that in the condition of
latency [conscious processes] are still something psychical. (71)

Freud obviously did *not* mean that the unconscious concept had a status equivalent to a conscious concept. Perhaps it is to his discredit that he dared use the term
"concept" at all; but he would not have fared better with words like "thought,"
"representation," or "idea." There is only so much of a traditional language, it
seems, that one can transform before the loss of sense becomes irremediable.

27. René Major examines this term in his "Le concept inconscient," in *La notion d'analyse: Actes du Colloque franco-péruvien, 30 octobre–6 novembre 1991*, ed.
Gérard Granel and Élisabeth Rigal (Toulouse: Presses Universitaires du Mirail,
1992), esp. 263.

28. See Roustang's introduction in Henry, *Genealogy of Psychoanalysis*, xvii.

29. As Levinas puts it, "what is essential in human spirituality does not lie in
our relationship with the things which make up the world." This forecloses that
thing in the world that is also a body. See Levinas, *Existence and Existents*, 19.

30. See Levinas, *Otherwise Than Being*, 127: "The way by which . . . the logos
arises to the concept of the ego passes through the third party. The subject as an
ego is not an entity provided with egoity as an eidetic structure." But note that the
reductions Levinas performs renders every discourse other than Freud's (and
even that one!) on subjectivity and "life" impossible. He is speaking of the psyche
"prior to any world" (against Heidegger; see 137). He frames "susceptiveness" as
"going against intentionality and the will" (against Husserl, Schopenhauer, and
Nietzsche, respectively; see 141); the transcendence of the other-in-the-self that
constitutes the "me" is "not convertible into immanence" (140); it is "already a psychosis" and "not an ego"; it is "possessed by the other, sick" (an anti-Freudian
pathology that is *not* meant to be a trope; 142).

31. "How would the contestation of the pretension beyond being have meaning *if this pretension were not heard?*" (Levinas, *Otherwise Than Being*, 156, emphasis
added). There is a permanent tension in Levinas between audition and saying,
and the strange seeing of revelation and the trace.

32. Marc Richir, "Phénomène et Infini," in *Cahier de l'Herne: Levinas*, ed.

292

BETTINA BERGO

Catherine Chalier and Miguel Abensour (Paris: Éditions de l'Herne, 1991), 231; "Phenomenon and Infinity," trans. Mark Gedney, "Levinas's Contribution to Contemporary Philosophy," ed. Bettina Bergo and Diane Perpich, special issue, *Graduate Faculty Philosophy Journal*, vol. 20, no. 2–vol. 21, no. 1, p. 160. Hereafter cited in the text as "PI" and "PaI," respectively.

33. See Jean Wahl, *Le malheur de la conscience dans la philosophie de Hegel* (Paris: Presses Universitaires de France, 1951). Wahl argues that the unhappy consciousness is a neglected form in Hegel's history and philosophical anthropology, equiprimordial with the master-slave dialectic. This form, being limited to certain "peoples" like the Jews, receives a highly localized qualification that misunderstands its significance.

34. As François Roustang said of Henry,

> If we cease to conceive of consciousness as experience understood as the relation of a subject to an object, but understand it rather as an appearing to itself or as auto-affirmation, then beneath the phenomenality of the visible, its original essence can be grasped. It is this that Descartes termed the "soul," that Schopenhauer named "body," Nietzsche "will to power," Freud "the unconscious," and what Henry prefers to designate as "life," that is, affectivity, that which is experienced in itself as pure immanence. (Roustang, introduction to Henry, *Genealogy of Psychoanalysis*, x)

35. Freud, "New Introductory Lectures," 22:86.

36. Ibid., 22:88.

37. I understand Henry's intent when he chooses the adverbial phrase "only in order to be made," but it is romantic to suppose that life "lives" somehow, at a human level, without consciousness. Of course it does, but not for long. It was Kierkegaard who recognized that as being-able-to, life is always already incipient *anxiety*. As such, life is consciousness even before this consciousness sets up an object for itself.

38. Levinas rejects the term "love" because it is already an intentionality, and because it can border on the erotic, or indeed because it is more ambiguous than being-for-the-other ever was. "The recurrence of the self in responsibility for others . . . goes against intentionality, such that responsibility . . . could never mean altruistic will, instinct of 'natural benevolence,' or love" (*Otherwise Than Being*, 111–12). It should be seriously considered how intense Levinas's apprehension of both *love and the erotic* remained throughout his long career, as though these would be the privileged keys opening the Pandora's box of an ontological permeation of the ethical. This repeatedly carries him close to *masochism:* "It is as though persecution by another were at the bottom of solidarity with another. How can such a passion take place and have its time in consciousness?" (*Otherwise Than Being*, 102).

39. Henry develops the contradictions in the relationship between drives, pleasure, and pain which unfolded over the course of Freud's career, especially between the "Introductory Lectures on Psycho-Analysis" (1916) and the "New Introductory Lectures on Psycho-Analysis" (1933). See Henry, *Genealogy of Psychoanalysis*, 298–316.

40. See Freud, "Beyond the Pleasure Principle," section 4: "What follows is speculation, *often far-fetched speculation,* which the reader will consider or dismiss according to his *individual predilection.* It is further an attempt to follow out an idea consistently, *out of curiosity* to see where it will lead" (*The Freud Reader,* 606).

41. Consider Freud's early draft on "How Anxiety Originates," which he sent to his friend Wilhelm Fliess. See Sigmund Freud, *The Complete Letters of Sigmund Freud to Wilhelm Fliess: 1887–1904,* trans. and ed. Jeffrey M. Masson (Cambridge: Harvard University Press, 1985), 78–83.

42. Søren Kierkegaard, *The Concept of Anxiety,* trans. Reidar Thomte with Albert B. Anderson (Princeton: Princeton University Press, 1980), 32.

43. As Levinas writes in "God and Philosophy" (1975): "If the intellection of the Biblical God . . . does not reach the level of philosophical thought, it is not because it thinks God as a *being* without explicating beforehand the 'being of that being,' but because, in thematizing God, intellection brings it into the course of being, whereas the Biblical God ignifies in an uncanny fashion . . . beyond being" (Emmanuel Levinas, *De Dieu qui vient à l'ideé* [Paris: Vrin, 1986], 95).

44. Simon Critchley, "*Das Ding:* Lacan and Levinas," in *Ethics, Politics, Subjectivity,* 198–216.

45. Freud's well-known and disingenuous obliviousness to philosophy is belied at many moments in "Beyond the Pleasure Principle," among other places. Note, in regard to the discussion of Levinas's "recurrence," Freud's avowal: "We have unwittingly [?] steered our course into the harbor of Schopenhauer's philosophy. For him death is the 'true result and to that extent the purpose of life,' while the sexual instinct is the embodiment of the will to live" (*The Freud Reader,* 618). A lengthy argument could show that Levinas's "Other" both resembles death, and functions in his logic to overcome death; moreover, the resemblance is not shed in the overcoming, and the latter is never complete. In a word, there is no rigorous separation between death and the other in Levinas's thought.

46. See Freud, "The Ego and the Id," 19:25.

47. This struggle takes various forms in Freud, but it is clear in later life. Note for instance, the 1930 essay "Civilization and Its Discontents." There, Freud argues against the necessity of defining the unconscious as what is closed to conscious access: "Since we overcame the error of supposing that the forgetting we are familiar with signified a destruction of the memory-trace . . . we have been inclined to take the *opposite view,* that in mental life nothing which has once been formed can perish—that everything is somehow preserved and . . . can *once more be brought to light*" (in *The Standard Edition,* vol. 21; emphasis added).

48. See Edmund Husserl, *Ideas I,* trans. F. Kersten (Dordrecht and Boston: Kluwer Academic Publishers, 1982), 110–111. He draws here the famous distinction between the "absolute being" of consciousness and the referred being of a world, especially a "world of transcendent 'res.'"

> In so far as its most universal sense is concerned, that has already been made clear by the exposition above. . . . A something transcendent is *given* by virtue of certain concatenations of experience. As given directly and with increasing perfection in percep-

tual continua which show themselves to be harmonious and in
certain . . . forms of thinking based on experience, a something
transcendent acquires, more or less immediately, its insightful,
continually progressive determination. (110–111)

Husserl assumes that the determinations of such a transcendent something can be effected by consciousness through its many "concatenations." Consequently, a transcendent "world," as utterly beyond the scope of "constituent mental processes," is not thinkable. In the place of the Kantian noumenon, we find an "adumbrated being" that might never be given absolutely, i.e., in all its *Abschattungen; and* a "necessary absolute being," consciousness itself, "essentially incapable of becoming given by . . . adumbration and appearance" (111).

49. Note Husserl's remark, "An object existing in itself is never one with which consciousness or the Ego pertaining to consciousness has nothing to do. . . . *Experiencableness never means a mere logical possibility,* but rather a possibility *rationally motivated* in the concatenations of experience" (*Ideas,* 106, author's emphasis; "rationally" appears in the margin of Copy "A").

50. Thereby reducing each phenomenon to the proper region in which it appears (eidetics) and bracketing logical and natural scientific assumptions about the unity of physical things and other "transcendencies" like Nature, universe, substance, or mechanical "laws" etc. (*Ideas,* 114 ff.).

The plural "phenomenological reductions" appears in *Ideas,* p. 66. Phenomenological reductions include here the phenomenological (60) and the transcendental *epoche* (65).

51. See Jacques Lacan, "Du 'Trieb' de Freud et du désire du psychanalyste," in *Ecrits* (Paris: Seuil, 1966–71), 851ff.

52. Louis Beirnaert, *Aux frontières de l'acte analytique: La Bible, Saint Ignace, Freud et Lacan* (Paris: Éditions du Seuil, 1987), 103 ff., my translation. Hereafter cited in the text as *AFAA.*

53. See Sigmund Freud, "Inhibitions, Symptoms and Anxiety," in *The Standard Edition,* 20:106–7, 124–26.

54. If I am under this judgment of the other, or the father, or God, I also and invariably forget the fact of this judgment. Is it absurd, then, to argue that it is "there" in some sense, perhaps unconsciously, and that we repeatedly discover it (or our moods disclose it as always already there)? This is the more compelling in that we do not discover it as a Perfect Being or a cause, but as a shaking up, a recurring remorse for the offense done, which is a remorse not reducible to everyday consciousness.

55. "The best [of Freud's] texts are those that flirt with the primacy of affectivity . . . , that speak of those tenacious memories of 'insults and humiliations,'. . . that in the return to consciousness of pathogenic memories emotion is reborn before its representative content" (Henry, *Genealogy of Psychoanalysis,* 316).

56. Freud, "The Ego and the Id," 19:23, including notes 2 and 3.

57. At one of the 1908 Wednesday night meetings, Freud praised Nietzsche for his prescience in regard to psychoanalysis. He added however, "What disturbs us is the fact that Nietzsche has transformed 'is' (*ist*) into 'ought' (*soll*). But such

an 'ought' is foreign to science. In this, Nietzsche remains a moralist and was unable to free himself from the theologians" (Paul-Laurent Assoun, *Freud et Nietzsche* [Paris: Presses Universitaires de France, 1980], 286 and 18).

58. There might be good reasons for supposing that psychoanalysis tends toward idealism, given Freud's assertion of laws in the unconscious. Freud encourages this at certain points. He writes, for example, in "The Unconscious": "The psycho-analytic assumption of unconscious mental activity appears to us . . . as a further expansion of the primitive animism which caused us to see copies of our own consciousness all around us, and . . . *as an extension of the corrections undertaken by Kant* of our views on external perception" (*The Freud Reader,* 577, emphasis added). Lacan explicitly rejects any such assimilation in his essay "Tuché and Automaton":

> [At] first sight, psycho-analysis seems to lead in the direction of idealism. God knows that it has been reproached enough for this—it reduces the experience . . . that urges us to find in the hard supports of conflict . . . the reasons for our deficiencies—it leads to an ontology of the tendencies, which it regards as primitive, internal, already given by the condition of the subject.
> (Jacques Lacan, *The Four Fundamental Concepts of Psycho-Analysis,* ed. Jacques-Alain Miller, trans. Alan Sheridan [New York: W. W. Norton, 1977], 53)

59. Perspicuous discussion of sensibility in Merleau-Ponty is found in Renaud Barbaras, "Le puissance du visible," in *Le tournant de l'expérience: Recherches sur la philosophie de Merleau-Ponty* (Paris: Vrin, 1998), 13–31.

Sensible Subjects: Levinas and Irigaray on Incarnation and Ethics

Diane Perpich

Can it be argued that embodiment is a necessary rather than contingent condition of the ethical relationship? And if so, then needn't we also conceptualize the ethical relation in terms of the question of sexual difference? That is, if ethical life has a meaning only for embodied beings and only on the basis of that embodiment, then isn't an ethics of sexual difference a necessary aspect of ethics? Two separate claims can be distinguished here, and will provide the focus for parts one and two of the paper, respectively.

The first claim posits the necessity of thinking the ethical relation on the basis of human embodiment. This could be interpreted as stating that human beings are, as a matter of (contingent) fact, embodied beings and that, therefore, an adequate theory of their relationships to one another will have to take this into account. In this form, the claim may be uncontroversial, but it is also fairly uninteresting, since it says little or nothing about how embodiment is ethically significant. Of greater interest would be a stronger claim to the effect that the very idea of an ethical relationship is meaningful only in connection with an understanding of subjectivity as embodied. In the first part of this paper, I contend that just such a non-contingent relationship between ethics and embodiment is at the heart of the philosophy of Emmanuel Levinas.[1] In particular, I want to argue that for Levinas the relation to absolute alterity—a relationship synonymous, for him, with ethics—is possible only as a relation between embodied or "carnal" beings.[2]

The second claim of the hypothesis, and the corresponding second part of the paper, considers the further necessity of thinking incarnation in relation to sexual difference. Here, too, it is possible to distinguish a weaker and a stronger version of the claim, and again it is the stronger version that is of interest. The weaker claim says something like this: since all living bodies are as a matter of (contingent) fact sexed bodies, then some attention will have to be given in any ethics of embodiment to the question of sexual difference. Like the weak version of the first claim, this says very little about the ethical significance of sexual difference, nor does it maintain an internal connection between an ethics of embodied subjectivities and the sexual specificity of bodies.[3] In the second part of the paper, I want to consider the stronger claim—central, I will argue, to the work of Luce Irigaray—that an ethics of incarnate beings is not secondarily or contingently an ethics of sexual difference, but from the first and necessarily so. For Irigaray, *only* an ethics of sexual difference will be sufficiently ethical. Where sexual difference is denied ethical relevance, where the sexually specific subject is replaced by the neutral or neutered agent, the formative experiences of ethical life—autonomy and responsibility, relations to oneself and to others—are distorted in the direction of an abstract, one-sided, and ultimately oppressive universality. In Irigaray's account, sexual difference is not only the exemplar or paradigm of a relation to alterity, it supplies the very morphology of that relationship.

Ethics and Incarnation: Levinas

On both sides of the Atlantic, the study of ethics has been marked in recent decades by a critique of subjectivity that rejects the abstract, disembodied ego of modern rationalism in favor of a concrete, particularized subject constituted by language and embedded in determinate material, cultural, social, and historical contexts. Within Continental philosophy, this "situated" or "decentered" subject has a long history associated first with the philosophies of Marx, Nietzsche, Freud, and Heidegger, and more recently with figures such as Lacan, Foucault, and Derrida. For Levinas and Irigaray, the critique of the modern subject, and the desire to reconceive the principal categories of subjectivity explicitly in intersubjective terms, form the shared horizon of their ethical projects. In this part, I want to outline the main elements of Levinas's reconceptualization of subjectivity, with particular attention to the way in which his reinterpretation makes embodiment central not only to our understanding of the subject, but to the possibility of an intersubjective ethical relationship. I will argue that, for Levinas, it is from the unique constituting-conditioned structure of embodied consciousness that ethics first arises as a possibility, and that, thus—and this is fundamental to Irigaray's appropriation of Levinas—ethics has a meaning only between incarnate beings and *on the basis of their incarnation.*[4]

In *Totality and Infinity,* Levinas develops an account of subjectivity that attempts to do justice to the ego as a power or spontaneity in the sense of Husserl's constituting consciousness, but that also recognizes the ego as an affectivity that finds itself in material and social circumstances whose meaning and intelligibility precede and condition it. On the one hand, the subject is a power or "work" of self-identification, a virile "I can" who not only grasps the world in thought, but actively confers a meaning on it. On the other hand, the subject is paradoxically dependent upon and conditioned by the very world it constitutes. The tension between these two poles is reflected in *Totality and Infinity* by the opposing intentionalities of representation and enjoyment.

Levinas's account of representation is based quite explicitly on the Husserlian theory of intentionality, and especially the distinction between *noesis* and *noema,* or between the act of representation and the object of representation.[5] Levinas recalls that for Husserl "the object of consciousness, while distinct from consciousness, is as it were a product of consciousness, being a 'meaning' endowed by consciousness, the result of a *Sinngebung*" (*TI* 123). The idea of a constituting consciousness expresses, according to Levinas, the rather extraordinary fact that in cognition or representation, "an object which is first exterior *is given,* that is, is delivered over to him who encounters it as though it had been entirely determined by him" (ibid.). Husserl's view, then, continues the tradition for which thought is always adequate to its object, though not in the sense that it actually grasps the object in toto. After all, Husserl argues explicitly that the object given in perception is never completely given, since I can never see all sides or aspects of it at once. Rather, the sense of adequacy here is that thought never fails to give itself the object as an ideal unity of meaning. Insofar as it thus delivers the object over to thought, representation shows itself to be a kind of creative mastering of the world in the production of intelligibility:

> Intelligibility . . . is a total adequation of the thinker with what is thought, in the precise sense of a mastery exercised by the thinker upon what is thought [such that] the object's resistance as an exterior being vanishes. This mastery is total and as though creative; it is accomplished as the giving of meaning. (*TI* 124)

The fundamental or characteristic structure of representation, then, is one in which the ego determines the other—confers a meaning on it, assigns it to its place in an intelligible order—without being determined by it in return. To be sure, it is not a question here of a creation or mastery that can project anything whatsoever onto the object; Husserl is clear that representation is guided or "motivated" by the object. But even as representation comes up against limitations, it constitutes these very limits as an object for consciousness, thereby reestablishing its primacy and recovering its position at the origin of intelligibility. Levinas thus describes the ego of representation as a "pure spontaneity" (*TI* 125) that reduces every exteriority to a moment of its own thought (*TI* 127).

Levinas argues, however, that representation is not the whole story of intentionality, and in fact, the picture of objectifying consciousness developed by Husserl—despite there being something quite right about it—presents an "uprooted" representation, or a view that detaches representation "from the conditions of its own latent birth" in a subjectivity that is not only theoretical but practical, and not only practical but first and foremost attached to or immersed in the world through enjoyment (*TI* 126). So long as it is conceived in abstraction from the corporeal subject, the mastery of representation seems complete and its spontaneity in the production of universal meanings seems assured. However, the notion of enjoyment that Levinas elaborates as the most fundamental structure of subjectivity belies this fantasy of totalization: "The naked and indigent body is the very reverting of representation into life" (*TI* 127). The subject that constitutes the world in an objectifying intentionality is nonetheless conditioned by that which it constitutes: the indigence and neediness of the body "affirm 'exteriority' as non-constituted" (ibid.), reversing the movement of representation.

> Representation consists in the possibility of accounting for the object as though it were constituted by a thought . . . In "living from . . ." the process of constitution . . . is reversed. What I live from is not in my life as the represented is within representation . . . If we could still speak of constitution here we would have to say that the constituted, reduced to its meaning, here overflows its meaning, becomes within constitution the condition of the constituting, or, more exactly, the nourishment of the constituting. (*TI* 128)

Hunger plays a constitutive role in Levinas's challenge to both the Husserlian and Heideggerian accounts of our mode of being in the world. To live from bread is not primarily to represent it to oneself, nor to act upon it or by means of it. Of course, food can be viewed as an object of thought or as equipment or fuel for the body, but only under exceptional circumstances or in contexts already determined by the demands of a theory. Levinas does not deny that one eats "in order to live" and that bread thus *does* exhibit the "in order to" [*wozu*] structure of Heideggerian equipmentality, but beyond that one also "lives from" bread, that is, one

enjoys it and lives in this enjoyment (*TI* 111). Even if the bread is constituted as an object for consciousness, its meaning is not exhausted in this
constitution. Levinas argues that the aliment, in both the enjoyment and
nourishment that it brings about, "overflows" every meaning that the subject bestows on it.

The surplus over meaning here "is not a meaning in its turn, [now]
simply thought as a condition" (*TI* 128). Certainly nourishing and enjoyment may become objects of representation; indeed, they may be represented as exceeding the very thought that thinks them. But this in no way
diminishes the surplus produced, according to Levinas: "The originality
of the situation lies in that the conditioning is produced *in the midst* of the
relation between representing and represented, constituting and constituted" (ibid., emphasis added). In living from the very world that I
seemed to create or bring forth in thought, in being nourished by the elements of this world, the "intentionality aiming at the exterior changes direction . . . becoming interior to the exteriority it constitutes" (*TI* 129).
The ego who constitutes the world must also be seen as a part of the world,
interior to it as its needs and enjoyment attest, but also always separable
from the world, able to seem to master it, even to produce it. This ambiguity, of a subject who is at once subjected to the world, but also free to
create and possess it, is the most fundamental characteristic, the lifeblood
as it were, of embodied subjectivity.

The question now arises, in what sense is this embodied subjectivity,
and the conditioned-constituting structure that defines it, the basis for
the ethical relation to the other? Why is the relation to absolute alterity—
a relation synonymous with ethics for Levinas—possible only on the basis
of this structure?

The ambiguity of embodiment, which enmeshes the subject in the
world even as it is the means of liberating oneself from this dependence
(*TI* 117, 164), produces a subject who is at the same time "open and
closed" (*TI* 148). On the side of "closed" subjectivity, the life of the ego in
the world is lived as the "reduction of every other to the same." Not only
constituting the world for itself in thought, the ego also possesses it concretely, reducing every object to a moment of its own economy. Things in
the world are undoubtedly other than me; however, their alterity is relative rather than absolute. The bread I eat or the landscape I contemplate
stand over against me, but "I can 'feed' on these realities and to a very
great extent satisfy myself, as though I had simply been lacking them.
Their *alterity* is thereby reabsorbed into my own identity as a thinker and
possessor" (*TI* 33). For Levinas, in acknowledged opposition to the Heideggerian description of understanding as a form of "letting be," com-

prehension is already a form of appropriation and mastery; it is the mode of being of an ego who is "at home" in the world, for whom the world is at his or her disposal.

On the other side, however, enjoyment leaves the subject open and vulnerable precisely insofar as a certain insecurity always threatens from the horizon. And while this insecurity "can not suppress the fundamental agreeableness of life," it does introduce a "frontier" into the interiority of enjoyment, a worry that is expressed as the "concern for the morrow" (*TI* 150). To enjoy the world is also to feel the threat of its disappearance in lack, pain, and ultimately in death. This is where the structure of embodiment becomes ethically salient: Levinas argues that only a being who is attached in this way to its enjoyments and who can be pained by their absence can be enslaved. And equally, only such a being is capable of an ethical relationship. Through enjoyment and suffering, the ego is laid open and made vulnerable to the Other.

In a discussion of willing in a late, and little-read, section of *Totality and Infinity*, Levinas argues that it is constitutive of the structure of willing that it does not fully coincide with itself; that is, the will cannot fully master the ins and outs of its own actions and products. In carrying out an action that it wills, the ego performs numerous other actions that it did not will. In pulling out the chair, one creases one's jacket or scrapes the floor. The action of moving the chair was willed, but the attending actions were not. Even more significantly, in work, the will produces an object whose future use and meaning it cannot control. "The fact that the will escapes itself, that the will does not contain itself, amounts to the possibility the others have of laying hold of the work, alienating, acquiring, buying, stealing it" (*TI* 228). This interval in which "willing escapes willing," in which the will is both open and closed, is a condition for violence: "Threat and seduction act by slipping into the interstice that separates the work from the will. Violence is corruption—seduction and threat, where the will is betrayed" (*TI* 229). Significantly, he adds, "This status of the will is the body" (ibid.).

It is not mere corporeality, but the manner in which embodiment entangles the ego in the world, making it both dependent and master, that is ethically significant:

> The will combines a contradiction: an immunity from every exterior
> attack to the point of positing itself as uncreated and immortal, . . . and
> the permanent fallibility of this inviolable sovereignty, to the point that
> voluntary being lends itself to techniques of seduction, propaganda, and
> torture. (*TI* 237)

Were the will only a constituting consciousness, a disembodied transcendental Reason, it would not be vulnerable to these attacks; the techniques Levinas mentions would fail to make an impact. But the contradiction in the will is not merely due to its being a rational will "housed" in an irrational or a-rational body. That Levinas rejects such a view is implied in the example of propaganda, which notoriously works through rational means in conjunction with material conditions. For Levinas, enslavement is an intrinsic possibility for a being whose mode of relation to the world is one of enjoyment (or embodied subjectivity); but so too is ethics possible and meaningful only for such a being. Only such a being is capable of the radical generosity of ethics.

In the first place, according to Levinas, it is not clear what two pure, disembodied reasons could give to one another, or do for one another, or need from one another. Indeed, Levinas observes that the very idea of *two* reasons is contradictory: "Reason has no plural; how could numerous reasons be distinguished?" (*TI* 119, see also 207). But second, and more to the point, only a being who is attached by its needs and enjoyments to the world could give anything to the other. Levinas sometimes makes this point by saying that only if I enjoy my bread can I give it to the other. The ethical moment in this lies not so much in my knowing the value of my gift, but in the possibility (which Levinas describes as exceptional) of tearing myself up from the order of being in order to be *for* the other.

If the meaning of the ethical arises in the extraordinary gesture of tearing the bread from one's own mouth to give it to the other, this is possible only for a being who "lives from" bread; that is, it is possible only for a sensible, incarnate subject who is conditioned by the world and involved in it in the mode of enjoyment, but who also maintains a reserve or a separation with respect to the world. What "counts" in this gesture—what is ethical in it—is that I give up my attachment, not for another stronger attachment, such as the pleasure of helping the other or out of sympathy or fellow feeling; what counts *as ethics* is the exceptional possibility of the ego's tearing itself up from being, despite itself, simply *for* the other. This possibility, which defeats the structures of both enjoyment and representation, and which cannot be reconciled within their methods of accounting, is the ethical possibility par excellence.

A full account of the connection between embodiment and the meaning of ethics in Levinas's thought would need to go on to consider the further formulations of the ethical relation and ethical subjectivity in *Otherwise Than Being, or Beyond Essence*. In this text, Levinas goes to even greater lengths to show the inseparability of the ethical relation from embodied, sensible subjectivity. At the moment, however, I want to turn to Irigaray's reading of Levinas in the essay "The Fecundity of the Caress," and specifically to her reinterpretation of his notion of incarnate subjectivity in a way that moves it in the direction of an ethics of sexual difference.[6]

Ethics and Sexual Difference: Irigaray

It should be noted at the outset that Levinas himself does not make the connection between an embodied subject and a sexed subject. Indeed, as is well known, the passages where Levinas discusses erotic love and the feminine other are among the most problematic in his work. The images employed to describe feminine alterity are stereotypically sexist, even in the way they contradict one another: the feminine is defined in terms of modesty and eternal virginity, but is also associated with voluptuosity, animality, and wanton nudity. The philosopher's own ambivalence toward erotic love is transmuted into ambivalence as the defining characteristic of the erotic, as Levinas argues that the erotic relationship is marked by equivocation and is both before and beyond the ethical relationship with a face. On the one side, erotic love is said to fall short of the transcendence of ethics: the couple in love produces a kind of solipsism of two and a return to the immanence of egoistic life; while the ethical relationship is said to be accomplished in language, the relation between lovers is described as lacking a language or as degenerating into cooing and laughter; the beloved does not command or draw the ego to responsibility, but threatens to drown him in an irresponsible animality. On the other side, in fecundity, the erotic relation is said to go "beyond" the face to face, beyond the ethical relation. In the production of a child—whom Levinas almost everywhere designates as the son—the subject enters into a relation with a being who is absolutely, irreducibly other, and yet who is also *mine*. In this sense, the transcendence of fecundity goes beyond even that of ethics.

Irigaray's reading of Levinas in "The Fecundity of the Caress" contests and reinscribes almost every element of this account. Categories such as voluptuosity, the caress, modesty, virginity, and fecundity are reinterpreted in a framework that valorizes the possibilities opened up in erotic love and that sees them as explicitly ethical. Further, whereas Levinas assumes that eros has an ethical component only where it is teleological, that is, only where it aims at and produces a child, for Irigaray, fecundity is not limited to reproduction, but is a fundamental ethical possibility of the self's own becoming.

Irigaray's essay is most often read as a critique of Levinas, but it might also be read—and it will be read here—as an enactment or production of the very sort of fecundity that is at issue in the essay. Describing the caress, Irigaray writes that it "weds without consum(mat)ing" and "perfects while abiding in the outlines of the other" (*ESD* 186). The caress neither consumes nor completes what it touches; it is a relation that follows the contours of the other, helping to define them, to show them to themselves, without either mastering or being mastered by the caressed body. The caress shapes and reshapes, "from within and from without, a flesh that is given back to itself in the gesture of love" (*ESD* 187). Irigaray's reading engages Levinas's work exactly in this mode of the caress. Abiding by the outlines of his text, Irigaray inhabits its language and structures, not as a parasite, or in order to subvert Levinas's text or force new meanings from it, but in order to reshape and adorn it. The alterity of Levinas's work will not be negated or reduced by Irigaray's reading, nor will his philosophy be completed as if it were merely lacking a full or adequate consideration of the question of sexual difference. Rather, Irigaray's aim is to make Levinas's ethics fecund, to regenerate it, to show it to itself differently.

In focusing on the erotic relation, Irigaray's reading is situated at the site of sexual difference in Levinas's text, but it needs to be recognized that this decision is not merely political. It is not just a matter of showing that the account of the feminine in Levinas's philosophy is false, distorted, or oppressive, or of then claiming the same rights and responsibilities for the feminine subject as are granted to the neutral ego of Levinas's descriptions. Rather, in returning to the site of the erotic body and in reinscribing it, Irigaray recovers a space within Levinas's thought for the becoming of feminine subjectivity—and for feminine subjectivity as becoming. Irigaray engages Levinas around the issue of the erotic not because this is a woman's issue or a feminist issue, or because Levinas has made it necessary for women readers to respond to this aspect of his work, but because it is from the vantage point of the erotic that it is possible to see, in Levinas's own terms, that the subject of the ethical relation is not just incarnate but is shaped from the first by and within a matrix of sexual difference.

"The Fecundity of the Caress" proceeds by means of a successive uncovering of the ethical meaning latent in the categories of the erotic or sensuous relationship. Primary among these is the sense of touch whose ethical possibilities are largely neglected by Levinas. In the opening lines of her essay, Irigaray writes: "On the horizon of a story is found what was in the beginning: this naive or native sense of touch, in which the subject does not yet exist" (*ESD* 185). For Irigaray, touch is more elemental, and more determinative of ethical subjectivity, than the category and structure of enjoyment. In enjoyment, even if the ego is conditioned by and dependent on what it enjoys, it nonetheless always retains the possibility of possession and appropriation of the world. The ego of Levinas's account may not be a subject "free as the wind," but it is a subject that "knows its objects and controls its relations with the world and with others. Already closed to any initiation. Already solipsistic. In charge of a world it enjoys only through possession" (ibid.). But touch belies this solipsism and the mastery or possession it promises. Touch, Irigaray insists, is in existence even "before orality"—that is, even before the subject can consume or introject its surroundings; "no nourishment [no enjoyment] can compensate for the grace or work of touching" (*ESD* 187). Essential to the structure of incarnate subjectivity, as Irigaray elaborates it, is the fact that the subject is touched before it is fully realized as an ego or an "I"; the subject thus preexists and precedes itself—not as potentiality precedes actuality, or capacity activity, but in a quite different manner unique to the mode of being of one who is *born*.

Eros and sensual pleasure return us to a site where there is an "evanescence of subject and object," a reversibility of toucher and touched that—in the manner of Merleau-Ponty's notion of the flesh—does not designate a confusion between orders or regions, but an intertwining without synthesis between interiority and exteriority. The touch of the caress is not a site where ego and other are fused or become one, but is the site where the boundaries between inside and outside, and thus between subjectivities, first come into being. This is what Levinas, especially, will have passed over or forgotten.

Irigaray writes that the other's hands first give me the contours of my own body. The famous "spontaneity" of the ego, which even Levinas feels compelled to give its due, is possible only after the fact, after the ego has been shown to itself, disclosed in its outlines by the hands that caress it without subjugating it. The child may accidentally find its own hands or its feet, but it is only when it is supported by the other's hands, shaped in and by them, that the infant ego has the possibility of discovering itself as a whole. Thus the caress gives birth to the self in the first instance, and later, after the advent of subjectivity, the lover's caress enables new discoveries, new births of the self: "The most subtly necessary guardian of my life is the other's flesh. Approaching and speaking to me with his hands. Bringing nourishment, the other's hands, these palms with which he approaches without going through me, give me back the borders of my body and call me to a remembrance of the most profound intimacy" (*ESD* 187). The caress is thus "prior to and following any positioning of the subject"

(*ESD* 186). It is the "call to birth" of the subject and the other, determining subjectivity as a "prolonged quest for a birth that will never take place, whose due date still and always recedes on the horizon" (ibid.).

Irigaray identifies this movement of becoming with the "fecundity" of love "prior to any procreation." Love "fecundates" each of the lovers in turn, giving each of them life. They are "reborn for each other," each one "welcoming" the birth of the other (*ESD* 190). This journey of rebirth and regeneration is a "perpetual transvaluation," an endless creation and becoming that Irigaray calls a "passage to immortality" or the divine (*ESD* 26–27).

The difference between these respective accounts of ethical subjectivity could easily be minimized; after all, both make sensuous enjoyment fundamental to the possibility and meaning of the ethical relationship. Moreover, both reinterpret the categories of subjectivity in a way that opens it at the center of its being to the encounter with the other. However, for Levinas, the ethical consists in the ego's tearing itself up from being and its enjoyments to make a gift of itself to the other. Ethics consists in a transcendent relation to an Other who separates or "absolves" himself from the relationship, remaining irreducibly and absolutely other. For Irigaray, the ethical relation is a relation to transcendence as well, but to what she calls a "transcendence in the sensible" (*ESD* 53), that is, to a becoming within the sensible, with and through another.

For Irigaray, it is touch, preceding enjoyment, that opens up the interval that constitutes the ego's relation to itself and to the other. It is not the attachment to the world that produces a subjectivity that is at once "open and closed," but the more elemental fact of touching and being touched, of a touching that goes beyond touching by calling forth, shaping and giving birth to the one touched. For Levinas, the subject's capacity to close itself off, to reduce every other to the same, is given a kind of primacy—at least in the descriptions of *Totality and Infinity*. Moreover, in both *Totality and Infinity* and *Otherwise Than Being*, ethics occurs as the reversion of self-sufficient egoism into vulnerability to and being-for the other. For Irigaray, the carnal subject who is born in the caress is first of all open, in the specific sense of being constituted by a certain porousness, neither interior nor exterior, but on or as the threshold which permits movement from the one to the other. The caress that brings the subject into being is from the first an ethical gesture: it "binds and unbinds" the ego and the other (*ESD* 186). And to the extent that it gives rise to subjectivity, the subject is from the first both an erotic subjectivity—a subjectivity born in the caress—and a subject thus implicated in ethics.

An Ethics of Becoming

One observation and two questions by way of a conclusion. First, Irigaray's idea of ethics as a "transcendence *in* the sensible" leaves ethics open to more ambiguity than Levinas sometimes seems to want. As an erotic relationship, that is, a relation carried out upon and through the bodies of subjects, between subjects who not only have but *are* their bodies, ethics on Irigaray's account always risks falling back "this side" of ethics. The caress which gives the subject to itself, showing it its own contours, always has the simultaneous possibility of turning the subject into a thing, treating it as mere matter or as a mere body. In other words, there seems to be nothing in this ethics that guarantees the difference between caresses and blows, neither the intention of the one who caresses nor the freedom of the one who is caressed.

Although Levinas insists on our seeing ethical subjectivity as embodied subjectivity, and stresses the manner in which the human will is fallible and permanently open to the possibilities of violence, he nonetheless tries in many respects to quell the ambiguity that arises from embodiment. This is most evident in the tensions that pervade the descriptions of the ethical relationship in *Totality and Infinity*—e.g., in the idea of a face that commands through destitution, or of a heteronomy that does not subjugate freedom but first permits it, and so on. It is not clear that in Irigaray we have this sort of command structure, or this desire for ethics as commandment. Ethics here would seem to consist not of my being *for* the other (being commanded to responsibility by the other), but of a being which is already with and through the other.

This brings me to my two questions, one of which has to do with the idea of sexual difference, and the other with the normativity of Irigaray's account, or of the sense in which it is an *ethics*. First, is the ethics that Irigaray proposes an ethics of sexual difference or an ethics of erotic difference? On the one hand, I'm tempted toward the view that this is an ethics of *erotic* difference, which is to say, of a subjectivity that is marked by or that bears an irreducibly erotic structure. Calling this an ethics of erotic difference might help, at least partially, to avoid a reductive reading of Irigaray's claims in terms of biological or physiological categories. Furthermore, the notion of erotic difference has the advantage that it allows for more than just one difference, not only the difference between two sexes but between a plurality of erotic bodies or sexually specific beings. On the other hand, I think there are important reasons not to erase the term "sexual difference" or the problems to which it gives rise. If the notion of erotic difference seems to open up the possibility for "more" difference in one register, it forecloses difference in another insofar as it suggests that there is one principal kind of difference—the erotic—and one common experience of subjectivity. Irigaray's rereading of Levinas is motivated precisely by the desire to show the plurality of subjectivity, to show the possibilities of thinking subjectivity *as* or through a plural becoming. Her reading requires us to rethink the constitutive relations or categories of subjectivity outside of or beyond the traditional oppositions between interiority and exteriority, self and other, identity and difference. And the carnal subject, born in the caress, is not just any subject whatsoever, is not a universal, abstract ego, but precisely this specific, incarnate, sexual, erotic being. Subjectivity is brought into being already in a relation to a sexually specific other (the mother), and this alterity (though not *only* this one) mediates the self's relation to itself and to the world. Thus, every subject is positioned and re-generated in a complex and fluid set of interrelations—of proximities, Levinas might say—that must be thought not only with the help of the concept of the erotic but also with the notion of sexual difference.

In the opening essay of *An Ethics of Sexual Difference,* Irigaray makes a number of rather bold claims on behalf of the notion of sexual difference. Citing Heidegger's observation that each age thinks through but a single issue, she suggests that "sexual difference is probably the issue in our time which could be our 'salvation' if we thought it through" (*ESD* 5). She claims it could "constitute the horizon of worlds more fecund than any known to date—at least in the West—and without reducing fecundity to the reproduction of bodies and flesh (ibid.). In order for this to come about, there must be a revolution both in theory and in action: "We need to reinterpret everything concerning the relations between the subject and discourse, the subject and the world" (*ESD* 6). Moreover, or especially, we must reconsider and reinterpret the categories of space and time insofar as these determine the problematic of the relation of interiority to exteriority, and thus determine subjectivity itself.

What would be the aim of this wholesale reconceptualization? Toward what or where would an ethics of sexual difference tend? Or, more simply, what *sort* of ethics is this? Irigaray concludes: "In order for an ethics of sexual difference to come into being, we must constitute a possible place for each sex, body, and flesh to inhabit" (*ESD* 17–18). Each one must be given a place, not as a way of solidifying or fixing identities, but as a place from which the self can make an "overture" to the future, a place that will constitute a threshold to a "growth and flourishing still to come" (*ESD* 19). The ethics proposed here, then, is an ethics of the future. Or perhaps better, one could say that this is neither an ethics of being, nor of the beyond being, but of the interval between—an ethics of perpetual becoming.

Notes

1. Works by Emmanuel Levinas cited in the text are as follows: *Totality and Infinity*, trans. Alphonso Lingis (Pittsburgh: Duquesne University Press, 1969); *Otherwise Than Being, or Beyond Essence*, trans. Alphonso Lingis (The Hague: Martinus Nijhoff, 1981). Hereafter cited in the text as *TI* and *OB*, respectively.

2. Treatments of Levinas's thought have not always recognized the importance of embodiment to his reinterpretation of the ethical relationship. The reasons for this oversight are legion, but perhaps the most important is the scant attention paid in the secondary literature to the sections of *Totality and Infinity* on enjoyment and interiority and of *Otherwise Than Being* on sensibility. Readings of Levinas sensitive to the important role of embodiment in his thought may be found in Rosalyn Diprose, *The Bodies of Women: Ethics, Embodiment and Sexual Difference* (London: Routledge, 1994) and Ewa Ziarek, *An Ethics of Dissensus: Postmodernity, Feminism, and the Politics of Radical Democracy* (Stanford: Stanford University Press, 2001), especially chapter 2.

3. For example, from the premises that all sentient beings feel pain, and that pain is undesirable, one could argue that we have a prima facie obligation not to cause sentient beings unnecessary pain. In this case, embodiment is ethically salient, but sexual difference may not be.

4. This essay leaves to one side the question of whether embodiment in the sense at issue here could serve as the basis for an ethical relationship between humans and animals. It is clear that Levinas himself restricts the ethical relationship to human beings, though he does so not on the basis of some exclusively human quality such as language ability or higher-order rationality. For Levinas, the problem of ethics is not that of accounting for the origin of my responsibility to the other, hence his philosophy cannot coherently be read as a matter of determining which qualities I or the other must possess in order to "count" as human or as worthy of moral respect. The problem of ethics, for Levinas, consists precisely in elaborating the ethical relationship as a relationship that outstrips the categories of metaphysics and of our relationships to things; it is thus a relation that is without a foundation not only in fact, but in principle.

5. Of course, *noesis* and *noema* are not reducible to the act and object of representation; as Levinas points out, Husserl accords a privileged place to representation in his account of the constitution of objects both in the *Logical Investigations* and in *Ideas*: "The thesis that every intentionality [whether willing, desiring, liking, avoiding, etc.] is either a representation or founded on a representation dominates the *Logische Untersuchungen* and returns as an obsession in all of Husserl's subsequent work" (*Totality and Infinity*, 122).

6. Luce Irigaray, "The Fecundity of the Caress," in *An Ethics of Sexual Difference*, trans. C. Burke and G. Gill (Ithaca: Cornell University Press, 1984), 185–217. Hereafter cited in the text as *ESD*.

Conditions: The Politics of Ontology and the Temporality of the Feminine

Tina Chanter

The metaphorics of sexual difference overtly orchestrates Levinas's critical response to Heidegger, but it also operates in ways that elude Levinas, whose self-commentary on other aspects of his own writing is so prevalent and so arresting. The way in which the feminine functions in Levinas's texts, often in an explicitly subordinate or supporting role to the dominant themes, would appear to exceed or refuse to be contained by the very structures that might seem to keep it in check. If the face of the other who calls me to infinite responsibility interrupts the metaphysics of presence in a dramatic and exceptional way, the withdrawal of the feminine from the categories of ontology effects its own interruption, and requires to be thought in relation to the more obvious exception to being that the ethics of the face to face exacts.

It does not seem to me to be adequate to treat the feminine, as the vast majority of Levinas's commentators have done, as subsidiary to the real import of Levinas's philosophy, by dismissing it as easily resolvable in a footnote or in an aside, or merely neglecting the theme altogether. Whether one approaches Levinas's work as defined by an ethics of alterity, as a critical engagement and confrontation with Heidegger's ontology, or as I shall approach it here—as a profound meditation on time that takes shape as a response to Heidegger's own reflections on being and time, the question of the feminine must be thought in its structural implications for Levinas's philosophy.[1] Nor is it adequate to treat Levinas's discussion of the feminine, in its various configurations as eros, in the dwelling, and as maternity, as if it constituted a seamless part of his philosophical interrogation, which can be unproblematically recuperated by the main contours of his ethical discourse.[2] Both alternatives underestimate the importance of the structural role of the feminine, and both leave aside the question of the politics of reading Levinas.

If, as Levinas claims, "I have access to the alterity of the Other from the society I maintain with him, and not by quitting this relation in order to reflect on its terms," and if "sexuality supplies the example of this relation" such that "the other sex is an alterity borne by a being as an essence and not as the reverse of his identity," how do social structures affect, inform, constitute, or condition the relation I maintain with the Other?[3] If sexuality is "accomplished before being reflected on" (*TI* 121, *TeI* 94), what is incorporated into the notion of accomplishment? Does Levinas exploit an ambiguity that allows him both to assume the social, sexual, racial, or political norms that are given in a particular society, so that he can endorse, without appearing to, a patriarchal and Zionist understanding of paternity and fecundity, by presenting himself as a philosopher who undercuts those norms by disengaging ethics from politics, and claiming not to prejudge the identity of individuals? If so, how are these two directions played out, and how are they implicated in Levinas's reflections on time and history?

Ontological Difference, Sexual Difference, and Time

> to be a body is to have time
> —Levinas, *Totality and Infinity*, 117

Heidegger's ontological difference has a central and lasting significance for Levinas. By tracing Levinas's insistent return to and recasting of the ontological difference not as a distinction but as separation, and as amphibology, it becomes possible to see that there is an important sense in which Levinas never completely overcomes the Heideggerian problematic. Levinas's philosophy of time must be read as a response to Heidegger's critique of the Western metaphysical concept of time. Heidegger maintains that metaphysics, from Aristotle on, has been sustained by a concept of time that is based on a confusion about being and time. He characterizes the tradition as adhering to a naive metaphysics of presence. The themes of sexual difference, corporeity, and the meaning of the instant play a structuring role not only in Levinas's early work (where they are investigated in terms of solitude, for example), but also in his later work, under the heading of sensibility, for example. Even those readers who have provided interpretations of Levinas which take up some of the earlier themes in order to follow through how they are recast in the later work have neglected, in my view, to explain the importance of the feminine and corporeity in Levinas's work, or to expand sufficiently on the relation between time and the instant.

In a 1977 preface to the second edition of *Existence and Existents*, Levinas remarks upon the passage between *Totality and Infinity* and *Otherwise Than Being* in terms of his attempt to rethink the ontological difference. One cannot simply reverse, he suggests, Heidegger's famous ontological difference by giving priority to beings over Being, as *Totality and Infinity* might be said to do.[4] Rather, and this is what Levinas identifies as the effort of *Otherwise Than Being*, one has to go beyond this initial reversal, and allow the infinite to signify from "beyond the ontological difference."[5] In a footnote, Levinas refers to the work of Jean-Luc Marion, and Marion responds to Levinas in an essay that first appeared in 1986.[6] Marion argues that Levinas's notion of "amphibology is substituted for that of difference because 'beyond or on the hither side' of Being and beings (*AE* 55, 63; *OB* 43, 49), an absolutely new term, as yet unnamed, insinuates itself. From the outset, the ontological difference no longer offers a goal, but only a point of departure, a given to be over-interpreted and destroyed" ("OI" 27). Marion continues:

> One result is decisively established: ethics is instituted by a new difference, a difference of the second degree, between, on the one hand, the entire ontological difference and, on the other hand, the Saying. Therefore, the beyond of the ontological difference absolutely cannot, here, be confused any longer with a reversal of the terms inside the ontological difference to the benefit of beings. ("OI" 28)

But to regard "the ontological difference" as "only a point of departure, a given" to be "destroyed" is, I suggest, to overlook the perpetual need that Levinas's philosophy exhibits to refer back to the ontological difference, if only to give it new meaning. It is also to risk obliterating the significance of all the work that Levinas does in infusing the corporeal and the temporal with a significance that Heidegger could not achieve, because his appeal to "ontological finality" (*EE* 42, *DE* 64) did not allow for any consideration of materiality apart from its significance in the overall structure of *Dasein*'s care for existence. If Heidegger "thereby failed to recognize the essentially secular nature of being in the world and the sincerity of intentions" (*EE* 42, *DE* 65), does not Marion neglect the bodily aspect of existence that facilitates the very idea of sincerity to which he wants to appeal, and does he not thereby short-circuit the very difficulty, to which he had earlier alerted us, of situating the ontological difference within Levinas's corpus? Marion says that

> sincerity phenomenologically destroys the terms of the ontological dif-
> ference: "A fission of the ultimate substantiality of the ego, sincerity is
> reducible to nothing ontic, to nothing ontological and leads as it were
> beyond or on the hither side of everything positive, every position" (*AE*
> 183, *OB* 144). Exactly as, for Heidegger, anxiety leads into the ontological
> difference, for Levinas, sincerity is excepted from it and liberates from it.
> ("OI" 31)

Does sincerity absolutely destroy the ontological difference, and is it completely liberated from it? What about the "ultimate substantiality of the
ego" to which Levinas refers us in the very quote that Marion provides, "an
ultimate substantiality . . . even in the very vulnerability of sensibility," as
Levinas puts it at the beginning of the section of *Otherwise Than Being*
from which Marion quotes?[7] What about the "constraint to give with full
hands, and thus a constraint to corporeality" (*OB* 142, *AE* 181)? It does not
seem to me that these references to substantiality, and position, to hands
and corporeality, are merely gratuitous.

The issue that Marion raises speaks to a central problem that has oc-
cupied other prominent readers of Levinas; that is, the question of how to
think ethics in relation to ontology.[8] One of the major theses of this paper
is that the relation of priority between the two cannot adequately be addressed without taking up the relationship between ontological difference and temporality. It will also be suggested that a thorough investigation of this relationship reveals precisely the import of corporeality in
Levinas's philosophy, another aspect which commentators have been slow
to elaborate. And finally, it is necessary, I maintain, to follow out the
theme of sexual difference, which structures Levinas's recasting of ontological difference and time from his early to his late work, but whose implications for his critique of Heidegger have also been largely neglected.

To see this more clearly, it is worth recalling that Levinas conceives
of his philosophy as an attempt to break with the notion of Eleatic being
that he thinks dominates not only Parmenides and Plato, but even extends to Heidegger's attempt to renew the efforts of Greek philosophy to
think Being.[9] Levinas's analyses of "sexuality, paternity and death" facilitate the break with Eleatic being because they "introduce a duality into
existence, a duality that concerns the very existing of each subject" (*TO*
92, *TA* 88). Paternity will answer to Levinas's attempt to conceive of a "plu-
ralist existence" (*TO* 54, *TA* 34). He says, "I do not *have* my child; I *am* in
some way my child. But the words 'I am' here have a significance different
from an Eleatic or Platonic significance" (*TO* 91, *TA* 86). Levinas thereby
elaborates anew the ontological difference, by showing that the task of

existing to which the existent (or, in Heidegger's terminology, *Dasein*) is in some sense condemned—in the sense that the self finds that existence is unavoidable and inescapable—is in another sense capable of encountering another dimension, an alterity that cannot be reduced to the identity of the I, or even to the knowledge that belongs to the I.

> The return of the ego to itself that begins with hypostasis is thus not without remission, thanks to the perspective of the future opened by eros. Instead of obtaining this remission through the impossible dissolution of hypostasis, one accomplishes it through the son. It is thus not according to the category of cause, but according to the category of the father that freedom comes about and time is accomplished. (*TO* 91, *TA* 86)

This is a remarkable claim. Without the category of the father, Levinas is saying, there will be no freedom and no time.

In attending to the function of hypostasis, and to solitude, and materiality, and enjoyment, Levinas not only reworks the ontological difference, but several other fundamental themes from *Being and Time,* such as the meaning of existence, world, everyday life, the for-the-sake-of, the role of the present, being-with-others, death as freedom, and forgetfulness. Thus, for example, "everyday life is already a way of being free from the initial materiality through which a subject is accomplished" (*TO* 63, *TA* 46), and "far from constituting a fall, . . . forms the very accomplishment of solitude. . . . [It] is a preoccupation with salvation" (*TO* 58, *TA* 39).[10] There is, in Levinas's reorientation of Heidegger's analysis, an insistent sexualization of two divergent aspects or tendencies of existence. On the one hand there is the virility of mastery, and on the other hand there is the passivity that Levinas will associate with the feminine. This differentiation is not to be thought of as a straightforward opposition between the active mastery of the subject and its passive submission, but rather as a duality that consists in the task of existing itself, or the necessity of having to be oneself. For what is at stake is precisely a rethinking of the ontological difference, which would preclude assuming a dichotomy between activity and passivity that already presupposes what is at issue in Levinas's return to the ontological difference, namely that the subject is already constituted in relation to a world of objects. In thinking through the ambiguous situation whereby a subject takes on its existence, Levinas no more assumes that the world is already constituted than he does that the subject is already imbued with the traditional characteristics of subjectivity, such as consciousness, freedom, and the capacity to know the world. The "I" is "neither a thing, nor a spiritual center" but "has to be grasped in its amphibological mutation from an event into an 'entity,' and not in its objectivity" (*EE* 79–80, *DE* 136). Bound up in Levinas's departure from Heidegger's rendering of death as ultimately the ground of *Dasein*'s virile, solitary, and masterful freedom is a reassessment of the meta-phorics of sight that accompanies it, and which is suggested by the word "lucidity." Levinas says, "Death in Heidegger is an event of freedom, whereas for me the subject seems to reach the limit of the possible in suf-fering" (*TO* 70, *TA* 57–58), and he marks the contrast by identifying Hei-degger's comprehension of death as masculine, while rendering his own as feminine. Thus, "Being toward death, in Heidegger's authentic exis-tence, is a supreme lucidity and hence a supreme virility" (*TO* 70, *TA* 57), while for Levinas "the unknown of death signifies that the very relation-ship with death cannot take place in the light" (ibid.).[11] Levinas thereby associates the unknowability of death with "the feminine" as "a mode of being that consists in slipping away from the light," or as "a flight before light," as "hiding" and as "modesty" (*TO* 87, *TA* 79).

Levinas explicitly counterposes the mastery that resides in "the viril-ity of grasping the possible, the *power to be able* [*pouvoir de pouvoir*]" (*TO* 82, *TA* 73), with death as "the limit of the subject's virility, the virility made possible by the hypostasis at the heart of anonymous being, and manifest in the phenomenon of the present, in the light" (*TO* 74, *TA* 62). The very terms that Levinas adopts to designate the mystery and unknowability of death insist that the "passivity" through which death announces itself is not just resistant to the language of experience and light (*TO* 70, *TA* 57), but that the vocabulary of light—and the concepts of vision, mastery, grasping, possessing, and knowing with which it is inevitably associated—are wholly inapplicable to the approach of death, in the face of which "we are no longer *able to be able*" (*nous ne pouvons plus pouvoir*; *TO* 74, *TA* 62). Further, Levinas wants to rehabilitate a notion of the present that does not simply fall prey to the idea of mastery that caused Heidegger to question the privilege of the present. Above all, it is the ambiguity of the present that Levinas is at pains to emphasize. "It is essential," says Levinas, "to grasp the present at the limit of existing and the existent, where, in func-tion of existing, it already turns into an existent" (*TO* 52, *TA* 32). Here we are returned, once more, to the ontological difference. By "positing the present as the mastery of the existent over existing, and in seeking in it the passage from existing to the existent" (*TO* 54, *TA* 34), Levinas wants to re-tain the complexity of the presencing of the present both as "pure event that must be expressed by a verb"—analogous to the verbal sense of being—and as a being "already a something, already an existent" (*TO* 52, *TA* 32)—analogous to *Dasein*, the being that exists. The ambiguity of the present is due to the fact that it is "a way of accomplishing the 'starting out from itself' that is always evanescence. . . . Evanescence would thus be the essential form of beginning" and yet it "result[s] in something" (*TO* 53, *TA* 32–33), it turns into an existent, and can be formed into time (*TO* 53, *TA* 33).[12]

There is, then, the aspect of mastery that Levinas associates with the present, and which he consistently marks as virile, and there is the limit or loss of mastery that Levinas associates with suffering, death, and love, and which he consistently marks as feminine. Thus there emerges a contest between the virile mastery of a self capable of preserving itself, and an effeminate self, one that finds itself unmanned, "unable to be able," deprived of all its powers, wounded in love (*TO* 89, *TA* 82), incapable of exerting its power of reason over the alterity that confronts it, be it in death, or eros. Before commenting further on this sexualized language, which (as will be clear by now) I take to have a significance beyond rhetorical embellishment, let me lay out in more detail what I have already hinted at, namely, the fact that Levinas does not assume that the subject is invested with freedom from the start.

Let me briefly restate the trajectory I am following. I am pointing out (1) how a sexualized language infuses Levinas's entire thought, his notions of self, freedom, and ethics; (2) how paternity is the privileged model of the relation to the other; and (3) how the sexualization of Levinas's discourse leads to complex questions about the conditionality of his philosophy that commentators have ignored to date for the most part. The father is the "category" that allows time and freedom to be introduced, but hypostasis is that which is somehow "before time" or allows time to appear. I will suggest that the feminine plays a similar structural role to the "before time" of hypostasis, but in a way that remains unthought by Levinas, and by his commentators. To thematize the "before" of the feminine both throws into relief the structural dynamic of the temporality of conditioning that allows Levinas to say what he is saying, and performs and enacts the aporetic relations that are inadequately framed as oppositions in Levinas's texts (ethics/ontology, infinity/totality, saying/said).

In this context, I cannot lay out his account in much detail, but Levinas puts hypostasis to work in a way that departs from its traditional resonance (as Llewelyn also notes). It allows Levinas to think how time, or freedom, or ethics first appear, and in trying to think this, Levinas's thought once again coincides with, even as it veers away from, that of Heidegger, who, in understanding Being as *Ereignis,* which in turn he renders as "appropriation or event of appropriation," cautions that we should "bear in mind . . . that 'event' is not simply an occurrence, but that which makes any occurrence possible."[13] Marking both the distance (insofar as

Heidegger's philosophy remains limited to a thinking of Being) and the proximity (insofar as it attempts to think Being as an event that makes any occurrence possible) between his own thinking and Heidegger's, Levinas claims that "everything that will be said of this *Ereignis* in *Zeit und Sein* is already indicated in §9 *Sein und Zeit*."

While Levinas distances himself from positing the Other as freedom, there is a sense in which he affirms the freedom of the existent, not as a free will, but as a freedom of beginning. The freedom of beginning is associated with virility. "As present and 'I,' hypostasis is freedom. The existent is master of existing. It exerts on its existence the virile power of the subject. It has something in its power" (*TO* 54, *TA* 34). Solitude is necessary for this virile mastery, for the "freedom of beginning" (*TO* 55, *TA* 35). But this first freedom has a price: "the definitiveness of the I riveted to itself" (*TO* 57, *TA* 38; translation altered), which Levinas identifies as a "great paradox: a free being is already no longer free, because it is responsible for itself" (*TO* 55, *TA* 36).[14] If this freedom is already a responsibility, in what sense does it remain free?[15] Levinas says, "Though it is a freedom with regard to the past and future, the present is an enchainment in relation to itself. The material character of the present does not result from the fact that the past weighs upon it or that it is anxious about its future. It results from the present as present" (*TO* 55–56, *TA* 36). So this freedom that is not yet freedom is at once virile and masterful, and passive and responsive.

Thus Levinas articulates two different modes by which an event is accomplished when he distinguishes between the event of hypostasis, "by which an existent arises" (*TO* 88, *TA* 81), associated with virility, freedom, power, and mastery; and the "event of alterity" (*TO* 87, *TA* 80), associated with the feminine, mystery, withdrawal, and modesty. "The existent" says Levinas, in a statement that is crucial for understanding what is happening in the sexualization of his discourse, "is accomplished in the 'subjective' and in 'consciousness'; alterity is accomplished in the feminine. This term is on the same level as, but in meaning opposed to, consciousness. The feminine is not accomplished as a *being* [*étant*] in a transcendence toward light, but in modesty" (*TO* 88, *TA* 81). By claiming that the feminine is "not accomplished as a being" Levinas appears to be privileging the feminine in a certain way, by situating it in a dimension, or allowing it to designate a domain that cannot be qualified as ontological. The feminine would thereby seem to indicate an escape from being; its otherness would be governed not by the powers of mastery that define the self, not by the freedom of self-initiative, not by consciousness, but would come from elsewhere. The feminine is the absolutely other. In this way, the feminine would seem to interrupt the language of ontology, and would seem to provide access to a new way of thinking ontological difference, by not immediately identifying itself with the turning of existence into existents, by resisting the illumination of the world. It would seem to stand for a mode of being's withdrawal.

Levinas's appeal to the feminine has therefore been heralded as radical. The "exceptional position of the feminine in the economy of being" (*TO* 86, *TA* 78) is celebrated, because it facilitates a break with being. Without wishing to entirely discredit or contain whatever radicality might be claimed for Levinas's notion of the feminine, I do not want to immediately grant its revolutionary status. Instead one would need to proceed more slowly, by asking about how the feminine functions for Levinas in relation to terms such as fecundity, paternity, and the son.

It is clear that Levinas does not want his use of the term "feminine" to function in a way that is reducible to a member of the female sex. His intentions in this regard are overtly stated, and have often been remarked. Ontologically, too, it seems clear that we would simply be mistaken to equate what Levinas means by the feminine with women as such. If the "feminine is not accomplished as a being," whatever meaning is to be granted to it cannot be assimilated with the empirical woman. It is rather a way or mode of being, a tendency, a regime. Levinas's intentions, and the ontological function of the feminine, might preclude feminist objections to his use of the term, were it not for the fact that intentions and ontology, as Levinas himself maintains, do not count for everything. And so we find Levinas resorting to language that, despite his disclaimer, does indeed assume the empirical woman (*TI* 155, *TeI* 128–29), and we find him affirming that "welcome in itself" is "the feminine being" (*TI* 157, *TeI* 131). Even if we take this to mean a being (male or female) that is feminized, the question remains as to how this being which is not quite a being is to be thought, and even more pertinently, who is to think it. Even if we keep in mind that it is the ontological equivocation of the feminine, or its very ambiguity (or perhaps, amphibology) as a being that is unknowable, or a being that is accomplished not in light but in modesty, still it must be asked, how the feminine is figured.

The fact that it is impossible to simply equate what Levinas means by the term "feminine" with individual subjects does not mean that all the problems raised by his use of this term, and his systematic differentiation of it from other sexualized terms, are resolved. To assert that the feminine is intended metaphorically, far from solving all the questions, merely reintroduces them at another level. As Sonya Sikka concisely asserts, "metaphors matter."[16] Neither is it satisfactory, in my view, to simply suspend the political questions that impose themselves as secondary to the ontological function that terms such as the "feminine" play in Levinas's philosophy, as if politics and ontology could be so easily distinguished, or as if the politics of ontology did not inform its very vocabulary.

Is there a way to read the feminine in Levinas's texts that avoids short-circuiting the resources it provides for breaking out of the closure of ontology, for disrupting its said, and at the same time refuses to naively bracket the implications Levinas's discourse has for feminism? Having begun to address this question with reference to Levinas's early work, I want to continue to perform this balancing act, initially by attending to the role of the feminine in *Totality and Infinity,* and then by moving on to some later texts, including *Otherwise Than Being.*

Levinas is critical of what he regards as the supreme virility of Heidegger's *Dasein,* and offers instead an account of subjectivity that remains open to the other, an account that privileges alterity over sameness, responsibility over freedom, infinity over totality. Rather than becoming a ground for the spontaneous or free action of a resolute *Dasein,* death retains an essential mystery for Levinas, remaining ungraspable, unknowable, and refractory to light. The future retains a genuine novelty of alterity that sets it apart from any present that can be mastered, or from *Dasein's* authentic realization of its own truth through the anticipation of finitude in anxiety. Levinas says:

> This future is neither the Aristotelian germ (less than being, a lesser being) nor the Heideggerian possibility which constitutes being itself, but transforms the relation with the future into a power of the subject. Both my own and non-mine, a possibility of myself but also a possibility of the other, of the Beloved, my future does not enter into the logical essence of the possible. The relation with such a future, irreducible to the power over possibles, we shall call fecundity. (*TI* 267, *TeI* 245)

Through fecundity, across generations, the privilege of the constant, self-identical, and masterful I breaks up, as the child offers the possibility of a new beginning that escapes every project I might have for him.

Levinas seems to offer a philosophy that is other-oriented, generous, and which prioritizes the ethical relation as one that is not chosen, but through which I am elected; he seems to break the hold of the subject of mastery, knowledge, and control.[17] His philosophy thus appears to share in common several affinities with feminism. The problem is that, on closer inspection, Levinas's version of alterity is permeated with a conceptual metaphorics that revolves around paternity, filiality, and fraternity by reinscribing the most traditional and patriarchal of Judaically inspired assumptions about the privilege of the father and his relation to the son, and the subordination of the feminine to the properly ethical and infinite relation. While providing a potential ally for feminists, he seems to endorse a position that is deeply problematic for women. I suggest that the feminine remains the privileged unthought in Levinas's philosophy, aporetically organizing his philosophy in a way that throws into question the adequacy of the traditional transcendental modes of thinking what conditionality means.

In *Adieu to Emmanuel Levinas,* Derrida suggests that whatever else can be said of the feminine, a certain indisputable privilege of the feminine as the welcome before all welcoming is not to be forgotten. He says,

> whatever we might speak about later, and whatever we might say about it, we would do well to remember, even if silently, that this thought of welcome, there at the opening of ethics, is indeed marked by sexual difference. Such sexual difference will never again be neutralized. The absolute, absolutely originary welcome, indeed, the pre-original welcome, the welcoming par excellence, is feminine: it takes place in a place that cannot be appropriated, in an open "interiority" whose hospitality the master or owner receives before himself then wishing to give it. (*AEL* 44–45)

In exhorting us to remember that the pre-original welcome is indelibly marked as feminine and in suggesting that this marking of sexual difference will never be erased, Derrida focuses his attention on the following passage from *Totality and Infinity:*

> The home that founds possession is not a possession in the same sense as the movable goods it can collect and keep. It is possessed because it already and henceforth is *hospitable for its owner.* This refers us to its essential interiority, and to the inhabitant that inhabits it *before every inhabitant, the welcoming one par excellence, welcoming in itself—the feminine being* [Derrida's emphasis].[18]

Let me make two further observations about how this passage is taken up by Derrida. First, having already gestured toward whatever else could be said of the feminine (a gesture that anticipates and defuses in advance the significance of "whatever we might speak about later"), Derrida does concede, later, that while the feminine claims a certain privilege as the preeminent welcome, it is through paternity that a relation with the infinite is maintained. Referring to the concluding pages of *Totality and Infinity,* Derrida says, "Where the feminine being seemed to be the figure of the 'welcoming one par excellence,' the father now becomes the infinite host or the host of the infinite" (*AEL* 94).

Second, Derrida indicates two disparate readings of this passage. One would "make of this text a sort of feminist manifesto. For this text defines the welcome par excellence, the welcome or welcoming of absolute, absolutely originary, or even pre-originary hospitality, nothing less than the pre-ethical origin of ethics, on the basis of femininity" (*AEL* 44). Notwithstanding Derrida's defusing of the paternal function that Levinas will go on to endorse, which in fact amounts to nothing less than a complete reversal, a thorough overturning, an exchange or substitution of the feminine face for the masculine, Derrida does not want to choose between a feminist reading and another reading, one which raises concerns about the "classical androcentrism" (ibid.) of Levinas's understanding of femininity. He asks, "Need one choose here between two incompatible readings, between an androcentric hyperbole and a feminist one? Is there a place for such a choice in an ethics? And in justice? In law? In politics? Nothing is less certain" (ibid.). By refusing to acknowledge any certainty about whether one can make a choice between a reading that would make of Levinas a spokesperson for feminism, or one that would criticize him for his traditionally androcentric views, has Derrida by default thrown his lot in with the privilege he, as a man, is free to assume? Perhaps there is no imperative for him to make such a choice. Or is he rather raising the question of the possibility of safeguarding a place for a feminist critique of Levinas? Perhaps he is pointing out that there can be no safe place for such a reading to situate itself, that no dwelling, no domicile, no home can protect such a critique, because wherever it might reside, wherever it might make a home for itself, inhabiting a domain that it can make its own, such a place is itself never exempt from critique. Any place that feminism marks out for itself is not exempt from calling itself into question. Feminism itself, far from being immune from the tendency to colonize, must be called to account for itself. In concluding, I will return to this issue. I want now to turn to an issue that Derrida raises, but one which he fails to thematize—what I am calling conditionality.

In order not to repeat the error of a philosophy of representation, which imagines its subject as sovereign and answerable to nothing outside itself, Levinas needs to think through the conditions of representation. The task is complicated not only by the fact that there is more than one condition of representation, and that the senses in which these conditions representation differ, but also (and partly as a consequence of the fact that there is more than one sense of conditioning at play here) because to think something as a condition is to reduce it to a meaning (to a said), and the sense in which representation is rooted in something other than a representation is precisely the sense in which representation finds itself conditioned by a surplus that it did not produce.[19]

Among the conditions for representation Levinas includes the dwelling, which, he says, "cannot be forgotten" (*ne saurait être oubliée; TI* 153, *TeI* 126–27). This formulation is worth pausing for. To say that the dwelling cannot, should not be forgotten, is also to acknowledge that it is forgotten, and (like Heidegger's question of Being) that it needs to be remembered. Indeed, the power of representation rests precisely upon the illusion of forgetting where it comes from; it presents its knowledge as if it were purified of any history or any legacy, as simply present. In fact, Levinas says, "the dwelling cannot be forgotten among the conditions for representation, even if representation is a privileged conditioned, absorbing its condition" (ibid.), thereby immediately conceding that although dwelling must not be forgotten, the privileged status of representation makes us forget it, by absorbing the very condition that facilitated it, allowed it to emerge, or (if we avoid thinking this phrase in the strictly transcendental mode, which reduces it to a thought) made it possible.

Levinas takes his distance from Descartes' categorical distinction between the physical extension of matter characteristic of bodies, on the one hand, and the thought that characterizes the mind, on the other hand, yet he does not want to follow Heidegger, whose notion of worldhood glosses over the distinction between the physical and mental. He departs from Heidegger precisely by retaining some aspects of the Cartesian differentiation of body and mind, even while not wanting to reproduce the distinction with any exactitude, neither adhering to Descartes' metaphysical commitments in this regard, nor maintaining the distinction as categorical. In this respect, Levinas's return to Descartes' understanding of bodies resembles Lacan's.

Levinas retains what he calls "the profound insight Descartes had when he refused to sense data the status of clear and distinct ideas, ascribed them to the body, and relegated them to the useful" (*TI* 130, *TeI* 103). According to Levinas, the "profundity of the Cartesian philosophy of the sensible consists . . . in affirming the irrational character of sensation, an idea forever without clarity or distinctness, belonging to the order of the useful and not of the true" (*TI* 135, *TeI* 109). Like Kant, who also separates sensibility from understanding, Descartes affirms that sensibility is not "situated on the plane of representation" (*TI* 136, *TeI* 109). Levinas calls the order of sensibility that of enjoyment, rather than experience (*TI* 137, *TeI* 110). He says, "The sensitive being, the body, concretizes this *way of being*, which consists in finding a condition in what, in other respects, can appear as an object of thought, as simply constituted" (*TI* 136, *TeI* 109).

For Levinas the body appears not, as it does for Descartes, "as an object among other objects, but as the very regime in which separation holds sway" (*TI* 163, *TeI* 137). The body is thus not wholly passive, as the classic interpretation of Descartes has it, nor is its active dimension circumscribed by Heideggerian equipmentality, which "presupposes a primordial *hold* on things, possession," without recognizing "the being established at the threshold of an interiority the dwelling makes possible" (ibid.). "In . . . paradisal enjoyment, timeless and carefree, the distinction between activity and passivity is undone in agreeableness [*agrément*]" (ibid.). There is a "primordial equivocation" that exists as the body (*TI* 164, *TeI* 138), so that "life is a body, not only lived body [*corps propre*], where its self-sufficiency emerges, but a cross-roads of physical forces, body-effect" (ibid.). Corporeal existence is not simply independent; rather, it "affirms its independence in the happy dependence of need" (*TI* 165, *TeI* 139). The paradox that Levinas had earlier understood as a freedom that is already responsible for itself is here recast as the indigence of the body, a body that is nevertheless capable and resourceful, with the ability not only to satisfy its needs, but to be happy in its enjoyment of food, walking, fresh air, or drinking coffee. "The body indigent and naked" changes or reverses the play of constitution (*TI* 129, *TeI* 102).

If dwelling, which frames and enables the being capable of satisfying its needs, and able to be happy in the enjoyment of the life it thereby lives, is among the conditions of representation, there is another condition that must be considered. The idea of infinity conditions everything that is said in *Totality and Infinity,* in that Levinas affirms its "philosophical primacy" (*TI* 26, *TeI* xiv). It is as infinite that the Other interrupts the presumption of Western philosophy that the self must be founded in the self. Levinas says, "To posit knowing as the very existing of the creature, as the tracing back beyond the condition to the other that founds, is to separate oneself from a whole philosophical tradition that sought the foundation of the self in the self, outside of heteronomous opinions" (*TI* 88, *TeI* 60). Contrasting representation and the welcoming of the Other, Levinas says, "The total freedom of the same in representation has a positive condition in the other that is not something represented, but is the Other" (*TI* 126, *TeI* 98). This Other commands my attention, yet, like the feminine other in the dwelling, who can (but should not) be forgotten, the infinity and transcendence of the Other can be forgotten. Levinas says that "the possibility of this forgetting is necessary for separation" (*TI* 181, *TeI* 156). The feminine can be forgotten because it is discreet (*TI* 170, *TeI* 145) and silent, but how can the idea of infinity be forgotten? Because of atheism (see *TI* 181, *TeI* 156), according to Levinas, or the idea that a free being can be created.[20]

Contemplation comes "after" the dwelling, that is, "after the suspension of the chaotic and thus independent being of the element, and

after the encounter of the Other who calls in question possession itself"
(*TI* 163, *TeI* 137). The problem I want to focus on here is what sense can
be given to this coming "after" or following on from both the dwelling and
the Other. In other words, in what sense does the dwelling, and the feminine welcome that gives shape to life as being at home with oneself, condition representation, and in what sense is the infinite Other a condition
of representation?

The Temporality of Representation:
After the Event

"A movement radically different from thought is manifested when the
constitution by thought finds its condition in what it has freely welcomed
or refused, when the represented turns into a past that had not traversed
the present of representation, as an absolute past not receiving its meaning from memory" (*TI* 130, *TeI* 103). This absolute past or "unrepresentable antiquity" is the "world which precedes me" (*TI* 137, *TeI* 111). A
"relation of myself with myself is accomplished when I stand [*me tiens*]"
(*TI* 37, *TeI* 7). I have already pointed out that representation rests on the
illusion that there is nothing outside itself, that it is answerable only to itself. But for Levinas, "the represented, the present, is a *fact,* already belonging to the past" (*TI* 130, *TeI* 103). Levinas is at pains to point out that
representation is not without conditions, among which he includes on
the one hand the dwelling, and the feminine or woman who conditions the
dwelling, and on the other hand the infinitely Other, whom I must encounter in order to "see things in themselves," and in order "to know how
to *give* what I possess" (*TI* 171, *TeI* 145).

What then is the relation between the discreet feminine presence,
and the infinite presence that forbids murder? Levinas never articulates
it as such, except inasmuch as he makes clear that the dwelling at home
with oneself that is the domain of the feminine is one that I must "be able
to free myself from" (*TI* 170, *TeI* 145) in order to "welcome the Other" (*TI*
171, *TeI* 146). The feminine is thereby relegated to the same, while the subject who has benefited from being in relation to it "is ashamed of its
naiveté" and "discovers itself as a violence" (ibid.). Is this being ashamed
of the feminine? Again, this is left unclear by Levinas, who does however
tell us that the "discretion" of the feminine "includes all the possibilities
of the transcendent relationship with the Other" (*TI* 153, *TeI* 129), without providing us with many clues as to what this could mean, or how possibility can be thought here. The gentleness, grace, and radiance of the

feminine face that provides the first welcome is meant to cut across formal and dialectical logic, according to Levinas (*TI* 150–51, *TeI* 124–25). But how exactly does it function? The feminine would seem to provide an implicit model for the giving that the I can only come to know through the infinitely Other who does not welcome me, but challenges me from above, from a height. Alison Ainley has pointed out that both Kant and Levinas draw on the feminine in similar ways, by seeing it as an initial, implicit, but informal ethical imperative.[21]

Levinas develops a formal comparison between representation and enjoyment in terms of their different relations to temporality. Representation is characterized as total presence. The same determines the other without being determined by it (*TI* 124, *TeI* 97).[22] "The same in relating itself to the other refuses what is exterior to its own instant" (*TI* 125, *TeI* 98). Thus,

> Every anteriority of the given is reducible to the instantaneity of thought and, simultaneous with it, arises in the present. It thereby takes on meaning. To represent is not only to render present "anew"; it is to reduce to the present an actual perception which flows on. To represent is not to reduce a past fact to an actual image but to reduce to the instantaneousness of thought everything that seems independent of it; it is in this that representation is constitutive. (*TI* 127, *TeI* 100)

The constitutive power of representation lies in its reduction of past and future to an intelligible instant, or a "pure present" that is "void of time, interpreted as eternity" (*TI* 125, *TeI* 98). By contrast, the "intentionality of enjoyment . . . consists in holding on to the exteriority which the transcendental method involved in representation suspends. To hold on to exteriority is not simply equivalent to affirming the world, but is to posit oneself in it corporeally. The body is the elevation, but also the whole weight of position" (*TI* 127, *TeI* 100).

Whereas in representation the same determines the other but the other does not determine the same, in enjoyment, the "same both determines the other while being determined by it" (*TI* 128, *TI* 101), but not reciprocally. Levinas uses the term "living from . . ." to designate this plane or "the way in which the same is determined by the other," a way which "is brought about by the body whose essence is to *accomplish* my position on the earth" (ibid.).

The formal comparison is complicated in part by the fact that one of the conditions of enjoyment is in fact representation, and that representation itself is conditioned by enjoyment, or "representation is conditioned by life" (*TI* 169, *TeI* 144). So although the intentionality of enjoyment reverses that of representation, "the body naked and indigent" is also "conditioned by its own representation of the world" (*TI* 127, *TeI* 100). Thus, representation reverts into the life that conditions it (ibid., and *TI* 169). In turn, representations themselves sustain life, and we live from them. The intentionality of the "world I live in" is thus both a "conditioning and an antecedence" (*TI* 129, *TeI* 102) in the sense that "I welcome" sensible objects "without thinking them" (*TI* 137, *TeI* 110–11), yet, as we saw, "conditioning is produced in the midst of the relation between representing and represented" (*TI* 128, *TeI* 101), and in this sense its conditioning is already caught up in constitution.

The order of sensibility as a mode of enjoyment recollected in the dwelling circumvents the present of representation, and in doing so, it engages with temporality in a way that does not conform to the model of mastery, domination, and conquest. Even if it is inextricably bound up with the constitutive time of representation, which reduces the past and future to a present, the intentionality of enjoyment also undercuts its virile movement, and in this way it offers a way of thinking time that is open to alterity. To take account of the peculiar conditionality of the feminine, the way in which the feminine both conditions ethics, and yet cannot be contained by the thought that thinks its status as a condition, must we say that there are two versions of welcome in *Totality and Infinity*? Must we say that each is achieved or produced by a movement that Levinas calls accomplishment, or must we distinguish between two modes of accomplishing left unspecified by Levinas? One mode of welcoming would occur under the sign of the feminine, while the other would take its place under the auspices of the masculine, having already made a home for itself thanks to the feminine. There would be the welcome of contentment, where a "relation of myself with myself is accomplished when I stand [*me tiens*] in the world which precedes me as an absolute unrepresentable antiquity" (*TI* 137, *TeI* 111). This first, feminine welcome of the dwelling would be associated with materiality, sensibility, and the corporeal. The second, masculine welcome would be the "welcome of the other by the same that is concretely produced as ethics which accomplishes the critical essence of knowledge" (*TI* 43, *TeI* 13).

Welcoming does not aim at the other as an object, it is not a thought; it is rather a way of the same being determined by the other. Although the first feminine welcome is replicated by the second, and moreover the second, masculine, ethical welcome takes place in virtue of the dwelling, the relation between the two is not clearly articulated by Levinas. This is, I suggest, because of the diachronic temporality that governs Levinas's thinking of the feminine, but in a way that remains inarticulate. While inarticulate, it nevertheless facilitates Levinas's saying. The dwelling, as that which is primarily enjoyed, rather than represented, cannot be thought strictly as a condition, which would reduce it to a thought. Is to think the feminine as a condition thus necessarily to destroy its openness to alterity, or its welcome, to reduce it to thematization, represent it as if it were a pure present, rather than an absolute past?

Must we say that ultimately the feminine that conditions the dwelling, facilitates recollection, provides a delay and a postponement, remains unthought and unrepresented? And if the feminine is unthought, is it unthought in the same way that the Other infinitely escapes representation? The Other contests my powers, but the feminine welcomes. The other calls me into question, but the feminine allows the appropriation of a domain for-me. The other requires that I think the condition of my life, but the feminine dwelling requires no thought; in fact it tends, as we have seen, to be forgotten. Can the feminine be thought only after the Other has made representation possible? But what would this "after" mean here, given that we are always already in the midst of representation, and others? To insist, as Derrida does in *Adieu,* that the third does not wait for the face, or to emphasize that the feminine is not understood by Levinas as outside of language, only as excluded from the "transcendence of language" (*AEL* 37), does not solve all the problems raised by the temporality of the feminine. To the extent that Levinas reminds us of the feminine, even if he maintains it as a silent, discreet dimension, he has uncovered a tendency, regime, or way that is usually neglected, overlooked, and ignored by philosophers. The feminine facilitates sensibility as a way of "living from" that runs counter to the mastery of representation, which puts the subject at the center of its world, reduces the object to *noemata,* reduces everything to the same. It thus offers a critique of the virile masculine will to conquer. Yet, the "very possession that the welcome of the Home establishes" is what the I must free itself from (*TI* 170, *TeI* 145).

Let me pose some questions to Levinas. If there always has to be some being—whether this is a way or manner of being, a particular being, or the female sex—to create a dwelling, does this being have to be the same being over time? Is its identity fixed by its function? Or can the role of the feminine be performed by different identities at different times— in which case, what sense can be made of retaining the term "feminine"? Can Levinas's notion of diachrony help to make sense of such a suggestion? By divorcing the term "feminine" from the empirical woman (insofar as he does so successfully), Levinas seems to point beyond a politics of identity. But in requiring that there be someone to perform the feminine function, without clarifying if this function can be shared, Levinas seems to require relations of domination and submission, however these are parceled out between the sexes. Can alternative communities be envisaged without someone to facilitate the dwelling? Is there a place to think the conditions of representation outside the home? Such questions return us to Derrida's concern, when he asks whether there can be a place for such questions in the realm of justice and politics. Derrida is right to suggest that the feminine in Levinas cannot be divorced from questions of national identity as they relate to the meaning accruing to the state of Israel. But perhaps the idea of the dwelling as refuge or exile that performs as a model for thinking Israel as a place for "political invention" marks the feminine as the privileged unthought of Levinas's philosophy.[23]

How can there be a present that is anterior to the time in which it is represented or known? The problem, which dominates so much of Levinas's philosophy, can be specified with reference to the temporality of the saying and the said, with reference specifically to the dual register of what Levinas, retrieving language he had earlier reserved for the feminine, calls in *Otherwise Than Being,* the "lapse of time." Time belongs to ontology, and yet, "In this said, we nonetheless surprise the echo of the saying, whose signification cannot be assembled" (*OB* 27, *AE* 38). Levinas both identifies the lapse of time with being and sees it as otherwise than being. "To explore an otherwise than being will still give an ontological said, in the measure that all monstration exposes an essence" (*OB* 44, *AE* 56). Rather than being hamstrung by the (apparent) dilemma—either the saying can only figure negatively and in opposition to the said, or it is completely subsumed by, contained in, and defused by the said—Levinas turns the problem around, and declares that "there is question of the said and being only because saying or responsibility require justice" (*OB* 45, *AE* 58), or that "one had to go back to that hither side, starting from the trace retained by the said, in which everything shows itself" (*OB* 53, *AE* 69). Thus the "saying has to be reached in its existence antecedent to the said, or else the said has to be reduced to it" (*OB* 46, *AE* 59).

What allows Levinas to claim that the "lapse of time irrecuperable in the temporalization of time is not only negative like the immemorial" (*OB* 51, *AE* 66)? The passage from the merely negative to the positive is marked by the "very patience of corporeality, the pain of labor and ageing" (ibid.), and by the exposure of "no longer dwelling" (*OB* 49, *AE* 95). Just as the welcome of the feminine face in the dwelling is not yet the ethical welcome of the face to face, if it is a pre-original welcome, and if enjoyment somehow precedes representation, yet discovers itself as always consequent upon the primordial status of the other, so maternity is not yet thought or consciousness, although "maternity, vulnerability, responsibility, proximity, contact—sensibility can slip toward . . . consciousness of . . . pure knowing" (*OB* 76, *AE* 165). Maternity thus prepares "the birth of thought, consciousness, justice and philosophy" (*OB* 128, *AE* 165) that

Levinas identifies with the "third party," without itself being identified with "this concern for justice" (*OB* 160, *AE* 204). There is a certain exorbitance in the "corporeality" and "materiality" signified in the "obsession by the other" that Levinas names maternity (*OB* 77, *AE* 97), as "body suffering for another, the body as passivity and renouncement, a pure undergoing" (*OB* 79, *AE* 100), as "wounded entrails." As the "ultimate sense of . . . vulnerability" (*OB* 108, *AE* 137), maternity indicates an attachment that is "irrecuperable" (*OB* 104, *AE* 137), and therefore resists representation. In the plot of sensibility as maternity, "I am bound to others before being tied to my body" (*OB* 76, *AE* 96). But what is the status of this before?

Maternity both describes "responsibility for others" (*OB* 106, *AE* 135) as a "complete being 'for the other'" (*OB* 108, *AE* 137), and at the same time it remains on the hither side of thought and consciousness, always preparatory. It can "slip toward" knowledge, but it is not yet knowledge. In the strategic role that is performed by maternity, which allows the textual progression to justice, to the third party, to the birth of thought (*TI* 128, *Tel* 101), but which itself does not measure up to the demands of justice, we have seen that the formal problem that Levinas confronts in sustaining the claims he wants to make about time is also reflected in his use of the language of sexual difference. I am suggesting that the relationship between time and sexual difference is not limited to a formal analogy, but is rather that which drives his thinking in a way that remains unreflective and resistant to his own otherwise infinitely careful articulation of language in relation to himself.

To give a charitable reading of how Levinas's rigorously sexualized, but relatively unthematized, language functions, would be to credit him with having seen the radical potentiality of the feminine to break up the categories of being, and create the possibility of ethics. A less generous reading would consist in recalling that Levinas reiterates the most traditional stereotypes when he characterizes the feminine as a dimension of silence, mystery, hiding, modesty, withdrawal, domesticity, and maternity.

The problem of the feminine comes into play at three different levels, which are necessarily interrelated, but also bear following out independently of one another, so far as this can be achieved.

1. First there is the textual movement facilitated or set in motion by the feminine, and brought to a resolution, completion, or closure by paternity. Thus the feminine is associated with the first (pre-original) welcome, in the dwelling, a welcome that breaks with the constituting intentionality of thought, and to this extent anticipates the welcome of the face to face, but it remains within the economy of the same, and in this sense does not approximate to transcendence of welcoming the absolutely

other. Similarly, eros prefigures the radical discontinuity of an infinite time that finds its fulfillment in the relations between the father and son. As a relation with mystery, the erotic relation with the feminine heralds the time of fecundity, in which the father presides over the birth of a son. Paternity is needed to complete the movement toward alterity that the feminine had begun.

2. Second, there is the formal or structural function of the feminine as it is invoked as an exception to being, as a breakdown of the systematicity of thought, as an interruption of totality. Thus the feminine is the withdrawal from being, a delightful lapse in being; unthinkable in terms of light, it is modesty and hiding. The face of the feminine is silent, without language, its presence is discreet. The sensibility of enjoyment, over which the feminine presides in the dwelling, cannot be adequately captured in the language of intentionality or phenomena. Structurally consonant with the infinite or the beyond of ethics, insofar as it cannot be contained by the language of thought and representation that nevertheless comes to represent it, the feminine is also that which defies comprehension.

3. Finally, there is the paradigmatic role that the feminine plays as preliminary, as a first sketch of the ethical, as a kind of prolegomena. The feminine seems to provide an implicit model for the break with totality that the ethical command of the other effects. Always preparatory, it never quite advances to the pure transcendence of absolute alterity, but remains indispensable as a kind of stepping-stone on the way to the infinite. Yet this preparatory role cannot be acknowledged as such, since to do so would be to lessen the radicality of the ethics it announces. The problem that the feminine names in Levinas's work can be stated more generally by referring back to the difficulty Levinas confronts in claiming that the present can signify outside of representation, or that diachrony is irreducible to the synchronization of thematization, or that the saying goes beyond the said, is otherwise than essence. As irrecuperable by ontology, the feminine would seem to retreat into the inaccessible, capable only of negative signification. Yet to subject the ineffable mystery of the feminine to the light of day, to render it accessible through thematizing it or representing it, would be to destroy its mystery. The feminine must both remain inexpressible and somehow communicate its energy to language, being, and the said. Here the feminine finds a parallel with the role that death plays for Heidegger in *Being and Time*—and it is perhaps not insignificant that the thought of death and the structures of finitude desert Heidegger in *The Basic Problems of Phenomenology* and thereafter, after having been a driving thematic in *Being and Time*. This retreat or withdrawal of what had been a decisive theme for *Dasein*'s authentic self-understanding finds an

echo in Levinas's denial of the feminine the status of the absolute other in *Totality and Infinity,* after he had designated it alterity par excellence in *Time and the Other.* If the feminine conditions reflection—by way of a conditioning that exceeds the thought that thinks it after the fact—who or what will provide a safe place for the feminine? Feminism cannot claim a safe place, free of challenge, nor should it. It must take responsibility, however, for thinking about which others it exploits, and how and why it does so, in making a claim for itself. Invoking "alternation and diachrony as the time of philosophy" (*OB* 167, *AE* 213), Levinas proposes that "truth is in several times" (*OB* 183, *AE* 231). A feminism that takes account of Levinas's diachronic notion of temporality should recognize both the need to maintain a disruptive effect in the refusal of the feminine to accommodate the categories of being, totality, or ontology, of never simply being a subject of knowledge, mastery, and recognition; and the need to assert that women must be recognized and thematized as subjects in the register of the said, taken account of by a history that, while covering over alterity, has also afforded its subjects the privilege of recognition.

Levinas's wariness of political identities grounded on identity, whether defined ethnically or otherwise, is more than understandable given the Nazis' reduction of people to their identities as a basis for their exclusion and annihilation from the nation state. Feminist theory has also grown wary of identity politics. If we take Levinas's rhetoric of sexual difference to signify beyond a merely rhetorical strategy, how then is the conditionality of the feminine to be thought in relation to an ethics that claims to be prior to and exclusive of its politics?

The question we are confronting here cannot be divorced from the question of how the political stands in relation to Levinas's philosophy in general. Can the question of politics ever be responsibly raised for Levinas, or does it always degenerate into an assertion of the privilege of egoism that Levinas so stridently denounces? More polemically, it could be asked whether ethics and politics are as discontinuous from one another as Levinas assumes. As Derrida suggests, the "border between the ethical and the political . . . was never pure, and it never will be" (*AEL* 99). If this is indeed the case, then it follows that we must regard with suspicion the distinction to which Levinas implicitly appeals when, having subordinated politics to ethics, he invokes another politics, a messianic politics.[24] This politics is supposed to be beyond politics as usual, beyond the politics of nationalism and universalism, and it allows Levinas to affirm Zionism, without appearing to make a gesture that can be reduced to the merely political (in the usual, and according to Levinas, non-ethical sense of the political).[25]

On the question of how to think Levinas's philosophy in relation to the political, Derrida suggests: "It might be asked, for example, whether the ethics of hospitality . . . in Levinas's thought would be able to found a law and a politics, beyond the familial dwelling, within a society, nation, State, or Nation-State" (*AEL* 20). It should be noted that this formulation already brackets certain pertinent questions about a feminist politics insofar as it eschews comment about how far the dwelling already contains the feminine. Derrida goes on: "This question is no doubt serious, difficult, and necessary, but it is already canonical." Not wanting to assume that a politics can be deduced from "Levinas's ethical discourse on hospitality," Derrida prefers to read the "hiatus" between politics and Levinas's ethics more positively, asking whether their disjunction opens "the possibility of another speech . . . where decisions must be made and responsibility, as we say, taken, without the assurance of ontological foundation?" (*AEL* 21). Following up on this question, Derrida says that "without the hiatus, which is not the absence of rules but the necessity of a leap at the moment of ethical, political, or juridical decision, we could simply unfold knowledge into a program or course of action. Nothing could make us more irresponsible; nothing could be more totalitarian" (*AEL* 117). Derrida also specifies the responsibility that Levinas calls for as one "where I alone must respond" (ibid.). If I am right to suggest that in the masculine privilege Levinas assumes, and which plays itself out conceptually in the fecundity of paternity, the scrupulous care that Levinas takes to speak in his own name, and not as a subject of any universal law, deserts him, and if the feminine pays the cost and bears the burden of this desertion, the responsibility that Derrida points to suffers a relapse, of which women are often the casualty.

By allowing women to signify otherness, Levinas continues a long tradition of male-authored texts which figure the feminine as unknowable, mysterious, ineffable, unrepresentable, and intractable. Does he thereby repeat, however unwittingly or unwillingly, the same exclusionary gesture that denies women language, and confines them to a gestural, corporeal, asocial psychosis? Or does his insistent privileging of alterity over sameness, even when it suffers a relapse at certain strategically predictable points, open up a space for the radical rewriting of the feminine? Certainly there are moments in Levinas's texts in which the virile economy of philosophical logic reverts to an affection and exposure of passivity to alterity, as in eros, or in the caress. Perhaps, in keeping with the vacillation of the saying and the said, a more ambivalent reading is called for, one that is both too generous, perhaps infinitely so, and one that is less than generous, perhaps necessarily so.

An infinitely generous reading of the trope of the feminine in Levinas would take its cue from the sense in which maternity hesitates between the saying and the said, as sensibility and vulnerability on the one hand, and as an irrecusable responsibility that is already an ethical response to the face on the other hand, already opening onto the political through the third party. One could perhaps read Levinas's notion of paternity as a model of generosity, although I am less willing to do so, because this possibility seems to depend upon leaving aside not only the context of the ultimately traditional significance Levinas attaches to the feminine, but also Levinas's attachment to a Zionist politics that passes for a politics of peace which would be nonpartisan.

I have also suggested, less generously, that the feminine as such remains captive to its preparatory role in Levinas's work, and in this way Levinas repeats the all too familiar gesture of confining women to the hearth, the home, the private realm, and excluding them from the public, political domain, which is reserved for the seriousness of masculine affairs. Thus the upright straightforwardness of the face to face is specified as the paternal relation to the son, and the discontinuity across generations is accomplished as fecundity, which, while requiring the feminine, still keeps the feminine in its subordinate place to the father and the son who complete the diachronous relationship. The feminine is entrusted with an initial interruption of the rhythms of the continuous time of history or totality, but only for the higher purpose of the properly transcendent masculine relationship that it initiates.

Both generosity and a lack of generosity are necessary in reading Levinas. There is a time for both, and these times are disparate. Diachrony does not efface their differences, or preserve them as part of a greater totality. It affirms their difference and it questions the priority and purity of the transcendental. There are moments, and in their novelty these moments can only present themselves to be decided at the time, when the infinite patience that Levinas exemplifies (if not calls for) is required, and there are moments when a political consideration is called for, one which will lack patience, discretion, or generosity.

What governs the relationship between generosity and a lack of generosity? I leave the question open, for one person cannot answer for another.

Lest this openness be misunderstood, let me merely say this. I am not suggesting that we should subordinate the philosophical to the political, and I am not issuing a rallying call. I am saying that to reduce the enabling function of the feminine in Levinas's philosophy to a formal oscillation that both exceeds and makes possible the ethical is to tame or homogenize the material and sensible disruption that is thereby recognized. The relation between the saying and the said, between the beyond and representation, must be kept in play in a way that leaves open the question of their priority at a particular instant, a priority that cannot be situated in advance, or according to a program, to be sure, but a priority that must be kept in mind as an irrepressible question. There is no simple equivalence between the tendency of the saying to congeal into a said, and the sense in which the modality of the saying both prepares for or conditions the said, and is the site of its reversion.

Notes

1. Jacques Derrida has recognized this in "Violence and Metaphysics," in *Writing and Difference,* trans. A. Bass (Chicago: University of Chicago Press, 1978), 79–153; "At This Moment in This Very Work Here I Am," trans. R. Berezdevin, in *Re-Reading Levinas,* ed. Robert Bernasconi and Simon Critchley (Bloomington: Indiana University Press, 1991), 11–48 (hereafter cited in the text as "AM"); and *Adieu to Emmanuel Levinas,* trans. P.-A. Brailed and M. Naas (Stanford: Stanford University Press, 1999), hereafter cited in the text as *AEL.*

2. Alain Finkielkraut, *The Wisdom of Love,* trans. Kevin O'Neill and David Suchoff (Lincoln and London: University of Nebraska Press, 1984), is representative of this tendency.

3. Emmanuel Levinas, *Totality and Infinity,* trans. Alphonso Lingis (Pittsburgh: Duquesne University Press, 1969), 121; *Totalité et infini* (The Hague: Martinus Nijhoff, 1961), 94. Hereafter cited in the text as *TI* and *TeI,* respectively.

4. Levinas says, for example, "*Being* before the *existent,* ontology before metaphysics, is freedom (be it the freedom of theory) before justice. It is a movement within the same before obligation to the other. The terms must be reversed" (*Totality and Infinity,* 47; *Totalité et infini,* 17).

5. Emmanuel Levinas, *Existence and Existents,* trans. Alphonso Lingis (The Hague: Martinus Nijhoff, 1978); *De l'existence à l'existant* (Paris: J. Vrin, 1984), preface. Hereafter cited in the text as *EE* and *DE,* respectively.

6. Levinas refers to Jean-Luc Marion's "*L'idole et la distance,*" and Marion responds in "A Note Concerning the Ontological Indifference," *Graduate Faculty Philosophy Journal,* vol. 20, no. 2–vol. 21, no. 1 (1998): 25–40, see esp. 26. Marion's response first appeared as "Note sur l'indifférence ontologique," in *Emmanuel Levinas: L'éthique comme philosophie première. Actes du Colloque de Cerisy-la-Salle 23 août-2 Septembre 1986,* ed. Jean Greisch and Jacques Rolland (Paris: Éditions du Cerf, 1993), 47–62. Hereafter cited in the text as "OI."

7. Emmanuel Levinas, *Otherwise than Being, or Beyond Essence,* trans. Alphonso Lingis (The Hague: Martinus Nijhoff, 1981), 142; *Autrement qu'être, ou au-delà de l'essence* (The Hague: Martinus Nijhoff, 1974), 181. Hereafter cited in the text as *OB* and *AE,* respectively.

8. See Jacques Rolland's essay in the 1982 edition of Levinas's *De l'évasion;* and Jacques Derrida, "A Word of Welcome," in *Adieu to Emmanuel Levinas,* 136n10. Der-

rida already raises the question of how to think the relation between ethics and on-tology in his earlier works, "Violence and Metaphysics" and "At This Moment." See also Jean Greisch, "Ethics and Ontology: Some 'Hypocritical' Considerations," trans. Leonard Lawlor, *Graduate Faculty Philosophy Journal*, vol. 20, no. 2–vol. 21, no. 1 (1998): 41–69; and John Llewelyn, *Emmanuel Levinas: The Genealogy of Ethics* (London and New York: Routledge, 1995), 29–30 and 176.

9. Emmanuel Levinas, *Time and the Other*, trans. Richard Cohen (Pittsburgh: Duquesne University Press, 1987), 93; *Le temps et l'autre* (Paris: Presses Universi-taires de France, 1983), 88. Hereafter cited in the text as *TO* and *TA*, respectively. By aligning Heidegger with the Platonic impulse to subordinate multiplicity to the one (see *Time and the Other*, 92; *Le temps et l'autre*, 88), Levinas articulates an as-sociation that has been taken up by other thinkers. Hannah Arendt also criticizes Heidegger for elevating *Dasein*'s self-individuation through its confrontation with its own death over the plurality of community, and she does so, in part, by show-ing that Heidegger remained committed to the Platonic celebration of the con-templative life (*bios theôretikos*) over practical affairs (*vita activa*). Perhaps unsur-prisingly—given that both thinkers were profoundly influenced by Heidegger, and both were forced to rethink their attachment to his thinking in confronting his Nazism—this is not the only parallel between Levinas's and Arendt's critiques of Heidegger. Arendt emphasizes the need to make nativity more central than being toward the end, just as Levinas emphasizes evanescence, and the impor-tance of new beginnings. Both of them criticize Heidegger for denigrating the world of work, and both of them provide accounts of the private, domestic sphere of habitation that are intended to correct Heidegger's neglect of these themes. For a valuable discussion of Arendt's critical interrogation of Heidegger (and one which shows signs of being influenced by Levinas), see Jacques Taminiaux, *The Thracian Mind and the Professional Thinker: Arendt and Heidegger*, trans. Michael Gendre (Albany: State University of New York Press, 1997). Julia Kristeva, in a pre-sentation informed by Taminiaux's work, took up the relation between Arendt and Heidegger in a paper presented at the 1999 International Association of Phi-losophy and Literature (IAPL), to which I had the privilege of being asked to re-spond.

10. Taminiaux points out that Heidegger's notion of "productive activity" which "reaches its accomplishment" in "the work itself" is a reworking of Aristo-tle's *energeia* (*Thracian Mind*, 5), and so, in turn, Levinas's understanding of ac-complishment might be read as a reassessment of productive activity, that is, of *techne* and *poiesis*. See also Levinas, *Totality*, 117; *Totalité*, 90; and Llewelyn, who dis-cusses the importance of the term accomplishment in *The Genealogy of Ethics*.

11. Levinas says that the alterity of death is "not unknown but unknowable, refractory to all light" (*Totality*, 75; *Totalité*, 63).

12. As Taminiaux says, quoting from Levinas's *Existence and Existents:*
Whereas the Heideggerian ekstasis is grounded in a process of temporalization which is focused upon the future of the end and deprives the present of all privilege, the point in Levinas is to grasp the hypostasis as an event which occurs thanks to "the very

stance of an instant" (17), an instant which is the "polarization of
Being in general" (18). In this new context, whereas Heidegger
puts the emphasis on the end, Levinas claims that "beginning,
origin and birth present a dialectic in which this event in the
heart of the instant becomes visible" (18). (Taminiaux, "The
Early Levinas's Reply to Heidegger's Fundamental Ontology," *Philosophy and Social Criticism* 23, no. 6 [1997]: 29–49)

13. Martin Heidegger, *On Time and Being*, trans. Joan Stambaugh (New York:
Harper and Row, 1972), 19.

14. See also Levinas, *Existence* 79, *De l'existence* 135; *Totality* 271, *Totalité* 249; and
Totality 303, *Totalité* 280. Freedom must justify itself, according to Levinas.

15. One could also ask, in what sense is this responsibility already ethical? It
would seem that responsibility is a term that already assumes the relation with the
other, just as freedom, in the full sense of the word, already requires the other.
And indeed, this will prove to be the case, for the feminine is already assumed by
the dwelling, and the dwelling is Levinas's attempt to rework the corporeity and
solitude of this provisional I that has a provisional freedom. By inhabiting the
home, the I has also been exposed to another.

16. Sonya Sikka, "Portraits of the Feminine," in *Feminist Interpretations of Emmanuel Levinas*, ed. Tina Chanter (Pennsylvania State University Press, 2001).

17. For a reading that emphasizes the positive aspects of Levinas's notion of
paternal election, see Kelly Oliver, *Family Values: Subject between Nature and Culture*
(New York: Routledge, 1997).

18. The translation differs slightly from Lingis's translation at *Totality and Infinity*, 157; *Totalité et infini*, 131.

19. The issue that I am thinking through here is also what I think is at stake
for Fabio Ciaramelli when he writes:

Through the notions of separation and recurrence, Levinas
alludes to the paradoxical past of subjectivity, which is the necessary condition or the presupposition of its constitutive activity.
The transcendental power of subjective constitution is thus conditioned by this prior presupposition which, itself always already
constituted, only afterwards turns out to be constituting. ("The
Posteriority of the Anterior," *Graduate Faculty Philosophy Journal*,
vol. 20, no. 2–vol. 21, no. 1, p. 410)

While I agree with Ciaramelli, I also want to emphasize the fact that Levinas does
not want to think recurrence simply as a transcendental condition, which would
reduce it to a presupposition that can be entirely contained in thought; he also
wants to claim the material excess of the anterior posterior. In this sense, Levinas
finds the language of the "constituted" and "constituting" inadequate to that
which does nevertheless become constituted, and thus comes to function as a condition (and thus is also constitutive), but this process of becoming part of the
movement of constitution is not without loss. Sensibility remains excessive to representation in a way that representation is never adequate to conceptualize or contain, even if it must be called upon to acknowledge even its own inadequacy.

20. As Anthony Steinbock points out in his essay in this volume, Levinas calls the judgment of God discreet (see *Totality*, 244; *Totalité*, 221). This suggests a point of convergence between the notion of God and the feminine that might seem to open up the potential for the feminine to take on an ethical connotation that Levinas elsewhere closes down.

21. See Alison Ainley, "Levinas and Kant: Maternal and Illegitimate Creation," in *Feminist Interpretations of Emmanuel Levinas*.

22. Levinas adds:

> To be sure, representation is the seat of truth: the movement
> proper to truth consists in the thinker being determined by the
> object presented to him. But it determines him without touching
> him, without weighing on him—such that the thinker who sub-
> mits to what is thought does so "gracefully," as though the object,
> even in the surprises it has in store for cognition, had been antici-
> pated by the subject. (*Totality*, 124; *Totalité*, 97)

23. Emmanuel Levinas, "Politics After!" in *Beyond the Verse: Talmudic Readings and Lectures,* trans. Gary D. Mole (Bloomington: Indiana University Press, 1994), 194.

24. As Bernasconi points out, this phrase is very rare, if not unique, in Levinas's texts. See Robert Bernasconi, "Different Styles of Eschatology: Derrida's Take on Levinas' Political Messianism," *Research in Phenomenology,* "In Memorium: Emmanuel Levinas," vol. 28 (1998): 3–19.

25. See Levinas, "Politics After!" 188–95.

Contributors

Bettina Bergo is an assistant professor of philosophy at the Université de Montréal. She is the author of *Levinas between Ethics and Politics: For the Beauty That Adorns the Earth*. She has written numerous articles on Levinas and aspects of French philosophy and has translated Levinas's *Of God Who Comes to Mind; God, Death and Time;* and *On Evasion*. She is currently working on a study of anxiety in psychoanalysis and recent philosophy.

Robert Bernasconi is the Moss Professor of Philosophy at the University of Memphis. He is the author of two books on Heidegger and numerous essays on Hegel, twentieth-century European philosophy, political philosophy, and race theory. He coedited *The Provocation of Levinas, Re-Reading Levinas, Emmanuel Levinas: Basic Philosophical Writings,* and *The Cambridge Companion to Levinas*.

Tina Chanter is the author of *Ethics of Eros: Irigaray's Rewriting of the Philosophers* and *Time, Death and the Feminine: Levinas with Heidegger.* She has published in journals such as *Philosophy and Social Criticism, Research in Phenomenology, Graduate Faculty Philosophy Journal,* and *Differences*. Her book, *Abjection: Film and the Constitutive Nature of Difference,* is forthcoming with Indiana University Press.

John Drabinski teaches philosophy at Assumption College. He is the author of numerous articles and the book *Sensibility and Singularity*. His current research concerns both questions of trauma, memory, and representation (especially in Claude Lanzmann's film *Shoah*) and issues raised by a Levinasian politics.

Wayne Froman teaches philosophy at George Mason University, where he served for ten years as Department Chair. He has published widely on phenomenology, including articles on Heidegger, Merleau-Ponty, Ricoeur, and Schutz. He is the author of *Merleau-Ponty: Language and the Act of Speech*. His recent paper "Rosenzweig and Heidegger on 'der Augenblick'" is forthcoming in a volume, edited by Wolfdietrich Schmied-Kowarzik, based on the 2004 Kongress "Franz Rosenzweigs Neues Denken: Grundlagen und Perspektiven." Froman was a Fulbright guest professor at the Hegel-Archiv during 1995-1996.

Margret Grebowicz is an assistant professor of philosophy at the University of Houston-Downtown, where she teaches postmodernism, philosophy of science, and feminist theory. Her current research concerns the relevance of contemporary French thought for feminist epistemologies, as well as for discussions of literacy and democractic education in the writings of African-American feminists. She is the editor of *Gender After Lyotard* and the co-editor of *Still Seeking an Attitude: Critical Reflections on the Work of June Jordan.*

James Hatley is a professor of philosophy at Salisbury University. He is the author of *Suffering Witness: The Quandary of Responsibility after the Irreparable.* He is currently editing a collection of essays to be titled *Interrogating Responsibility: Ethical Turns in Merleau-Ponty.* Hatley is also publishing pieces on the significance of repentance in the thought of Levinas and is working on a manuscript in environmental philosophy to be titled *Walking Mountains Thinking.*

Antje Kapust teaches at the Ruhr-Universität-Bochum. She is the author of numerous articles about Levinas, Merleau-Ponty, violence, and war. Her first book, *Berührung ohne Berührung,* will soon appear in English translation from the Northwestern University Press. Her second book *Der Krieg und der Ausfall der Sprache* was published in 2004.

Claire Elise Katz is an assistant professor of philosophy and Jewish studies at Pennsylvania State University. She is the author of *Levinas, Judaism, and the Feminine: The Silent Footsteps of Rebecca* and the editor of *Emmanuel Levinas: Critical Assessments.* Her current research focuses on what Jewish philosophy and Continental philosophy can bring to bear on contemporary questions in the philosophy of education.

David Michael Kleinberg-Levin is a professor of philosophy at Northwestern University. He is the author of numerous journal studies and books, including *The Body's Recollection of Being, The Opening of Vision, The Listening Self,* and *The Philosopher's Gaze.* His latest work, *Gestures Befitting the Measure: Physiognomies of Ethical Life (Hölderlin's Question After Heidegger)* will soon appear in the Meridian Series, Stanford University Press.

Alphonso Lingis is a professor emeritus at Pennsylvania State University. He is the author of *Excesses: Eros and Culture; Libido: The French Existential Theories; Phenomenological Explanations; Deathbound Subjectivity; The Community of Those Who Have Nothing in Common; Abuses; Foreign Bodies; Sensation: Intelligibility in Sensibility; The Imperative;* and *Dangerous Emotions.*

Leslie MacAvoy is an assistant professor of philosophy at East Tennessee State University. She works on issues in phenomenology, hermeneutics, and philosophies of dialogue and is currently doing research on subjectivity and the phenomena of meaning, value, and responsibility within the phenomenological and postphenomenological traditions, with particular attention to the work of Heidegger and Levinas.

Eric Sean Nelson is assistant professor of philosophy at the University of Massachusetts Lowell and has taught at the University of Memphis. He has published articles on Kant, Schleiermacher, Dilthey, and Heidegger. He is currently cotranslating Heidegger's *Einleitung in die Philosophie* (Indiana University Press) and coediting the anthology *Rethinking Facticity* (SUNY Press). He is also working on one book on the early Heidegger and a second on Kant and Levinas.

Diane Perpich is an assistant professor of philosophy at Vanderbilt University. She has published essays on Levinas's relation to various figures in the Continental tradition, including Kant, Merleau-Ponty, Derrida, and Irigaray, and was the coeditor of a special double issue of the Graduate Faculty Philosophy Journal devoted to Levinas's thought.

François Raffoul is an associate professor of philosophy at Louisiana State University. He is the author of *Heidegger and the Subject* (Prometheus, 1999), *A Chaque Fois Mien* (Galilee, Paris, 2004), and has edited and co-edited several volumes on Heidegger and Lacan, including *Heidegger and Practical Philosophy* (SUNY Press, 2002) and *Rethinking Facticity* (SUNY, forthcoming). He has co-translated numerous works of French philosophers into English, such as Jean-Luc Nancy, Philippe Lacoue-Labarthe, and Francoise Dastur, as well as Heidegger's last seminars, *Four Seminars* (Indiana U. Press, 2004). He is currently preparing a book on a phenomenology of responsibility.

Jill Robbins is a professor of comparative literature and religion at Emory University. She is the editor of *Is It Righteous to Be? Interviews with Emmanuel Levinas* and the author of *Prodigal Son/Elder Brother: Interpretation and Al-*

terity in Augustine, Petrarch, Kafka, Levinas and *Altered Reading: Levinas and Literature.*

Michael B. Smith is a professor of French and philosophy at Berry College. He has translated numerous works by Levinas, including *Outside the Subject, In the Time of the Nations, Proper Names, Entre Nous* (with Barbara Harshav), and *Alterity and Transcendence.* Duquesne University Press will publish his book *Toward the Outside: Themes and Concepts in Emmanuel Levinas* in the spring of 2005.

Anthony J. Steinbock is a professor of philosophy at Southern Illinois University at Carbondale. In addition to articles in social, political, and phenomenological philosophy, he is the author of *Home and Beyond: Generative Phenomenology after Husserl* and is the translator of Edmund Husserl's *Analyses Concerning Passive and Active Synthesis: Lectures on Transcendental Logic.* His recent work, in preparation, includes *Verticality and Idolatry,* which concerns religious, moral, and ecological experience, and *The Phenomenology of Hope.*

Kent Still is a doctoral candidate in philosophy at Emory University and co-editor of *Minima Memoria: In the Wake of Jean-François Lyotard,* forthcoming from Stanford University Press.

Bernhard Waldenfels is a professor emeritus at the Ruhr-Universität-Bochum. He is the author of numerous books in phenomenology and on Husserl, contemporary French thought, ethics, and politics, including *Phänomenologie in Frankreich, Antwortregister, Deutsch-Französische Gedankengänge,* and the four-volume *Studien zur Phänomenologie des Fremden.* His most recent books are *Das liebliche Selbst* and *Verfemdung der Moderne* as well as *Bruchlinien der Erfahrung* and *Phänomenologie der Aufmerksamkeit.* In addition to his numerous articles published in English, his book *Ordnung in Zwielicht* has appeared in an English translation, *Order in Twilight.*

David Wood teaches philosophy at Vanderbilt University and is Honorary Professor at the University of Warwick, England. He is the author of *Philosophy at the Limit, The Deconstruction of Time,* and *Thinking after Heidegger.* His book *The Step Back* is forthcoming (SUNY Press, 2005). He has edited many books, including *Derrida: A Critical Reader* and (with Jose Medina) a volume on truth.

Consulting Editors